S0-CBA-758

AN OUTLINE OF
ABNORMAL PSYCHOLOGY

An Outline of
Abnormal Psychology

REVISED EDITION

Edited by

Gardner Murphy, Ph.D.

Director of Research, Menninger Foundation

and

Arthur J. Bachrach, Ph.D.

Director, Division of Clinical and Medical Psychology,
University of Virginia

THE MODERN LIBRARY · NEW YORK

THE MODERN LIBRARY
is published by RANDOM HOUSE, INC.
BENNETT CERF • DONALD S. KLOPFER

Manufactured in the United States of America by H. Wolff

Foreword

A fundamental revision of the 1929 *Outline of Abnormal Psychology* in the Modern Library is obviously called for. Not only have the specific contributions contained in that volume grown old and musty; the very temper of the modern approach to abnormal psychology has altered and quickened to an extraordinary degree. It is not enough to drop some parts and add others, like Aristotle's jackknife, in which sometimes the blade, sometimes the handle, was replaced. Rather it is necessary to reconsider the whole effort. I have been fortunate, indeed, in achieving the collaboration of a clinical psychologist deeply imbued with the enthusiasm which I share for making available to the thoughtful reading public a glimpse of some typical contributions to modern abnormal psychology: Dr. Arthur J. Bachrach of the University of Virginia at Charlottesville. The entire task of selecting appropriate material for the present edition lay in the hands of Dr. Bachrach, with whom I constantly exchanged ideas. The spirit of his work and of my own earlier work is similar, but the present labor is his own.

Parallel to the *Outline of Abnormal Psychology*, the Modern Library has for many years made available an *Outline of Psychoanalysis* edited by Dr. J. S. Van Teslaar. This volume is in the process of revision in the hands of Dr. Clara Thompson. The reader interested in

abnormal psychology will find it appropriate to compare the two volumes closely with respect to content
and aim, and to check constantly on his conception of
the relation of psychoanalytic to other approaches.

G.M.

Contents

ADOLESCENCE

ADULT

Introduction

I

What is abnormal psychology? At one time it was conceived to be the "psychology of abnormals" or the "psychology of abnormal people." More and more the thinking of modern psychiatrists and psychologists has tended away from such a definition. More and more clearly it has been evident that the abnormalities of the withdrawn schizophrenic and of the compulsive drinker or drug addict are not basically different at root from psychological dispositions which "come with the package" wherever human beings are found. A great many of our common abnormalities are due to small or large defects in constitutional abilities or emotional dispositions, or to small or large accidents, mistakes or tragedies in the process of growing or learning, especially in picking out goals and models upon which to base one's life. A great many of the more serious tragedies, leading to crippling types of mental disorder, are related to profound and repeated frustrations, with consequent inability to live normally, and with no opportunity, at the time of frustration or crisis, to find a way out into a happier and more effective adjustment. It seems to us, then, that abnormality, as was suggested long ago by Hippocrates, father of medicine, is essentially a matter of defect or of exaggeration. We can all find ourselves exaggerated, reduced or transformed in some manner or other in every sick human personality. In some cases, the difference between ourselves and the nervous or disturbed person is not very large, and we can easily put ourselves in his place, "empathize" with him. At other times, especially when his disorder is due to constitutional defect or to some gross physical tragedy like brain injury or the wasting process of old age, we may find ourselves more annoyed, more alien than friendly and close. Nevertheless, our study of the range of human variability makes us aware that we can have something in common even with those who are most alien to us.

A few words about the origins of abnormal psychology. From our pre-literate ancestors through the Greco-Roman period and through the medieval period, abnormalities of the mind tended to be regarded as of supernatural origin and as calling for recourse to supernatural techniques, e.g., the driving out of demons. Nevertheless, a small number of thoughtful physicians began at least as early as the fifth century B.C., to regard mental disease naturalistically, subject to natural causes as were other diseases. The "revival of learning" brought with it the development of anatomy and physiology—Vesalius, Leonardo da Vinci, Harvey—and the sixteenth and seventeenth centuries brought an amazing medical effort to understand mental disorder. One thinks of Burton's *Anatomy of Melancholy*, written in the age of Shakespeare, and of Shakespeare's own extraordinary studies in mental abnormality as they appear, for example, in *Hamlet* and *Macbeth*. General medical progress during the seventeenth and eighteenth centuries made possible a full-fledged naturalistic approach to psychiatry in the work of the French physician Pinel in the period of the French Revolution.

In a dramatic act, Pinel, in 1791, struck off the chains of the wretched inmates of the Bicêtre, the great institution for the insane in Paris, symbolizing the emancipation of body and mind from the shackles of traditionalism and demonism and the whole conception of the inherent dangerousness and moral depravity of those afflicted with mental disease—an act commemorated in a well-known painting shown in countless psychiatric settings. The naturalistic attitude toward mental disease which had been gaining rapidly in the eighteenth century was expressed in careful studies in anatomy, histology, and physiology, which made great strides during the nineteenth century, and were enriched by the evolutionary principle and by the growth of experimental medicine.

During the same epoch, psychological rather than purely biological approaches to human adjustment likewise made great gains, notably in the French psychiatry of the third quarter of the nineteenth century. German experimental psychology joined forces with systematic "clinical psychiatry" toward the end of the nineteenth century in the huge labors of Emil Kraepelin.

Shortly thereafter, the brilliant creativeness of Sigmund Freud resulted in the development and elaboration of the psychoanalytic method. This method, utilizing the analysis of dreams and slips of speech, and taking note of the instinctual life of the child and of the interpersonal relationships in the family, accepted the evidence of unconscious dynamic psychological processes, unconscious struggle and conflict. Such conflicts were seen to be frequently handled unconsciously by the individual in terms of a development of symptoms or gross misinterpretations of reality, requiring a systematic analytical procedure. The reader is referred to the Modern Library *Outline of Psychoanalysis* for a further discussion of these approaches; but he will find in the present volume, notably on pages 132 and 271, demonstrations of the psychoanalytic way of thinking.

Psychoanalysis developed as a medical discipline at first in the German-speaking world, then in the English-speaking world (during and after the First World War), and began to influence the thinking of thoughtful people everywhere during the twenties and thirties. Experimental psychology, which had during this period been systematically studying psychological processes such as those of perception, learning, and thinking, began more and more to be influenced by psychoanalysis until an actual fusion of psychoanalytic thinking with the thinking of experimental psychologists began to be evident in many quarters. The reader will find at many points in the present volume (page 16, page 223, page 377) instances in which the thinking of psychologists has been profoundly colored by the work of their psychiatric confreres, especially the psychoanalysts.

The conception that human nature can be the subject of systematic scientific study is a recent one, for the ideas still prevalent in our society regarding human abnormalities are to a large degree survivals from the pre-scientific era. At the outset of his study of abnormal psychology, the reader will find a continuous struggle between two ways of looking at persons suffering from abnormalities. He will at times feel strongly tempted to judge them moralistically, to think of their behavior as unjust, unreasonable, unfair to others, or depraved, brutal, or contemptible. At the same time, he struggles to use the method of science, which has proved so generally useful in dealing with our human problems, and will attempt to postpone his moralistics to another occasion, allowing himself the uncertain luxury, as he studies, of a genuine effort at scientific understanding. The difficulty of this latter approach to the problem may be shown in our response to almost every day's accounts of the crimes which make the headlines, our impulse for blood vengeance competing with the still small voice which moves for understanding.

II

It may be helpful to offer a rough classification of "abnormalities."

Let us begin with mental defect. Individuals who are defective in their ability to learn are found in mammalian species generally; and human beings at all cultural levels are familiar with the problem of the stupid or "half-witted" person. A careful investigation has, however, shown that intelligence is not something you "have" or "don't have." It is a question of degree. It moves through steady gradations, from the very lowest to the very highest levels. There is consequently no sharp break which differentiates the defective from the normal. The psychologist thinks in terms of the individual's level of intelligence as compared with the social group as a whole; and in the case of the child, he thinks of the relation between the intelligence of a given person and that of other children of the same age. He has, therefore, invented the conception of "mental age." One's mental age goes up as one grows. An average child of six has a mental age of six (as shown in intelligence tests); an average child of eight, a mental age of eight, etc. From this viewpoint, a child who is quite bright for his age might be only six years old, yet have a mental age of eight. A dull child might have an actual chronological age of eight and a mental age of only six. One divides the mental age by the chronological age. Thus, for example, the eight-year-old who only has a mental age of six would have an intelligence quotient of .75, rather than 1.00 (the decimal point is customarily omitted).

The intelligence level is very roughly the same thing as the general ability of the individual to learn. Consequently, one cannot expect the mentally defective child, that is, one with a very low intelligence quotient, to learn as average children do. Actually, however, one must also go on to say that average children do not learn as very bright children do. One has to be content with a general statement that there is no sharp line anywhere between classes or types of intellectual level. There are simply *degrees* of brightness or of ability to learn. For social convenience, IQ's of below 70 are frequently treated as representing mental deficiency, and in some States this is the characteristic point at which one may draw the line, saying that the child below such a point should be institutionalized. It is, however, completely impossible to make any such absolute rule. Many children, especially in rural districts, can function pretty well with IQ's considerably below this, and where special training is possible, a child's intelligence quotient has often been pushed up to a considerable degree. The question of amount of gain to be expected will depend, of course, on the kind of facilities available, and the raw stuff, the intrinsic capacity, which may be overlaid or hidden by a long period of difficulties or of a gross insufficiency of opportunity. The issue of the amount of gain to be expected under optimal conditions remains controversial. We can, however, state that there is nothing absolute or fixed about an intelligence quotient, and that the latent potential of the individual may be released or developed in greater or lesser degree, depending upon all sorts of helpful and stimulating environmental conditions.

But the psychology of the feebleminded is more than just a question of a low level of intelligence. The child who is somewhat retarded has wit enough to realize that his situation is difficult. He cannot compete effectively with average children, may be the butt of many a practical joke, and may, in all sorts of ways, develop emotional problems which are as important as (or more important than) the intellectual one. The mental defective, then, is not just a problem for special schooling. He is a problem for our deeper and more generalized social sympathies, understanding, analysis and training.

What is the basis for mental defect? In a few cases, birth injury; in a few cases, an abnormally small head (microcephaly), or a head distended by intracranial fluid (hydrocephaly); in a few cases a thyroid defect (cretinism). Sometimes there is a disorder in prenatal development which shows itself in various abnormalities of hair, skin, eyes, tongue, etc., as well as in mental stunting—a picture called "mongolism." But in the majority of cases of mental defect there is no injury and no special or distinctive physical abnormality; there is simply mental defect. In order to understand the problem, a few words must be said about the laws of heredity.

In the tiny germ cells of male and female which unite
to produce a new individual are minute rodlike structures known as chromosomes. Twenty-four of these
from the father and twenty-four from the mother enter
into the heredity pattern of each person. Within each
chromosome are the "genes," the actual determiners of
heredity traits. The work of these genes has been extensively studied in various species, and the concept of
"defective genes" has been shown to be useful in ex-
plaining defects in teeth, hair, etc., and likewise in the
nervous system. It is possible to identify in the germ
cells the location and something about the attributes
of the genes upon which the properties of eye, skin
color and nervous system depend. In the case of man,
while it has long been suspected that there are defective genes as related to emotional, muscular, intellectual
and other properties, we must admit that we have paid
far less attention to the problem of heredity than we
have to the heredity of domestic animals, and we rely
mainly upon the labors of a few medical men and students of heredity who have a special interest in some
special problem.

But it appears likely that there are genes related to
defective development of the brain, and that certain
classes (definitely not all classes) of mental defectives
owe their condition to defective genes. It appears likely,
also, that both defective and abnormal genes of various
other sorts play a very considerable role in the origins
of some of our major types of mental disorder, to be
discussed in the appropriate place in this book. The
evidence regarding the exact genetic contribution in
the causation of our costliest and most tragic mental
disorder, schizophrenia, remains a controversial issue

upon which the reader will find appropriate references below (page 360, and page 361).

We cannot give our primary attention here, however, to the matter of causation, partly because the material would be too technical for such a book, and partly because the psychologist is, for the most part, concerned chiefly with psychological description and analysis of these conditions, while it is the biologist's task to investigate the role of heredity.

Heredity and environmental factors act together, not in isolation. Broad general factors in the environment, like unfavorable climate, inadequate sleep, physical wear and tear, may have obscure but nevertheless important effects in preventing adequate development of the nervous system. Far more important is the fact that social conditions may be so very dull and unstimulating as to reflect themselves in the inadequate intellectual level of the child, as is often seen among the "Southern Appalachian whites," as well as in Negro children of the rural South—in fact, the same comment may be made on limiting and unstimulating environments every-where. While we cannot adequately measure such influences, we must recognize their reality. In the same breath, we may recognize that many environmental factors causing strain or shock—such as violent punishment, extreme prudery and restriction in the child's emotional development, and his eagerness to understand the world and make some sort of contact with it—may be reflected in inadequate mental functioning. One must actually see the child with a blocked or frustrated mind to realize the insidious effects of adult efforts to stifle the child's yearning to understand. The conception that a child must be "seen and not heard," and must *never* "argue back"—in other words, have and express opinions of his own—may not play a prominent place in the textbooks of psychiatry, but the alert teacher and parent have a chance to witness the results of this process.

III

Our next concern is with those persons whose intellectual level is not defective but who gradually or suddenly begin to exhibit mental disorder of the sort which popular speech characterizes as "insanity." Technically, these persons are said to be "psychotics" or to be suffering from "psychoses." They are regarded by the law as irresponsible, incapable of making a valid will, undependable as witnesses, and many are treated as essentially suffering from a living death, especially if they have long been in a grossly disturbed or deteriorated state indicating the "hopelessness" of the outcome. We may rapidly run over some of the types and classes of psychoses.

Brain changes late in life, in some stocks and some families, lead into pre-senile and senile changes in which there is an inability to make new impressions, although one may remember the events of childhood; a general impairment of thinking; and often a sense of helplessness and ineffectiveness, with resulting peevishness and sometimes character changes. Aside from the more general changes which are known as "senile," one must also take into account brain conditions related to hardening of the arteries (arteriosclerosis) which likewise belong mainly to the later years. There is often no such general blunting of intellectual powers, but there may be memory losses and quite considerable personality changes.

Other types of organic changes in the brain (changes which can be discovered by post-mortem examination or other physical techniques) include responses to gross injury involving damage to the brain, and the effects of toxic and bacterial agents. These often lead to states of confusion or bizarre conduct. These conditions may sometimes be handled by medical or surgical means. They are not of major interest to abnormal psychology today, because they have not been very systematically studied from a psychological viewpoint. Formerly, a rather large group of patients consisted of those suffering from syphilis of the central nervous system, notably, the psychosis known as "general paresis," but these conditions have come somewhat under control through modern medical methods.

Another set of conditions having a definite physical agency, but this time on the basis of the body's own chemical processes, are those related to the "glands of internal secretion" (or "ductless glands" or "endocrines" —see the study below on page 282). The chemical regulating effects of such endocrine glands may at times lead to toxic consequences, with gross disturbance of both physical and mental and, especially, emotional function; or at times, as in the case of hypothyroidism (see page 174), may lead to gross insufficiency of growth of the central nervous system. Very often, indeed, however, such endocrine disorders *express* rather than *cause* emotional difficulties (cf. page 269).

So far, we have been describing "organic psychoses" and those psychoses which have "some organic basis" which is more or less understood. It must, however, be admitted that the majority of patients suffering from psychoses suffer from no such easily described physical agencies. We shall attempt now a description of those psychoses not classified as organic, and make a few cautious comments on their possible origins, regretting the brevity of treatment in view of the complexity of the known and unknown factors.

All human beings are subject to swings of mood from one extreme to another—from gaiety and light-heartedness at the one end to the gloom or despair of a depressed state at the other extreme. These swings of mood (cycloid tendency) may often enough cause some maladjustment, although the individual may have some insight into his condition, and may realize that though gay today, he will be sad tomorrow, or vice versa. When the condition becomes exaggerated one may refer to cyclothymia or cycles of mood. Exaggerate this further, and one finds oneself in the region of a psychosis—the manic-depressive psychosis, characterized by its extremes in mood. Waiving for the moment the problem of origin or deep-level dynamics, we may note that in mania, or the manic phase of this condition, one confronts what appears to be rapid tempo of thought and action, frequently combined with restlessness and agitation, and with chattering, laughing, or excited buoyancy which suggests elation. At the other extreme one encounters an apparent retardation of thought and action, a tendency to fixed preoccupation with the somber and unbearable in life, and a mood of deep distress, often taking suicidal form. The reasons for grouping together these contrasting conditions are first the fact that they have in common the exaggeration of mood to a point where the person is overwhelmed by the mood, rather than capable of coping with it; and second the fact that the person may pass from one to the other of these conditions. Such conditions tend to recover, but they also tend in many individuals to recur. There is considerable evidence of a predisposing hereditary factor with regard to the manic-depressive condition, but this does not mean that environmental factors are of no importance. On the contrary, both the protection of the individual from situations which exaggerate changes of mood, and the creation of some insight into the condition, permitting one to foresee dangerous situations which would tend to bring on an attack, are among the constructive factors available. Somewhat related to the depressed condition is a serious disorder of the later middle years, known as involutional melancholia, involving extreme gloom or despair, and until recent years regarded as predestined to consume many years of the patient's life before a recovery could be expected. The various modern therapies have cut down the extreme suffering of depressed and involutional conditions in many cases. These conditions are sometimes grouped together under one name as in the phrase "benign affective psychoses." They make up together the second commonest form of psychosis.

Commoner still, and by far the greatest waster of human life known to psychiatry, is a kind of loss of the ability to distinguish reality from unreality, and a tendency to withdraw from contact with the real world in favor of fantasies or delusions, to which the term *dementia praecox* was earlier given, and today ordinarily the term *schizophrenia*. The condition is far too complex to be adequately described, even in a substantial volume. The modern point of view recognizes the very wide diversity of forms, some authorities believing that we are dealing basically with different diseases which have superficial similarities, and some believing that the same basic maladjustment takes varying superficial forms. We shall content ourselves here with the observation that there is again considerable research evidence for a hereditary predisposing factor, and likewise considerable evidence that environmental factors are of great importance and may be used effectively in protection of the individual from the onset of the disease and in connection with therapy if he does succumb.

Sometimes following from a long history of frustrations which have given the individual a sense that he simply cannot live effectively and must retreat into his shell, sometimes following in an inexplicable way from a life which has previously been happy and effective, schizophrenia is likely to appear in the teens or in the early years of maturity, although it may, in fact, occur at any time in life. The characteristic signs are typically a gradual inability to maintain sound and realistic social contacts, a tendency toward suspiciousness, misinterpretations of the environment, a loss of what the psychoanalysts call the capacity for "reality testing." With this may appear brooding, rumination, preoccupation with ideas more and more bizarre and out of touch with the current mode of thinking of one's friends and associates, sometimes taking the form of unsystematized or systematized delusions. A common illustration is the belief that one is being plotted against, as by the family or by some social group, such as the Catholics, the Jews, the Socialists, the Masons, or some other rather large and powerful group with which the individual feels that he cannot cope.

The full-fledged disorder ordinarily requires hospitalization, but very mild forms of this condition pass for near-normal. The general tendency to make inadequate social contacts, to develop a loss of realism with regard to one's place in society, a tendency to ruminate, verbalize, and play fantasies off in an unrealistic direction is sometimes called schizoid. A number of people in any community are likely to be schizoid, and this does not in itself portend psychosis. There is, however, no very sharp line to be drawn between schizoid tendencies and actual schizophrenia, and every hospital and every private practitioner encounters many "borderline" cases, in which it is touch and go as to whether the person will have a "psychotic break" or not.

It must, of course, be heavily stressed that the general reader is even less qualified to diagnose a schizoid condition than he is to diagnose diphtheria or typhoid fever. One can give a recognizable popular *description* which may prevent some gross misunderstandings, but whenever the problem of potential psychosis comes up, the problem is a problem for a psychiatrist. Relatively few medical men are trained in psychiatry, but the ethical medical man will refer such problems to a qualified psychiatrist, to whose field they belong.

If now you counted all the persons in the United States suffering from any of the conditions so far described, conditions so severe that they require constant care, you would have a couple of million people—very roughly one might say a million mentally defective and a million psychotic, with schizophrenics by far the largest contingent in the latter group.

IV

But what about the people who are neurotic, disturbed, frightened, confused, compulsive, rigid, anxious, harried, suffering from a thousand ills the human flesh is heir to, but still capable of functioning in society at a reasonably adequate intellectual level and without any disorder which could be classified as a psychosis?

A large proportion of these people are today called psychoneurotics. They defy adequate description and classification. There is, nevertheless, some value in a few gross pigeonholes, the partitions of which will undoubtedly be battered down as psychiatric progress continues. We may distinguish between the following major groups: first, the compulsives, who are overwhelmed by something that has to be done. They can never get their hands clean enough, or make sufficiently sure that all the gas-jets are turned off, etc. They may have to be at their appointments ahead of time. They may have to go through a ritual before they may answer a simple question or carry out a simple act. Often the compulsive condition may be combined with an obsessive condition in which one is harried to death by an idea which will not leave the mind—an idea of uncleanness or guilt, or still more frequently an idea of some sort which plainly keeps the individual from dwelling on the painful idea which has been shoved out of the consciousness; thus Lady Macbeth thought of the idea of the spot on her hand because the horrible fact that she was a murderess could not be directly held in consciousness, but only the surrogate idea of a stain upon her skin. The obsessive-compulsive conditions usually take a long time developing; in fact, they can often be seen in children and adolescents, and they may dog the person through life. But they may gradually yield to situational changes, or may be assisted through psychotherapy of one sort or another.

Next to be listed are the hysterical conditions—conditions marked by extreme sensitiveness to the environment, picking up one's cue from the situation either in the dramatic form of laughter and tears, or through alerting oneself to certain attributes of the environment while shutting out others. Thus the individual may look at things and not see them, or his skin may be touched by things which he cannot feel, or he may have failures of memory or be partially paralyzed—in all these cases shutting out certain functions while he is alerting himself to something else. For every full-fledged case of hysteria of this sort there are many people with mild hysterical tendencies.

Material on all these conditions will be found below on pages 262, 274. It is, of course, the study of conditions such as these which played such a major role in the initiation of psychoanalysis over a half century ago. In general, it was Freud's genius to perceive that in all these instances the person is fighting a battle with himself, particularly against the recognition of something painful about himself which he cannot allow into clear consciousness. Often in Freud's experience it was a direct or concealed sex wish against which the individual was struggling. Some broader dimensions of this problem appear on page 248 below.

We shall not attempt, here, to detail the other types of psychoneurotic conditions so numerous, so protean in form. Rather, our interest in the volume presented here is in the psychoneurotic conditions which appear in more normal, or less disturbed, persons—the less fully developed aspects of hysterical, obsessive, and compulsive behavior (page 268 and page 518).

At the time that the first edition of this book was presented, one would find in the textbooks a brief consideration of persons suffering from "constitutional psychopathic inferiority." These were people like the fire setters, or pyromaniacs; the compulsive stealers, or kleptomaniacs; the morbidly brutal or feelingless people who carry out inhuman crimes without conscience, the people who do what they want to do on the spur of the moment without any "impulse control"; broadly speaking, the people who, though of normal intelligence, cannot accept and live in terms of the ordinary rules of social living. They are often referred to as having "character disorders." One can, of course, if one likes, include alcoholics and drug addicts in this group, but it is confusing to do so; there are some patients with character disorder among these alcoholics and the drug addicts, but the special conditions under which relief through drugs may be sought mark these problems off for separate treatment. The character disorders are, however, rather common. One finds in almost every army or merchantman or prison a certain number of individuals who simply do not emotionally understand what discipline is about, and who cannot be controlled by the ordinary, or even extraordinary restraints which would inhibit normal men through the fear of punishment. The conscienceless type of character disorder, so common among children who have grown up in the chaos of war without parents and who have never deeply incorporated within themselves the rules and decencies, the regard for the feelings and needs of others, has taught us dramatically within recent years how a type of behavior which looks like an innate defect can actually be bred rather easily by the absence of normal warm family life, social support and guidance in the early years. Material below (page 261) will develop this point more fully.

V

Now for a few words about the ways of caring for people with mental abnormalities in our society. They are cared for primarily by psychiatrists, aided by other medical men and social workers; and by psychologists.

Since the reader will have noticed that references to psychology are freely mixed with references to the medical specialty known as psychiatry, it may be of interest to say a few words first about the relations between psychiatry and psychology in the United States. For the medical man, psychoanalysis (and more broadly, psychiatry in general) is an aspect of the healing art and a part of the broad medical definition of the physician's responsibility for the patient. From the psychologist's point of view, the broad problems of human adjustment and maladjustment are aspects of the science of psychology, and problems of abnormal psychology, mental hygiene, and psychoanalytic dynamics come up in these contexts. There is, therefore, a large overlapping as far as medical and psychological preoccupations are concerned. For the most part, actual training in the diagnosis and treatment of mental disorders has been relatively easy for medical men to get, and difficult for psychologists to get, since the training is available mainly in medical centers. Despite this fact, there has been an increase, notably during World War II and thereafter, in the number of psychologists devoting themselves to problems of "clinical

psychology"—that is, problems involving a psychological background and then a specialization in problems
of diagnosis and care of mentally afflicted persons.

The rule is that the psychologist works in a coöperative relationship with medical persons and with
psychiatric social workers, nurses, and others, rather
than actually participating in "private practice" in competition with physicians. Nevertheless, grave questions
have to be worked out still as to the actual role of clinical psychologists. The clinical psychologist does not, as
a rule, assume the whole responsibility for the patient's mental health; he usually works in a team directed by a psychiatrist; and he does not, of course,
attempt to deal with "organic" conditions. Both in organic and in all other conditions he must be ready to
work closely with medical colleagues. Here and there
he can obtain the full training which is ordinarily available only to medical men. In most centers, the clinical
psychologist plays a large part in the total work on
behalf of the patient through his administration of special tests and the gathering of data which throw light
upon the patient's problem. He likewise also frequently
assists in therapy, as does the psychiatric social worker.

In many special groups, such as college students,
"counseling" involves personal as well as vocational and
educational guidance, and becomes an assumption of
responsibility for mental health. The "client-centered
therapy" of Carl Rogers of the University of Chicago is
a prominent example. In this instance the clinical psychologist *does* carry the responsibility ordinarily carried
by the psychiatrist.

In hospitals, child guidance centers, etc., not involving "private practice," hundreds of clinical psychologists
are engaged in therapy, and the number who are quali-

fied for responsible positions on their own (not requiring supervision) is daily increasing. Custom and law
have not yet crystallized into a code defining what he
may and may not do, and in many States the clinical
psychologist is very uncertain regarding his future.

Remembering, then, that at present the work of the
clinical psychologist takes the form of assisting in diagnosis and participation in group work rather than of full
responsibility for psychotherapy in private practice, it
may be worth while to give a paragraph to the operation of the clinical psychologist in the development of
tests and their application, and in the field of research.

The development of intelligence tests by Binet and
others at the beginning of this century led to a larger
and larger variety of tests to be used with children and
adults encountering a wide variety of different problems. The properly prepared modern clinical psychologist obtains training during his four or more years of
graduate work in the administration of at least 15 or
20 different tests of intellectual functioning, and intensive work with at least two of these—ordinarily the
Stanford revision of the Binet test, and the Wechsler-
Bellevue test. He likewise receives training today in a
large number of *personality tests*, a few of which consist of paper and pencil schedules in which the person indicates attitudes and feelings, but the majority
of which consist of "projective tests," in which the patient simply looks at or listens to certain material and
indicates how it strikes him. He looks, for example, at a
series of inkblots and tells what he sees in them, or he
looks at a series of pictures and makes up stories as to
what the characters in the pictures are doing. He looks
at cartoons of frustrating situations and indicates what
the frustrated person probably said. He sees incomplete

pictures, and sketches in the lines to finish them; or he encounters unfinished sentences and adds a few words to make sense. In all these cases he shows his own slant on life; he "projects himself into" the material. It is a long and complex process to learn what can and what cannot be done by the projective tests of today; to learn the criteria for the sound development of such tests; and to learn how they may be combined in practice for the benefit of any individual type of adult or child who may need help. The working up of the data on a patient typically takes several hours, and the report is usually transmitted to psychiatrists and social workers and discussed at staff meetings. The psychologist thus plays an important part in the diagnosis and in the plan for therapy.

More and more also in recent years, *research* in abnormal psychology tends to be the responsibility of psychologists rather than of any other professional group. Several recent studies of research grants administered by the Veterans Administration and by the United States Public Health Service show the same story that is obvious if one reads the various technical journals— namely, that most of the research investigations into the factors at work precipitating mental disorder, the nature of the problems which patients confront, and the process of psychotherapy (to see how well it works and with what results) are today the work of psychologists. The division of labor in which the psychiatrist has the main responsibility for the individual patient and the psychologist looks at matters in long-range research terms, may or may not be ultimately desirable. We are in no position to make a judgment today. We should, however, note that while for the most part it is through the medical man specializing in psychiatry that the pa-

tient is cared for, the long-range assimilation of data as to what actually works, tends more and more to be in the hands of research clinical psychologists.

It should again be added that social workers, especially the psychiatric social workers prepared specifically for the job, also play a very considerable part today in therapy, regularly serving as assistants to psychiatrists in the gathering of data and in the carrying out of a plan for the benefit of the individual and his family. And insofar as we are turning today to an emphasis upon culturally oriented studies of the background of mental breakdown (page 27 and page 558) we draw more and more upon sociologists and other social scientists collaborating with psychiatrists and psychologists to participate in basic research on the causes of mental disorder, and research upon the effectiveness of social therapies—education, better housing, recreation facilities, mental hygiene, etc.—in curbing the mental disorders of our troubled civilization.

The ultimate decision, of course, regarding the types of assistance offered for the development of these branches of knowledge and fields of science will depend upon the consumer-citizen, whose understanding of the immense problem, and of the scientific approach to its solution, will determine the conditions of healthy living which are the best preventives of mental abnormality, and will provide the wherewithal for the therapy and reëducation of those who need help.

GARDNER MURPHY

CHILDHOOD

Problems of Infancy and Early Childhood[*]

BY *Erik Homburger Erikson*

***

Outline: Epigenesis
The Organismic Basis of Infantile Behavior
Social Relativity of Behavior Problems
Growth and Anxiety
Child Training and Culture
Suggestions

Introduction

The current division of labor in the care of the child places him alternately in the hands of training, curing, and teaching adults. In accordance with what they have learned to consider their function in his life, his problems are variously interpreted: He "just does not know better," is "bad," "physically sick," or "mentally sick." However, under the influence of psychiatric enlighten-

[*] From *The Cyclopedia of Medicine Surgery and Specialties*, 1945. Reprinted by courtesy of the author and publishers, F. A. Davis Company, Philadelphia, Pennsylvania.

ment, the importance of inter-relations between *well-being, well-behaving,* and *well-learning* are being increasingly understood: It is conceded that a child's capacity to learn may decline because of an undiscovered disease; that a naughty child may be hounded by fears or be the victim of a broken home; that a sickly and irritable one may be craving for attention at any price. The "whole child" should be studied.

What is known scientifically of human behavior problems has its source in *psychopathology* (especially *psychoanalysis*) and in *psychology.* These branches of science tell how an individual behaves or what he says about himself and his life only (1) if he feels sick enough to *surrender himself* to the guidance (hypnosis, suggestion, psychoanalysis, etc.) of a therapist; (2) if he, for one reason or another, is ready and capable of *lending easily isolated* parts of his mind or body (vision, audition, memory, learning, etc.) to a tester or experimenter. In either case he is not the person met with in the give and take of a family situation.

There are indications that even regarding its most disturbing subject, man's emotions, science is arriving at methods comparable to the use of x-rays in the investigation of the organism, which allow for the study of vital mechanisms under circumstances not constricting or disturbing the integrity of the personality. But today the practitioner, turning to established psychologies to learn what a child is, still finds himself confronted with strange pictures—which either depict an aggregate of psychological mechanisms in the state of pathological insurrection, or synthetic robots reconstructed from single isolated reflexes, instincts, and growth patterns. Each robot functions only in terms of its own terminology, and without a complete mastery of this terminology, the way back to the problems of the living child is often far from clear.

What is a virtue in science, namely scepticism as to what can be known, unfortunately in practice often turns into inhibitory fatalism in regard to what may be done. The individual child is rarely as good or as bad as the tests show him to be; there is a large field of balance and chance provided by human contact, which makes practice, inspired and corrected by research as it is, an art in its own right, developing in and by its own experiences.

In this sense the present chapter can only attempt to offer a few guiding concepts which the writer found basic to much that is being done in practice as well as in research, and to problems of the misbehaving as well as the untrained or mentally sick child.

I. Epigenesis

We begin with an analogy taken from a time of life when the human being cannot possibly be thought bad or stupid, and when a differentiation between physical and emotional sickness is meaningless, namely the fetal stage. What can fetal development teach us about the hazards of all growth?

Embryology has developed from the concept of the homunculus, a minute, but completely preformed man waiting *in utero* to be awakened, to expand and to jump into life, to the present understanding of what is called *epigenetic development,* the step by step growth of the fetal organs.

In this development each organ has its time of origin, as important as the place of origin. If the eye does not arise at the appointed time "it will never be able to express itself fully, since the moment for the rapid outgrowth of some other part will have arrived, and this will tend to dominate the less active region, and suppress the belated tendency for eye expression." (1)

After the organ has begun to arise at the right time, still another time factor determines the most critical stage of its development: "A given organ must be interrupted during the early stage of its development in order to be completely suppressed or grossly modified . . . After an organ has arisen successfully from the anlage, it may be lamed or runted, but its nature and existence can no longer be destroyed by interrupting the growth."

The organ which misses its time of ascendancy is doomed not only as an individual, it endangers at the same time the whole hierarchy of organs. "Not only does the arrest of a rapidly budding part, therefore, tend to suppress its development temporarily, but the premature loss of supremacy to some other organ renders it impossible for the suppressed part to come again into dominance, so that it is permanently modified . . ." The result of normal development is proper relationship of size and function among the body organs: The liver adjusted in size to the stomach and intestine, the heart and lungs properly balanced, and the capacity of the vascular system accurately proportioned to the body as a whole. Through developmental arrest an organ may become disproportionately small; this upsets functional harmony and produces a defective person.

If *"proper rate"* and *"normal sequence"* are disturbed, the outcome may be a *monstrum in excessu* or a *monstrum in defectu:* "The fact that the normal individual stands between these two arbitrary classes of abnormalities has no significance other than that the abnormal *deviations* are simply modifications of the normal condition resulting from unusual reductions in the rate of development during certain critical stages."

II. The Organismic Basis of Infantile Behavior

The most critical time in terms of possible organic monstrosities are the months before birth; once born, the body has "successfully arisen from its anlage," or can soon be diagnosed as being too defective for integrated maturation. Still a "precerebrate" bundle fit only for a slow increase of limited kinds and intensities of stimulation, the infant has now left the chemical exchange of the womb for maternal care within the training system of his society. How the maturing organism continues to unfold, by developing not new organs, but a prescribed sequence of locomotor, sensory, and social capacities is being described in the child development literature. (2) Psychoanalysis has added to this the understanding of the less normative, often seemingly less normal and always more individual "habits" of strong positive or negative emotional tone.

Animals with a long, protected childhood play most. Least prepared for rapid adaptation, and protected longer than any other being, man begins to learn by means of play, experiment, and speculation. The changing aspects of his bodily growth, and the constant increases in his ability to perceive, to touch, to grasp, to manipulate, to vocalize, cause him to "invent" new forms of playful activity involving his body, objects, imaginary or real persons. These activities are characterized by periods of exclusive fascination and endless repetition;

they shall be called here *developmental habits*. Whether they are the child's official habits, for which tests have been found because they are obvious steps to certain skills, or his unofficial, which become the delight or the concern of mothers, *it is first of all important to realize that in the sequence of these habits the healthy child merely obeys, and on the whole can be trusted to obey inner laws of development, namely those laws which in his prenatal period had formed one organ after another, and now (as these organs meet the extrauterine world) create one behavior item after another. Proper rate and sequence are the critical factors in their successive man-ifestations as well as in those of intrauterine growth.*

The first problems of extrauterine behavior are dic-tated by organismic facts; they are problems of *incor-poration, retention-elimination,* and *intrusion.* These "organ-modes" develop as the organ systems express-ing them first become capable of coördinated activity. Thus the urge to incorporate parts of the outer world is expressed first in the inborn receptivity of *mouth* and *senses,* including the whole *tactual* surface of the body; the discrimination between what portions of this world are to be held on to (retained) and what pushed away (eliminated) is a matter of the more mature *muscle* system including the *sphincter* muscles; while intrusion into the sphere of other beings becomes a major issue when the *locomotor* system is more mature and some *genital sensitivity* established. These systems in which the growing periphery of action and the acculturation of the vital orifices become integrated require detailed attention.

(A) INCORPORATION — According to the cephalocaudal growth tendencies already effective *in utera,* the oral-respiratory zone is the first organ system ready to act coördinately when stimulated by tactual sensations. From the moment the first breath of air is inhaled, the baby is dependent on the delivery of environmental "materia" (air, food, warmth, sensory stimuli, emotional stimuli) right to the doors of his organism, so that he can incorporate them and—in constant assimilation—mature. The baby's first vital and pleasurable experiences are feeding (including its olfactory, tactual, and gustatory part functions) and sensations such as touching, stroking, rocking, singing, if they are below the threshold at which joyful acceptance changes so abruptly into diffused muscle defense.

Degree and kind of this peripheral stimulation (just as much as degree and kind of oral stimulation in connection with feeding) influence the integration of breathing, digestive, metabolic and circulatory adjustment. (3) They lay the foundation for further development, determine variations in such development—or lifelong deficiency.

The eyes and then the hands follow in the coordinated search for objects. Whatever goes into the mouth serves the baby's oral and visual curiosity. Thus the radius of and the initiative in incorporation are increased.

(B) RETENTION-ELIMINATION — In learning ever more actively to incorporate, to bite, and to grasp, the infant gradually develops the ability to express individual discrimination for incoming objects more coördinately. However, if the environment's way of delivering or withholding desired objects has not already irritated him during the oral phase (i.e., by early insistent removal of the thumb from the mouth or by forced feeding), the zone of the body most apt to dramatize stubborn discrimination, especially if interfered with too abruptly is the anal zone which at this time in many children has become the seat of sensual and cathartic experiences (initiated also by more formed stools). The general impulses dominating this period can express themselves rather violently. Unlike the previous stages, when incorporation at any cost seemed the rule of behavior, now strong, sometimes "unreasonable," discrimination takes place; sensations are in rapid succession accepted, rejected; objects are clung to stubbornly or thrown away violently; persons are obstinately demanded or pushed away angrily—tendencies which under the influence of equal parental stubborness easily develop into temporary or lasting extremes of self-insistent behavior.

It is at this stage that the undisturbed infant, after having experienced delusions of omnipotence and panics of impotence, comprehends "power"—his own and that of others. Also after having clung to and disposed of things not belonging to him (and this includes the food which he considers his divine right and the feces which his own inside has manufactured) he experiences what "property" means. While during the incorporative stage the infant's main character development depended on contact and reassurance, much depends now on the experience of a sense of muscular mastery—and of firm environmental limitation; on a sense of inviolability of his own body and "property"—and on a clear delineation of that of others.

(c) INTRUSION — New problems arise out of the increasing mobility of the child's body and growing curiosity. Suddenly feeling himself in the possession of what must appear to him to be an unbounded mastery over space, the child follows new ideas of attacking and conquering; he wants to be everywhere, to enter everything, and to know all secrets.

It is in this period of violent activity that a divination of what it means to overwhelm and to be overwhelmed (in acts which are felt to be cruel or sexual or both) takes possession of the child. This is the time of increased genital masturbation, since the genital zone, destined later on to search for a partner, together with the locomotor system, has taken over some of the cathartic function for all otherwise frustrated impulses, which before were concentrated on incorporative and eliminative organ systems. For children who have been or are denied too many aspects of self-satisfaction and self-expression, and who are therefore hounded by too many unpacified developmental fears, the genitals are the last zone to hold on to—and that literally. To the girl this latter stage offers special problems, since it is during this period of stronger intrusive tendencies (tomboyishness) and increased curiosity that the girl senses her role as the inceptive object of male intrusive tendencies, but also the potentialities of the maternal role.

This is the stage when mental curiosity, locomotor vigor, manipulative skill, libidinal and social urges gradually draw the child away from the nursery in the home. Cultures, in various ways, underline this emancipation and utilize the child's larger social potentialities.

Incorporation, assimilation, retention, elimination, and intrusion are some of the basic problems of organismic existence on all biological levels. In every world contact, be it physical, emotional, or intellectual, some part or stimulus of the outer world will pass through the individual, and his attitude toward this (wished for or imposed) foreign body entering his personal sphere is one main expression of his individuality. Physical as well as emotional and intellectual self-preservation demand that one accept, keep, digest, and eliminate; give and receive; take and be taken *in fair ratio*. This ratio is the firm organismic foundation for the later development of an infinite variability and specialization of modes in human existence.

The under or overdevelopment of one impulse system decisively and systematically changes the organization of all the others: Thus—always maintaining the fair ratio —the emphases of child training systems create collective types and individual deviations. There are "suckers," "biters," "retainers," "expellers," and "intruders"; and types of personality which suffer from impotence in one or more of these impulses. Severe disbalance leads to characterological *monstra in excessu* and *monstra in defectu*.

If after infancy, the bodily functions and impulses have successfully arisen in all their importance as intermediaries between inside and outside, the *procreative organs* are the only ones to be arrested by the so-called latency period until adolescence (the last epigenetic crisis), and to unfold only then their full physiological and experiential patterns. In latent genital sexuality are also latent all the associations with the critical experiences of his earlier development. In future sex life, there is no mode or zone which cannot play a role in healthy (preliminary) sex play or make itself an independent subject for perverse (final) gratification. It is here that the individual, hunting for the sensual experiences and the self-assertion missed in the sequence of childhood pleasures, is most apt to be driven to seek—and at the same time to be blocked in seeking—fulfillments, the mere idea of which must be suppressed before it ever entered full consciousness (repression). (4)

Prolonged infancy and latency are both specifically human and intimately connected with man's ability to learn and to create. On the other hand, his initial helplessness and his retarded sexual maturation are also strong factors in his mental suffering.

III. Social Relativity of Behavior Problems

From the beginning of man's helpless life, his every move is relative to the actions of his milieu: The first succession of bodily sensations is also the first sequence of social experiences. In fact, according to recent research (5), not even the fetus lives in absolute social exclusion. Significant changes in the mother's nutritional, glandular, and emotional status (which are part of her milieu) become part of his nervous endowment. After birth the physical or emotional status of an individual clearly depends on how he changes in relation to what changes around him.

This social relativity is difficult to formulate. Because of historical habits of defining cause and effect according to older physical theories, we again and again find ourselves trying to decide what in a given case one factor (*i.e.*, in society) did to another factor (*i.e.*, in the individual) or how one item (*i.e.*, in the body) is a function of another (*i.e.*, in the mind). Yet we are never able to isolate pure factors and one-way functions. It seems clinically more fruitful to think of every item of human behavior as being simultaneously determined (6) by three organizing principles:

1. The organism is a *mammalian organization* of organ-systems (as we saw, in the time-space arrangement of epigenesis). It varies in "size and rate of growth, muscular equipment, nervous reactivity, sensory acuity, energy level, etc." (7)

2. Societies are *socio-economic organizations* of organisms (in the time-space arrangement of geographic-historical units). They vary in their provision for and demands on individuals, in their guiding ideals and threatening evils.

3. The individual functions by force of the *ego organization* of his organisms' unique experience in a particular society. As physical and mental equipment develop, the learning ego develops varied mechanisms of adaptation and defense.

These organizations exist by and are relative to each other; variations in one of them changes the meaning of the others. To protect each from dysfunction and all three from mutual disintegration, danger signals (*pain, anxiety,* and *panic*) warn of physical weakness, inner conflict, and disintegration of group coherence, each of which may be fatal to the coherence of the others.

Let us consider the problem of infantile thumbsucking. Here, possible future pain is anticipated by paternal warnings. It may be presented as a medical complaint: "It makes his teeth crooked, it is going to spoil his bite and his digestion." The complaint may be a social one: "I can't stand his sitting there sucking away, it is going to make him a weak character (sucker)." Or there may be a psychological query: "What do you think is bothering him, so that he needs to do that?"

In response to the complaint, medical science will decide whether or not certain kinds of thumbsucking lead to lasting physical defects. Social anthropology will inquire in what types of human organization thumbsucking exists at all, and where it is ignored, condoned, or condemned. The science of child development will determine at what age children in this society suck their thumbs, as it were, normatively. Psychoanalytic child psychology will indicate what frustrations and fears make the child dependent on this easily available object, his thumb, and what this temporary or lasting fixation might do to his personality. Each of these disciplines will promote its own explanation of thumbsucking—as an inherited tendency to self-indulgence or an accidental event; as imitation or the outcome of spoiling; as a natural expression of oral erotism or a neurotic expression of anxiety.

It is, then, the *meaning* of thumbsucking within this relativity and not its "cause" or "effect" which should determine diagnosis and treatment. Any attempt at correction will reveal this clearly enough. One may be convinced that the infant's teeth, if further pushed, will be crooked. But will the family be able to help in the correction without sympathetic leniency or moralistic violence, either of which will make the child hold on to his thumb—or something else? This prediction, in turn, is relative to the stage of the child's development and to his ego's ability to moderate between the need for pacification, the anxiety of frustration, and the guilt of transgression. If, however, one sympathizes with the parents' or the grandparents' horror of the habit, one again has to outline a course of gradual correction that takes into account the child's health and development, the grandmother's nerves, and the child's position in between. And if, finally, one should be inclined to let an infant suck it out—will his family or neighborhood or nursery school let it pass peacefully or will somebody's tenseness cause the child to become only more frightened? And will his ego be able to integrate permissiveness in this one aspect with prohibition in others?

Before we can state such problems more adequately, we shall have to consider the subjective aspects of epigenetic growth.

IV. Growth and Anxiety

Experimenting in physical safety, the infant expands (step by step) the limits which are his protective womb and his prison—until these limits coincide with the adult world in which he finds other members of his society sharing his newly found securities and fears. Until then he is often hounded in a most lonely, individual manner by fears which are never verbalized though he may later find them taken care of by religious cults and historical, political, or scientific myths.

Anxiety is for the personality what pain is for the body: A sign that coherence and integration are endangered by what is happening to one part of function. Since the child, in the changing worlds of his growth, has the continuous task of reëstablishing coherence, integration, and mastery while threatened with physical perils and psychological frustrations, he is apt to experience moments of anxiety which must be considered normal.

Psychoanalysis teaches that from the point of view of the child's ego each of his main developmental preoccupations, during its exclusive ascendancy (a) has the driving character of an impulse manifestation (instinct); (b) is, at the time, singularly pleasurable (libido); (c)

serves as a release of irritation from other sources (catharsis); (d) helps to master experience (ego); (e)
leads to playful trial-and-error experiments with things
and people (learning); (f) is accompanied by omnipotence fantasies. It will be apparent how much these attributes resemble those of mature sex acts in adults.
However, the child's experiences are transient and develop part functions, the exclusive importance of which
will have to give way to others and await final integration. Certain mechanisms determine fate: "Reaction formations" ward off unwelcome excess: *i.e.*, loathing
prevents certain oral desires; cleanliness, anal ones; pity;
sadism. "Sublimations" bind energy in permanent values: *i.e.*, oral satisfaction may strengthen the confident
anticipation of new experiences, while oral training may
augment caution, restraint, and taste in their acceptance. However, each trend can also become a potential
"fixation" point, to which a later "regression" may be
oriented, if and when later trends are traumatically arrested. The incompatibility of fixation and progression
is the kernel of later neuroses, the manifestations of
which often dramatically demonstrate, like a needle
in the grooves of a broken record, the attraction of the
fixation point and the repulsion from the point of arrest.

Thus many of the child's first fears are the subjective
aspects of growth, *i.e.*, they express the *anxious expectation that in a moment of realignment of forces he may
be overwhelmed by a power without or within himself,*
that functions of the self or the body may either *not be
allowed to manifest themselves fully* or, if unchecked,
overwhelm the whole child.

Best understood are those based on the infant's helplessness and slowness in coördinated defense; anything
too loud, too bright, too sudden or quick, etc., seems to

cut through his senses right into the heart of his existence. Dependent on being fed, he often seems to be
overcome by a panicky rage if nourishment is not forthcoming, and it may be concluded from psychopatholog-
ical observations that there is an anxiety that he will be
left empty and helpless in the face of overwhelming
impulse demands. Having filled his stomach all too eagerly, he appears to be bothered by a desperate feeling
that he cannot assimilate or eliminate the foreign body
quickly and sufficiently enough (an overanxious mother
seems to the child to share these fears); later, forced to
empty his bowels at appointed times, he may feel deprived of vital possessions. He is, of course, afraid of being dropped, or of falling; on the other hand, he soon
hates to be held too tightly, or to be held back, and this
ambiguity is basic for the quandary of his extrauterine
existence in general.

The continuous change in time and space perspective
often makes for insecurity in the mind of the child as to
what part of development is predestined, what dependent on human will. Will he grow too much or too little?
Will parts of him grow monstrously or shrink again and
disappear altogether? Who tells the baby when to be
born? Who makes girls out of boys? When does a baby
begin; when does a dead person stop living? Already a
small child seriously though unsuccessfully theorizes
about sex and death, the two incomprehensible dangers
which seem to wait at the end of every road of feeling
and reasoning.

Except in play, the child rarely verbalizes his world.
Only he who enters the child's world as a polite guest
and studies play as a most serious occupation learns
what a child thinks when he is not forced to adapt himself to the verbalized and classified world. It is the great

function of fairy tales that they make play, in safety, of what is too big to be mastered in the child's own play. In *Alice In Wonderland,* probably, the child finds most of his developmental fantasies verbalized—and played with.

A child, though unable to verbalize that much, knows more about adults (in so far as they are children without suspecting it) than adults know of him. But because of their verbal and mechanical virtuosity, they also assume them to know more than they do. He expects adults, especially those against whom he harbors fantasies, to know or feel his thoughts, and, furthermore, to have the right and the means to do to a child what the child can only dream of doing to them. Thus the smaller child's only protection against the constantly changing perspectives of dangers arising within or without himself is the experience of meeting on each of his various levels adults who deal firmly and *consistently* with him; only thus can the gradual incorporation of adult standards and characteristics lead to the formation of a stable person consistent in himself.

A child is especially terrified of sudden changes in adults if he lives in an overprotected atmosphere, which means usually one hostile to impulsive expression, so that he has never learned to size up how far the adult actually may go in a really fought-out issue. His confusion is increased if impulsive acts on the part of the parents are denied or rationalized (such as parental ill temper explained as being indulged in only "for the child's good"). He is overwhelmed by the sudden experience of an adult flaring into an impotent tantrum, or giving in to panicky moods. He is appalled to observe sexual activities in which the parents seem overwhelmed by what he has been taught are dirty impulses. "Who then is the really big adult who defends order against chaos?"

It goes without saying that for a child who is frightened by his own impulses and fantasies nothing is "accidental." If he has been threateningly warned against a certain act, any accident or sickness or any kind of traumatic impression experienced in connection with this act is more than accidental; it is Nemesis. Furthermore, if a slight injury is suffered, an accident observed, or a new dangerous fact is discovered (for example, the difference between boys and girls) which has a specific association with the impulses and fears of the period in question, it may take on overwhelming dimensions. Anything can be felt as personal guilt; the mother, having given birth to another child, has "bought another baby because I am not good enough for her any more"; the (dead) grandmother or the (dismissed) nurse "went away because I was not nice to her"—and so on *ad infinitum*.

It must be obvious that these fears, if fed by unwise and inconsistent restrictions, lead to an increase of habits as *pacifying activities in moments of extreme subjective danger*. Developmental habits, such as sucking and biting mannerisms, body-rocking, head-banging, wetting and soiling, spitting, smearing, motor restlessness, tic-like mannerisms, genital or anal masturbation, speech mannerisms, lying, etc., become fixed under the influence of unresolved anxiety, *i.e.*, become *compulsive habits*. If they then are "broken," the unresolved anxiety is a strong potential contribution to a neurotic regression, a character deformation, or one of the many psychosomatic disturbances.

No form of temporary play, habit, or fear is the origin

of a neurosis, or is dangerous to the child who is not already neurotic; and for the neuroses, it is always the totality of the child's life situation that should be blamed, or better, should be investigated. If anything traumatic does happen to a child, be it an accidental, peripheral happening, or a specific threat to body or self, *the tendencies just "budding up" are the most severely hit, excessive or defective variations in the child's personality are created, and the developmental fears corresponding to his stage of growth and maturation are associated to build a nucleus of the spreading system of anxiety.*

Personality disturbances only in rare cases appear to have been created by any one single factor in body or mind, in heredity, constitution, or environment. Human beings, and especially children, are seen to defend their psychic integrity most successfully in the face of one or more great handicaps. Only where several of these factors unite in crushing the psychological defense system of a personality, real emotional crises are created. The most dangerous combination of such factors implies the coincidence in time and the mutual aggravation of the following groups: (1) Changes in the *body* during periods of rapid growth, or of sickness, resulting in new or stronger impulses or fears; (2) changes in the constellation or emotional temperature in the *environment* (*i.e.,* birth, death, sickness, moving, trips, visitors, change of nurses); estrangement or separation of parents; tension or panic-like states in family or community; (3) changes in the person's *conception of his psychological status in the world,* i.e., a tightening of the rules of conscience (guilt feelings) or a change in the conception of psychological causality (inferiority feelings, projective

misunderstandings, etc.) because of the irrational association between one's bad deeds, wishes, or fears,
changes in body environment.

It has been pointed out that nothing appears to be
accidental to the anxious child. It is also important to
understand that the child's conscience (later on an important part of his unconscious) does not preserve what
the parents actually said or meant to say, but what the
child, with the selective perception of his particular
stage and state of mind, understood them to say.

Thus a boy with strong aggressive characteristics, during an especially disquieting period of muscular growth,
may be fascinated and terrified by mystifying tales of
crime and police; if during such a phase something happens to a relative or friend against whom he has recently
shown or felt hostility, he may take this so much to
heart that he will try to inhibit himself beyond his constitutional capacity for self-control. His disturbed psychobiological economy may react with formation of a
symptom, potentiality for which has been latent in his
makeup, *i.e.*, tics, convulsions, or obsessions.

V. Child Training and Culture

In the center of the epigenetic description stood the
growing body; in the center of the consideration of social relativity naturally is placed the figure of the protecting and training mother. Whatever developmental,
whatever accidental factor may have delighted or disturbed the child, he is sure to have experienced it in
relation to his mother. Especially if anxious, he is always
in flight to her or away from her—a characteristic remaining with neurotics for life (with a transference of

the mother-image on other persons or on institutions).
The mother stands between the baby and the world;
she is the first to gratify and to frustrate, to be loved
and to be hated, to be idealized and to create disillusionment. To secure the mother's affection by remaining or *appearing helpless* like the small siblings; to
secure her undivided attention and some form of physical contact with her, even by *provoking* corporal punishment; to secure her admiration by doing *"big" deeds*
like the older siblings and the father; *to be like her* to
the extent of feeling and suffering with her, or *to be
liked by her* physically and mentally at any price, even
that of turning against otherwise loved rivals (especially the father, who thus may become an object of
fear); these are the changing aims for the attainment of
which a child often goes far out of his natural way. Only
a motherly combination of friendliness and firmness in
the face of constantly changing provocation can prevent
him from getting stuck in any of his roles, and can help
him—always changing, experimenting, pretending, and
playing—to become himself. As these tendencies appear
and disappear on the surface of behavior, they may result in not so easily observable *lasting identifications*
with father, mother, or other important members of the
household. If a person of the other sex is the leading
image, special conflicts arise.

In the first few years the child is very susceptible to
physical and emotional change in the mother, gradually
also to that in the father. Often his problem is only a
part of a disturbance in the mother (for example, her
anxiety over food or dislike of dirt), as his body was
once a part of hers; in this case their common anxiety
may bind them together to such an extent that interference from outside is impossible; or a queer estrange-

ment may push them apart. A mother and a child are never alone; through the mother's conscience, generations are looking on, integrating the relationship with their approval or dividing it with their disapproval into countless disturbing details. It is always useful to know in what educational constellation the mother and father grew up: whether in a family dominated by the grandfather or by the grandmother; whether the grandparents lived for their children, or made the children live for them; whether the parent was the only child or there were many children; whether among them there were one or many brothers, one or many sisters, etc. What did the grandparents expect or hope of the parents; what do the parents expect or hope of their children and how are these hopes related to what parent and child could or would be? Often the mother and father are fighting educational battles with their children which have remained undecided in their own childhood. Often, very often, the mother fights them alone, with the father in a state of prebelligerent neutrality.

Small differences, jealousy guarded, preserve the virtues and the latent panic of generations, classes, nations: they are symbols of status and identity and to many, especially in times of change in the structure of society, identity becomes as important as food, security, and sexual satisfaction.

The various experiences described in the previous chapters are not fixated on any one zone or function for a long time unless there are arresting constitutional and environmental factors. A sensible valuation of habits and fears, one would think, would be based solely on the time and duration of their existence. Different habits should be expected from the baby whose mouth is the zone of the body most urgently demanding experiences by cutaneous contact, than from the infant whose muscles, developing quickly, make him enjoy contraction and relaxation and allow him the first successful acts of self-willed muscle aggression. Different habits should be expected in the child who is just able to move toward fascinating objects (property or not property), and in the child who, still rightfully mistrusting the ambiguity of language, has to experiment with truth and reality by asking and telling more or less humorous nonsense or lies. Habits of an earlier stage should even be expected to return now and again when a later stage passes through a crisis, or a child is tired, frightened, or sick. However, possessed as he is by sensitive zones, developing functions and increasing social awareness, the child inadvertently reaches into the sphere of adult concern by his intolerance of being interrupted and the stubborn expansion of his activity into what is called naughtiness or diagnosed as a symptom. An anxious quandary arises: When is he misbehaving, when disturbed, when abnormal?

The easiest answer to this question is given by the voice of tradition; if this voice fails, great anxiety arises. It is as if everybody felt that tradition (as long as it is a part of a living culture) establishes channels of mutual self-regulation between body and mind, adult and child, individual and culture—poles of existence which are hard to comprehend rationally.

Lack of tradition or conflicting traditions put enormous demands on the flexibility and maturity of parents. Consider, that one and the same mother must offer her baby, at first, a place in her body; then, intensive physical contact; later, a wise routine of presence and absence; and finally, active encouragement to go out into the world, and assurance that she will be there,

as refuge and as guide. Not all mothers, by temperament, can be all of these things equally well. Furthermore, where children are not perceived as a trust (of a
deity or a society), the mother's individual predilections
will emphasize one stage or another. Some women like
to be reproductive, and consider the baby a means to an
end. Some like to cuddle babies but abhor dirty children. Some ignore babies but enjoy playing with older
children. Some like to dress girls, some like children
only if they are cute or placid or clever or clean, or under the condition that they please the neighbors or do
not resemble this or that relative (i.e., the husband).
On the other hand, to some the devil's very materializa-
tion resides in voracious eating, in excrements, in noise,
in nakedness, in the slightest gleam of masculine sexuality. (The case histories of "psychoneurotic" war cas-
ualties show what aberrations of maternal individualism
and puritanism have done to many boys.)

It is no mere accident then that the branches of science most concerned with what seem to be irrational
manifestations of the human mind, i.e., psychopathology
and recently also anthropology (9), began to focus their
attention on the early training problems of the child in
their relation to his total individual and cultural potentialities. To the psychopathologist, and especially the
psychoanalyst, the dangers of interrupting the child's
behavior development unwisely seem to resemble those
in all epigenetic development: If anything is *suppressed
at the beginning*, then characterological and mental
potentialities may be destroyed and characterological
monstra created. The matter is complicated, however,
by the fact that spoiling in any single respect, by which
is meant active help in overindulgence rather than
mere patience with one habit or a group of habits, has

the same total effect, because it makes it impossible for the experience involved to find its proper status among other experiences.

Since the forms of neurosis appear to be the price paid in psychological currency for membership in civilization, it seems worth while to compare our training and education with that of primitives.

Primitive people are relatively freer from the educational guerrilla warfare of Western homes, and frequently abhor civilized methods of child training. They seem to be lenient with the child, strict with the adult. Nevertheless, their children experience, early, sometimes cruel restrictions. But students of their societies realize that, far from being arbitrarily lenient or cruel, these educational systems are logical in the sense that they tried to create a human variation which seemed to be the *optimum* under the natural and historic conditions of the tribe. (10) Thus, in simple cultures, training of the individual and preservation of the tribe appear to regulate one another automatically. Primitive societies cannot be used as an argument for hostility to training as such. On the whole, however, they seem successfully to avoid both *the early deep estrangement between body and self in the individual and between children and adults of a generation*—the commonest background of anxiety in individuals. The secret of their highly successful educational methods, regardless of the type of frustration imposed, seems to be the unquestioned promise of a participation in the prestige possibilities of the community.

Western education, in comparison, tends not only to suppress single acts of infantile habits, but also to devaluate in the small child the subjective potentialities of epigenetic development, namely, *pleasure and will as such.* It need only be remembered that the child's personal integrity is violated by calling *bodily expression as such "bad" or "sinful";* the security of the child-parent relationship is jeopardized by the threat (to the very small child) of *physical harm or psychological isolation coming from the parents themselves.* Then he is encouraged to become an individualist.

In view of the critical importance of the time element in development, it must be questioned how much of the individual's biological endowment is risked if it is tried to *mechanize out impulse life* along with the surroundings. Very early training, it is supposed by many, leads to automatic compliance and maximum efficiency. It is argued that the method works with dogs. Dogs, however, are trained to serve and to die; they will not be forced to represent to their young what their masters represented to them. Children will train their children, and any impoverishment of their impulse life will have to be considered not only in its value for a functioning without too much friction during one lifetime; generations will depend on every procreating individual's ability to face his children with the feeling that he was able to save some vital enthusiasm from the conflicts of his childhood.

There is a tendency in the obstetric world to help young mothers who are in conflict with the tasks of their maternal functions to rationalize the deprivations which they impose on their babies (*i.e.,* withholding of nursing or caressing), by considerations of comfort or career. This meets the tendency of many pediatricians to sidetrack the issue of moral authority by shifting training to that earlier time of the baby's life when it seems more an automatic issue.

Such procedures are now being carefully revised;

however, it must be kept in mind that some of the conflicting and unreasonable demands made on infants are
not mere signs of adult malice or ignorance, but are an
outgrowth of historical habits and socio-economic goals.
They are strengthened by the fear that a revision of
educational attitudes might jeopardize—to mention only
one strong set of trends—the development of the Anglo-
Saxon kind of decency (which often prefers breaking
to bending), of minute reliability and mechanical precision, of fraternal humility, of respect for women, etc.
—all of them felt by many to be basic virtues in this nation and a necessary balance to unselective immigration
and the boisterous free-for-all of continental and economic expansion. Therefore, while it is apparent that
no society can for long afford to nip in the bud too many
impulses with measures causing emotional impoverishment in too many individuals, scientific revision can
succeed only with due consideration for the (unconscious) unity of child training and national and economic goals. Certain groups, it is true, implore the
professions to replace the nation's search for more inclusive identities with any suggestions that could be
rationalized with new terminologies. This trend, too, has
to be responded to with a cautious appraisal of its historical meaning.

A comparative science of child-training is needed
which offers a body of scientifically established facts to
a world now being brought closer by equalizing systems of production and communication and by a sense
of wider identity. On the other hand, the physician and
psychotherapist must know that all of our children's
"problems" cannot be taken care of case by case, even
if guidance technics promise more intensive care for
larger numbers. He must become aware of the cul-

tural meaning of his profession, so that he may be instrumental in the gradual replacement of tradition by planning.

VI. Suggestions

A physician, constantly called by complaining parents to a sickly or naughty child, may ask himself whether he has not been given a role in a drama, the plot of which is unknown to him. If he knows the family background, he may be able to reconstruct it and—more than anybody else—to influence the outcome.

The understanding of the two principles of *epigenesis* and *social relativity* forms a basis for child care firm and flexible enough to allow for amendments and interpretations in specific cultural or individual circumstances. These very concepts forbid the formulation of advice for specific situations; their application grows out of clinical experience. Small issues will often show what aspect of training is compulsively overemphasized in a child's milieu: "First of all he must eat as much as possible"; "First of all he must obey when told to eat"; "First of all he must enjoy his food"; "First of all no food should be wasted"; "First of all he should be clean, learn to eat nicely," etc. In these cases it is well to look at the child and to determine what he needs most at his developmental stage and in his state of health. The child may appear to be spoiled and a period of firmer training more advisable than any consideration of his physical health or his I.Q. In another child it may be the relationship to the mother which has to be built anew to the exclusion of other factors. A child who has been sick might need nourishment even if he has to be spoiled in regard to the choice and delivery of his food, while another child may appear so restricted in all his expression or so backward in his abilities that new experiences and play adventures must be planned.

But the work is only half done when the advice is given. Deep-seated difficulties in the parents may lead any advice *ad absurdum* by the exaggeration of one aspect of it, or the neglect of another. Thus the therapist has to observe the development of his suggestion when put into actual practice.

In trying to guide, the physician cannot avoid making certain parents dependent on him, while estranging others. This and other aspects of his profession may at the moment make it impossible in most cases to do true guidance work; his may not be the psychological experience or the cultural role of the "family doctor"; but physicians will find it difficult to avoid the role thrust on them by questioning parenthood.

While sometimes a state of anxiety in a smaller child can be traced to known and observable changes in body, mind, or environment, an older child often cannot be understood without a psychoanalytic inquiry into the extent and depth of *regression* to earlier stages in which his personality feels safer from inner and outer dangers. Processes of this kind are rarely verbalized even, so it seems, in the child's own mind; they are an unconscious retreat along early established (often preverbal) developmental routes and direct questioning is fruitless. The physician can only try to study the child's total situation to provide him with the stimuli which will encourage him to advance again.

Several promising developments may be mentioned here: (1) Guidance clinics which keep the records of the whole family for reference even when various

specialists have entered the case, or the family has
changed residence; (2) extensive and intensive longitudinal studies of infantile problems in various social
milieus (3, 7); (3) study groups and committees (5)
of practitioners and research workers; (4) nursery
schools. As present-day conclusions in regard to the psychological importance of early childhood are tested, and
diagnostic and therapeutic methods improve, early diagnosis by attending specialists of problem children in
nursery schools can be provided. Proper treatment in all
degrees, ranging from slight changes in routine or play
activities to psychoanalytic treatment (if available in
the form authorized by one of the psychoanalytic training institutes), may then be advised and much unbal-
ance kept from becoming chronic. Residential nursery
schools promise special therapeutic possibilities and scientific returns.

In the treatment of unwelcome or dangerous habits it
is first of all necessary that the physician form a conviction in regard to their danger; only then can he give
parents (prejudiced for or against their own upbring-
ing) authoritative security that temporary habits in
themselves, i.e., without environmental overemphasis,
are not dangerous, and that in general an individualistic
approach to matters of early child training does not
necessarily imply a leniency that is apt to "spoil" the
child.

Neurotic habits differ from developmental habits
mainly in quantitative factors, i.e., they may occupy
most of the time and attention of a child who should be
getting ready for other habits; interference with them
may create deeper desperation or tighter closing up or
further regression in the child, etc. They require careful investigation of the total lifetime and life space of

the individual child. While various forms of not too sudden and not too rigid interference are known, these interferences should be adjusted to the biological and cultural peculiarities of the case; it is never wise to apply them without considering at the same time where in the total picture undue pressure is exerted on the child in terms of the stage of his development and the vulnerability of his personality. Of special and natural help are the new interests which are always ready to be awakened in a child and can draw his fearful attention away from the habit in question. The impulse to be modified can be guided into physiologically or socially less dangerous channels. (If, for example, the habits are characterized by destructiveness, paper and breakable objects of little value can be given to the child; in general, a corner in home or garden should be assigned and a period in his day provided where he has to be neither too careful nor too clean.)

It is especially important to remember that habits of long standing are seldom abandoned without the creation of transitory substitute habits which, in terms of the child's development, are less severe, but often more of a concern to the environment than was the old habit. (It may be found, for example, that a child who has given up bed-wetting may masturbate for a while, but in many respects appears more alert and more active.) A violent interruption of this new habit can only throw him back to the old one, or, if the way back is definitely closed, to worse habits or a general personality deformation. New habits should be expected and parents prepared for them. The important thing is not that a child become "faultless" overnight, but that he move forward.

Parents often need to be reminded that play is the

greatest balancing factor in a child's life; it is his most serious occupation. Disturbances (acute anxiety, restless shifting, lack of concentration, etc.) in his play are the clearest indicators of deeper disturbances.

The adult dealing with a child helps him most by being playful while playing with him, but realistic when representing future reality. Therefore, as the child grows older, play has to be balanced by regular talks in which the adult says what he knows and what he does not know, but first of all encourages the child to verbalize his changing ideas and fears. Misconceptions of growth, sex, and death cannot be corrected by a didactic attitude on the adult's part; they must correct themselves in repeated discussion in which the adult answers what he is asked—not more and not less.

If respect for children's play and their vivid interests is based on the understanding of their function, certain rules will be kept intuitively, which will allow the child to cross the border between his world and the adult's without too great difficulty. It is wise, for example, to give playing children some warning in advance if an eating or sleeping period is nearing. After giving them time "to wind up their business," compliance may be urged firmly. Other rules, pleasantly formulated and ready to be handed to mothers (as for example: "Don't take the child for a walk, go with him," or "Don't laugh at the child, laugh with him") can be found in Susan Isaacs' *The Nursery Years*. (11)

The essence of all these rules is of importance for the physician's relationship to the child: Things which *are done to the child* must be balanced by situations in which he is *actively leading or understanding*. Thus even in his direct contact with the child, it will be rewarding for the physician to take the time to make a game out of what he has to do to the smaller child; while unavoidable painful sessions may be followed by some game, suggested by physician, nurse, or patient, repeating the medical procedure with, this time, the doctor, parent, or doll the patient. The older child's confidence and consent can often be gained by truthful explanation and an appeal for his intelligent help rather than by assurances later belied. Play therapy immediately following hospitalization should be considered.

One can hardly help concluding that man's irrational outbursts, as well as the grandiose structure of his culture, are rooted in his prolonged childhood experimentation. To be overwhelmed—from within or without —is the growing being's most serious fear. When aroused, it stimulates the impulse to overwhelm, which, in the helpless human infant, can lead only to impotent, frustrating rage, or, if then inhibited, to meekness which, is only a patient way of waiting for a really worthwhile revenge.

References

1. Stockard, C. H.: *The Physical Basis of Personality,* W. W. Norton and Co., Inc., New York, 1931.
2. Gesell, A. and Armatruda, C. S.: *Developmental Diagnosis: Normal and Abnormal Child Development,* Hoeber, New York, 1941.
3. Ribble, Margaret A.: "Infantile Experience," and Murphy, Lois B.: "Childhood Experience," in *Personality and the Behavior Disorders,* edited by J. McV. Hunt, The Ronald Press Company, New York, 1944.
4. Freud, S.: "Three Contributions to the Theory of Sexuality," in *The Basic Writings of Sigmund Freud,* Modern Library, New York, 1938.

5. "Proceedings of the Conference on the Psychosomatic Status of the Infant at Birth," *Psychosomatic Med.* 6:151, (April) 1944.
6. Frank, L. K.: "Man's Multidimensional Environment," *The Scientific Monthly*, LVI, 1943.
7. Macfarlane, Jean W.: "The Guidance Study," *Sociometry*, 2, No. 3, 1939.
8. Freud, Anna and Burlingham, Dorothy: *War and Children*, International Universities Press, New York, 1942.
9. Mead, Margaret: "The Primitive Child," in *Handbook of Child Psychology*.
10. Erikson, E. H.: *J. Psychol.* 7:101, 1939.
11. Isaacs, Susan: *The Nursery Years*, George Routledge and Sons, Ltd., London, 1932.

Avoiding Behavior Problems*

BY *Benjamin Spock, M.D.*

Serious behavior problems seldom arise abruptly in later
childhood. The maladjustment in the child and the
tension between him and his parents have usually accumulated step by step as the child passed through successive stages in his development. In tracing the origins of
emotional disturbances, one encounters again and again
stories of friction developing in infancy and early childhood around certain typical everyday situations. The
commonest are: feeding, weaning, thumb-sucking, toilet
training, anxieties incidental to development, sibling
jealousy. It is helpful for physicians to know ahead of
time where and when these difficulties are likely to arise
and to give routine advice calculated to avoid or minimize them.

* From *Journal of Pediatrics,* Vol. 27, pp. 363–382, October 1945.
Reprinted by courtesy of the author and publishers, C. V. Mosby
Company.

Early Feeding Problems

Feeding problems seem to be the commonest behavior disturbances among American children. They not only cause much unnecessary malnutrition but also create tensions in mother and child which often predispose to other emotional disturbances outside the field of feeding. A majority of these problems begin during the first two years in the child's life. This is the age in which to expend the greatest prophylactic effort. It is during this period that the infant most regularly and frequently comes under the care of the doctor and nurse.

An early occasion for a feeding problem arises if the mother takes home her new baby along with a formula which is a little too large. When the baby, blissfully satisfied, falls asleep, the mother, instead of being pleased, holds the bottle up in alarm to see how much is left. She attempts to awaken him again by snapping the soles of his feet. When he opens his mouth to squawk she reinserts the nipple. If he tries to go to sleep again she stirs the nipple vigorously in his mouth.

Probably the reason that more problems do not develop in this newborn period is that the baby's appetite is increasing so fast that he catches up to the formula in a few days, usually before his mother has taken away his appetite completely. Occasionally, however, a feeding problem becomes well established at this early stage, more often in the case of the premature baby, because of the inverse ratio between the baby's size and the mother's anxiety. If a child has been systematically robbed of his desire for food from the very outset, the mother may be quite truthful when she reports that the child, now 5 years of age, has never shown any appetite.

Prevention is always easier than cure. The mother in the hospital is in a state of relative relaxation and calm compared to the tenseness which is so apt to envelop her when she takes her first baby home. This is the time to implant wholesome ideas about the naturalness of feeding and about the baby's capacity to know his caloric needs. The physician can refer casually to the formula as a rough approximation of what will satisfy the baby's hunger. Specifically he must explain that the baby will be a better judge than parent or scientist of the quantity he wants at each feeding, that the parent should not try, after the baby is no longer eager, to get in one more drop.

While he is suggesting a casual attitude toward bottle feeding he might well discuss also the philosophy of the feeding schedule. Infant feeding during the last forty years has been dominated by the idea of extreme regularity. This was a natural development in a phase devoted to bringing scientific order out of the ignorance and confusion of the past. But gradually an awareness has arisen that the swing to regularity has gone too far, that the insistence on rigid routine ignored the variations in functional capacity of individual babies and created, at least temporarily, frustration in those who had difficulty conforming to the schedule. Long-lasting has been the harmful effect on countless mothers who have been encouraged to become tense, authoritative, and intolerant in their attitudes toward their children.

The pendulum has begun to swing in the opposite direction. Various physicians, parents, and psychologists in rebellion against arbitrariness are experimenting with the so-called "self-demand schedule" according to which the infant is fed whenever he appears hungry. The clock is determinedly ignored.

Only time will show how far the pendulum will swing and how acceptable the method will prove to be. At the present time, the implication of anarchy in the method disturbs many who forget that until the twentieth century the young of the entire human race, in common with the rest of the animal kingdom, always determined their own feeding time without disastrous results.

As a matter of fact, observations of infants fed at their own demands indicate that most babies put themselves on a "regular" schedule very shortly. The baby may take a five-hour interval at one time of the day and a three-hour one at another time, but the pattern tends to repeat itself day after day, and the baby is on a regular schedule which is not predetermined by the physician and mother.

But even if we eventually go back to feeding at the infant's demand, it should be recognized that there will be a transition period, and that at least part of this generation of mothers imbued from their own infancy with the moral obligation of regularity cannot suddenly be cast adrift with the advice to feed the baby when he is hungry, without feeling insecure. There are other busy mothers for whom regularity has great practical value. It seems possible to retreat from the rigidity of the recent past, to allow for individual variations in both babies and parents, and still give the mother a framework of schedule within which to work. The mother might be told the following before she assumes the care of her infant:

"The feeding schedule is primarily for your convenience and to guard against excessive overfeeding. It is not a moral law. One baby adjusts to the four-hour interval from the start, another takes weeks to become regulated. You can wake the baby if he is asleep when feeding time comes. This seldom arouses balkiness because young infants, waked after four hours, will always show hunger within a few minutes. But if he wakes half an hour early or an hour early on occasion, and seems really hungry, do not be afraid to feed him then. He may compensate by a longer sleep the next time so that you can get back on schedule. Even if the schedule is accelerated all day, he will make up the time during the night. If he regularly is hungry in about three hours, he is a baby who temporarily needs a three-hour schedule. If he wakes at 2 A.M. or thereabouts, feed him. This does not establish a habit. All babies will give up the 2 A.M. feeding as soon as they are getting enough calories at the other meals to allow them to sleep through the night. Some babies can do this at the age of one week, others not until they are a month old." Such middle-of-the-road advice not only gives the mother who wants definiteness a tangible pattern to aim at, but also makes allowances for the baby's need. The mother who prefers to let the baby dictate can construe this system very liberally.

In attempting to remove some of the unwholesome apprehensiveness with which the new mother is apt to face the whole matter of the formula and the schedule, it is helpful to ask her to imagine how baby feeding proceeds in a primitive society without pediatricians or cows. The baby sleeps until he is hungry. He wakes and cries. The cry does not just give vent to the baby's feelings but also arouses a sense of urgency in the mother. In putting him to the breast she relaxes the tension in the baby and in herself. The baby nurses until he is satisfied and that satisfies the mother too. She does not worry about how much he has taken or about how much he has left. If a mother can visualize this picture at all, it will help her to understand that a civilized baby might also be trusted to take only as much as he wants at each feeding, to understand that minor irregularities in schedule do not violate the laws of nature or create spoiled personalities.

A more common time for the beginning of a feeding problem is when solid foods are first introduced. Most babies are at best doubtful about the first few mouthfuls. They wrinkle their brows, screw up their faces, and clack their tongues against the roofs of their mouths with at least a shade of disgust. The food is oozed out onto the chin. This bewilderment is understandable. The taste is strange, the consistency is strange, and the spoon is strange.

After two or three days the majority of babies seem to decide about cereal, which is the traditional first food, "It's strange but it's calories so I will take it." Within a week or two they are enthusiastic. But there are other babies who, on the second day, dislike the cereal more than on the first day, and on the third more than the second. If the mother persists in her efforts to force the substance in, the baby's obstinacy increases apace. When such a struggle has lasted for ten days the mother may call the physician with considerable alarm to say, "Doctor! Not only has the baby refused to take his cereal but this morning he refused his bottle too!" This example of how resistance once thoroughly aroused will spread to other areas, throws light not only on the development of feeding problems, but also on other behavior problems as well.

To prevent this battle over the first solid food

the mother can be advised at the time the solid food is prescribed, "Take it easy. It will require several days, perhaps several weeks, for the baby to get familiar with and enthusiastic about this new food. There's no hurry. The only important thing is to ensure that he will eventually like it. A mere taste a day is plenty until he becomes eager."

Cereal so often causes rebellion that I have in recent years routinely suggested a fruit like applesauce or mashed banana as the first solid food. Fruit is nearly sure-fire. The baby may be puzzled for a day or two, but then almost invariably becomes enthusiastic. After a couple of weeks when he has become thoroughly prejudiced in favor of the idea of solid food, cereal can be added too. He is now in a mood to take cereal or anything else equally unpalatable. Whereas if he has started with cereal and has fought it for two weeks, he will in turn fight fruit or any other delicacy on principle.

The time when feeding problems most commonly begin is around the age of one year. The 6- or 9-month-old baby is usually so hungry at mealtime that he opens his mouth and leans forward for whatever his mother puts on the spoon. Many 12- or 15-month-old children lose this avidity, at least in spells. They have time to ask themselves, "What appeals to me today?" Another factor is the growing egotism and negativism which are normal and desirable developments at this age. The less ravenous appetite and the increasing arbitrariness in expressing choices bring to the surface the normal and sometimes surprising variations in appetite, which Davis (1) observed in her experiments on self-selection of diet by children.

The conscientious, well-instructed mother cannot "take it." She knows something about what a well-balanced meal consists of and she has been led to believe that it is her duty to get it ingested. She complains bitterly and incredulously to the doctor, "Last week he loved his spinach best of all, but today he wouldn't even touch it." The foods most commonly refused or taken in reduced quantities are vegetables, cereals and milk. These three have always seemed to the mother the very foundation of health and growth. She dare not let them be slighted. She urges or forces. The baby's obstinacy increases. It is already too late to ease the situation completely at the next routine medical visit. Mother and baby both have their backs up. Each has become disillusioned about the other. All this is hard to undo.

The mother should be warned *before* the change occurs. In fact, it is wise to repeat the caution each time the baby is seen between 9 and 15 months. You say, "Don't be surprised if the baby's appetite falls off and he becomes more choosy. This is normal, otherwise he would become an obese monstrosity. He may turn against half his vegetables. Do not worry. Serve him the others. He may reject all his vegetables for days or even weeks. If this happens I wouldn't even serve them for two weeks. It will infuriate you to buy, prepare, and serve them only to have this whipper-snapper turn up his nose; and it will tempt you to try to force them. While he is off vegetables, serve him fruit twice a day. His fruit and his cod-liver oil will make up for the vegetables. He may temporarily cut down his milk intake to a pint a day or even less. A pint is enough anyway. If he goes below for any length of time you can serve it in milk puddings, milk-made cereal and cheese. His milk intake will probably go up again sooner or later if you don't turn it into an objectionable food.

by urging it. Instead of cooked cereal you can offer dry cereal, bread, potato, macaroni, tapioca, rice. Even if he wants none of these starches for considerable periods he will not suffer. If you will let your baby go on thinking of food as something always to be enjoyed, his nutrition will take care of itself, even though his appetite varies considerably in amount and in kind. But if during this period when he becomes more choosy you urge and force and make him feel that half the foods are his enemies, there's a good chance that you will make him thin and 'cantankerous.' "

There is one other occasion when feeding problems commonly begin and that is after an illness. A few days of a febrile disease may take all the color out of a baby's cheeks and a lot of the fat off his ribs. To the mother who has set great store by his plumpness and color this is deeply distressing. One day the fever is gone and the doctor says, "Now you can give him some cereal." The mother is overjoyed. She brings in the cereal, all eagerness, but the baby gives it a fishy eye and turns away. His gastrointestinal tract tells him it is not ready for cereal yet. His mother thinks either that he has forgotten how or is too weak to eat and that she must get him started. Forcing food in the face of the anorexia of illness creates a disgust reaction even more quickly, more intensively, and more permanently than forcing during health. Again prophylaxis is better than belated efforts at cure. At the end of each of the child's first illnesses the physician would do well to remind the mother that it often takes several days for the appetite to recover, but that when it does return it will not only be intense enough to ensure the child's former rate of growth, but also it will probably be abnormally great to ensure the recovery of the weight lost.

Weaning Conflicts and Thumb-Sucking

A story of a stormy battle over weaning will often be found in the past history of children with severe behavior disturbances, suggesting that the kind of resentment created by this particular struggle may be unusually long-lasting and bitter. Certainly the pediatrician is familiar with the common complaint that a feeding problem centering around milk started abruptly at the time of an attempted weaning to the cup.

How should weaning be managed and at what age? Experience suggests that there is no simple or single answer. Babies are born with a strong instinct to suck quite apart from the instinct of hunger. In some babies this desire to suck appears to weaken and disappear in the last half of the first year. Others seem unwilling to begin to give up sucking until the first half of the second year. The baby will show in various ways how ready he is for weaning from breast or bottle, and it seems fair that his readiness should be the main guide of parent and physician. If one questions mothers of 8- or 9-month-old infants about their attitudes toward the bottle, toward the cup, and toward thumb-sucking, the answers fall between two extremes. Of one baby the mother will say, "He seems to be bored with the bottle. Half the time he only chews on it or plays with the nipple. When I offer him milk from a cup he takes it enthusiastically. He isn't doing any thumb-sucking." At the other extreme is the baby whose mother says, "Oh, Doctor! How he loves his bottle. All the time he is eating his food, he is watching the bottle out of the corner of his eye and when it's time for the bottle, he's all eagerness. He clutches and fondles it while he's drinking and always finishes it to the last drop. He's very suspicious of milk in the cup and will take only a sip at most. It's not that he doesn't know how, because he takes his orange juice well from the cup. He is doing a lot of thumb-sucking." Many babies of course fall between these two extremes, and the thumb-sucking is not necessarily so highly correlated with the other signs of sucking need.

For the sake of the discussion let us consider the two clear-cut types. The baby who at 8 or 9 months is getting bored with breast or bottle and is taking milk eagerly from the cup seems ready for weaning and it would seem entirely proper to tell his mother, "Gradually over a period of weeks, put more and more of his milk in the cup at each meal until the bottle is done with." Another gradual method is to substitute the cup for the bottle first at breakfast, then at lunch, then at supper, allowing a couple of weeks between each change. If during the process the baby shows reluctance to go further, the mother should follow his cue. There is often a temporary increase in the desire to suckle during illness, during the miserable stage of teething, or during any episode which upsets his spirits.

If the baby at 9 months still loves his bottle dearly and is suspicious of milk from the cup, present-day teaching emphatically advises against attempting to force the issue. Experience with forced weaning shows that many babies will react violently with an absolute and often long-lasting refusal to tolerate the cup. An occasional baby will go on a complete hunger strike for several days and another may become generally resentful and hostile. It is true that many babies who have been deprived of a bottle against their wishes, will, after holding out for two or three days, apparently decide to let bygones be bygones. But one cannot tell ahead of time which will give in and which will remain adamant. From the sharp distinction that many a baby makes between orange juice and milk from the cup, it is clear that he is not primarily suspicious of the cup itself. He apparently feels deeply that milk from bottle or breast has been and still is his chief emotional gratification and perceives that milk-in-cup is a threat to its continuance.

It will help to prepare the infant for eventual weaning to offer him a sip of milk a day from the cup beginning at 5 months. At that age he will try almost anything. At 10 months he has become wise enough and opinionated enough so that he is apt to object to anything newfangled on principle. Unfortunately, however, the babies who seem destined to be long sucklers may take the sip a day for several months and then turn sharply and indignantly against the cup at about the age of 10 months.

If a baby falls into the group of those who are still devoted to the bottle and suspicious of the cup at 9 or 10 months, the chances are good that he will stay of the same opinion until he is at least 14 or 15 months. Then he will relent gradually. But even when initial progress is good he is apt to want the supper bottle for several months more. It is important that during this age of suspicion of the cup, between, say 10 and 15 months, that the mother refrain from urging the cup or withholding the bottle, since this seems to increase his dependence on the bottle and postpone his readiness for weaning.

Thumb-sucking is obviously related to the sucking instinct and the problem of weaning. Until recent years it was universally considered just a bad habit which ought to be broken quickly before it became ingrained. Levy (2) collected evidence that the baby sucks his thumb because he has not gotten enough satisfaction from the breast or bottle, that babies whose bottles took a long time to empty were less apt to thumb-suck than those who drank their bottles quickly through large nipple holes, and that babies who had few nursings in the twenty-four hours were more apt to thumb-suck than those who had frequent nursings. He showed that puppies, deprived of the chance to suckle through being fed by a medicine dropper, sucked vigorously on various parts of their own and each other's bodies. I have repeatedly seen thumb-sucking begin at the period when an infant was able to reduce his bottle time from twenty to ten minutes because of his growing strength and the aging of the nipple, or when he was suddenly weaned to the cup at an early age. I have the impression that there are two other etiological factors. First, there seem to be wide constitutional differences in the amount of sucking craving in different babies. Second, the important time to insure complete sucking satisfaction is in the first three or four months of life. Many babies are unable to get their thumbs into their mouths except by accident before the age of 3 months and therefore can give their mothers only vague signs of their unsatisfied craving at the period when correction is most vital. Incidentally thumb-sucking that occurs only just before feedings seems to be merely an expression of hunger.

If thumb-sucking in early infancy is primarily the result of a deficit in sucking satisfaction at breast or bottle, the prophylaxis and treatment should consist in providing longer and more frequent opportunities to nurse. For the breast-fed baby this means allowing him to nurse as long as he feels the urge rather than stopping at any aribitrary number of minutes. Sometimes a baby taking both breasts at each feeding and being removed after ten minutes on the first, stops spontaneously after five minutes on the second because he is too full (with the initial copious flow), even though he has not had his quota of sucking. In a few cases this can be solved by prolonged nursing at only one breast. But if the milk is insufficient at least the baby can be allowed to nurse much longer on the first breast before being shifted to the second.

Just as soon as the bottle-fed baby begins to suck his thumb, or, more important, shows signs of *trying* to, one should inquire whether he has recently been able to drain the bottle in a shorter time and suggest a new set of nipples with smaller openings.

Occasionally one can suggest more frequent feedings in the young infant if he is willing to take them and his mother to give them. Few mothers, however, take kindly to the idea of reverting to a three-hour schedule unless they are excessively alarmed by thumb-sucking. It is sensible though, when the baby is beginning to thumb-suck, to advise against omitting the 10 P.M. and the 6 A.M. feedings for a while longer, even though the baby seems ready for the change in other respects.

If the feedings are lengthened or made more frequent and the thumb-sucking still persists, the hypothesis that the baby is trying to make up insufficient nursing time will dictate emphatically that no effort should be made to interfere with the thumb-sucking. The aim, of course, should be to give the baby every opportunity to suck by any means that he can use.

By the time a baby is a year old thumb-sucking appears to be no longer primarily a need to satisfy the sucking instinct but has become a comforter. He no longer sucks it a certain number of minutes every day but only on special occasions: when he is going to sleep, when he is fatigued, when he is frustrated, when he is bored. There is no longer any point in trying to increase his nursing time. The constructive thing with the 1-, 2-, or 3-year-old child is to survey his daily life to see whether he has enough playthings, play space, and playmates to make life absorbing. Is he being treated at home in such a way that he feels secure and happy? Whether or not constructive changes can be made in his daily routine and handling, it seems wise to advise the parents to make no direct efforts to stop the thumb-sucking. The normal tendency is for the child to give up the habit gradually as he acquires inner security and interest and absorption in the world around him. Efforts to stop the habit from the outside, whether they consist of physical restraints, punishment, nagging, or teasing, seem only to increase the child's need of his thumb. Sometimes a child who has practically given up thumb-sucking does it only when a certain relative is near by who has always made most fuss about it. We all know dozens of cases where every form of physical restraint and moral intimidation were used without beneficial effect. If the parent objects to this "laissez-faire" attitude toward thumb-sucking on the basis that the teeth are being made crooked, the answer again is that letting the child alone is often the quickest way to stop the thumb-sucking and the threat to the teeth.

A physician might summarize his discussion with a mother about weaning and thumb-sucking as follows: "Every baby is born with a strong instinct to suck. The intensity and duration of this instinct seem to vary in

different individuals. We should consult the baby about
the time for weaning from the breast or bottle. One infant at 9 months is bored with the bottle, enthusiastic
about milk from the cup. He seems ready for gradual
weaning. Another at the same age rejects the cup and
shows a deep devotion to the bottle. He may not be
ready until 15 months or later. Do not force for fear of
making him balky or resentful. Urging may prolong his
dependence on the bottle. Thumb-sucking in the early
months suggests that the infant is not getting sufficient
suckling satisfaction at breast or bottle. At the first sign
try to prolong the nursing time and to retain frequent
feedings. By the age of one year thumb-sucking appears
to have become a comforter when the baby is tired,
bored, or frustrated. Constructive treatment consists in
insuring that his life is as happy as possible, counting on
him gradually to give up the habit as fast as he is able.
In a persistent case efforts to interfere directly seldom
succeed and may prolong the habit."

Bowel Training

There is a widespread but unfounded belief that
good health is acquired through meticulous regularity
of bowel movement. In order to get the baby started
early on this mythical road to health, and also for the
sake of general elegance, it has become the style in
our twentieth century American civilization to put a lot
of effort into and to take great satisfaction from early
and rigorous toilet training. Often to the parents' despair training has broken down at a later stage of the
child's development and the child has resisted retraining until an abnormally late age. The psychoanalysts
have felt that in certain individuals these over-vigorous

training efforts created permanent distortions of the personality.

In the early months of infancy the movement of the bowels is a fairly simple reflex. It is true that when the reflex evacuation occurs at a predictable time of day the assiduous mother can catch the movement in an appropriate vessel. But it is more the mother who is trained than the baby. As the infant gets into the second half of the first year and acquires voluntary control of the lower half of his body, he acquires more voluntary control of the bowel movement too. For instance if the mother rushes him to the potty too abruptly he may become startled and cease pushing. As he gets into the second year he acquires not only further control, but also a genuine interest in the movement as well. He turns around to see what he has done, babbles about it, even plays in it if he has not been inhibited. He gradually takes a possessive proprietary attitude toward it, brings his mother in to admire what he has done.

Each of us has been told by at least one happy-go-lucky mother that her baby trained himself to the toilet in the second half of the second year without her making any effort. The child, naturally, in the course of his social development reaches a stage where he wants to deposit his movement in the same place that the rest of the family use, just the way he wants to use his mother's toothbrush or mop.

Observation of children trained for the bowel movement at different age periods suggests that the age at which the baby is first set on the toilet is not of primary importance. There are babies trained early who stay trained without gross evidence of personality distortion. There are babies trained early who rebel during the second year and suffer tragic changes in character during the prolonged conflict with a severe parent. And among the babies whose training has been postponed until after the age of 12 months some get into trouble and others do not. It seems to me that the most important factors are *how the mother goes about it and how the baby feels about it during the second year.*

If during the second year when the baby is becoming more possessive of his movement a stern and exacting mother is going at his toileting hammer and tongs, it is clear why a conflict will occur. It is as if the grim mother were saying by her behavior, "It isn't your movement, it is mine. You must produce it for me, when I say, where I say." This seems to offend his sense of proprietorship and arouses the negativism which is his handiest weapon at this period. It doesn't take an outrageously demanding mother to start a conflict during the second year. Many babies at this age get so sensitive about their rights and interests that they rebel against minor degrees of maternal insistence.

There are other factors in toilet rebellion besides the mother's demanding attitude. Of vital importance is the comfortableness of the bowel movement. The baby who has had painfully hard movements on frequent occasions will naturally dread the toilet seat as soon as he learns what is expected of him there. The request, "Now do your duty," when translated by his experience means, "Now hurt yourself." It is no wonder that he resists sitting down, or if sitting, that he procrastinates. I believe that a large proportion of the babies who resist training come from the group who have had painful movements. This puts on the physician the responsibility of carefully preventing or curing all painful constipation throughout the first two years of life.

Another factor of great importance is whether or not the infant is naturally regular. The baby who always moves his bowels within ten minutes after the first meal of the day is practically never a training problem. He moves so quickly and thoughtlessly that there is no reason for his mother to become insistent. It is when the movement occurs without any regular rhythm that the mother is tempted to become overstrenuous and demanding in her efforts to put him on the toilet often and to keep him there for long periods, to use strong disapproval when he fails, and to act as if he had redeemed himself when he succeeds.

There are three common forms that the resistance against training takes. The first is reluctance to sit on the toilet or even to go into the bathroom. The reluctance may be mild and transitory or it may develop into violent rage and terror. Another baby is more subtle and "polite." He may sit down willingly but nothing happens so long as he is on the toilet, whether he is kept there five minutes or fifty. The movement occurs promptly after he has gotten up. Mothers complain, "He seems to have forgotten what he's put there for." But a baby who has been performing well for several months does not forget that easily. There is more indication that he has moved on to a new phase of awareness and resolved to get matters back under his own control. The third form that resistance commonly takes is for the infant to retain his movement not only while he is on the toilet but afterwards, too. He acquires a constipation of purely psychological origin. The retained movement, however, becomes hard and painful to pass. He now has two reasons for withholding.

At this stage the determined mother is apt to use suppositories or enemas. Almost invariably this intensifies his resistance and alarm. A suppository used for two or three days in the first stages of toilet training may not be harmful though some would prefer not to use them even then. But suppositories or enemas after the child has begun to resist training are dangerous in the extreme and should never be recommended.

What does happen to a small child's personality in the course of a long struggle against training? He is first of all made unduly obstinate and hostile. This in itself is an unfortunate influence at such an impressionable age. But worse than the hostility is the insecurity which usually keeps pace with it. The small child cannot consistently defy his mother without becoming uneasy and guilty and this throws his whole personality out of balance. Such is the case when a boy of 4 has developed a compulsion to touch constantly the seat of his pants and then sniff his fingers. He is obsessed with the fear that he has soiled his pants even though he has not actually done so for a couple of years. In less dramatic form it shows up in the little girl who runs crying to her mother every time she gets a speck of earth on her hand. The fear that was impressed on her in the earlier training period has spread to include dirtiness in any form.

One might summarize a sensible discussion with the parent about bowel training as follows: "It is normal for many individuals to move the bowels irregularly. Do not try to change this as long as the movements are comfortably soft. Every child gradually acquires control of his bowel function and becomes willing to dispose of his movement in a way that is locally conventional. You do not need to become concerned about this process. It seems unnatural to do anything before the baby can sit up. It is important to keep his bowel movements soft so that he will not dread defecation. When you begin to put him on the chair or toilet, do it casually and briefly. This means putting him on it at just the right moment, an easy job with the regular baby, but one calling for ingenuity or postponement of the whole program when the movement comes at any time of the day. Do not make it a moral issue. Between 1 and 2 years it is normal for the baby to acquire a proprietary interest and pride in his movement. During this period he may show resistance to your efforts to capture his movement. He may object to going to the bathroom or wait until he gets up to move his bowels, or become constipated. Relax your efforts gracefully until he feels more coöperative. Your persistence, especially if you resort to suppositories or enemas, will only increase his rebellion and distort his personality."

Urine Training

Control of the urinary bladder, like control of the bowels, is something which the child gradually acquires by himself through physiologic development. The most that the parent can accomplish is to persuade the child to void in the conventional receptacle a little earlier than the child would have gotten that idea by himself. During most of the first year the bladder retains little urine and voids frequently though there is considerable variation in different individuals. A great majority of babies do not retain their urine for as long as two hours until they are approximately 15 months old. By this age they have usually acquired enough conscious awareness of urination to comprehend the purpose of toileting if the mother has gone at it in a sensible way.

At this period, however, the mother has to take all the responsibility. The child becomes aware of what is about to happen only a few seconds ahead of time and participates voluntarily only to the extent of standing still. During the second half of the second year he shows increasing voluntary control. If his mother has been teaching him that she expects the urine to go into the toilet, he now retains the urine for a few seconds beyond the stage of comfort and may signal his mother with some sound that signifies urgency. He may on the other hand forget to warn her until it is too late. Most children still need to be watched and reminded into at least the first part of the third year.

Night control is not usually acquired until after the child has taken over the responsibility of keeping himself dry during the daytime. But as should be pointed out to parents, retention of urine at night is a normal development in the inherent maturing of bladder function and has little to do with whether the child is picked up during the evening. It is true that a dry bed is secured a little earlier if the long night interval is broken. But the child would not be caught dry, either at 10 P.M. or at 7 A.M., unless the bladder were already tending to longer and longer retention. That it is not the parents' training efforts that make the child dry at night is shown in another way by the rare child, usually a girl, who jumps the gun and becomes dry at night before the age of a year and before her parents have made any move at even daytime training.

What are the causes of delayed control both day and night? First of all there is the apparently wide variation between individuals in the maturing of bladder function as is shown not just by individual cases but by the observation that on the average boys are slower than girls.

Training itself, if it is done in the wrong spirit, sometimes works to postpone voluntary control. The child between 1 and 1-½ who is rigorously set down once an hour and kept there for long periods sometimes rebels against this unnatural imprisonment and becomes firmly determined never to void in the proper place. This resistance shows up more often in prolonged night wetting. A 2-year-old son of ambitious parents is at first caught dry about half the time at 10 p.m. and 7 a.m. At first their zeal is rewarded but after a few weeks of this night work, coupled with exhortations and admonitions during the daytime, he gets wetter and wetter. Instead of being warned by these negative results the parents resolve to torture themselves and the poor child even further and take turns getting him up every two hours right through the night. Again there is partial success at first. But after a while the boy's resistance becomes so ingenious even in his sleep, that he wets before even two hours are up.

At least in some individuals tension and uneasiness of many kinds seem to be readily communicated to the bladder, rendering it less capable of relaxing and of retaining urine. It is common for the 2- or 3-year-old who has been dry at night for six months to begin wetting again temporarily when he moves to a new house, or when his mother leaves him to go to the hospital, or when the new baby sister comes home, or when he is frightened by a dog, or after he has gone to the circus. This mechanism is no more mysterious than the frequency of the adult athlete before the race. If almost any kind of emotional disturbance, small as well as great, can cause a child to relapse temporarily into enuresis, it is easy to see why a child who lives in a constant state of tension during his early years never has sufficient equanimity or inner relaxation to become dry in the first place.

When the physician is consulted because a young child is still wetting his bed, the first question should be whether there are tensions operating to postpone the child's normal inherent progress to dryness. In one case the child needs only a little more time to feel at home in a new situation. In another the friction between himself and his parents centers around a feeding problem. More commonly it is apparent that the mother's handling all day long is characterized by pushing, nagging, and unnecessary interference. Occasionally the only problem is that the parents are expecting perfect control at an age when a good proportion of children are still wetting regularly or intermittently. Certainly if the parents are going at the enuresis by intensive methods that are bringing diminishing returns they should be called off. This is done not with the promise that this new technique will bring immediate success, but that in the long run it will work in the right direction. In the meantime less harm will be done to the child's personality.

The physician is often troubled with the question of whether he should recommend a complete urological examination. There are cases, of course, where the symptomatology or the results of urinalysis demand further investigation. But in a great majority of cases of slow bladder control there is no reason to suspect an organic cause. The point is that hospitalization, anesthesia and instrumentation, with or without pain, are all alarming to small children. This danger should be given serious consideration in deciding whether or not to investigate further.

One might summarize a discussion of urine training with the mother as follows: "Urine training is largely accomplished by the child himself. His bladder function, through a normal process of maturing, comes to retain urine for longer periods. Simultaneously the child acquires a conscious control of voiding. Your baby, if he is average in this respect, will, in the neighborhood of a year and a quarter, begin to retain his urine for about two hours at a time. He will also be wise enough at this stage to see what you are after when you put him on the toilet. If you put him on only when he is dry after two hours, you will insure three things: (1) His bladder function is ready for coöperation. (2) His bladder at that moment will be full. He will urinate soon. Therefore you will not have to antagonize him by keeping him on for a long time. (3) Your training efforts will be gradual since you will only find him dry occasionally at first. After some months he will begin to take the responsibility of telling you when he needs to urinate. In time also his bladder will learn to retain urine throughout the night. Inner security and emotional relaxation are necessary for this progress of bladder function."

Anxieties in the Early Years

The fears of children shift with age. The newborn is alarmed by loud noises and loss of support. By about 5 months he can recognize the difference between friends and strangers and may cry with anxiety if approached too suddenly.

By a year babies are apt to show that they now realize that they depend on their mothers for comfort and safety. Mothers often complain at this stage, "He is getting so he cries every time I go out of the room." Usually the child who cries this way is confined in his crib or play pen. The mother hopes to keep him in the pen for many more months because it is practical. Some mothers even think that confining a child by himself will develop his capacity for independence.

It seems to me wiser when the baby has reached the stage where he is no longer happy in his pen and feels lonesome every time his mother leaves the room to admit that he has reached a new phase in his emotional development and to let him out on the floor. When he wants to be near his mother he can creep or toddle after her. Then when his need for security is satisfied he gets the urge to do a little independent exploring and moves into the next room. After ten minutes his hankering for company reasserts itself and he scrambles back to his mother again. By degrees he increases his independence, partly by the very process of satisfying his need for dependence as soon as he feels it. It seems to me fair to say that the baby who is kept crying in his pen while his mother is out of the room is only becoming more convinced of his own insecurity. If the physician suggests letting the child play on the floor as soon as he becomes unhappy in the pen, the mother will immediately protest that the baby will break things or hurt himself. The answer is that eventually the household furnishings must be rearranged anyway to allow him scope for exploring without too much danger to himself or the bric-a-brac. Why not now when he shows he needs it? He will not be more reasonable at a year and a half.

There is another side to the insecurity which develops around the age of a year. As the infant becomes more conscious of his dependence on his mother he also is apt to become much more suspicious of strangers. In the physician's office a majority of the babies who at 8 or 10 months were quite unafraid, now between 12 and 15 months leap to their feet in alarm as he approaches and try, howling, to climb onto their mothers for safety. The child who between 1 and 2 sees little of anyone besides his parents, tends to retain this suspiciousness both of adults and children. Then when he is thrown among outsiders at 2 or 3 he shrinks back with a look of alarm and tries to hide behind his mother. At best it will take him a long time to learn that other grownups and other children are fun too. Some overprotected children never do learn the joy of give and take even in adulthood.

The baby at 1 year, even though he has an initial timidity about anyone strange, nevertheless has also a great passion to approach, to make friends. This outgoing urge overcomes his caution if he is allowed time. A mother should be encouraged to give her year-old baby plenty of opportunity to get used to outsiders, especially children. Of course he will not develop much capacity for *coöperative* play before the age of 2 but if he learns before 2 that there are other children in the world and how to play in their presence, he will by 2-½ be ready for give and take when that phase is due.

There appears to be a new phase of increased dependence that crops out between the ages of one and three quarters and two and a quarter. Mothers often complain at this stage that their children are getting more tied to their apron strings and shy with strangers, showing reluctance to being left alone at bedtime, sometimes calling out or climbing out of the crib and joining the family a dozen times during the evening. Some of the children who start nursery school before the age of 2-½ cry at first when their mothers leave them there and take a longer time to feel at home with the group. This tendency to greater dependence around 2 makes the child more sensitive to any sudden or prolonged separation from the mother or other close adult. This should be taken into consideration if the mother is thinking for example of taking a job, going on a trip, or having an elective operation. If the right preparations are not made her absence may create a real anxiety state in the child, particularly if he is an only child or already overdependent.

Here is a typical story of a badly handled separation: A mother abruptly takes a job leaving her 22-month-old boy in the care of a woman with whom he is not familiar. The first day he is well behaved but when his mother returns that evening he hangs on to her like a leech, refusing to let the other woman come anywhere near. The next morning there is a scene when his mother leaves and in the evening he not only refuses to let her out of his sight but also he refuses to be put in bed. If she tears herself away he may cry anxiously for hours. If she sits by his crib he lies down only as long as she sits still. Her slightest move toward the door brings him instantly to his feet crying.

Anxiety about wetting often seems to play a part in these cases. The child keeps begging to be taken to the toilet throughout the evening or when he wakes later. One is apt to jump to the conclusion that he is using this merely as an excuse to hold the parents near but it probably has another significance too. It is when the child is about 2 that the adults are apt to express definite concern about having him stay dry. It may be that his fear that he will displease his mother by wetting gets linked up with his fear that she will go away and leave him again. Once an anxiety over separation from the parent is started it is difficult to allay. Letting the child "cry it out" may take months, is agonizing to the mother, and probably further destroys the child's security. The only solution I know of for the severe bedtime anxiety, and it is not an easy one, is to have the mother settle down beside the crib until the child is *surely* asleep, even if it takes hours at first, and to count on his slowly returning confidence to shorten his anxious, wakeful period by gradual steps.

I think that such anxieties can be largely avoided if the emotional dependence of young children is understood and respected. This brings up the whole subject of parental, foster parental, and group care. (In this discussion age divisions are used arbitrarily for simplification.) In the first place mothers should understand clearly that the young child, particularly up to the age of 3, derives his greatest security from a sense of belonging intimately and irrevocably to his parents. Generally speaking a mother should be discouraged from going to work during the child's early years unless it is really essential from the point of view of finances or of the mother's morale, and unless there is a relative, maid, friend, or foster mother to take her place who is familiar, loving, comfortable and can be counted on to last at the job, or unless there is excellent nursery school care to which the child is mature enough to adjust.

If the mother must leave him in the care of a stranger coming into the home the important thing is to accustom him to her, to transfer his dependence to her by

gradual degrees especially if he is in the sensitive period around 2 years. Ideally he should have a chance to
get used to the stranger's presence before she even tries
to do things for him which itself may take a couple of
weeks or more. Then gradually she participates in his
care. When he accepts this his mother can begin to
leave him first for only half an hour, then lengthening
her absences as the child adjusts to them. Many children stay secure without these precautions which may
seem overfussy but I think they are worth while in
order to avoid the occasionally bad outcome.

Needless to say the person to whom the child is to be
entrusted should be chosen not primarily on the basis
of experience, training, or cultural level but for qualities
that are vital to the child: a capacity to love him
warmly without smothering him, to handle him easily
wihout nagging or severity.

It is wise I believe to avoid the usual type of *day
nursery* care, certainly before the age of 2 or 2-½ years.
In the first place it is doubtful whether any child before
2 can get enough sense of being really cherished from
ten or twelve hours a day of *group* care of even the
best quality. Furthermore few day nurseries have staffs
of teachers trained in modern concepts of children's
needs.

On the other hand, first rate *nursery schools*, well
equipped and with a sufficient number of trained teachers selected on the basis of temperament and understanding, have a contribution to offer the 2- to 6-year-old
children of working or nonworking mothers. They supplement the modern child's life where it is most often
lacking—in play space, in variety of toys and apparatus and materials, in companions of the right age,
in opportunity to learn the fun of coöperative play and

to lose self-consciousness and overawareness of parents. Here for a few hours (three to four) a day the child may gain much but it is important to accustom the child under 3 to nursery school gradually. If the teachers are understanding and know their job, they will encourage the mother of a sensitive younger child to remain at school for part of the day and then take him home herself for a sufficient number of days until he comes to feel at home and gradually shifts some of his dependence to the teachers. The commonest mistake is for the mother to try to sneak away on the first or second day just as soon as the child is half absorbed. When he discovers her absence he feels abandoned.

The ideal arrangement is when school runs for half or three quarters of the day, leaving a number of hours when the child can be with his mother. All-day nursery schools may be necessary where mothers have to take full-time jobs but this long separation is less desirable, especially for the child under 3. Practically all children benefit from first-rate nursery school care by the age of 2-½, and most do so by 2. There is an occasional child of 2 who is so intensely dependent that he cannot tolerate the separation from mother or the immersion in the group even when it is gently done. He requires a more gradual weaning: a slow familiarization with one or two playmates in the mother's presence and a few more months of maturing. If his mother must work he may do better until he is 3 with an excellent foster mother. The baby or small child up to 2, 2-½, or 3, who *must* be left *outside* the home with strangers for all-day care, may better be placed in a private home ("foster care" or "foster day care") that is supervised by a conscientious agency in the care of a proved, motherly woman who is able to give one or two young children the kind of attention and affection that approximates the mother's own. The mother and child should together visit the foster mother until confidence in her is built up.

The anxieties that a child is liable to have by the time he is 3 or 3-½ are more complex. He may acquire a sudden fear of dogs without ever having been attacked by one. He hears that someone has died and after a few questions about what death is asks anxiously, "Do I have to die?" The sight of a cripple fills him with dread. He has reached a stage of mental and emotional development where he can imagine and apply to himself dangers which he has never experienced.

These fears appear to develop more often and more intensely in children who in their earlier period have been overprotected or who have been made tense by struggles over such matters as feeding or toilet training. It is as though what previously had been a vague inner uneasiness is now able to be crystallized by the imagination into a specific phobia. If this is all true then the prophylaxis of fears at 3 consists in the wise handling of a child from birth on.

There are further possibilities of prevention in one particular group of fears. The 3-year-old is not only alarmed by truly crippled and malformed people. His limited experience and fertile imagination sometimes make him misinterpret the natural physical differences between boy and girl and jump to the conclusion that some injury has befallen the girl. This misunderstanding worries girls as well as boys, and in both leads at times to a preoccupied, anxious handling of the genitalia.

It is important for parents to know that questions

about bodily differences occur to children around the age of 3 and to answer the first questions cheerfully, reassuringly, making it clear that girls are *meant* to be one way and boys another. If the parent tries to hush the question it will confirm the child in his suspicion that something terrible has happened. The little girl needs extra reassurance because at her age it seems better to have something, whether she was intended to have it or not and this is a good time to tell her that girls can have babies of their own when they grow up.

If physicians realize that worry about bodily differences is a common cause of preoccupied handling of the genitals in early childhood, they can then not only give helpful constructive advice to parents but they will recognize also the importance of refraining, when possible, from operations or treatment in the genital region. It has been traditional to blame masturbation on local irritation and to recommend circumcision for the boy or vaginal treatments for the girl who has evidence of mild inflammation. Handling of the genitals itself often produces mild infection but this is effect rather than cause. If the child is doing it because of worry that some injury has happened or may happen, then the worst possible treatment is actually to operate. What the child is dreading comes true. It is clear also why the parent should not attempt to combat the masturbation with threats that it will cause injury. Many modern parents, having heard that it is considered wrong to make a moral issue of masturbation, slip into the alternative of telling the child that the practice will hurt his genitals. With this new reinforcement of his fear he may cease handling himself. But the psychological effect is bad and may result in sexual maladjustment later. The parents' efforts should be directed to understanding why the child masturbates, to reassuring him about his anatomy and to making his daily life satisfying and absorbing. It is better to say nothing to the child about the masturbation. But if they feel that they must say something at least to stop his masturbating in public, let them confine themselves to some remark such as, "People don't think it is very polite."

To summarize then: It is helpful for physicians and parents to know that children become liable to characteristic anxieties at different ages. These are by-products of various stages of emotional development. The baby around a year is becoming aware of his dependence on his mother. His increasing interest in things around him will wean him of this if he is spared too much parental concern or domination and is allowed freedom and contact with other adults and children. His need of his mother acquires a new intensity at about the age of 2 years. Abrupt unprepared separation from her may precipitate an anxiety state. Mothers should be discouraged from going to work when their children are young unless the need is imperative and unless the child can be left with an ideal and familiar substitute either in the home or in a foster day home. *All-day group* (nursery) care before the age of 2-½ is generally unsatisfactory. First-rate nursery schools have much to contribute but because of the greater dependence of children up to 2-½ or 3, their introduction should be gradual and all-day attendance should preferably be avoided.

The 3-year-old's imagination makes him apply all kinds of real and fantastic dangers to himself. Anxiety about his genitals is common and often leads to preoccupied handling. This calls for understanding and wisdom on the part of parents and physician.

Jealousy of the New Baby

Many severe behavior problems spring from a corrosive jealousy of a new baby in the family. The jealousy is more apt to be intense when the older child is under 5 years of age. This is the period of his life before he has formed strong attachments and interests outside the home, when his main security comes from his close emotional dependence on his parents. There is also a greater likelihood of severe jealousy when the older child is the first in the family. He has been the recipient of all the adoration and fussing of which his parents are capable. He has taken this attention for granted and tacitly assumed through no fault of his own that he was the center of the universe. The impact of the arrival of a competitor may be shattering. One child becomes aggressive and vengeful; another loses all his joy in life and mopes disconsolately for months. Even when the child eventually makes good progress in digesting his jealousy, his personality throughout the rest of childhood and adult life is apt to show sensitive spots from the old hurt.

Jealousy is one of the facts of life and cannot be wholly prevented by any bag of tricks. Most depends, of course, on the wholeheartedness of the parents' love for each of their children. Advice from a physician cannot make up for defects in the parents' attitudes. But the physician should do what he can both by practical suggestions and, more important, by so interpreting the older child's predicament that the parents, sympathizing, will handle the situation with a maximum of understanding.

It is better for the child to know ahead of time that a baby is expected so that he can get used to the idea gradually. This helps less than an adult would expect because the small child's imagination may not create anything like the reality. He may visualize an animated doll to tote around or a full-fledged companion. Even if he knows and loves a neighbor's baby, he is apt to find that his mother's baby evokes entirely different feelings. Most professionals in the children's field feel that the child should know that the baby is growing within the mother's abdomen. This is not primarily for the sake of abstract honesty but because it is known that many children beyond the age of 3 and some under 3, suspect the truth anyway, through a combination of shrewd observation, slips in the conversation of adults, and perhaps a touch of intuition. One supposedly innocent 3-year-old will call attention to this mother's changing girth with hints, partly questioning, partly accusatory. Another will suddenly hit at her abdomen as if already jealous of what he suspects is there. The child who is hesitantly coming to his own conclusion that the new baby is growing in the mother is likely to become troubled. It is not that he cannot take the truth. What worries him is his mother's evasion in continuing to talk about the stork theory or the hospital theory in an unconvincing tone when he is pretty sure the baby is coming from elsewhere. Many parents refrain from telling the child the truth for fear that it will open the door to other embarrassing questions. This is an unjustified fear. The child before the age of 6 years will not put his parents on the spot to explain conception. The likely question will be, "How did the baby get in there?" to which at this age the most understandable answer is that the baby grew from a seed which was there all the time. To the question, "How will it get out?" the answer might be, "Through a special place." Incidentally, parents should be warned against predicting the sex of the baby ahead of time since a wrong guess may lead to long-lasting disappointment.

Some mechanical readjustments in the household are usually necessitated by the arrival of a baby. Wherever possible these should be made several months before the baby's birth and presented to the older child as evidence of growing up. If he is to move into another room or into a big bed, he should graduate to them because he is a big boy and not be dispossessed by the rival in person. If he is to enter a nursery school he should become well established there before his mother's confinement. Then when the baby arrives, even though the older child feels somewhat slighted at home, his satisfying life at nursery school will help to ease the pain. If he is sent off to nursery school after the baby's arrival, he may resent it as banishment, resist going, resist fitting in.

It is vital, particularly when the older child is in the neighborhood of 2 years, that he feel comfortable and secure with the adult who will care for him while his mother is in the hospital. If a relative or maid is coming into his home, she should either be someone whom he knows well and loves, or she should come two or more weeks ahead of time and take over his care gradually. When a very young child is abruptly left in the care of a stranger, he may behave well while his mother is away, but when she returns all his latent anxiety suddenly comes to the surface. Such a state may last for many months and make even more difficult his other problem of adjusting to the baby.

First impressions are most important. When a mother and father bring the new baby home from the hospital there is usually a great deal of hectic confusion for at least an hour. The older child is lost in the shuffle. No one has time to fuss over him and he stands by, looking wretched. If possible he should be off on an excursion during this time and come home when his mother is able to take him in her arms and give him her undivided attention.

Now that the baby is at home what are the parents' cues? The first principle is to play down the importance of the baby. This means talking about him as little as possible, enthusing over him as little as possible, taking care of him casually when the older child is around. The hardest thing for many children to take is seeing the baby nursed, especially when this is at the breast. Often the older child will want a bottle, too, and it is a wise mother who cheerfully provides it. If this is well handled the child will not repeat the request often since he finds that the bottle is not really a delight.

Even though one advises the mother to feed and care for the baby as much as is practical when the older child is preoccupied with other activities, she should, of course, be equally warned against shutting him out of the nursery whenever he has the desire to see what is going on there. If there is a relative or nurse helping out in the early weeks, it is usually best to have this person taking care of the baby, allowing the mother to give as much attention to the older child as she used to.

Then there are the other relatives. When the father comes home from work he should resist the natural impulse to greet the older child in the front hall with the question, "How's the baby been today?" but should stop to play with him for a while before he drifts in to see the newborn. When Aunt Nellie telephones to arrange a visit to the baby, the mother can remind her that the older child is still counting on being her favorite and will appreciate a present much more than the baby will.

So often Aunt Nellie in her thoughtless enthusiasm greets the older child with the breathless question, "Where's that darling baby sister of yours? I have brought her a present." For these situations the mother might have a box of ten-cent store toys from which to produce a gift each time one arrives for the baby.

Many parents have already heard of the value of letting the child share in the ownership and care of the infant. It is fine for the older child to bring the bottle from the icebox or the towel to the bath provided he enjoys this work and does it spontaneously. Another child will overcome the feeling of being an outsider by an elaborate care of her doll which follows her mother's care of the baby to the last detail.

It will help the parents to know what different forms jealousy may take. Everyone knows what it means when a child grabs a heavy object and whacks the baby over the head with it. But many mothers think it is clumsiness when the child hugs the baby with an embrace which begins gently and ends with a grip which brings a squawk from the infant. One child turns all his resentment against his mother and grimly empties the flowerpots on the living room rug. Another loses all joy in his usual pursuits and follows his mother from room to room sadly sucking his thumb. Children frequently revert to wetting by night and by day and some even soil themselves, for which there are several explanations. There is the element of defiance. There is the desire to receive the same tender care by imitating the baby. But it must also be realized that any severe unhappiness, without the elements of resentment or imitation may lead to a dramatic regression to infantile behavior.

The mistake is sometimes made of thinking that because a child shows affection for the baby there is no possibility of jealousy. There is always some latent jealousy to be guarded against even when all is love on the surface. And the child who has shown nothing but hatred for the baby at home may defend him like a lion outdoors if a stranger approaches. It must also be remembered that a child may show wholehearted delight in the baby for months until the day when the baby snatches one of his toys.

It is generally believed by psychiatrists that a strong destructive instinct like jealousy will be better coped with if it is allowed to stay near the surface. It will do more harm to the personality and persist longer if it is deeply repressed from the outset. What is a mother to do then, when her child makes a cruel attack on the baby? The common impulse is to shame the child, to overwhelm him with a feeling of guilt. If such a maneuver succeeds too well, the child, dreading the intense disapproval of his parents, will not dare to show or even let himself feel his jealousy. The emotion, however, is not dissipated but only driven underground. A case in point is that of a 2-½-year-old girl who for months after the birth of a baby sister wandered around in a sort of daze. She entered into no games herself but only watched the other children in a preoccupied way. When she saw a small boy riding a tricycle she would murmur, "Susy (her baby sister) has a bike." When a dog passed she murmured, "Susy has a dog." She was obsessed with Susy and objects in the world around her served only to remind her quite illogically of the baby.

If it is unwise for the parent to shame the child, to scare him out of expressing his jealousy, what is she to do when the child makes a physical attack on the infant? She has to jump in and use physical restraint, but she can turn the restraint into a hug and say to the child comfortingly, "I know how you feel sometimes. You wish there were no baby here at all. I love you just the same." This tends to reassure him and lessen his jealousy. For jealousy is not just hatred of the baby. It is hatred of the baby for fear he will monopolize the parents' love. If the parents can be helped to put themselves in the child's position they will begin to see that his cruelty and mischievousness are not simply matters of impoliteness or cussedness but are reactions to severe anxiety.

There are three further points which may seem partly to contradict what has been said before. First, some conscientious parents become so fearful of causing jealousy that they feel positively guilty about having produced a new baby at all, develop an uneasy apologetic manner toward the older child and fall all over themselves trying to appease him. This attitude does no one any good and specifically convinces the child that his parents have done him wrong. The parents' cue is tact, not abjectness. Second, the new baby will of course need an increasing share of attention and affection and acceptance as his waking hours increase. The older child should be increasingly able to tolerate this if a good start has been made. Finally, jealousy is not entirely a destructive experience. Probably everyone has to go through a certain amount of it. If it is not too bitter and is solved constructively, the result should be a more resilient, adaptable, tolerant personality.

References

1. Davis, Clara M.: *Am. J. Dis. Child.* 36:651, 1928.
2. Levy, David M.: *Am. J. Orthopsychiat.* 4:203, 1934.

Treatment of a Withdrawn Girl*

BY *Jacob P. Kahn, M.D.*

This is the case of Ann L, who was seen in therapy for 14 months at the James Jackson Putnam Children's Center.† Ann's mother brought her to the Center in March 1949 at the suggestion of her nursery school because she did not play with children, sucked her fingers, wet the bed, and had temper tantrums. Ann was then 4-½ years old, and had one sibling, Mildred, aged 6-½ years.

The mother gave the following history:

Mrs. L was nauseated during the pregnancy, which was unplanned. She vomited and had low blood pressure and varicose veins. Delivery, however, was easy

* From *The American Journal of Orthopsychiatry*, Vol. XXIII, No. 3, July 1953, by permission of the author and American Orthopsychiatric Association.

† The James Jackson Putnam Children's Center, Boston, Massachusetts, treats only preschool children and their parents. Treatment of the child consists of individual sessions with a psychiatrist, as well as placement in a nursery school which is an integral part of the Center. The parent is usually seen by a psychiatric social worker.

and labor took only two hours. But the mother had breast abscesses and was unable to nurse Ann.

The child was a feeding problem in infancy. She could not suck milk from a bottle. Although she had weighed 8 pounds, 3 ounces at birth, she was a "dried-up little mummy" at four months and weighed only 6 pounds. At that time, she was tube-fed for one month, after which she began to take milk and cereal by mouth.‡ At one year, the child weighed 25 pounds.

According to the mother, Ann was born with flat feet, was knock-kneed, and had ankles that turned over. She started to walk at fifteen months. When Ann was three, Mrs. L took her to the orthopedic clinic of a children's hospital. Thereafter, she wore special shoes and her feet improved.

Toilet training started at one year and was completed at two, at which time daytime wetting stopped also. However, Ann wet the bed at night.

The child began to have severe temper tantrums, apparently unprovoked, at the age of two. During these, she would cry, clench her fists and beat them up and down, yelling the while. Mrs. L felt she neglected Ann during this time, but she was busy getting the maternal aunt, who was living with them, properly placed in school, and much of her time was taken up.

The mother dismissed her own early life with the

‡ A letter from the pediatrician who attended Ann in infancy did not disclose any significant information about the feeding difficulties, the lack of sucking, or the tube-feeding. A copy of the records of the Army hospital where she was born also did not disclose any significant findings. The child was a full-term normal delivery. It does not seem probable that the mother could be mistaken about this matter, which she discussed at some length with the social worker. Nevertheless, the fantasy, if it was that, was certainly significant in revealing the mother's feeling about Ann.

statement that it was a mess. The maternal grandmother was an unhappy person with six children, of
whom Mrs. L was the second child and the oldest girl.
Much of the responsibility for the care of the younger
siblings fell upon her, which she resented. She said she
was a "horrible child, just like Ann." Mrs. L thought
that she herself was "normal" now and that it would not
help to discuss unhappy things in the past. At the time
of Ann's birth, the father was in the Army, the maternal grandmother had died recently, and as stated, the
maternal aunt was living in Mrs. L's household. Judg-
ing from the mother's statements, the father was
warmer than the mother in his attitude toward Ann.
He and Ann had formed a club—the "greenies." It was
he who had insisted that Ann, as well as Mildred, should
get new clothes for Easter.

Work with Mother

The mother was seen by the psychiatric social
worker, usually in weekly sessions, some forty times.
Because of unavoidable departures, she was seen by
three different workers.

Mrs. L had always thought Ann was an odd child. She
and the father had become reconciled to her dullness.
The mother felt Ann would never equal her sister Mildred. It was very difficult for her to accept the social
worker's assurance that Ann had done well in a psychological examination and was of normal intelligence.
The mother talked about the importance of understanding things. When the social worker said feelings
were important too, Mrs. L replied that she had no

feelings, but that she admired people who did have feelings. She told the social worker that she had "failed" as a mother. She had not wanted Ann in the first place and had withdrawn from her when she was born. She stated she had given Ann excellent physical care, but had not given her the things she needed. She knew it was not right at the time but could not help herself. She wished Ann were like other children and felt she was terrible to be so critical. We understood Ann at the Center, but many people did not. It was painful for Mrs. L to see Ann left out of things because other children thought she was different. It was hard to dress her attractively because she was so awkward and looked like a bear cub. Mrs. L had bought a new coat for Mildred for Easter, but Ann did not need one because she could wear the one Mildred had the previous year.

In the last few months of therapy, Mrs. L told the social worker that she felt she had come a long way. She thought she had changed a great deal and said she felt more comfortable and more at ease. She had stopped expecting specific advice on how to handle her child. She said that probably all of Ann's problems were not over as there was no way of creating a life for a child without problems, but together they would be able to meet them better now. The mother said that she and Ann had "grown" together and that if she were careful, things would be all right.

Mrs. L told the social worker also that she was pregnant and expecting the baby in November (1950). The mother said she was pleased, but the social worker felt she was trying to convince herself of this. Mrs. L had talked with Ann about having a new baby and Ann had said she did not want one. The mother had not told Ann that she was carrying the baby.

Work with Child

Ann was seen some eighty times, usually twice a week, over a period of fourteen months. Therapy, as indicated, consisted of a threefold approach: treatment of the child in biweekly individual psychiatric sessions, usually lasting half an hour; placement of the child in the nursery school* twice a week, involving her remaining there usually several hours in either the morning or afternoon; and treatment of the mother by the social worker.

I saw Ann for the first time toward the end of March 1949. She impressed me as a rather heavy-set, stolid, lumplike child, with little spontaneity or sparkle and with a tenuous contact with others. Her mousy-blonde hair never seemed well combed, and she had a sad and sulky expression. Her clothes were unattractive and she wore special shoes. She walked heavily and stumbled often. Her ability to play with other children was nonexistent. She talked very little, either not responding at all, or perhaps nodding or shaking her head. Her speech, when she did talk, was fairly clear, although this too was not constant. She would often suck her fingers. This was particularly noticeable whenever she

* The nursery groups are small (not over half a dozen children at the most). The problem of the child, the structure of the group, and the personality of the teacher, as well as the chronological age of the child, all enter into determining to which group a child is assigned. There may be two or more teachers in charge of each group. There is little organized group activity and demands are made only as the child is able to meet them. The emphasis is on reëducation of the emotionally disturbed child in a group setting. A yard is available for outdoor play sessions. For a more detailed account, see Rexford (7).

met with any sort of frustration. Most of the time she wanted her mother to be with her. Once outside, however, she would go to all parts of the yard as long as her mother was in sight. Her behavior suggested that she had very little physical fear. She would climb on the jungle-gym in an intrepid fashion and use the slide without hesitation. When she hurt herself, which was not infrequent because of her poor motor coördination, she would cry, and would deny any pain.

When I first saw Ann, she was unwilling to go to my office-playroom with me, but I succeeded in swinging her a bit in the yard and then in following her on the slide and jungle-gym. She uttered practically no word during this first play session and only when I was leaving and her mother spoke, telling her to say goodbye, did she look up and say goodbye in a small voice.

When I next saw her, she impressed me as being somewhat brighter, less flat, and more outgoing than she had been the previous time. However, when we got to my office and I pointed out the various toys to her, she simply stood in a corner with a dull expression on her face and a few fingers in her mouth and responded thereafter only by nodding or shaking her head. This continued in the nursery room too. Ann did not want to play with anything and just stood about. In the yard, she did use the slide and the jungle-gym. I would tell her now and then what a pretty coat she had or what a pretty ribbon she was wearing in her hair, but she would not respond. She did not speak or initiate any activity. She would suck her fingers during this time and sometimes would bite her nails.

The following time, Ann was seated at a table in the nursery room with some clay in front of her. She made no response when I greeted her. I made a bear out of

the clay and presented it to her. She refused to accept
it, shaking her head. However, she went into the yard
with me. When I asked if she would like to take the
bear with her, she nodded, and I brought it to her. In
the yard, Ann seemed to enjoy the slide. Back in my
room she became interested in some of the toy bureaus
and in opening and closing the drawers. She was surprisingly clumsy at this. When our time was up, she remembered to take the clay bear with her.

The next time I saw Ann, I had some chocolate bits for
her and thereafter would always have some. She would
smear her face with chocolate and had a habit of taking
a handful of them and shoving them into her mouth.
This time Ann did not do anything but sit in a chair and
eat her chocolates. Throughout, she sucked her fingers.
She did not want me to read a picture book to her.
This pattern continued for a number of sessions.

Never would Ann intitiate anything, and only at some
suggestion from the therapist would she sometimes enter into activity and even then not constantly. On one
occasion I got her interested in rearranging the furniture in the dollhouse, but she would do this only in con-
junction with me. Occasionally she would be in the
nursery room when other children were present and
playing and then she would stand around and look at
them wistfully, but never make any attempt to join in.

Around the middle of May, when I had seen her
about two months, I went down to the basement to see
Ann, who had been asking for me. She was riding
around on a tricycle. She looked up eagerly when I
greeted her and said she had been waiting for me. During this time I would continue to comment on her
clothes, telling her how nice her dress was, or noticing
the color of her hair ribbon. She would respond a little

more than she had at first and would look pleased. At times she would even smile in response. Once, at my instigation, Ann played with a jigsaw puzzle, and the following time, she began to do one without any encouragement from me. This was the first time that she had ever initiated any activity in my presence. This play with jigsaw puzzles kept on for a great number of periods. Ann did not learn too well from her previous experience with the puzzles. She usually had trouble in assembling them, although she might have done them a half-dozen times before. Usually with some help from me, she would finally get them done, but now and then she would get stuck. At those times, Ann would suddenly look up and say that she wanted to go down to the nursery room. Ann's reaction to separation, even the momentary separation involved in my speaking briefly to another doctor, was also withdrawal. It was necessary to concentrate on her completely and exclusively if contact was to be maintained. Even when this was done, however, she had the faculty of withdrawing and then perhaps reëstablishing contact in an extremely fluctuating way.

The child's activities around the end of May consisted of doing puzzles, and of sliding, cycling, and swinging in the yard. Many times while I was swinging her, she would be only in semicontact. Around the middle of June 1949, as I was swinging Ann, I started to sing a song. I asked Ann to join me and together we sang the song over and over again ("A Tisket, A Tasket"). The following time, after I initiated the singing, Ann sang around twenty different songs. She has a voice like a small frog, but nevertheless it was a remarkable performance with a pathetic and poignant quality. Now and then I could see her looking toward her mother. I had the feeling during this period that she was more in contact with me than at any previous time. Other children would come into the yard, but Ann kept on singing. The next time, she spontaneously burst into song and thereafter she would sing during many of our sessions.

Mrs. L would sometimes ask Ann if she could remain in the waiting room or in the nursery room while Ann and I went off. Ann almost invariably said no to this. The mother would usually sit in the yard in a sort of immobile, stony silence. All of Ann's attempts to be affectionate would, in effect, be repulsed.

On her last visit before summer vacation, Ann was accompanied by her sister. The latter was much more alert and attentive than Ann. She spoke easily and played eagerly. There was a competitive, almost phobic attitude on the part of Ann toward Mildred. Ann had to do everything that Mildred did, and wanted her to be near.

The Center was closed during the month of August and Ann did not return until near the end of September. At that time, I was not infrequently able to get her away from her mother, who would go with the social worker. Ann was more alive and animated, less phlegmatic, and her facies was more expressive and mobile. She would now respond with a negative or affirmative or some comment in answer to me. She told me about her vacation. She demonstrated a sense of humor for the first time. One of the doctors was attempting to ride a tricycle in the yard. Ann said it seemed a little small for him and laughed. She had started to kindergarten in September and was going three times a week.

Early in October, Ann was willing to go with me without her mother. Her activities in the yard consisted of singing, swinging and tricycling. She would often

stand and look at another child but would make no attempt to communicate. She had stopped sucking her
fingers since her return from summer vacation. She was
still quite unspontaneous and lacking in joyousness. In
October also, she began to demonstrate affection more
often to her mother and the latter's relationship with
her seemed somewhat warmer and softer. Ann would
sometimes kiss her mother and Mrs. L would have a
smile on her face. I had the impression that the mother
was dressing Ann in more attractive clothes. During this
month, Ann made friends with Betty, a very narcissistic
and exhibitionistic little girl. For the first time, there
seemed to be some participation with other children on
Ann's part although in a rather passive fashion. She
began to be somewhat more spontaneous in her ver-
balizations. Around the middle of October, she sought
physical contact with me by putting her hand in mine as
we were going downstairs. This too would fluctuate,
however. She would wave back at me when I waved as I
was leaving. The singing in the swing continued, as did
Ann's friendship with Betty. Ann was often preoccupied, but always seemed to be in better contact when
singing.

I often had the feeling that Ann was singing *out* to
children in the yard. Sometimes when we were the only
two present, she would sing in a low voice or hum.
When others entered the yard, she would begin to sing
more loudly. Often her singing seemed to wax and
wane with the presence or absence of the nursery-
school teacher in her vicinity. Late in the year, Ann began to do jigsaw puzzles again. Now, however, when
frustrated she was able to say that the puzzles were too
hard.

In December Ann began for the first time to build

with blocks and made some towers. She also made a house. Her structures had definite form and configuration. She followed other children in getting on a ledge and jumping down. She took my hand as she jumped. She succeeded, with my support and that of the nursery-school teacher, in defying an aggressive child. Ann would wander circuitously about the room, which seemed to be an attempt to enlarge her horizons. She would go from the phonograph to the piano, thence to the table, then to the window. She would ask where other children were. She gave a feeling of being part of the group with the other children in the nursery room. At Christmas time I gave her a gift. She opened it immediately, eagerly, and was pleased with it. She had brought a present for me. She informed me she was going to have a part in the play at the kindergarten Christmas party.

Ann would often be occupied in watching the very exhibitionistic Betty, whose activities undoubtedly often stimulated her fantasies. Betty would raise her dress and show her pink panties. Ann would become a little more withdrawn. She would cease to talk and stop whatever she was doing.

In January 1950, Ann was changed to a new nursery group because of a change in the therapist's schedule. In the new group, she met three new children. She adjusted very well to the change and gave no indication of being disturbed over the separation from Betty. During this month also, Ann's capacity to hold a conversation was tremendously improved. Her expression became increasingly less stolid and more mobile. Around this time, I gave another child whom I saw some chocolates. Ann saw me, waved, came over, and tried to take the chocolates away from the child. She would fre-

quently wave at me now and greet me when I was seeing other children in the same nursery room. At this
time also Ann would go to the waiting room where her
mother was, greet her, and sometimes sit in one of the
chairs. She was more vivacious, and would often smile
and give a joyful laugh. She continued to fluctuate,
however, in the degree of her contact and not infrequently would stop talking or playing or would again
seek refuge in activities which for her showed isolation,
such as swinging or jigsaw puzzles.

During February, Ann would often say that she
wished to see her mother and she wanted to be with
her much of the time. Mrs. L seemed warmer and more
accepting of Ann. The child's activities still were tentative and tangential. She gave the impression of trying,
although not very definitely or clearly, to broaden her
sphere of consciousness and widen her range of activity.
She made some candy for me, which she brought to
the Center.

In March, Ann appeared with a new haircut, which
transformed her appearance. The inner process, however, had been going on for a long time. She looked
far more alert and alive and showed her pleasure in
her appearance by calling my attention to the curls at
the end of her hair. I had never seen her so spontaneous
or aggressive. She inverted a cup of chocolates so that
they spilled. Then she threw the cup down the stairs.
In the basement, she ordered me around and would
kick at things in her way as she tricycled. She pounded
with hammer and nails at the workbench as she held
a conversation with me. She played in the swing with
other children. Her expression had a pleased, excited
quality.

As time progressed, she continued to look well, almost

puckish. Once she wanted her mother to come with us to my room. Mrs. L vacillated. Ann kissed her and the mother came with me. Ann was displaying a sense of humor more often. Mrs. L told Ann that she was tired and wanted to continue with her knitting. Ann replied that the knitting would not talk to her. Her behavior generally was freer and more spontaneous. She was able to handle her competitive feelings about my seeing other children without withdrawal or denial. In the nursery room, Ann painted such distinguishable objects as an Easter bunny, a flag, and a girl with red hair. She used bright colors. It was interesting to compare these with the indiscriminate, drab, formless paintings Ann did when she first came to the Center. She showed the pictures with a good deal of pride to her mother and said she was going to take one home to Daddy.

Around the middle of April, I saw another child first. Ann came up to me and asked, "When are you going to see me?" She still fluctuated, however, in her ability to stand physical contact with me, often moving away when I sometimes put my arm around her. Ann would play in the sandbox and make mud pies. She was able to hold conversations with people about her.

During the spring, when it was time for me to leave her, she looked at me and said, "Why do you have to leave so early?" Around the end of April, Ann's sister again accompanied her to the Center. She seemed to have less sparkle and to compare less favorably with Ann than the previous year. Ann was pretty much in control this time and Mildred was the uncertain one. I felt that the difference between the two girls now was a measure of the change that had occurred in Ann.

During this time, Ann had been singing and using the swing, but these activities had not occupied *all* of our time together and she had been able to stop them and go on to other pursuits. She still fluctuated but had less marked swings. She still retreated at times, but less completely. Most of the time Ann would speak to me and maintain communication.

As spring progressed, she would play with sand and water, make "cement," and order me to get her a ladder and "cement" the roof of the little hut in the yard. She was using the wading pool also. She would swish her bare wet feet in the sand. Her play had become freer. She began to show jealousy of the nursery teacher's attention to other children, and at one point went over and threw a handful of sand at a little girl the nursery teacher was swinging. Ann was still a heavy, rather awkward child, but was more secure in activities requiring fair motor coördination. She was also better able to stand physical contact with me and at times would seek it. She was speaking to other children whom she did not know well. She gave some of her chocolate bits to a new little girl. She climbed a porch railing and jumped down into my arms. However, immediately after that, she ran over to the nursery-school teacher and threw her arms around her.

More and more Ann began to demonstrate a will of her own and would do the things that she wanted. In June, Ann became more aggressive and boisterous. She began to bang doors and would slap at the nursery-school teacher's palm. I wondered about the effect of her mother's pregnancy on Ann. Because there was never any indication in her behavior of what her fantasies about this might be, I did not bring the matter up with her. Ann was seen three times in June. She played in the sand pile without shoes or stockings. She picked flowers for her mother and was easy and relaxed. She carried on conversation without any difficulty. I spoke to her about her leaving the Center and said I hoped that she would come to see me. Ann said she would. The mother told the social worker that Ann had expressed hostility to the expected new sibling in the form of such questions as, "What would happen if no one fed it? If someone hit it on the head?" Mrs. L apparently was not disturbed about this and felt it was something she could handle.

The last time I saw Ann she was somewhat boisterous, without being hypomanic; aggressive, without having her aggression overwhelm her. She was capable of receiving and giving affection. We had a party and Ann was quite natural and gay and easy. She had presents for the nursery-school teachers and for me. Ann opened her gift to me, which consisted of handkerchiefs, and asked me eagerly if I liked them. When it was time to go, she gave us all a hug and then gave me a kiss. She was noisy as she went down the stairs, shouting and yelling, and was, I think, trying to cover up some of her feelings at leaving the Center.

Comment

There were moments when the mother appeared to be making an effort to talk more, to ask questions, to participate in the interviews. There were times when she seemed more genuinely comfortable and relaxed. But actually, since her coming to the Center, her quiet reserve and underlying tension had changed but little.

Mrs. L dismissed her life previous to her marriage with the remark that she did not like to talk or think about it, nor did she like to think about her own mother.

One will recall that the mother said she herself was a "horrible" child—"just like Ann." Her identification with Ann was clear and her rejection of Ann was really a rejection of herself. It is a question whether the feeding difficulties during the first months were precipitated by the mother's rejection, or whether the difficulties came first and intensified the mother's identification with Ann. Although it is not possible to know with certainty, in the light of the mother's statements that she had not wanted Ann in the first place and had withdrawn from her when she was born, it would seem that the rejection preceded the feeding difficulties.

Ann represented the unacceptable, painful part of Mrs. L. Her feeling that Ann would never amount to anything was part and parcel of her feeling that she herself did not amount to much. Her protest about Ann's unhappiness was a protest against her own unhappy childhood. Yet she was unable to give Ann what she herself lacked as a child. She could react only in accordance with the pattern familiar to her, that of her own mother about whom she did not like to think or speak. Certainly she gave the feeling and also implied that she had had a tremendously adverse childhood to combat.

To the last, Mrs. L had difficulty in believing that she had married and deserved the "wonderful man" she had for a husband. One wonders whether she utilized so much libidinal energy in improving her state and securing it that she had little left for Ann. Why did Mrs. L feel that Mildred was the exceptional child? Perhaps because Mildred was the first and came just when the mother felt that her life was going to be more fortunate than she had anticipated. It may that the mother was capable of loving only one child. She does, how-

ever, seem to have been reasonably consistent in her
rejection, and in that consistency is perhaps one explanation of why the child was not even more withdrawn. A mother whose attitude is consistent, even if
this attitude be one of rejection, affords the child relatively more security than a mother whose attitude vac-
illates between partial rejection and partial acceptance.
The swinging ambivalence gives the child a less secure
base for making relationships. It may be, however, that
the main reason for Ann's not being more withdrawn
was the contact with the warmer father and with her
sibling.

We have felt that there was somewhat of a depressed
quality about Mrs. L. It may well be that she was depressed after Ann's birth. As stated, her husband was in
the Army at this time. The maternal grandmother had
died recently, and the mother's younger sister had come
to live with her. Mrs. L stated she knew she was doing
wrong, but she felt unable to caress or love Ann. It may
be that the death of the maternal grandmother revived
guilt feelings against the younger sister so that Ann became the scapegoat for her mother's feelings. Perhaps,
in order partially to protect herself from being immo-
bilized by her depression, she projected some of her
feelings onto Ann.

The mother-child relationship bears some consideration. Mrs. L referred to Ann as a "dried-up little
mummy." She felt that Ann needed no attention and
got little. Ann was "like a lump" until two years of age.
She was an ugly baby. No one ever made a fuss over her
even from the beginning. The parents had even made
bitter concoctions and had sewed up Ann's pajama
sleeves to try to stop her finger-sucking, without success. Since Mrs. L made these remarks, all essentially

rejecting, when Ann was 4-½ years old, it is not difficult to imagine the emotional barrenness of the child's earlier environment.

We know that an affectionate, consistent attitude on the part of the significant adult is necessary for the infant to begin to direct its libido outward, to start to differentiate between itself and the outside world. In the absence of this, emotional development is inhibited and retarded. It seems clear that Mrs. L did not caress or handle the child, except minimally, nor was she able to be a warm, relatively unambivalent, accepting mother. Enough has been said to indicate that there was considerable emotional isolation between Ann and her mother. We believe that Ann's withdrawal and retreat into her inner world were the result of this emotional isolation rather than of any constitutional or inborn factors.

There was during the 14 months of Ann's treatment a fairly steady, but often slow progress with transient periods of obvious improvement, sometimes followed by slumps. Her one tremendous forward spurt will be indicated. It was not possible to correlate Ann's behavior at the Center with happenings and behavior at home. Nor, because of the gradualness of the improvement for the most part, was it possible to divide the therapy into sharply separated segments except possibly those natural divisions due to seasonal variations in the activity of the Center.

We feel that the part played by the nursery school in Ann's treatment was extremely significant. It gave the child an opportunity to establish relationships with her contemporaries according to a sort of self-dosage schedule and under optimal conditions. We do not feel that her isolation was such that the impact of the group drove her into further retreat. In addition, the nursery school offered Ann a substitute mother in the form of the nursery-school teacher who, like the therapist, met her needs for unconditional acceptance.

Only rarely did Ann allow us to perceive the nature of her inner life. Rarely was there opportunity for interpretation, for seizing the "therapeutic moment" to do or say the right thing in any very active sense. Treatment consisted primarily of a consistent acceptance of Ann, of an attempt to understand and meet her needs. This essentially was the presence of a warm, accepting, unambivalent adult so that the child could realize that it was possible for her to make a meaningful relationship with an adult without fear of disappointment or frustration. The therapist tried to show her that there was safety and security in the relationship. At the same time, there was an attempt not to intrude too much upon her withdrawal or her fantasies, or to make demands upon her which we felt she could not meet.

The strong bond with the therapist was followed by greater ability to make demands and to initiate activity and express hostility and aggression. There was a gain in ability to tolerate frustration without retreat. The development of activities progressed from those involving kinesthetic, autoerotic satisfactions to those involving increased awareness of and interaction with the outside world. This was paralleled by the increased use of play materials in general, as well as by corresponding changes in Ann's behavior in the nursery school.

Ann's ability to accept and demonstrate affection to the various people at the Center with whom she was in contact seemed to be in inverse proportion to her closeness to the person. This applied also to her ability to tolerate physical contact. This, of course, was minimal when she first came to the Center. It was only in the later stages of treatment that she was able to accept and to respond to the affection and tentative physical closeness, such as an outstretched hand, offered her by the therapist. I think that her initial inability to receive or offer affection was due to her fear of rejection and frustration. Later, her ability to accept and respond to affection from people other than her therapist was due in large part to her closer bond with him and her unconscious oedipal wishes toward him.

Ann's repetitive play (with puzzles) allowed her to indulge in withdrawal. The finger-sucking and the activities like swinging pointed to her need for auto-pleasures to make up for the satisfactions she felt she could not obtain from the outside world. I believe she used her singing to attain contact and also to maintain distance. All of these activities decreased as therapy progressed.

Ann's seeming slowness and stupidity were essentially a matter of her withdrawal. We know that learning is in great part a libidinal process, as well as an aggressive act, an incorporation. It involves a cathexis of objects and people. Ann was clothed, as it were, in a veil of pseudo stupidity which served to isolate her still further from her environment. To this inversion of her libido, we relate also her seemingly greater capacity to endure physical pain. Perhaps also, her isolation served as an insulation against the mother's only partially repressed rage toward her.

The child's extreme fluctuation was primarily a defense against even the threat of disappointment or frustration—she was always in readiness for flight, for retreat. This was her primary reaction to frustration and included physical withdrawal. Communication, both verbal and nonverbal, became limited, as a mode of defense. Passive behavior was preferred because activity was dangerous and fraught with disappointment. Ann's rage, frustration, and jealousy as she realized the difference in her mother's feelings and attitudes toward Ann and her older sister found expression in temper tantrums, which began at the age of two.

The difference in Ann's physical appearance as therapy progressed was rather striking. When she first came to the Center, she was a stolid, heavy-set, unspontaneous, stupid-appearing child, with no grace whatsoever to her motor activities. After three months of therapy, Ann first began to be more alive and animated, her face more mobile and expressive. During this time also, besides the contact with her contemporaries at the Center, she had contact with other children her own age at kindergarten. It was not until the following March, however, that her appearance really seemed transformed. This change paralleled the onset of the mother's pregnancy. Perhaps her pregnancy lessened Mrs. L's identification with Ann so that it then became possible for her to allow Ann to become less bound to her and more of an individual. One of the difficulties in treatment of this type of child-mother unit is that the child is never really a separate entity. The mother has never separated the child from her own psychic image. It may be also that the mother's becoming pregnant again indicated that the work of mourning for the maternal grandmother had become completed and Mrs. L was able to become a mother to Ann.

The change extended to Ann's general motor activity so that she was less clumsy than she had appeared in the past. I think this was due to Ann's increased capacity for contact and communication, to her greater awareness of the external world, and the development of a more sharply focused body image, with consequent better general muscular control.

One can speculate as to the reasons for Ann's increased progress at this point. Perhaps she felt that now there would be another child who would be the least favored one. Perhaps she imagined that the new baby would be her ally. It may be that the forward spurt would not have occurred if the mother had not found it possible to allow Ann greater self-identity.

Concomitant with this change in Ann's physical appearance and motor activity was an increased spontaneity, a lessened need to have things go according to a prearranged plan. There was greater ability to cope with situations as they arose.

Many questions remain. We wonder why, after a month of tube-feeding at the age of four months, the child was able to take food well enough so that she weighed 25 pounds at one year. Were physical factors operating or had the psychological situation changed? We know that both mother and father were taking part in the feeding. Was the emotional contact with the warmer father making the difference? One wonders how important the tube-feeding was in the establishment of this child's passivity and her later manner of feeding, characterized by an indiscriminate mass oral stuffing of whatever she was eating. Why did Ann reveal so little of her inner life by either word or action? Was it primarily a matter of her passivity? Was it connected with her general withdrawal, her unspontaneous, repetitive, auto-oriented play? We believe this is so and that Ann, with her inward-directed libido, had a rich, though unexpressed fantasy life.

It may be that Ann's greater self-identity, which was

the real turning point in her improvement, would have occurred later even had Mrs. L not become pregnant. But certainly the pregnancy acted as a catalyst by cutting the psychic umbilical cord to Ann, thus making it possible for her to move forward and consolidate the gains she had made during treatment. Her progress would not have been possible, however, without the strong relationship she had developed with the therapist.*

Discussion

Irving Kaufman, M.D.:† It is always difficult to communicate all the elements which go into the treatment of a patient. I had the opportunity to observe Ann with Dr. Kahn. It was very clear that Dr. Kahn liked Ann. This essential element was one of the most important experiences for her.

I, too, feel that the mother was depressed at the time of Ann's birth. She had lost her mother, and her husband was in the Army. She reported many of the typical characteristics of a depression. These included withdrawal, hostility, and difficulties in relating.

Ann showed these same symptoms at the time of referral. She was not only retarded in her psychological development, but also appeared withdrawn, hostile and depressed. Apparently, up to the time of treatment, the mother had not resolved this depression and Ann showed the effects of this pathology in the mother. It was very clear that the mother identified Ann with her-

* When I saw Ann again in follow-up sessions during the next fall and spring, she had maintained her improvement.
† Judge Baker Guidance Center, Boston, Massachusetts.

self—the depressed devalued part of herself. As the child grew older, the behavior patterns which were then established became cumulative in their effects, and Ann appeared clumsy, stupid and withdrawn.

Her mother was withdrawn and preoccupied during Ann's developmental years. She was unable to give Ann the necessary stimulation for an adequate emotional development. She also identified Ann with her deprived depressed self and so the child, instead of being a source of gratification to this mother, could only be painful to her. This lack of positive emotional interaction interfered with Ann's turning from the narcissistic to the object level of development. Ann's mother could not cope with the emotional and painful elements in herself. She said she could not tolerate any feelings. She treated Ann in the same way and could not tolerate any kind of emotional interaction with her. This too interfered with Ann's ability to turn to objects in a positive way. The child then had to turn her libidinal and aggressive drives back upon herself. For example, she bad temper tantrums, sucked her fingers, or withdrew into other autoerotic and autoaggressive play. The transformation of autoerotic and autoaggressive drives from the narcissistic ego to external objects represents the major accomplishment of treatment. Ann was transformed from a withdrawn girl with temper tantrums into a child who could relate to others in a constructive coöperative way.

The technical aspects of the therapy with this child with her anaclitic type of depression particularly interested me. As Dr. Kahn said, the therapy rarely included the more usual bringing to consciousness of emotional conflicts and working them through by play and verbal techniques. The therapy here appeared as an undoing of the whole traumatic pathologic process which occurred to this child.

The first and most important aspect of the treatment was Dr. Kahn's positive feelings for Ann which he obviously communicated to her. One can assume that Ann's positive relationship with her father facilitated the positive relationship to her therapist. Dr. Kahn's sensitivity to the child's needs was obvious. However, he did not wait indefinitely for the child to verbalize her problems, but took the nonverbal cues and acted upon them. He talked to her, commented on her pretty coat, etc., and not only conveyed to her his positive feelings, but also gave her the psychic and emotional stimulation that had been lacking in her relationship to her mother. This was, in a sense, a restorative phenomenon.

I was particularly struck by the mother's description of Ann as a bear cub. When Dr. Kahn made the clay bear and gave it to Ann, he symbolically stated the problem in so concrete a way that she could know he understood it. With this therapeutic technique, he was able to indicate to her early in treatment that he could accept her as she was.

Dr. Kahn continued to initiate activities and invited Ann to participate. The sensitivity to realize at what pace this child could move marks the difference between a successful and unsuccessful result.

Ann repeated her mother's behavior by reacting to separation from her therapist by withdrawal. Ann demonstrated her inhibition and withdrawal in the following areas and ways: 1) in the motor area by hypoactivity; 2) in the intellectual area by stupidity; 3) in the emotional area by showing no pain. Although Ann's withdrawal was not as severe as that of some of the atypical children, in some ways she appeared borderline. In her tenuous relationship, disturbed communication and type of isolation she was similar to the atypical children. However, she never seemed to reach the severe degree of their disturbance.

As Dr. Kahn accepted Ann—the devalued part of mother—the mother then was helped symbolically to accept this part of herself. As Ann progressed and became able to accept Dr. Kahn's affection, she became able to go to her mother and be affectionate to her. As the mother saw this part of herself accepted, she was gradually able to respond, and this benefited Ann.

I feel this is an extremely interesting and valuable case, particularly from the point of view of the technique Dr. Kahn used to undo the anaclitic type of depression shown by Ann.

References

1. Benedek, Therese: "Adaptation to Reality in Early Infancy." *Psa. Quart.*, 7:200–215, 1938.
2. Pavenstedt, Eleanor, and Irene N. Andersen: "Complementary Treatment of Mother and Child with Atypical Development," Workshop. *Am. J. Orthopsychiatry*, 22:607–641, 1952.
3. Putnam, Marian C., et al.: "Case Study of an Atypical Two-and-a-Half-Year-Old." Round Table. *Am. J. Orthopsychiatry*, 18:1–30, 1948.
4. Rank, Beata: "Aggression," in *The Psychoanalytic Study of the Child*, Vol. III/IV. Internat. Univ. Press, New York, 1949.
5. ———: "Adaptation of the Psychoanalytic Technique for the Treatment of Young Children with Atypical Development." *Am. J. Orthopsychiatry*, 19:130–139, 1949.

6. Rank, Beata, Marian C. Putnam, and Gregory Rochlin: "The Significance of the 'Emotional Climate' in Early Feeding Difficulties." *Psychosom. Med.*, 10: No. 5, 1948.
7. Rexford, Eveoleen N.: "The Role of the Nursery School in a Child Guidance Clinic." *Am. J. Orthopsychiatry*, 19:517–524, 1949.

Neurotic Depression in a Child *

BY M. R. Harrower,† Ph.D.

Introduction

The unusual aspect of the psychological examination of this 13-year-old female patient, Vivian, lies in the fact that it was possible to subject to a similar battery of tests not only the patient's younger sister Betty, age 11, but also her father and mother. Thus the patient's difficulties, as revealed in the tests, are seen against the background of the inevitable rivalry with her younger and considerably more intelligent sister, and also against the background of the recently precipitated marital difficulties of her parents.

The testing situation was completely "blind"; that is, the examiner knew nothing of the family problem, did not know in fact which member of the family was the patient. In the case of the two children, contrary to the

* Reprinted from *Case Histories in Clinical and Abnormal Psychology* by courtesy of the author, the editors, Dr. Arthur Burton and Dr. Robt. E. Harris, and publishers, Harper & Brothers.
† With the collaboration of Lawrence S. Kubie, M.D.

usual practice, a joint report rather than two individual ones was prepared, for the very nature of the material seemed to demand presentation in such a way as to make the interrelation of the two children's lives of primary importance.

The test findings have been presented first, just as they were originally reported. It will not be difficult for the reader to anticipate that the elder child, Vivian, was in fact the patient, and that the younger, Betty, was judged clinically as exceptionally well adjusted. While no detailed psychological report is given on the parents for want of space, the relevant data from the clinical findings have been included to give as complete a picture as possible of Vivian's psychological environment at the time of examination.

Throughout the report the girls are spoken of by ages rather than by names in order that the difficult situation in which the elder finds herself may be most clearly emphasized. As will be seen in detail by the reactions to the various tests, it would seem that there existed a situation of the following kind: The older girl, whose intellectual equipment is considerably less than the younger's, is constantly threatened and challenged by the latter. But it is more than this; for the younger child is unusually artistic, gifted, and spontaneous, whereas the older child is becoming increasingly anxious, increasingly unhappy and withdrawn, because in no area can she compete successfully with her sister or establish herself in her own right. Where the younger child is able to give vent both to her effervescence and enthusiasm and to her somewhat explosive but relatively unsustained bursts of aggression, the older is concerned more and more with controlling a smoldering resentment which, as it were, seeps out, permeates and poisons the world around her. Whereas the younger child is openly and fiercely competitive, with a naïve joy in her own achievements and performance, the elder has given up the unequal struggle overtly but has become concerned with it at a deeper level.

Intellectual Evaluation

Both children were given the Stanford-Binet, Form L; three performance tests from the Wechsler-Bellevue and the intellectual aspects of the Rorschach were studied in detail. The results from the Binet show the younger to have a considerably higher I.Q. than the elder, 126 as compared to 104. Moreover, the younger, age 11, has a mental age of 14.4 and the elder, age 13, has a mental age of 14. Not only, therefore, is the younger child considerably brighter for her age but also, judged by absolute standards, her mental age at this moment is higher than that of her sister. It should be noted that the older child is by no means backward, and that her performance is clearly "good average." In neither child's record is there any indication of gross psychopathology. Both children coöperated excellently in this test.

The examiner made the comment that the elder was "precise, proper, and polite," whereas the younger was "alert, alive, interested." A further comment on the younger child was that she was so exceedingly responsive to the environment that in order to name objects she went over to the window to get ideas. This unusual activity is characteristic of her fantasy, and is seen in several of the other tests. On the other hand, the comment on the elder reads, "She is good on things that she has learned, but fails on things requiring immediate concentration or effort."

Both children easily completed the three performance tests from the Wechsler-Bellevue Scale. However, in this as in all tests, the younger child's performance was superior. Table 1 shows the difference.

TABLE 1. *Comparative Time Scores on Three Wechsler-Bellevue Performance Subtests* (IN SECONDS)

YOUNGER	OLDER
100	115
20	50
45	150

I had the feeling in watching the younger child perform that, in a sense, every situation is for her a competitive one in which she expects and desires intensely to excel in her performance and "beat" her sister.

Intellectual Aspects Revealed in the Rorschach

There is really considerable difference here in what I would call the basic organizational ability of their respective minds. The younger child has a quick, almost intuitive grasp of abstract relations; the older child is uninspired, and more than any other characteristic lacks the ability for abstract thought. The younger child has a surprisingly easy grasp of total situations. More than any other one thing, I feel that this stacks the cards against the elder child in an almost hopeless way. Her apprehension and anxiety in relation to the younger sister is in a sense wholly justified, having its roots in the incontrovertible fact that the younger child can outdo her in every field.

Bender Gestalt

Although not strictly an intelligence test, the Bender Gestalt is added here in this connection. This very simple procedure was taken much more seriously by the elder child, and her drawings are much neater and more accurate. Her general retrenchment, withdrawal, and submissiveness are seen in the reduction of the space between the dots. On the other hand, her reproduction of one figure and her spacing of the entire series are perhaps her only point of clear superiority to the younger girl. Their attitudes toward this somewhat prosaic procedure differed in accordance with their degrees of control, a factor which is one of the main differences in their personality structure.

Personality Structure: Rorschach

The personality structure of the younger child is very favorable—favorable, that is, in terms of her own development, but constituting difficulties for her sister. This child is the potential "artist" in the widest sense of the word. She has unusual imaginative gifts, and a happy, spontaneous, uninhibited approach to life. (Both the animals and the people of her fantasy world "dance" often "around a fire"; that is, warmth and emotional expression related to instinctual and imaginative life are not destructive or frightening.)

The personality type is definitely dilated, and, with

the inevitable defects of such qualities, she tends toward a lack of control. She will surely give frank expression to her moods, both joyous and those of occasional resentment and hostility. Because of the ease with which her resentment is expressed, it leaves no scar.

In some ways she is a little precocious; there are indications of adolescent problems, rather than those of the preadolescent period. Sensual stimulation produces a mild "shock." But she is in no way disrupted by these undercurrents.

The personality structure of the elder child is much more constricted and inhibited. Moreover, there is evidence of considerable anxiety which is completely lacking in the younger girl. There is also an undercurrent of depression which is in sharp contrast to the almost ebullient, "slap-happy" mood of the younger.

Although she has a surprisingly rich fantasy, she is far less productive than the younger child. She does not possesses either the unusual, individual artistic flair or the intellectual grasp of the younger, and she is really impeded by her anxiety. Her whole approach to life is lacking in spontaneity; she reacts with the characteristics of an individual who has been badly hurt. She lives in a world of half tones which are in sharp contrast to the world of gaiety and bright colors of her sister. Her tendency is toward overcontrol and a more tentative approach.

One of the most interesting features of this record is the way in which the hostility that she feels toward the younger child is reflected. She finds, for instance, "children looking angrily at each other," and again "children glaring at each other." Again she sees animals as "fighting." In all probability the younger child will give vent spontaneously and quickly to her annoyance at or dislike for her sister, but I feel that perhaps the elder one is not even aware of the extent of her own hostility. Thus it finds expression indirectly in her record, in a way that does not appear in the younger's. In the record of the older girl the depressive tone and the increasingly menacing aspect of the environment are seen. Animals are "dead," branches are "cut off," the "house is struck by lightning." (This last response, occuring in the "vagina" area of Card VII, would seem to suggest that undercurrents of anxiety, with specifically sexual reference, are added to the generally disturbing picture.)

Thematic Apperception Test

The TAT shows a very sharp distinction between the spontaneous and uninhibited stories of the younger child, and the restrained and in some cases almost impoverished comments of the older. As a merely quantitative example, one of the pictures is described by the younger child in 12 lines, whereas the elder child uses only one sentence of less than one line for the same picture. The most outstanding feature in the older girl's fantasies is the theme of wanting, waiting, missing, and the general sadness which dominates all the stories. It is a groping for something of whose exact nature she is not aware. One of the most significant remarks was made about a picture with two girls. Here she says, "The girl running has something that the girl standing wants" (Picture 9GF). This I feel is very significant, for the implication is that of the active child getting what the more passive one so badly needs—love, affection, attention, and prominence. In another story

she says, "The woman is thinking of someone she loves.
. . . She is very poor, but I think she is intelligent"
(Picture 8GF). Again she says simply: "I think that the
child has died" (Picture 3GF). And about the picture
of a little girl she repeats twice, "I think she is waiting
for something . . . waiting for something." Asked directly what the girl is waiting for, she says, "To see
someone she has not seen for a long time" (Picture
3GF).

The tone of the younger child's stories is entirely
different. "People go home tired but happy" (Picture
9GF). There is always a happy ending. A woman who
"thought she could not go to France . . . sees a good
friend who gets her a passage . . . so she goes right up
the gangplank" (Picture 13G). The girl "whose career
was to have been modeling" gets "very excited, and
finds she can go on a mission" . . . on the "mission she
finds that helping people makes her much happier than
modeling" (Picture 8GF). In contrast to the elder sister's story about the little girl "waiting for something,"
the younger has a wonderful "success-story daydream."
In this picture the mother is "reading aloud to the little
girl the published story that the little girl has written"
(Picture 3GF).

Man, Woman Drawing and Story

The drawings (Figs. 1, 2, 3) speak for themselves.
That of the older girl shows much better than average
ability for her age, but those of the younger are really
outstanding. Her choice of a clown for the man may be
significant in that she would seem to identify herself

FIG. 1. *Vivian's Drawing in Response to the Instruction "Draw a Man and Woman" on Separate Sheets.*

with the masculine figure. Her description of him as "someone always very cheerful, who likes to eat" is not unlike herself.

Report on Handwriting Specimens *

"Vivian's writing is forced and stylized. She is soft, submissive, yielding, but withdrawn. A real heaviness is in her; she cannot easily make up her mind but has to lean on others, while she has lost most of her pri-

* Handwriting specimens were analyzed by Dr. Meta Steiner.

FIG. 2. *Betty's Drawing in Response to the Instruction "Draw a Man."*

mary, instinctive contacts with people. She is intelligent, but not a fast thinker. Occasionally, she leaps off into a dream world. She is serious and resentful, with no opportunity to abreact; no sense of humor. Her attempts to get love and attention are frequent, but end in a rejecting attitude from fear of being rejected. She has a strong sense of justice and duty, watchful all the time lest her feelings and personality should be hurt. She controls her sudden flashes of temper rigidly, but still they are likely to break out at times.

"Betty is a girl in a revolutionary stage, stressing independency and individual freedom, while still very

FIG. 3. *Betty's Drawing in Response to the Instruction "Draw a Woman."*

immature. Her revolt is much more obvious than her sister's, but so is her self-assertion. She is certain to win. Although not open, she is basically warm and confident. An intelligent and gifted girl relatively mature for her age; more subjective than her sister and more capricious. She too, is sensitive, but naïve in her reactions. She can accept the world as it is. She will try to dominate, not to withdraw. She has a remarkable sense of beauty and sensuality."

Clinical History

Vivian's parents have been married for about 15 years. Until the war they had almost never been separated from each other or from their children; they considered themselves, and were generally considered, to be exceptionally happy and well mated. Shortly after the outbreak of the war, however, the father left to undertake some special work in the Orient. Unaccountably, he failed to write to his home, friends, or former associates for many months; and while on a brief visit home his manner toward his wife was distrait and distant. She suspected that he had been having an affair with another woman, a suspicion which he subsequently confirmed. After he left again his wife entered into an affair, at the height of which her husband returned permanently. His return precipitated a period of intense emotional upheaval for both parents, with considerable anxiety, mutual recriminations, and repeated efforts at reconciliation.

Vivian presents a problem in both emotional adjustment and school life. At home she shows a diffuse affective flattening, with an almost total lack of enthusiasm about games, sports, books, and people. In school this is not equally true. She is immaculate in person, clothes, and details of her work; but the content never seems to penetrate. She seems to resent being taught school work or games and maintains an air of quiet, depressive grievance and tragedy. She lays great stress on wealth and material possessions, in opposition to the mother's emphasis on the importance of acquiring skills for self-support and independence. She has a sloppy, shuffling walk (perhaps a characteristic of the paternal family), is a nail-biter, and suffers from a recurrent dream in which a robber ties her against the wall, goes out to get a first-aid kit, and then returns to untie her and take care of her scratches. There is some tendency toward fantastic lying.

All these tendencies have been apparent in some measure for a long time, but have been sharply increased in the last two or three years. The accentuation of her symptoms may date from the time her father went away; a further increase occurred when the mother became interested in another man. At the same time that her father left, Vivian's governess also went away. The mother took care of her and made every effort to give her a great deal of special attention. This did not seem to make any difference in Vivian's emotional reactions; she remained resentful and full of jealousy, fight, tears, and hurt feelings.

At nine months Vivian had rigid, breath-holding spells which were quickly eased by a change of regimen. At one year she fussed over her meals. At one and a half years she had a "hysterical" disturbance over the departure of her nurse, who had been with her only three months and had been the only person who ever struck her. At this time she also screamed and cried whenever her mother left the apartment.

She was completely trained before her sister was born. While the mother was in the hospital, Vivian became ill. When the mother and the new sister returned, in spite of the mother's efforts to make Vivian feel secure in her love she vomited, had bowel movements in bed every night, and screamed herself to sleep. She lost weight, ate poorly, and turned angrily away from people. In subsequent years these reactions continued. She would say, "Go away I hate you," to many people, and she kicked her dog until it had to be sent away. The soiling of her bed continued for some time, and in her periods of upset she called her mother a "dirty woman and a liar." Once at the age of four she had a tantrum in which she locked the door of her room, threatened to jump out of the window, and smashed a lamp to make the sound of breaking glass.

At two years of age she had her tonsils and adenoids removed, and at six much additional lymphoid tissue was removed, following which she developed asthma. She became a "fantastically good patient," submitting to sinus irrigations and other difficult and painful treatments with an ease which amazed the physicians. In all other situations and relationships she was difficult, whereas her younger sister won everyone with ease and confidence. Physical and laboratory examinations by the highly competent family physician revealed no relevant abnormalities.

Clinical Summary

This is a chronic neurotic depression arising out of an unusually early conflict, with stormy rage and jealousy of a younger sister. The many evidences of regressive involvement at anal and oral levels indicate the possibility that psychotic disturbances may ultimately supervene unless intensive treatment is instituted. The conflict clearly drains off all free energy, and limits the patient's ability to use her intellectual capacities, her capacity for imaginative fantasy, or her emotions.

Private daily tutoring by a psychiatrically informed tutor is recommended to keep her ahead of her younger sister. Psychoanalysis should be started as soon as it can be arranged for.

Treatment in Child Schizophrenia: Presentation of a Case[*]

BY *J. Louise Despert, M.D.*

Introduction

Recent Recognition of the Disease Entity

It cannot be overemphasized that the recognition of child schizophrenia as a disease entity is very recent and in many countries, and even in certain sections of the United States, the disease is not fully accepted as a clinical entity. For example, in the literature references to "schizophrenic-like" diseases in children are not uncommonly found. The earliest specific mention of schizophrenia in children in the American literature goes back less than twenty years to the article by Howard W. Potter, "Schizophrenia in Children," which appeared in the *American Journal of Psychiatry* in 1933 (5).

[*] From *Specialized Techniques in Psychotherapy*, 1952. Reprinted by courtesy of the author and the publishers, Basic Books, Inc.

Need for Differentiation

It is important to differentiate between "schizophrenic-like" illness in childhood and the true schizophrenic illness. In the former, there may be some isolated behavior, thinking, or feeling manifestations which are of a psychotic character, but the total personality is not involved in the disease process, as it is in childhood schizophrenia. The latter, that is, true schizophrenic illness is to be defined in terms of pathognomic changes taking place in the personality, as related to the loss of affective contact with reality.

Central Core of the Disease Process

At the first international congress concerned with child psychiatry in 1937, a survey of twenty-nine children admitted to the New York State Psychiatric Institute from 1930–1937 and diagnosed as schizophrenics, was presented (1). An attempt to define schizophrenia in childhood was made. The definition may be inadequate in that it lacks reference to psychogenetic factors, yet it is sufficiently descriptive of the process, and it offers possibilities as a working definition. It has proved helpful in the course of several years of experimentation with psychotherapy.

Schizophrenia in childhood was thus defined: ". . . a disease process in which the loss of affective contact with reality is coincident with or determined by the appearance of autistic thinking and accompanied by specific phenomena of regression and dissociation." With the advance of Kanner's concept of early infantile autism (3), (4), the definition could be modified to include both the failure to develop affective contact with reality, and the loss of affective contact.

To the author it appears then that the first task in child schizophrenia is by any and all means to establish affective contact with the patient, to break into the child's autistic world with a keen alertness for possible associations which might offer insight into the unconscious as it is revealed, yet not legible, in external manifestations. This means also a breaking-down of apparently unintelligible neologisms, the interpretation of which can subsequently be given to the patient. On the whole, this is a very active process but once the contact has been established its activity can be relaxed; interpretations and other techniques as carried out in severe neurotic illnesses can be used.

Types of Therapeutic Approach

In looking over a fairly large series of schizophrenic children since their treatment and/or diagnostic evaluation, it is immediately apparent that from the point of view of therapeutic approaches a differentiation must be made between two distinct categories: the children in whom mutism and negativistic features are foremost; and those in whom the opposite manifestations are found, that is, excessive and distorted verbal behavior.

In the first category which offers additional difficulties since language is such a potent means of communication and contact, the approach is through the observation of subtle changes of facial expression, involuntary gestures, changes in motor reactions to interpretations offered by the therapist.

In the second category, difficulties of an altogether

different nature are encountered. The child usually presents motor restlessness in addition to the verbal behavior. It is difficult to approach him even physically long enough to communicate with him. His compulsive outbursts are apparently meaningless verbal content. The irrelevancy of his speech which expresses his extreme ambivalence makes it difficult to offer an interpretation. Furthermore, when interpretation is available and can be offered, one may find it impossible to place a word edgewise into the flow of speech in order to introject the interpretation. From the point of view of treatment, these two categories of children present distinct differences in the order of approach and difficulties.

The extreme ambivalence of the schizophrenic who is torn between emotionally opposite drives will present a similarity between the two categories.

Presentation of the Therapy in One Illustrative Case

The patient discussed here was briefly referred to in a previous communication (2). Peter K. was at the time of admission, and still is, an only child. He was three years ten months when first seen. He was referred by the pediatrician who had been attending him since birth, and who was now administering barbiturates for reasons shortly to be given.

Complaint

Three weeks prior to admission the child suddenly manifested excited behavior, acute anxiety, and stupor-like states, alternating with excitement. He seemed to hear but did not answer. He had always been an anxious and excitable child. Furthermore, because of a congenital dislocation of the hip, he had been from age four months to ten months in a cast which extended from midthigh to neck. He had had several illnesses. There was great tension in the home mainly because of clashes in personality between the mother and her own mother (the latter had practically brought up the boy). In this background of tension and poor emotional adjustment the child developed the acute symptoms which led to admission, as follows: for about a week (at Christmastime) he had been a little more excited than usual. The whole family (mother, father, maternal grandmother) was "on edge" because on the night after Christmas he had slept very little. The following day he asked his father to take him to the Museum of Natural History. There he saw totem poles in the American Indian section. He came home very excited, referring to crocodiles in an incoherent fashion. The next night he appeared dazed for a long period before finally falling asleep. For approximately one year he had been sleeping in his room together with his grandmother, who was in the habit of telling him stories. The second night after the visit to the museum, he refused the story, then suddenly clutching the bed he shrieked, "Mummy, I can't be by myself!" He would not let his mother go out of the room. He spent the whole night lying on his bed, dazed, and staring at the ceiling. During the following day and night the same behavior was shown but with alternating periods of acute anxiety when he mentioned "rhinoceros" and "Indians with sticks." Since that time he had continued in a dazed, stuporous condition with outbursts in which he referred to hostile feelings he had toward his mother, but had never expressed before, such as, "you don't let me shovel enough snow," and "you stay too long in stores," all of which referred to specific past episodes.

Parents

The father (age 41) is a professional man, a mild-mannered individual with quiet speech who practices corporation law and is mildly successful in a job which does not require much contact with people. He appears quite even-tempered but his veiled hostility is very close to the surface and on occasion breaks through, to be controlled quickly again. He has centered his life interests on the patient. He had great drives to achieve success, put himself through college, married at twenty-five; through the nearly seventeen years of marriage, at least up to the time the patient was born, he had great doubts as to whether he had "made the right marriage." This refers to considerable tension because in the past his wife, the patient's mother, has had periods of depression and he has had to "nurse her through" these periods. Sexual relations have become very infrequent and unsatisfying. He drives himself as an escape. He is the second of two boys. He states that he had a happy childhood, admired his own father, a compulsive man "who had to do it all himself" and who died when he, the patient's father, was ten years old. The grandfather's death changed the social and economic position of the family, and after it the patient's father determined to rely upon himself for his college education and other aims. He was very close to his mother who died of a cardiac condition in her 60's, a few years after his marriage. She was affectionate, and both her sons were very attached to her. The patient's father has been "all wrapped up" in the patient and considers that his sole happiness comes from him.

The mother (age 38) is the most important member of the family background. Her own family was highly neurotic. Her father died at 46 when she was twenty-four years old. Following his death she had a severe depression. The maternal grandmother is high-strung, given to violent temper outbursts. The mother had an ambivalent feeling toward her own father: she admired him but feared him because of his unpredictable, violent behavior. The grandmother is close to 60, lives with the family, and has had more to do with the bringing-up of the patient than the mother herself. She indulges the boy, but at the same time frightens him by telling him gruesome, worrisome stories, and is in constant conflict with the boy's parents. The maternal grandmother was always "anxious and worrisome, had hysterics," but has been much worse since, at 40, a trolley-car accident caused a fractured skull which exacerbated her personality difficulties. The accident took place shortly after her husband's death and shortly before her daughter's severe depression.

The patient's mother is the older of two sisters, a woman who would be attractive were it not for her constant depressed expression. She speaks in a whining monotone with occasional outbursts of very aggressive speech. She was the favorite of both parents presumably because she was conspicuously more attractive than her sister. Owing to economic difficulties, she did her college work at night, soon after her marriage at twenty-one-and-a-half years. She has done secretarial and editorial work in various non-profit fields. In the past few years she had been a clerical assistant in the public school system which she joined in the hope of securing paid holidays, a hope which was never realized because approximately at this time, after thirteen years of marriage, she decided to stop working and have a child. She had frequent mild depressions with one severe and long period (about one-and-a-half years following the death of her father and her mother's injury). At the peak of the period she had suicidal impulses which were precipitated by the suicide of a woman, unknown to her, who lived in the same house.

Patient

The patient is an only child, born after thirteen years of marriage (mother 34, father 37). On the conscious level this was a wanted and planned pregnancy; however, there is evidence through associative material that the purpose of the pregnancy was to consolidate a shaky marriage. The mother stopped working in the fourth month. Although she was given to frequent mild depressions, she was physically well during her pregnancy. She describes herself as more emotionally stable at this time than at any period of her life.

One month premature, the baby was born after short labor, middle forceps. He was not breast fed, presumably because of some physical difficulty with the mother's breasts. He slept and fed well but was noted to cry "fiercely" for an hour before feedings. As already mentioned, he was in a cast from 4 to 10 months of age, sat up at 14 months, walked at 16, was precocious in every other respect. At 22 months he could recite many rhymes, but also at approximately this time had severe stuttering. Because of the additional difficulty created by the congenital dislocation of the hip, the maternal grandmother was called in to take over. ("It was wrong to have her come.") There has been a continuous conflict over the patient, mostly between the mother and the maternal grandmother. The elimination training was initiated late because of the cast and was met with "terrific resistance."

On admission the child was still enuretic at night. Vigorous thumb-sucking started at the time the night bottle was taken off, and was forcibly interrupted. Masturbation, which has been varying in frequency and severity, has been a major problem to the parents, and in particular, to the maternal grandmother. Repeatedly the patient was told that he would "hurt his penis." Shortly after he was put in the cast he began to sleep poorly, and in recent years this has been accentuated. He also has had frequent nightmares, following a herniotomy at two years, four months. His grandmother sleeps in his room, she responds when he screams, never his parents. The mother has been overanxious, overprotective. She reports, for example, that with the appearance of any minor symptom she frequently "imagines he is going to die." Death wishes toward the patient are thus very close to the surface.

The child has always been very active and has gradually become very destructive, throwing books around, and breaking toys apart, stuffing a variety of objects into the toilet bowl and wash basin. Regressive behavior (tempers, rocking, speaking incoherently) seems to have appeared a few days before the acute onset mentioned above, although the parents do not agree on this point. The father "never saw anything abnormal" prior to the visit to the museum. The mother saw insidious changes for several months prior to the acute onset. During the reporting of the developmental data it became apparent that the mother was depressed, with intense aggressive impulses, generally under control, with openly expressed strong guilt feelings ("It's my fault, even if it was the grandmother, it's again my fault."). In addition, there was strong rivalry between the mother and grandmother; and also the mother resented both the affection that her son showed to the grandmother and the grandmother's affection to the boy ("He does not respond to me"). While he does not respond to anyone in the family, when he is acutely frightened he is apt to run to his grandmother.

Therapeutic Approach

In advance of the first interview with the child it was suggested that the mother refer to the child's fears and tell him that she would bring him to a lady who would help him as she helps other children. In spite of these recommendations the mother brought the patient, with the sudden, advance announcement to him that: "It's so windy, let's go up and see a lady."

The mother was asked into the playroom because of the child's clinging to her for protection, and the obvious anxiety of the mother at the thought of separation. It appeared that the mother was clinging to the boy more than the boy to the mother, an observation which was confirmed later.

He was an attractive, large-boned, very alert youngster, with pupils widely dilated. There were sudden rigid attitudes of the body which were revealing of the intense anxiety experienced by the patient. It is difficult indeed to give an adequate picture of the intensity of the anxiety, which a good deal of the time was equivalent to an acute panic. His speech was incoherent;

however, amid the jumble of words and disconnected syllables, it was possible to make out distinctly a full sentence: "I am not afraid of anything." The mother was asked to sit in a corner of the playroom and as much as possible not to participate actively in the therapeutic session, yet to respond to the child's demands, if any.

The patient let the physician undress him, holding himself in a characteristic way with brief muscular rigidity and intervals of intermittent screaming.

His uttered answers were incoherent for the most part; he had an extensive vocabulary, both for his chronological age level and as shown in single words and those sentences which were coming through with some degree of legibility, even when it was not possible to ascertain the meaning. The associative links could not be made out, but out of the jumble of words, references to a variety of experiences, realistic and fantastic, could be reconstructed.

There was evidence of visual and auditory hallucinations, as when, staring at the ceiling with a frightened expression, he was seen to cock his ears to listen, and at such moments did not respond to any stimulus. There was catatonic posturing and drooling.

Some of the verbal content which illustrates the nature of his anxiety could be made out in the following expressions: ". . . different . . . things the same . . . things different . . . the wrong floor . . . go to another room . . . crocodiles . . . animals in the same place . . . I am not afraid of anything . . . Indians . . ." With attention for any utterance, single or grouped words which could be made out, reassurance and protection were repeatedly offered: "The physician would not let the animals hurt Peter. Things were different indeed: the bathroom is different, the room is different, I am a new person, but the room also looks different because Peter feels different." When he said that he was not afraid, the physician offered that "Peter was not afraid, but what was the little boy afraid of?" The answer came in the form of incoherent words with the one clearly articulated word "animals." It was offered to him that the little boy was afraid of animals and that the physician would not let the animals hurt him. The whole while the physician kept as close to the child as would possibly be accepted.

Animals and other toys were put on the floor, but the child at first would pay no attention to them. He began to take note of them (after repeated suggestion) and out of a variety of toys he picked the animals and held on especially to a dog and a snake. While handling these toys he announced several times, "must be the same" and seemed to attempt to disarticulate them, concentrating especially on the eyes. He was told that he wanted to see if the animals were alive, that he was afraid of live animals but these were "pretend" animals and they could not hurt him. The concentration on a toy dog and the associated anxiety aroused the suspicion that although the dog was the object of anxiety at the unconscious level, possibly it was involved also in a realistic episode. In the course of the second interview with the parents (that in which evaluation of the problem and the suggested treatment were discussed), it was learned that a dog left with the family by a maternal aunt had frightened and bitten the patient several times. The word "Echo" which had been used several times in connection with the toy dog was the name of the actual dog. Incidentally, it was suggested that the dog be removed from the environment.

Diagnosis

The pathological manifestations met the criterion for schizophrenic illness as described above. The first steps in therapy were to establish affective contact with the child. Then to relieve the intense anxiety associated with primitive fantasies, such as the fear of being destroyed or devoured, and the loss of self. In particular to provide therapy aimed at bridging realistic, traumatic, conscious experience with the underlying anxiety arising from unconscious fantasies. It was indicated to the parents that the treatment would be a long process and that it could be ascertained within a few weeks whether the child responded or not. The parents, leaning on the suggestion made by the pediatrician that they send the child to an upstate farm, were briefly resistive to the plans formulated, and throughout the treatment showed some ambivalence to the plans. However, because the child improved rather early, he was kept in treatment.

During the initial period he was seen with the mother present three times a week for the first two months, then twice a week for the next four months. The summer vacation intervened; following this, the child was seen alone once a week for a year. The mother was allowed to remain in the playroom not only because of the child's screaming, but also because he fastened himself so tightly to his mother that the result was a sort of physical symbiosis. Some contingencies could not be controlled: such inordinate screaming might be tolerated on the in-patient service of a hospital, but was hardly acceptable in a non-clinical ambulatory set-up.

In one of the initial interviews with the mother she made a statement that was very revealing of the relationship between the mother, the child, and the therapist. She said specifically, "After I saw you with Peter —you were so beautiful, such a beautiful job—I thought, 'she loves children, she hates parents.'" This was presented to her as reëstablishment of her own family relationship, in which the physician was the mother and she saw the physician in rivalry with the patient, as if the physician were her own mother (her awareness of her conflict with her mother helped her to accept this interpretation).

It was suggested that the barbiturates which had proved ineffecutal be discontinued.

The various relationships in the family were discussed, generally in their superficial aspects; the conflict between the mother and father, mother and maternal grandmother, was pointed up. It was suggested that the maternal grandmother might gradually become less indispensable. The parents were considerably relieved that the child was not to be sent to an institution, which they had feared.

The father, though compulsive, did not seem to have too disturbed a personality and since it was impossible to consider treatment of the whole family, owing to economic limitations, it was decided to deal mostly with the mother. She was the one most in need of therapy. However, intensive therapy was ruled out because of the possibility of a psychotic explosion and even suicide. It was therefore planned that the work with the mother would be on the basis of supportive therapy, with the mother-son relationship as a foremost consideration. It was thought that after the child's improved condition brought some release of the family tension and particularly of maternal anxiety, more intensive therapy for the mother might be considered.

The mother, who had been a secretary, was made to feel useful in the therapeutic situation when she was asked to make notes as she wished; and it was explained to the child that the mother would be helping the physician by taking down some of the things that were being said. This was explained to the boy as "mother helping us." Indeed, in a relatively large series of child schizophrenics treated, this is the only case in which the presence of the mother during such a long period of treatment was deemed necessary. While this was unusual and presented certain liabilities it was also an asset in some respects; for example, it was of the greatest interest to the physician to compare the type of information that the mother would select as significant, with what had actually taken place, in that it revealed areas of emotional blocking which could be used for analysis and interpretation.

The immediate and most important job was to begin with Peter. From the beginning, it was possible to get the child to respond even though this was the briefest sort of response. Owing to his passive attitudes, it was possible to cuddle him and demonstrate affection to him even at such times as he was completely out of contact. This was a considerable asset if one compares such passivity with the negativism and muscle rigidity frequently encountered in child schizophrenics. This asset was exploited to its full possibilities.

The mother, who had been asked to turn to the physician for every minor problem or question that might come up day by day, had reported to the physician one morning that the child had remained awake the major portion of the previous night and that he frequently referred to a dog when he was in a stuporous state. The physician therefore deliberately opened the interview with a toy dog and the child immediately identified with the dog, growling, snarling, in a complex facial pattern which seemed to indicate such complete impersonation as to erase any human facial features. This was dramatized in a situation of acute anxiety which alternated in a mechanistic manner between being the dog and being the victim. He would spell the word "growl," point to the closet door referring to "wild animals in a cage," to "rhinoceros" and "Indians." At intervals he shrieked without verbal content. Again and again it was pointed out to him that he was afraid of being devoured by the animals, especially the dog, not only devoured, but that he feared that other worse things (castration anxiety referred to, but not mentioned) would happen to him and that to stop the dog from devouring him and doing these other things he wanted to be the dog himself. Then again, he was told he was afraid to be the dog because the dog would be doing these bad things. The tenor of the interpretations is merely indicated here; the interpretations had to be repeated again and again, and dramatized. It was evident at once that these interpretations afforded a penetration into the child's fantasies; he would suddenly stop and stare intently at the physician and briefly respond to her in a more positive body contact.

Everything around him was a cause of anxiety because of misinterpretation of objects in the environment. For example, the bathroom fixtures were the "sticks"; "Indians with sticks" which he had frequently referred to. The physician explained to him that the sticks were really something else to him, and, that he was afraid that some bad things would happen to the sticks. He was encouraged to come and touch the pipes, etc.; thus his anxiety was fully recognized, but also evidence of objective reality was offered. This handling of the child's anxiety associated with fantasies and distortions of the reality world, illustrates an approach which was used over and over to the point of monotony and perseveration, namely, the need to establish a distinction between reality objects and fantasies projected into the reality objects. The reaction was always a more positive body attitude and sometimes, though rarely, a verbal acknowledging of the interpretation given. At any rate, the result was clearly a breaking into the autistic world of the child.

It is impossible for lack of space to multiply the illustrations which were all of the order of reality-testing. As an example, when he handled the dolls and seemed intent on pulling them apart and tearing the eyes out, especially in acute anxiety, his confusion about reality and unreality, living and not living, his own concern about himself not being real, not being himself, the people not being live people, was brought up over and over again. This loss of identity of self, extended also to the people around him, as when he referred to his mother as a statue. Once he turned to her in the midst of play and said, "I'll plug you in" (which besides the sexual connotation and in the light of the total context, referred to his feeling that his mother was inanimate).

At the beginning of the treatment the mother was very anxious for the boy to be treated daily. She would "do everything, no matter what it cost," even bring a lunch box for the physician if the latter did not have time to cook, etc. As will be seen from later developments (request for a consultation, insistence on application of shock therapy as suggested by the family physician, etc.) her attitude toward the physician and toward therapy was very ambivalent. Incidentally, the physician was willing to accept the consultation but indicated firmly that it was either shock therapy and severance of all contact with her, or continuation of the current therapy. Following this, the family dropped all further suggestions.

The boy continued hallucinating, laughing irrelevantly, staring into space, shrieking in anxiety, all in rapid succession. Every coherent statement which was made was immediately seized upon for an interpretation of his anxieties. When, for example, he was heard to say, "I am everybody's boy, all people's boy," the physician pointed out to him that he was afraid he was not his mommy's boy, but that he was also afraid to be that.

Pictures of a dog and a rhinoceros were drawn for him again and again, and the drama of a dog and rhinoceros trying to bite or eat a little boy was enacted, always with the reassurance that the rhinoceros (or the dog) was not real but that the little boy was afraid it was real. Through this period (approximately three weeks) it was reported that at night the stuporous periods were considerably shorter; the content was indicated by the following words which were distinctly heard: ". . . dog . . . bone . . . growl . . . it's dangerous . . ."

The mother was especially disturbed by the fact that the patient addressed her almost as though she were a thing. He would suddenly ask her to stop in the midst of some activity with such comments as, "You can be a statue . . . don't move, I can't use you now . . . I'll plug you in . . ." (the latter as he played with electric fixtures). Considerable time was spent with the mother in an elucidation of the "inanimate" delusion, and it was pointed out that this was a safety mechanism which enabled him to save himself pain, but that it was also the result of his own loss of self.

During this period, while he was not completely sleepless at night, he stayed awake a good deal of the night. Then, in the morning he would be "worn out" and would make such statements as, "Nothing lets me sleep and I want to sleep so hard." These comments were all utilized in the therapeutic situation.

The mother alternated between two opposite attitudes: one of extreme anxiety about the severity and hopelessness of the child's illness, and belief that a short period of contact with the physician would be sufficient to bring him back to normal. "I am sure if you could look after him he would be OK in one week."

During this initial period (the second or third week), the physician initiated the session by taking a boy doll out and asking what the little boy thought about when he was going to sleep. A then cryptic statement came forth: "Elissa with the pokers." Since the pokers had previously been associated with the sticks of the American Indians, this was again brought up in connection with anxiety about the sticks and what the sticks stood for. It was formulated that he feared that the sticks would be used to hurt him and that bad things would happen to the sticks. The meaning of Elissa was not immediately ascertained but was later recognized as standing for an old woman about whom additional reference is forthcoming. At one moment, he pointed to the bathroom door and insisted it must be closed because "Echo (the family dog) might come in and bite you." Actually, the physician pointed out, he said this because he himself was afraid that the dog might come in and bite him. His response to this was immediately to turn into a dog and a wolf, growling, snarling, in space as well as at the physician. This activity was interpreted to him as having to be the dog or the wolf in order to do some of the things he was afraid he might do. It can be said that each interpretation of the kind illustrated here brought responses different in degree, but generally at least some reaction.

The general pattern was one of absence of contact and verbal incoherence; for example, there often was a reference to "an animal a long time after the war" which could never be elucidated and interpreted. Since the anxiety relating to animals was dealt with in a general way, it did not seem imperative to pursue the specific meaning of many references to animals which were at times unintelligible.

The notes taken by the mother during the sessions provide an interesting opportunity for insight into the mother's personality. She was emotionally involved in the dramatization of fantasies, etc., and was singularly blocked in her reporting of them. Of significance is the following: "Peter was glad to see you and advised you on questioning that the wind had given him his red cheeks." The child's dramatization of fantasies related to the wind had been completely omitted. The child on that day showed great anxiety and most of his speech was incoherent. The following is selected from otherwise unintelligible material: "The wind and the sun came to say 'Happy New Year' and the little old lady tapped on the door . . . I was asleep in the bathroom in the toilet . . . I saw the dog eating and then he lifted his leg . . ." At that point the child had acted so realistically and lifted his leg, and the physician pointed out that Peter wanted to know about the dog's penis, wanted to make sure it was there, and he was afraid his own penis might not be there. The castration anxiety which had repeatedly come up in various symbolic ways was thus for the first time pointed out.

At this time the associations with "little old lady" were not intelligible. However, later, when he stated, "I am not going to be afraid of the little old lady," the physician pointed out that the "little old lady" might be a woman whom she (physician) did not know, but she was also like his mother, grandmother, and the physician herself. At a later session it was learned that the "little old lady" was a rather dilapidated woman whom he had seen in the country a year or before. This particular association was brought in reference to a pump (there actually had been such a connection with the dilapidated old lady). Whenever he expressed anything relevant, the physician was quick to pick it up and hold on to it, to talk about it over and over, dramatizing both sides—the frightening and the frightened. In relation to the little-old-lady fantasy and through bits of associative material it was acknowledged that someone gets into his bed, specifically the little old lady (as he was mentioning) but also it was indicated that the little old lady was not real. In regard to this double dramatization he stated, "Another little old lady comes in the middle of the night. I won't get scared of her; she'll get scared of me." He was encouraged to feel that he could now deal with the little old lady.

He frequently expressed his anxieties by projecting them. Once he said, "You must not talk because something bad will come to you and bite you." This was quickly seized upon to point out to him that it was he himself who was afraid and not the physician, and also that he thought that by asking her not to talk the danger would be removed from himself (magic thought). About this time he frequently expressed an intense anxiety about the physician putting "pennies" into him. He would shriek in a tone of terror, "Don't put pennies into me." Although at the time the delusion was totally unintelligible, it was possible to assume, in view of the total content, that he was referring both to "pennies" and "penises," especially as often the "s" was pronounced to point to the latter interpretation. At first he was told of the double meaning and of the associated anxiety, but the complete analysis of this delusion was made only after additional information was secured. As has been previously reported, this delusion was the end-result of a condensation-phenomenon commonly encountered in schizophrenia. The child, as indicated above, had hallucinated a "little old lady" identified both with his grandmother and with an actual dilapidated old woman. The grandmother had brought a dog, and there was anxiety associated with this dog. The grandmother had often over-dramatized the story of the Three Little Pigs and the child had, even prior to his illness, identified with the little pig eaten by the wolf; and lastly, he owned a penny bank, in which pennies were frequently dropped. Each fragment was brought up for analysis and abreactive release with the "pennies" content at first only mentioned, and the "penis" content held in abeyance for evidence, later secured, regarding the castration anxiety. This was in a short while brought in by the child in the form of a neologism which will be later described.

Illustrations too numerous to be related here (at first unintelligible, incoherent statements) were analyzed, dissected, as it were, and wherever possible, replaced in their relationship to reality, fantasies, unconscious expressions, etc. One more illustration is given: He kept repeating "lock happening . . . happen . . . it happened . . ." During one of these expressions (always associated with severe anxiety) he glanced toward the closet door and was told that he was afraid to be locked, that if he were locked he would not be able to come with his mother nor his mother to come with him, that he would be alone, strange, and not himself, and that he was also afraid that he might be locked, perhaps alone, perhaps not alone. His reaction to this was some incoherent garbled language with two distinct words which gave it a specific meaning: "cage . . . cage with wild animals . . ." Again this was an expression of his anxiety about being devoured, but, as was learned later, it also referred to an actual event which had taken place several months before the onset of his illness when he locked himself in a closet and had been released almost immediately. At the moment he had appeared very frightened but no after-effects had been noted.

To illustrate the technique in the utilization of apparently unintelligible statements, the analysis of a neologism which was of the greatest importance in the understanding of this child's problem is here offered: Toward the end of the second month, he began to use a neologism, the phonetic rendering of which would be "benishghellaman." It was noted that "Benjamin," the name of his father, came up from time to time in the flow of unintelligible language, and seemed to belong with this neologism. It would be impossible except with mechanical recording to give a faithful reproduction of these phonetics, but some of what seemed significant or intelligible at the moment was taken down by the physician in the course of several sessions, and it became clear that the neologism expressed the fear of castration at the hands of his father. Incidentally, at no time did he refer to his father as "father" or "my father," but rather as schizophrenic children will often do, brought him in descriptively, via a reference to a gesture or special function more or less characteristic of him, in this case, the fact that his father brought in the mail at night. It was only after constant interpolation from the physician, regarding the association, that he finally referred to his father specifically, and to what his father might do to him. When he finally connected his father with the neologism, within a mass of unintelligible material, the castration anxiety emerged, could be, and was, interpreted: "There is benishghellaman . . . the kind that bites off your penis . . . the kind that spoiled your benishghellaman . . . last year . . . don't touch my benishghellaman . . . then Benjamin comes home . . . the night-carrier . . . my daddy's name . . ."

Conspicuous, following the interpretation, were the draining of the anxiety, the improved contact, and the amelioration of intelligibility. This was the end of the second month and the beginning of the third. His contact was much improved and he had become spontaneously affectionate, at intervals.

Throughout the initial period, as condensed above, he appeared at times to have amnestic aphasia. For example, he would place a number of animals on the radiator, look at them with a very anxious expression, seemingly to identify each one, and obviously laboring to find the proper name. Then with a helpless expression, he would wail, "I don't know all the words."

As the contact improved, negativism, which at first had been mild, increased and there was a great deal of perseverance in activity as well as in verbal expression. Throughout, drawings had been used by the physician, in preference to those of the child, whose productions

were at first of the scribbling type. The drawings made
revolved mostly around a boy, his mother, his father,
and animals suggested by the patient's current verbal
comments. He sometimes took the pencils, adding protu-
berances at any part of the body, which were clearly
the penises he had mentioned and were so interpreted
to him in later sessions. He began to refer to "the other
boy inside" and this was again and again used to point
to the split in himself between the other boy who used
to have bad thoughts, etc., and the boy who now was
beginning to be more comfortable with himself.

Through this period (two months to two-and-a-half
months) he went through regressive and aggressive behavior, biting, mostly his mother. This was interpreted
to the mother as identification with the dog and other
animals in order to control his anxiety about being bitten
and castrated. It was a difficult period for the mother,
as the scenes, temper tantrums, and biting activities
worried her considerably. When he was told he was
playing "doggy" because he was afraid of a dog and
what the dog would do to him, he seemed at first startled, then smiled in acquiescence and his play lost the
"vicious" character (a note that the mother herself entered in her "report").

Toward the end of the third month he began to play
constructively with the toys and to dramatize play
scenes in which his hostility toward his mother, his anxiety relating to his father and to his grandmother were
more clearly coming through, with the primitive fantasies associated with totem poles, Indians, etc., appearing infrequently. Whenever the latter were manifested,
the mother's own anxiety was of such severity as to
constitute a problem in the therapy situation. She was
particularly disturbed by the fact that his facial expres-

sions were so realistic. She was also watchful of such identifications outside the playroom and reported, for example, on one occasion that "he makes a face like a totem pole and shouts, 'I don't want anybody in the street.'" At this time, he made frequent references to his mother at home regarding: ". . . going up . . . don't send me up . . ." which were associated with the "totem poles," "rhinoceros," etc. His father had bought him earlier a small bronze rhinoceros, and the physician asked the mother to bring it. This was used for dramatic abreaction for several sessions, during which Peter would reassure himself with, "It's not a rhinoceros from the museum." Then he made it go up and down a thin block which he called a "stick." When it was suggested he might want to go again to the museum, he said he would, "if you take me with you because it's dangerous." Actually, the plan was not carried out, owing to unavoidable circumstances.

In the course of treatment, about the middle of the third month, a light was thrown on an interesting condensation-phenomenon which involved the mother figure, a woodpecker instrumental in the castration fantasy, and, coincidentally, the gradual growth of his hold on reality. He had made frequent references, mostly unintelligible, to a "little lady—and the little old lady who looked like a woodpecker . . . the woodpecker and the benishghellaman." He asked the physician to draw pictures of these very subjective experiences and she proceeded to render the requested scenes as best she could, during which the child dramatized more and more comprehensibly this half-realistic and half-fantastic experience. In this connection he made it evident that the lady-woodpecker represented a current hallucination which seemed to be on the wane. He said that the little old lady still "climbed in my bathroom window," then she "melts away." Many abreacting activities at this time (drawing, play, and dialogue) involved the little old lady as woodpecker, or the big wolf and the little boy. He had, for instance, taken the physician's hand to go to her bathroom, which he identified, on the occasion, with his own. "I will have to take you there—now the little old lady is gone—she used to talk 'lad talk.'" Incidentally, while it could be assumed that the "lad talk" referred to threats addressed to a little boy, and was so interpreted, the use of the word in this context was never clarified.

He would also play for a short period with chairs in a "cage arrangement" and was at first in a panic when the physician "opened the door" by removing a chair. His anxiety was interpreted in the light of his ambivalence in wanting to retain the safe closing-in around himself with the mother figure, the fear that he could be closed in with the animals that could devour and injure him, and the fear that he could himself be let loose, abandoned, on his own. This was substantiated again and again by acts such as the drawing (requested by him) of a woodpecker next to a little boy, when he suddenly interrupted the activity to draw a heavy black line around the woodpecker in order to protect the little boy.

By the end of the fourth month (he was then being seen only twice a week) there was no evidence of hallucinations, but reality-testing continued in a manner somewhat akin to that of the normal 2-3-year-old child who experiments on the "real" and "pretend" objects of his world. An interesting episode which took place at this time illustrates the point: The mother came in on that day with a heavy bandage on her finger. She had reported that she had seen the child holding a broomstick toward the ceiling light in a play which she did not understand, but which had made her anxious. In the sudden movement she made to remove the stick from his hand she had broken the bulb. The child was anxious and guilty over the mother's minor injury and was asked at the beginning of the session to explain the mother's bandage, etc. This enabled him to reënact the scene and to ventilate the tensions attached. A very illuminating comment regarding his relationship to the therapist was, "You should have hurry up."

With the summer breaking into the therapy, he was not seen for two months, and the mother was prepared to let him come to the playroom alone.(Sessions once a week were started at this point.) The separation, difficult for the mother, was relatively easy for the child because of the positive transference and also because he had in the meantime become relatively independent of his mother. The reality-testing continued for approximately another two months; for example, he would from time to time in the course of dramatization of the family relationships take a large doll and say that she was to cry, then that "she can't really cry—her eyes are wood—my eyes are not wood because I am real, but the doll is not real." The improvement was considered sufficient to warrant his attending school. After initial apprehension in the new setup he adjusted well, made friends, but displayed a tendency to flare up in excited play. This tendency the teachers were able to control readily.

Vacation time arrived (he was then five years four months), and the whole family moved to the country for a two-month period which was very happy for all. In the fall it was impossible to get the parents to continue with treatment, the reason given by the mother being that since he was so well, further contact with psychiatry would be harmful. Against advice she had insisted that the school be uninformed about any of the youngster's problems. She did not maintain contact with the physician, not even for information, a contact which was actively sought by the physician for a whole year, then given up.

The determination to remain incommunicado continued for four years, when a frantic call came from the mother. The child was then nine-and-a-half years old. The mother explained that he had rather suddenly developed obsessive-compulsive neurotic symptoms. The mother cried on the telephone, making a significant statement: "Don't punish me . . . please see him again . . . etc." Seen several times on this occasion the boy manifested none of the psychotic behavior reported in this communication. Since it was impossible for the physician to take him on for continued treatment at this time, he was referred to an outside therapist working under her supervision. The child is still under treatment; after several months he is considerably improved, and is now seen once a week. He has made a very good adjustment in his family; and for the first time went to a summer camp, where he was happy and free of symptoms.

Conclusion

This case was selected because it represents a typical case of child schizophrenia with acute onset in a background of insidious changes.

The therapy, as illustrated, is also typical, with the exception of the unusually long time that the mother was permitted to stay in the therapeutic situation, for reasons previously given. (This is a unique exception.)

The abrupt severing of the therapeutic process was accomplished by the parents, based on their assumption that the child's improvement was sufficient. Such severing is an occasional feature of parental attitudes; it represents an additional obstacle to total therapeutic success.

It has been shown through a number of representative illustrations that the breaking-into the child's autistic world, into his primitive fantasies, and into the initially impenetrable defenses of his neologisms could be and was accomplished. This is considered by the author to be the core of the therapeutic approach in child schizophrenia. The transference relation was built up on this basis of the establishment of contact; otherwise such a relationship could not be realized.

The patient was thus able gradually to achieve subjective delineation between reality and unreality, and ego-boundaries reëmerged. It was also feasible to drain the excessive anxiety attached to the primitive fantasies, which thus made possible the realization of self. When the above was accomplished, therapy could proceed along the more familiar lines, not here elaborated upon, of the therapy of severe neurotic illness.

Bibliography

1. Despert, J. L.: "Schizophrenia in children." *Psychiat. Quart.*, XII, 366–371, 1938.
2. ———: "Psychotherapy in child schizophrenia." *Am. J. Psychiat.*, CIV, No. 1, 36–43, 1947.
3. Kanner, L.: "Autistic disturbance of affective contact." *Nerv. Child.*, II, No. 3, 217–250, 1942–1943.

4. ———: "Problems of nosology and psychodynamics of early infantile autism." *Am. J. Orthopsychiat.*, XIX, No. 3, 416–426, 1949.
5. Potter, H. W.: "Schizophrenia in children." *Am. J. Psychiat.*, LXXXIX, 1253–1270, May, 1933.

Psychological Problems of Children with Organic Brain Disease[*]

BY *Lauretta Bender, M.D.*

When a child comes to the Children's Service of the Psychiatric Division of Bellevue Hospital with a behavior problem associated with an organic brain disorder (1, 2, 3) there are always other social and emotional problems in his life situation severe enough to account for the behavior disorder on a dynamic interpretation alone. Our follow-up studies on children with inflammatory encephalitis (4, 5) and traumatic encephalopathy (6, 7) have led us to emphasize the dynamics of personality development and inadequacies in early childhood emotional experiences as contributory factors in the subsequent behavior disorder. Also it has been our experience that some children with acute traumatic or encephalitic disturbances who were cherished in adequate homes showed no subsequent behavior disorder (8, 9, 10). Consequently we have come to a more fa-

[*] Reprinted from *American Journal of Orthopsychiatry,* Vol. XIX, No. 3, July 1949, by courtesy of the author and the publishers, The American Orthopsychiatric Association.

vorable and positive evaluation of the brain-damaged child than the literature has generally advocated, provided the child has not suffered from social and emotional deprivation as well.

This positive evaluation has also depended on a considerable body of knowledge accumulated from many fields. 1) It must be possible to evaluate the nature of the organic damage from its effects on the functioning brain and on the developing child in his motor, perceptual, impulsive, and emotional behavior. 2) It must be possible to determine the special needs of such a child and how these needs can be met. 3) We must be able to anticipate from sufficient clinical experience what may be expected ultimately for the brain-damaged child.

There must be a thorough well-grounded organic neurological approach on the basis of the following neuropathological insights: 1) the epidemiology of childhood diseases and traumas, 2) the observation and evaluation of the patterned neurophysiological reflex behavior, 3) the motor maturation of the child (Gesell 11, 12), and 4) the meaning of motor play and the pattern of impulsiveness or impulse to action (Schilder 13). There must be knowledge gained from the motor-perceptual psychology, patterned as the Gestalt school of psychology teaches (14) with maturation and configuration, including the body image concept of Schilder (15), as in the drawing of a man (Goodenough 16) and in other projected behavior patterns whereby the child makes articulate his responses to the environment and his inner fantasy life. There must be knowledge of the personality maturation, patterned in terms of the relationship with the mother or parent figure and ultimately with society, together with the knowledge of the development of the emotional life and conceptual thinking, and the signs and meaning of anxiety where normal maturation is frustrated.

Children with various biological problems have common psychological problems. These common problems are best described as: 1) difficulties in patterned behavior in motor, perceptual, and emotional-social areas with tendencies to regressed or retarded maturation; 2) a severe anxiety, also poorly patterned (17); 3) a greatly increased need for human support in all these areas. This formulation gives us all that we need for diagnostic evaluation, prognostication, and therapeutic approach to the psychological problems. There will not be time to discuss the differential diagnostic techniques, or the analysis of each clinical syndrome, or possible therapeutic regimes or probable life courses for the different kinds of organic brain disorders. The emphasis will be on the common problems.

My own experiences have led me to include the following with the biologically or organically determined behavior disorder: childhood schizophrenia (18), language retardations or lags (including reading disabilities), motor lags (the so-called palsies, the mental defects or congenital deviations, epilepsy, as well as inflammatory encephalitis (with burn encephalopathies (19)) and traumatic encephalopathy (including birth injuries, prematurity, and cerebral anoxia).

Any knowledge gained about children in any of these biologically determined problems will lead to a better understanding of all other biologically determined problems, and incidentally in all problem children and growing children without problems. For example, the relationship between anxiety and the regressive motility patterns and projection of the body image preoccupations in the art work of the schizophrenic child teaches us about the dynamics of the process-determined conflict. It is then easier to understand other children with different pathology who show much of the same clinging, grasping behavior even though combined with focal neurological disorders referred to one or another part of the body. Efforts to express body image problems in art often are frustrated by difficulties in drawing in children with gross encephalopathies, but the drawings will still show some of the same features. The scattered, somewhat infantile patterning in all areas in the maturation curve of the preschool child who later develops a reading disability, with compensation by wild, asocial, clowning behavior and highly articulate drawings, makes it easier to understand the retardation in personality of the motor lags and certain of the early-determined encephalopathies. Some of these problems . . . I have discussed elsewhere. I am to limit myself to a consideration of the psychology of the traumatic and inflammatory encephalopathies and those congenital motor deviations which are especially closely allied.

It is necessary to emphasize that the examination of the brain-damaged child requires different techniques from those used with adults; this is especially true of the neurological examination. One must really forget about the reflex arc and tendon reflexology, as well as the usual tools of a neurologist, and think in terms of observing neurophysiological patterns as exemplified by the postural reflexes. These must be related closely to the dynamics of the evolution of locomotion and motor and nutritional independence. Grasping, sucking behavior or manual manipulation and oral activity must be evaluated in the same ways. The neurological examiner must also observe the child at play, cognizant at each age level of normal motility, degree of activity, tonic states, ability to relate, or to be independent. Organically damaged children tend to give way to impulses for primitive reflex patterns and to reflex play such as whirling postural response, or motor impulse to action which leads to perseverative and compulsive phenomena, as well as to unusual grasping, touching, pointing, and devouring. Some diffuse organic disorders merely lead to a psychologic clinging or dependency, a tendency to relate too closely and identify with every object and cause.

A neurological examination of a child is not complete which does not include an examination of the way the child relates himself to the adult. Does the child use the adult's body to compensate for his own organic disability and disorganization? Is he clinging, physically dependent, cohesive? Is he plastic or resistive to bodily manipulation, fondling, lap-holding, and to permissive indulgence in reflex motor play, such as whirling, bouncing, tossing, and swinging against gravity? These responses in children more than two years of age are reliable signs of the disorganization of the motor maturation and indicate retardation or regression in motor development. There may also be more or less choreoathetotic motor behavior and tonic changes of muscles which can only be evaluated by intimate observation and actual manipulation of the child's body. They will never be detected by any physician whose careful neurological examination is performed on a prone child, covered with a sheet to his chin, and with the physician's hands busily engaged with tuning forks, percussion hammers, ophthalmoscopes, etc. Incidentally, the organic child is a clever deceiver and has more ways of concealing his symptomatology than the unwary physician has of revealing it. This is one reason why the neurological signs in early childhood organic diseases fluctuate from day to day.

The neurological examination is not complete that does not also take into consideration the child's anxiety and his way of dealing with it. All organically disturbed children suffer profoundly from anxiety because of the disorganization, the difficulty in relating themselves to reality, and the frustration in achieving normal maturation. There may also be difficulties in making articulate the anxiety that stems from unknown inner sources rather than a reality situation in the environment. I have come to the formulation that any severe anxiety in a child which cannot be readily accounted for and corrected by a reality situation is invariably pointing toward a threatening and disorganizing illness. I include schizophrenia in this category. I have never seen a conversion hysteria or major anxiety hysteria in childhood which could not be accounted for by an organic illness. A four-year-old girl was sent to me with a diagnosis of an hysterical paralysis on the basis of a castration anxiety. I observed that the profound anxiety of the child could not mobilize her to the use of her limbs. A four-year-old girl might certainly feel herself castrated by the loss of use of her limbs from severe systemic disease (although undiagnosed) but not by the knowledge of the little brother's unimpressive genitals. Unfortunately, the interpretive psychotherapy which this child nevertheless received did not save her life from the leukemia which was subsequently diagnosed. I do not doubt, however, that the therapist gave the child some supportive help through a trying period, in the warmth of the therapeutic relationship.

My earliest insight into the psychological problems

of children with organic brain disorders came with the observation of children with cerebellar disorders (20). Cerebellar disorders often exist in relatively pure form and are not complicated with other perceptual or impulse disorders. They therefore lend themselves especially well to the study of the effect of motor disorders on the personality development. They help us recollect that the mother in the first months of life functions not only to give birth, food, affection, and personal care to the child but also to support the child in all its motor functions. The infantile relationship of the child to the mother is as much determined by the slow development of the motor system as it is, for example, by the dependency on her for nutrition. In a cerebellar disorder it is necessary for the mother to give motor support to the child for a much longer period of time, not only in regard to locomotion, but also in feeding, dressing, and even in speech. Such children tend to cling to the mother or a substitute and as a result are capable of deep emotional attachments and dependency relationships. These children are brought to us because of the difficulties arising out of the dependency on the so-called oversolicitous mother. Often not until the child was actually separated from the mother did it become evident how great was the child's need for the solicitous care of the mother, and that her apparent excessive care was actually only a response to this real need. Similar problems are seen in other motor disabilities including the extrapyramidal disorders, the choreoathetotic disorders, the choreas, and the pyramidal tract paralyses. The grasp reflex in these children serves the purpose of obtaining support from the mother's body as well as protection for the child from the pull of gravity. The grasping reflex is related, therefore, both to the feeding responses and motor development. This is especially true when maturation has been impeded. The psychological counterparts are readily seen in the psychological clinging and dependency and the deep attachments. Profound anxiety states are induced by threats to deprive the child of the needed support.

Thus the child with the cerebellar dysfunction is held back to a more primitive stage in the development of equilibrium as well as in its emotional life. Clinging and dependency occur in both fields. This is related to non-specific motor difficulties, lack of equilibrium due to cerebellar asynergias, muscle weakness, and disturbed tone distribution plus tendencies to maintain or regain postures. The effects upon the personality are more profound since cerebellar disorders are usually present from birth and yet are developmental lags which tend to correct themselves. If the infant's greater needs have been recognized and met, and he has not been left helpless or unaided in his efforts to attain and maintain posture and equilibrium, there are usually no subsequent difficulties in giving up the dependency relationship when it is not needed. The clinging does not remain in the motor sphere alone, but becomes a psychosexual clinging which is easily transferred from mother to other love objects. Only the child whose need for help in solving the motor problems has not been met is likely subsequently to show hysterical features.

Schilder, in his study of grossly brain-damaged children in 1931 (21), and his experience with adult obsessional neurotic problems (22), concluded that unsolved motor problems in infancy concerning security and equilibrium may well be one factor which leads to an anxiety neurosis later on, and unsolved problems in the patterning of impulses may be connected with compulsive and obsessional neurosis.

Many of the developmental lags classified with the congenital palsies represent more extensive system involvements than the cerebellar diseases and include the pyramidal tract as well as other extrapyramidal systems. Such developmental lags are nearly always more severe on one side than the other and in either the upper or lower part of the body. For this reason the diagnosis of diplegia or monoplegia is often made although careful examination will show that the motor disability is general. The organism is presented with problems similar to those of the child with cerebellar disease. These are problems in maintaining and regaining posture and equilibrium, the control of tonic disorders, relating to supporting agents, and acting out of impulses and experiencing patterns interwoven from all of these factors. Similar problems are often produced by encephalitis and other encephalopathies early in infancy. These problems are quite independent of the specific motor disability which varies in every child, and supportive care is indicated for individual disabilities, in addition to any specfic treatment or program for motor retraining.

In 1942 (4) I reviewed the problem of encephalitis in children and came to the conclusion that there were three major problems.

1. The motor or motility disturbance which was mostly extrapyramidal and tended to progress.

2. The specific intellectual defect which was based on difficulties in gaining patterned behavior through perceptual experience.

3. The personality disturbance related mainly to the hyperkinesis and deficiencies in social orientation.

The postencephalitic child shows difficulties in perceptual experience in the psychometric patterning which is fairly typical for most organic brain disorders. There are difficulties in spatial orientation, visual or auditory memory, and baragnostic sense. These are all patterned perceptual-motor functions. Specifically, there are failure to copy a diamond or even a square (especially in younger children), poor memory for digits especially backwards, inability to reproduce designs from memory, and often failure to distinguish weights (IX Stanford-Binet, 1916 revision). The visual motor gestalt test (Bender 14) is of diagnostic value because of its specific perceptual motor nature. Most significantly the Goodenough drawing of a man is usually two years or more below the mental age on the Stanford-Binet (Bender, 1940) (23). This indicates a specific imperception for body image which is defined as a performance of total integration of various perceptions of the whole organism. There is no difficulty in perceiving as such, but in integrating perceptions from the various fields into meaningful wholes. The drawing of a man is not the man seen, but a self-portrait or the inner man experienced by integrating all experiences. The specific difficulty in integrative function gives some clue as to the frustration which the organically sick child suffers. The constant drive to make contact with the world and to use one's body in action and perception does not come to a final pattern and does not give satisfaction. This, in turn, leads to an increase in drive to contact and to experience contacts and in itself accounts for the hyperkinesis with the drive to touch, see, hear, feel, and finally to devour and destroy every object which cannot otherwise be appreciated. It also increases the drive to cling which arises from the inadequacy in the motor fields for independent posture and locomotion. This inability to appreciate the perceptual experiences, and the frustration that rises from it, increases the anxiety.

In some organic brain disorders, the ability to draw a man is not impaired due undoubtedly to different localization of pathology. These children draw compulsively—like some schizophrenic children or those with reading disabilities—and often draw unusually well. However, the drawing of a man nearly always reveals the neurological disorder or motility problem, or expresses the presence of an unsolved problem in motor impulses with compulsive features.

Finally, one may say that the hyperkinesis may be understood as an effort continually to contact the physical and social environment, to reëxperience and integrate the perceptual experiences in a continual effort to gain some orientation in the world. The asocial behavior may be understood as the result of a lack of capacity to live out normal psychosexual drives and build up some understanding of one's place in the world in a longitudinal pattern, through learning from past experience and building up concepts for future satisfactions.

One can reconsider these matters from the point of view of unpatterned impulses to perception and to action. The emphasis has been on the hyperkinetic or hypertonic disorders. One sees as many hypokinetic children and hypotonic conditions. One sees children who part of the time are hypokinetic and part of the time are hyperkinetic, depending upon excessive external stimuli and mounting frustration with anxiety. Hypokinetic children show apathy, blocking, and mutism frequently with daydreaming and compulsive behavior. Overtalkativeness with confabulations, swearing,

obscenities occur with increased oral impulses together
with biting, spitting, kissing, and devouring. Some
encephalitic children will show a continuous flow of
impulses which cannot be controlled, increased, or diminished. Such a child was Eileen, whose mother complained that she demanded too much attention. Her
mother even had to think and act for her. Eileen
showed many compulsive features as the only way of
organizing her too slow but steady impulse stream. She
talked constantly but monotonously and engaged in
endless daydreams when she did not have an audience.
Her prepuberty daydreams concerned themselves with
the awkwardness in her motility, her difficulties in competing with other children, and difficulties in her relationship with her mother. In puberty, they dealt with
sexual matters and unrealistic fantasies of building her
own family life. She was a compulsive reader and compulsively drew human figures in the complex social situation with which she could not deal. The heads in her
drawn figures were always pulled to one side, as Eileen's
was in reality by her tonic neck responses and the impulse to carry out postural reflex patterns. She also had
compulsive tendencies to hit, touch, and point while
she talked, either aggressively against children or toward genitals—her own or others'. Such acts, however,
were never completed.

The training and treatment of such children depend
on establishing satisfactory patterns within the flow of
impulses. Basic is the relationship with the mother
through the infantile periods when the actual needs of
the child are being ministered to. Basic also is the relationship with whatever therapist or tutor the child
needs in order to correct special disabilities. Ordinarily, special psychotherapy is not indicated. A dynamic

interpretation of disordered behavior may indeed be an accurate description of the dynamics involved, but still does not indicate the cause of the disorder (White-horn 24). Interpretive psychotherapy may be comforting, or it may add to the disturbance and make further difficulties in more basic interpersonal relationship. It will not be curative.

Edward, a seven-year-old Negro boy was referred to Bellevue because of sluggishness, inability to learn, dullness, and a tendency to go to sleep in class. His parents were of unusual mixed cultural and racial background, and as a result appeared to be in conflict, although they formed a solid, warm, family group who showed high levels of attainment. Edward, because of the school problem, had been sent to a rigid grandmother in the country. He had an I.Q. of 130 but no educational accomplishments. It was easy to arrive at a dynamic formulation of a conflicted child reacting to anxiety and rejection with blocking and inhibitions in learning. We had already learned that Negro children (25) respond to anxiety with blocking, inhibitions, and sleeping. Some such interpretation was made to the child and parents who were encouraged to keep him in their own family circle. He returned two years later, at nine years, because of increasing attacks of sleeping in school, and still was unable to read.

A more careful study revealed that there was a severe illness with pneumonia at 3 months and 5 months of age in which the child was prostrated and after which he remained apathetic for a long period. Repeated neurological examinations showed fluctuating disorders in oculomotor control and postural responses. The electro-encephalogram was diagnostic for narcolepsy. Further psychodynamic investigation disproved psychogenic

features in the narcolepsy. This was treated with benzedrine. The learning difficulty was recognized as an
independent developmental lag or reading disability.
He was sent home again when a school was arranged
that would provide necessary remedial tutoring.

Two years later, at eleven years of age, he was seen
again. He was at this time a happy member in his family,
school, and community group. He had learned to read,
and in these two years had brought his school work up
to a grade placement suitable for his chronological age,
though still below his higher mental age. Benzedrine
helped to control his sleepiness though a sufficient dose
made him mildly toxic. We are now trying to make further adjustments in his pharmacological therapy.

This case is important in demonstrating that a dynamic interrelation may describe the psychological
problem, but still does not touch the cause. It is also important in indicating that two independent biologically
determined processes may be present in one child and
still be independent; that each must be evaluated on its
own merit and treated specifically; that the prognosis
is dependent upon applying the specific treatment and
also upon meeting the general need of supporting the
child in his own group and emphasizing the worth of
the individual.

It is also important in showing that while an organic
illness may have its own specific residual symptom due
to focal pathology, like Edward's narcolepsy, it also
tends to exaggerate the personality problems which belong to the individual because of his heredity, constitution, and cultural background. At first Edward seemed
like a very good example of blocked, inhibited, withdrawn, anxious Negro boy in a conflicted family. The
father said, "I was just like him as a boy. I was slow in

reading, and stubborn and lazy, and slept, and I've always been the black sheep in the family." It appears that the organic process, because of the increased, poorly patterned flow of impulses and the diffuse, nonspecific anxiety, tends to exaggerate the dynamic problem and make the individual more vulnerable to stress and strains and less able to manipulate his own relationship to reality. There is also the factor that the organic child clings psychologically to the mother or father and other adults. This leads to a close indentification, and the parent often responds in kind. Eileen's mother said, "She is a replica of me and I was like her when I was a child; clumsy, slow, daydreaming and lazy." Actually Eileen was a caricature of her mother as well as her mother's concept of herself.

The question of anxiety in the brain-damaged child has been very much misunderstood except for the work of Greenacre (17). The anxiety is of a diffuse nonspecific type, and the child, too, becomes inured to it and conceals it as he has learned to conceal many of his neurological signs. In my early work with the organic child, I too undervalued it. I have already indicated that the diagnostic evaluation of the child organically sick must include the anxiety and the way the child deals with it. The presence of anxiety not readily related to a reality situation and not responding to an attempt to correct the reality situation is an indication of an organic illness (including schizophrenia). Even though a dynamic interpretation may be made, this is not sufficient evidence of the cause or origin of the anxiety. However, an organic illness which interferes with normal maturation in any field, such as motor function, perceptual integration, or in relating to reality, will give rise to anxiety. The earlier the illness, the more physiological or nonspecific or nondynamic is the anxiety. It increases all the other psychological problems of the brain-damaged child—his clinging to adult figures, the unpatterning of impulses, and the drive to overcome these difficulties with further activity and regression of pattern.

Greenacre postulated the predisposition to anxiety as a physiological tendency to anxiety due to organic suffering at or near the time of birth with a heightened basic anxiety and a secondary anxiety arising from frustration and the inadequacy of the neurotic defense. The concepts of facile identification and of mirroring and weak relationship to reality are all similar to the experiences which we observe directly in the organically brain-damaged child.

This anxiety is best met by a close and continuous stream of well-patterned support in the earliest years with a prolongation of the infantile period. It should be realized, however, that the security gained for the child in support of posture and motility and relationship with the environment is not an end in itself but only a means for subsequent independent action. The impulse for action is as basic as the need for security (Schilder 21).

There are many remarkable things about the organic brain-damaged child which also remind us of the miraculous capacity of all children to grow up, to maturate, and to be as normal as they are. The drive for normality and for living through a regular maturation pattern as a global response of the biological unit is much stronger than the disorganizing tendency resulting from other focal or diffuse structural pathology or destructive and depriving influences in the environment. Deviations or pathology in the central nervous system tends to produce a general kind of disorganization of behavior patterns even in the motor activity or personality function with resulting primitive unpatterned responses. Often, therefore, there are none of the usual neurological signs sought by the neurologist. Observation will, however, show immature, retarded, or regressed motor play, loco-motion, postural reflexes, or the grasping, sucking reflex pattern. The impulses for action are inadequately patterned for the growing individual. At the same time the total personality is impelled to strive for normal maturation. Because of the need for motor support, as well as related emotional problems, there is a prolongation of the infantile period with a need for dependency on the mother or mother figures and on the total environment for support. Failure to receive such support leads to inadequate patterning of behavior with increased anxiety. This, in turn, leads to the so-called oversolicitous mother who is responding to the special needs of the child often, of course, with resentment because she does not understand either the situation or the criticism it brings upon her. The pathology may also show itself in other areas of disorganization. At the motor level there is an increase in regressed motor play with whirling and other kinds of reflex play. The unpatterned motor impulses meet the compulsive, repetitive, or perseverated tendencies which have been looked upon as the hyperkinesis of brain damage.

Summary

The psychological problems of the organically sick child are dependent on these fundamental factors:

Motor or motility disorders make the child dependent on the mother in a prolonged infantile relationship and promote deep emotional attachments.

Perceptual or intellectual problems are due to difficulties in organizing or interpreting and appreciating the totality of perception, which lead to frustration due to a poor relationship to reality. Drives to contact the world and obtain satisfaction from perception and reality experiences account for the hyperkinesis and asocial behavior.

Further difficulties in organization or patterning of impulses lead to distortion in the action pattern with final compulsive features.

Anxiety is a central problem basic to the physiological disorganization and secondary to the frustration and lack of satisfaction and to the difficulties in the relationship.

The answer to the problem is to give mothering support to the organism from the earliest period and for as long as needed; to avoid isolating experiences; to give specific aids for specific disabilities which will increase the patterning in motility, perceptual fields, or personal relationship, as indicated.

The dominating drive of the organically sick individual like the normal individual's is for normality in development and freedom for independent action; every normal and pathological process will be bent to this goal.

Bibliography

1. Bender, Lauretta: "Organic Brain Conditions Producing Behavior Disturbances," in *Recent Trends in Child Psychiatry* (Nolan D. C. Lewis and B. L. Pacella, Eds.). Internat. Univ. Press, New York, 1946.

2. ———: "Neuropsychiatric Contributions to Mental Hygiene Problems of the Exceptional Child." *Ment. Hyg.*, 26:617, 1942.

3. Bender, Lauretta, and Helen Yarnell: "An Observation Nursery." *Am. J. Psychiatry*, 97:1159–1174, 1941.

4. Bender, Lauretta: "Post-Encephalitic Behavior Disorders." Chap. XIV, 361–385, in *Encephalitis. A Clinical Study* (Josephine Neal, Ed.). Grune & Stratton, New York, 1942.

5. ———: "Cerebral Sequelae and Behavior Disorders Following Pyogenic Menengo-Encephalitis in Children." *Arch. Ped.*, LIX: 772–784, 1942.

6. Bender, Lauretta, and A. A. Fabian: "Head Injuries in Children: Predisposing Factors." *Am. J. Orthopsychiatry*, 17:1, 1947.

7. ———: *Personality Problems and the Head-Injured Child.* Unpublished.

8. Blau, Abraham: "Mental Changes Following Head Trauma." *Arch. Neurol. and Psych.*, 35:273, 1936.

9. Bowman, Karl M., and A. Blau: "Psychiatric States Following Head and Brain Injuries in Adults and Children." Chap. XIII in *Injuries of Skull, Brain and Spinal Cord* (Samuel Brock, Ed.). Williams and Wilkins, Baltimore, 1940.

10. Schilder, Paul: "Neurosis Following Head and Brain Injuries." *Ibid.*, Chap. XII.

11. Gesell, Arnold, and Frances L. Ilg: *Infant and Child in Culture of Today.* Harper, New York, 1945.

12. ———: *The Child From Five to Ten.* Harper, New York, 1946.

13. Schilder, Paul: "Brain and Personality. Studies in the Psychological Aspects of Cerebral Neuropathology." *Nerv. and Ment. Dis. Monog.*, No. 53, New York, 1931.

14. Bender, Lauretta: "Visual Motor Gestalt Test and Its Clinical Use." *Research Monog.*, No. 3. Am. Orthopsychiatric Assoc., New York, 1938.

15. Schilder, Paul: "Image and Appearance of the Human Body." *Psyche Monog.*, No. 4. Kegan Paul, London, 1935.

16. Goodenough, Florence: *Measurement of Intelligence by Drawing*. World Book Co., New York, 1926.

17. Greenacre, Phyllis: "Predisposition to Anxiety." *Psa. Quart.*, X:1 and 4, 1941.

18. Bender, Lauretta: "Childhood Schizophrenia." *Am. J. Orthopsychiatry*, 17:1, 1947.

19. ———: "Burn Encephalopathies in Children." *Arch. Ped.*, 60:75, 1943.

20. ———: "The Psychology of Children Suffering from Organic Disturbances of the Cerebellum." *Am. J. Orthopsychiatry*, 10:287, 1940.

21. Schilder, Paul: "Psychological Implications of Motor Development in Children." Proc. Fourth Institute on the Exceptional Child. Child Research Clinic of the Woods School, October, 1937.

22. ———: "Structure of Obsessions and Compulsions." *Psychiatry*, 3:549–560, 1940.

23. Bender, Lauretta: "The Goodenough Test (Drawing a Man) in Chronic Encephalitis in Children." *J. Nerv. and Ment. Dis.*, 91:277–286, 1940.

24. Whitehorn, John C.: "The Concept of 'Meaning' and 'Cause' in Psychodynamics." *Am. J. Psychiatry*, 104:289–293, 1947.

25. Bender, Lauretta: "Behavior Problems in Negro Children." *Psychiatry*, 2:213–238, 1939.

Mongolism[*]

BY *Theodore H. Ingalls, M.D.*

The story of mongolism is a medical whodunit. In the 85 years since the condition was first recognized as a classifiable defect by Langdon Down, an eminent British neurologist, many theories have been proposed as to the cause and possibilities for cure of this dread affliction. One of the most popular theories has been that the condition is due to "defective germ plasm." The phrase caresses the ear with the sweet ring of reason, but it possesses little scientific meaning. If the defect is in the germ plasm, is it hereditary or acquired, and if acquired, how and when? The germ-plasm theory is a fence-straddler that leaves the basic problem untouched.

About two of every 1,000 babies born are found to have mongolism. The marks of the condition are stamped plainly on the victim's face—a foreshortened skull, a flattened nasal bridge, folds at the corners of the eyelids. This Oriental-like cast of the features was dragged as a red herring across the trail, in the standard

[*] From *Scientific American*, Vol. 186, No. 2, February 1952. Reprinted by courtesy of the author and publishers, *Scientific American*.

tradition of detective fiction, at the very beginning of the story. Down seized on this feature to name the disability "Mongolian idiocy," and early in this century a

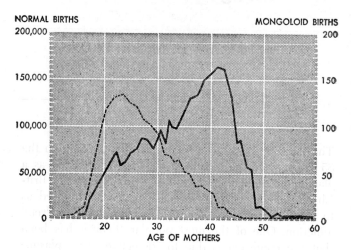

Mothers of mongoloids (solid line; from 2,882 cases) *tend to be older than mothers with normal infants* (dotted line; from 1934 U. S. births).

melodramatic scientist, carried away by the name and the sloe-eyed appearance of the patients, wrote a popular work entitled *The Mongol in Our Midst*. The condition was portrayed as an atavistic throwback through Oriental forebears toward the orangutan. Although patently an unjustified, unscientific slur on Oriental peoples, the name, now softened to mongolism, has stuck like a burdock in the beard of the Western physician.

It is the mental retardation, due to malformation of the brain, that makes the disease so tragic. The mother of a mongoloid baby slowly learns with heartaches and secret tears that her child will never be capable of caring for himself or bringing the usual pride and joy to his parents. Hope for a "cure" dies hard, but it is only fair to admit that the task of therapy for mongolism baffles the scientific imagination. How can one expect to reform the intricately disordered gyri of a brain that is nourished by anomalous blood vessels, is contained in an abnormal skull and looks out at the world with eyes that are already markedly defective at birth? Let the surgeon try with his knife, let the pediatrician try with his endocrines, but let them not allow their research activity to be misinterpreted as promising or even hinting of promise, for the evidence is all against the possibility of a cure in the foreseeable future. In this era of vitamins, hormones and antibiotics it is no feat at all to make mongoloid children taller, longer-lived and healthier than they used to be, but to restore missing cells to crippled brains and eyes is asking too much of "miracle drugs."

One can, however, speak optimistically about the possibilities of prevention. In searching for the means of prevention it is necessary to keep constantly in mind a basic principle of modern epidemiology—namely, that there is never a single cause for any disease. This truth has been ably expressed by the famous epidemiologist Karl Meyer: "Today, the doctrine that there is a single specific cause for each disease entity is untenable. A purely bacteriologic (or chemical) explanation pays little heed to the fact that the essentials of disease are two—an animal and an organism (or a physical or chemical agent); these interact, react, and are acted upon by external forces. The more quickly it is recognized that causation is a constellation of predisposing, provoking and perpetuating factors, the more certain will progress be made."

In short, disease is a complex process that depends on the interactions of an injurious agent, a susceptible patient and a particular environment. Not everyone exposed to syphilis, for example, gets the disease. Not all people who contract syphilis get it in the same way or exhibit the same symptoms—for social, economic, anthropological or constitutional reasons that have nothing to do with the germ. The old may differ from the young, men from women, the colored from the white, the rich from the poor, the educated from the uneducated, military from civilian populations. By the same token, a given disturbance may be produced by several different agents. Boiling water from a broken pipe or scalding oil from a kitchen pot may cause exactly the same kind of burn. Suffocation from lack of oxygen may be caused by hemorrhage, diphtheria, carbon-monoxide poisoning, drowning, flying in the stratosphere or swinging too long on a gallows. In each of these conditions, despite the differences in causation, the end result in terms of the oxygen content of blood and tissues may be identical.

All this emphasizes the unreasonableness of trying to incriminate a single cause for mongolism—whether it be a poison, a virus, hypothyroidism, "uterine exhaustion," something inherited or something the mother ate. Three cases chosen almost at random illustrate how various the causes may be. A mother who bore mongoloid twins recalled in a letter to me that about the eighth week of her pregnancy she had suffered a uterine hemorrhage in an automobile accident. Another mother of a mongoloid child reported that she had had a tooth pulled, and been made sick by the anesthetic, during the seventh week of pregnancy. In the third case, the mother of a mongoloid child had undergone a thyroidectomy for a large tumor before her pregnancy. Although it is not claimed that these events were the sole cause of the offspring's mongolism in each case, the three cases obviously are different.

The causes of mongolism can be investigated along three lines—clinical, epidemiological and experimental. The clinical, of course, involves the examination of individual patients (meaning both mother and child) and their symptoms. The epidemiological approach means the study of the incidence and manifestations of the disorder among groups of people over periods of time and in the social and geographical context. The experimental line is the testing of hypotheses in the laboratory by work on animals.

The analogy between medical investigation and dectective work recalls an observation made by Sherlock Holmes, who, between puffs on his pipe and passages on his violin, once remarked: "When you follow separate trains of thought, Watson, you will find some point of intersection which should approximate the truth." In the investigation of mongolism the point of intersection of the clinical and epidemiological trains of thought lies somewhere in the first three months of pregnancy; that is to say, this seems to be the critical period for the origin of the disorder. It is significant that many of the secondary defects associated with mongolism—absence or stunting of one or both nasal bones, frequent lack of the second permanent lateral incisor teeth, dwarfing of the middle phalanx of the little finger, defective compartmentation of the heart—involve structures which begin their budding during approximately the eighth week of the embryo's life. The inference, of course, is that this is the period during which the mother's health and the condition of the embryo should be scrutinized most carefully in the search for causes.

Let us see what clues epidemiology provides. The mean age of mothers of mongoloid babies is 41, an age at which chronic disturbance of the endocrine system begins to become common in women. It is probably significant that malfunctioning of the thyroid gland is more frequent among mothers of mongoloid babies than would be expected on the basis of chance alone. Nearly 10 per cent of the mothers of mongoloid babies have had acute infections in or about the eighth week of pregnancy. The Australian ophthalmologist Ronald Lowe, after a study of eye defects in 52 mongoloid persons, concluded that these defects must be established at about this stage of pregnancy.

In about 25 per cent of the mothers of mongoloid babies the uterus has been found bent backward to a significant extent, which may affect circulation between the uterus and placenta, though whether it actually does so is not known. About 20 per cent of mothers of the defective babies are known to have had vaginal bleeding during the first three months of pregnancy; this should not be construed, however, to mean that a mother who bleeds in early pregnancy is in danger of producing a mongoloid child, for the over-all risk of mongolism, as the statistics show, is small.

The epidemiologic evidence suggests, in other words, that mongolism may stem in part from an acute injury to the embryo due to placental hemorrhage, threatened abortion or infection, or from a chronic disturbance resulting from abnormal functioning of the uterus or of the thyroid gland. The embryologist George W. Corner has pointed out that a mechanical disorder of the uterus which does not allow sufficient space for development of the embryo is likely to result in an anatomically abnormal child, if it succeeds in being born. The statistics indicate that 90 per cent of the time chronic rather than acute disturbances of pregnancy are the underlying causes of mongolism. A severely deformed or backward-bent uterus, disturbed metabolism or significant anemia—any such influence may act as one of multiple triggers to blight the "fruit of the womb."

At first it is difficult to conceive how investigation of the causes of mongolism can be approached experimentally in the laboratory. How, for example, could one recognize mongolism in a mouse, even if he could produce it? Actually the investigation is not impossible, for the investigator can produce gross cerebral and skeletal defects in animals of a kind similar to those associated with mongolism. In other words, it is possible to study, not mongolism as such, for that is restricted to the human species as surely as stuttering, but the principles governing both hereditary and acquired congenital deformities.

In 1910 the Cornell University biologist Charles R. Stockard found that he could produce cyclopia (a single, central eye) in fish by exposing fish eggs to the action of a solution of magnesium chloride at a critical moment, between the 13th and 15th hours of the fertilized egg's development. Further, he demonstrated that various other agents—alcohol, chloroform, ether—could likewise cause eye defects and anomalous development of the central nervous system. His work showed not only that a particular defect could be induced by different agents but also that, in fish at least,

characteristic and specific defects are directly related to
a particular moment in development of the embryo;
they can be produced only by injuring the embryo at
that moment.

During the past 15 years many experiments have
made clear that congenital anomalies can similarly be
produced in higher animals. In the laboratory of the
Department of Epidemiology at the Harvard School of
Public Health Richard Prindle and the writer have done
such work on some 300 pregnant mice, bearing a total
of about 2,500 embryos. Within a plastic chamber the
pregnant mice are subjected to rarefied atmospheres
deficient in oxygen. Each mouse is exposed for five
hours on a single occasion. In this manner from 10 to
20 litters have been subjected to intra-uterine anoxia
on each of the first 17 days of pregnancy. On the 18th
day the young are delivered by surgery (when defective offspring are born naturally, the mother usually
devours them). The delivered fetuses are then examined for gross defects. The quantitative aspect of the
method is its important feature. One fires bullets, so to
speak, at the embryo during selected stages of its development rather than subjecting it to a continuous dietary or metabolic disturbance. In this way it is possible
to ascertain quantitatively the result of an acute rather
than a chronic upset, not only at the cellular and clinical level but at population levels of the epidemiologist
and geneticist.

We find a whole series of deformities in these fetuses,
the nature of the defects depending on the intensity,
duration and timing of the oxygen deprivation. Of the
litters subjected to anoxia on the eighth day of development, about a third have members that are born with

grossly defective brains. Those injured on the 14th day of development may produce offspring with a cleft palate; those so treated on the 16th day produce significant numbers of mice with a defect known as "open eye."

This experimental method also makes it possible to study genetic susceptibility and resistance to abnormalities. For example, in a study that the writer made during the summer of 1951 with Francis Curley, Fred Avis and Howard Temin at the Jackson Memorial Laboratory at Bar Harbor, Me., fetuses of the so-called *dba* strain of light brown mice were exposed to anoxia on the 7th, 8th and 9th days of gestation. Over 15 per cent of them developed umbilical hernia. Normally from one to two per cent of fetuses of this strain have this defect. On the other hand, among more than 2,500 young of an albino strain that had been subjected to anoxia at the Harvard School of Public Health none had umbilical hernia.

The investigation of mongolism is part of the much broader problem of congenital anomalies in general. Mongoloids, Siamese twins, "monsters" without a brain or with only one eye and infants with lesser defects, such as congenital heart disease or a cleft palate, give every suggestion of being naturally related as members of a family of anomalies. The anomalous individual is only an isolated unit of a larger dynamic process, like a single "still" removed from a moving-picture strip, or like a person with congenital syphilis. The evidence suggests that many anomalous children have survived a period of anoxic distress, just as the mouse with cleft palate has survived a period of anoxic distress. Others have survived infections, metabolic upsets or nutritional deficiencies.

In any event, modern research has clearly demonstrated that environmental factors account for a
substantial proportion of all congenital anomalies and
crippling defects. The pendulum which, as a result of
Gregor Mendel's classical discoveries, swung away from
the Lamarckian preoccupation with environment toward a fruitful concentration on the genes, seems to
have swung too far in that direction. Actually heredity
and environment are overlapping influences; as Theo-
dosius Dobzhansky has remarked: "The so-called
nature-nurture problem is not to distinguish which traits
are genotypic and which environmental, for all traits
are genotypic and environmental." The indications are
that every human embryo is a potential candidate for
mongolism, just as he is for measles, sunburn or an
auto accident. I am in full accord with the statement
by L. S. Penrose of University College in London
that "at the present time the mode of action of the
hereditary background is obscure and is much less important, from the point of view of preventive treatment, than the environmental factors dependent upon
maternal conditions." In his introduction to Penrose's
book *The Biology of Mental Defect*, J. B. S. Haldane
says: "It is entirely possible that a suitable hormonal
treatment of elderly mothers could halve the frequency
of mongolism." There is more to the problem than the
use of hormones, however. Present knowledge suggests
that coördinated and energetic study of congenital defects will result in a significant contribution to public
health. The objective is an improved quality, rather
than quantity, of the human race—the kind of thing we
might hope for were the application of eugenics as prac-
ticable among mankind as it is among pets and beasts
of burden.

ADOLESCENCE

The Mental Health of
Normal Adolescents*

BY George E. Gardner, Ph.D., M.D.

You will note that I have selected as my title "The Mental Health of Normal Adolescents." I did this deliberately, because it is my feeling and my experience that 90 per cent of the so-called "problems" of adolescents have to do with *normal* reactions or *normal phases* through which the adolescent passes in his journey toward adulthood. I feel that this must be true because certainly 90 per cent of our adolescent children do get through this stage of development without any serious emotional upset, though I'm not so sure that they get through it without a few emotional scars.

I feel so strongly the need to emphasize these problems as stages in development because I believe that mental health itself is for all of us a continuing problem that we all—including the adolescent—must work at year after year. Our mental health and the mental

* Presented in the Judge Baker 1947 Lecture Series, April 25, 1947. Reprinted from *Mental Hygiene,* Vol. XXXI, October 1947, No. 4; by courtesy of the author and publishers, The National Association for Mental Health, Inc.

health of the adolescent are not static conditions. In other words, I want to bring to you a point of view regarding mental health in general and the mental health of adolescents in particular that will be a dynamic point of view. It is a point of view that looks upon the adolescent and all the rest of us as biological organisms with certain drives and motives and instincts that determine what our behavior shall be, and with needs that not only have to be satisfied, but, more important, have to be re-satisfied again and again as we go through life. That is my first emphasis as regards the point of view I wish to convey.

My second emphasis would be that there are two types of problem having to do with the adolescent that set themselves as tasks for him to solve. There are, in the first place, the general problems that he has been trying to solve all along from his earliest infancy and that are probably more fundamental and of more concern to him in adolescence and thereafter than are those of the second group that I will mention.

These general problems of the adolescent, I will say briefly, have to do, first of all, with the child's need for the establishment of a sense of security. It is that security that comes to the child when he learns that he is wanted and loved, that he has fair treatment by his parents in relation to his brothers and sisters and all other children his own age; when he recognizes that his home is a stable one, and that his parents not only love him and his siblings, but also love each other and demonstrate it by showing for each other that consideration and care that they bestow on him, the child; and, finally, when he reaches the stage at which he is able to appreciate that he can predict a continuing security in his home because, due to the consistency in their dealings, he can in large part predict what the behavior of his parents toward him is going to be from moment to moment.

This, then, is one of the general problems that precede adolescence, but it is by no means confined to the pre-adolescent years. It is a process that continues in adolescence—in fact, through all our lives—and feelings of insecurity relative to the parents and the possible instability of the home are just as poignant and upsetting in adolescence as they are in the earlier years. Furthermore, the basis of security or its lack that is established in early years will be the base line from which may start, or the frame of reference to which may be referred, the particular problems of adolescence which come up only at that time and with which we will deal shortly.

A second general problem of mental health that antedates adolescence, but that also has a tremendous effect on adolescent adjustment, is the problem of control of the instinctual expressions of sex and aggression. At this point I would particularly emphasize that the child learns from earliest life onward to stand frustrations—to limit, delimit, or even give up entirely certain goals of instinctual expression in the face of justified parental objections. Now his immediate reaction to this frustration in infancy is with aggression—aggression toward his parents, aggression toward his brothers and sisters, his teachers, or whatever may be the source of his frustration. A very prominent task of early life, then, is to acquire a workable method of handling this aggression, and the method outlined then will receive some very severe testing in puberty and adolescence and, in fact, in every other emotionally toned situation or stage of development throughout life.

In addition, let me state briefly that not all the problems relative to sexual adjustment are solved at the
time of adolescence; many of them are solved in infancy and early childhood—and certainly a foundation
of truthful fact and of trusting reference to parents in
such matters will very largely determine how upsetting
will be the actual maturation of the heterosexual instinct
in adolescence. Pleasures later referable to the sex instinct are certainly present in diffuse form in infancy
and childhood, and their meanings and their control
are part of the child's very early education.

Such, then, are some of the general problems of
mental health that face the adolescent, the partial solutions of which in early childhood aid or hinder him in
their re-solution in the newer settings of adolescence
later on. In short, what I am driving at is that these
early problems *re*-present themselves for continual *re*-
solution.

Now let us turn to the mental-health problems or
tasks that we are more likely to associate with the adolescent boy and girl—that is, the particular problems
that set this age off as a unit or stage in development.

The first problem of great concern during adolescent
years is the drive for emancipation and independence,
and, as I stated before, a successful solution of it is
dependent upon, and in large part influenced by, solutions that have previously been made in earlier life to
the aforementioned problems of security or insecurity,
aggression, passivity, and the emergence of infantile
sexual components. In other words, if the earlier adjustments to these have been inadequate, the problem
of adolescence and freedom from parental control, the
overcoming of dependence and the gaining of a state

of self-sufficiency, will be much more difficult. However, the internal pressures within the child, and the pressures from his colleagues, from his own parents, and from society as a whole *insist* that he find a solution to these problems in adolescence. It is as if a new drive or a new instinct for independence had been implanted within him.

Now the drive for adult status in adolescence immediately sets up certain serious conflicts that have been hinted at in various ways in our literature. On the one hand, the adolescent feels driven to be independent of his parents, to make his own decisions regarding his comings and goings, to choose his own friends, to determine his own academic and educational future. Everything about him and everybody—including his parents, really—insist that he *shall* assume these responsibilities, and he himself feels strongly that he should do so.

On the other hand, there are always many, many fears that contemplated independence brings to the mind of the adolescent boy or girl, and these we are very likely to overlook, for we note only the brave—perhaps even foolhardy—attempts on his part to throw off parental controls. But I assure you that adolescents have the parallel or concomitant fear of losing or giving up the parents and all the material and spiritual gifts that they can bestow. They fear also the possibility of making the wrong decisions, choosing the wrong type of friend, or perhaps selecting the wrong vocation on the basis of some temporary whim. And though they may carefully conceal all these in their braggadocio, any child psychiatrist will assure you of their presence. This conflict makes for the typical state of adolescence, which is best described as a state of continual indecision and fluctuation of needs and desires. It is, in short, the characteristic indecision that we see in our boys and girls.

But equally important, it seems to me, is the simultaneous conflict that is set up within us, the parents of our adolescent children. We, in turn, wish for the independence and self-sufficiency of this child of ours, but we also fear the loss of love that a removal of his dependency upon us creates. We, too, are subjected to internal and external pressures in both directions, and we, too, have a great stake in the outcome. So, paralleling the conflict of the adolescent boy and girl, we also note in ourselves the same conflict of independence versus dependency at work within us.

The most prominent feature of this drive for emancipation from parents and for independence of action—particularly in its early stages—is seen to be a marked devaluation of the parents that adolescents seemingly must first make if they are to advance and progress toward adulthood. These devaluations of parents involve just those areas of action, those ideas, and those ideals with which parents have been vitally concerned in their attempts to bring up their children in an acceptable—and mentally and socially healthy—way, and the blows of devaluation that are received are hard for the conscientious parent to take—at least in good-humored fashion; though the parental head may not be bloodied by them, the parental head from time to time is certainly bowed.

Let us look at these normal "phases" of adolescent devaluation of parents in order that all of us, being forearmed by an appreciation of their normalcy—i.e., be cause we know that they constitute necessary phases or steps in development—will not be too alarmed by their appearance. I have not tried to place these normal phases of devaluation of parents—or, more pointedly speaking, of "parent-belittlement"—at certain ages in adolescence. They may come early or late—from ten or eleven years through the teens—but come they will. I shall try to do justice to girls at this age level, too, though, as you can guess, my own particular practice concerns largely adolescent boys.

As you will see, much of the repudiation of the parents and their training that is aimed at by this behavior may also be accompanied by, or associated with, a desire to repudiate the whole growing-up process—to deny maturity, to cling to infantile ways of acting, or to ward off as long as possible the assumption of the responsibilities and conflicts that becoming a man or woman in the biological sense imposes.

Take, for example, the disheveled phase of adolescence or, much better perhaps, the dirty and disheveled phase which is of such concern to parents of boys in the earlier teen years. (Of course, of late years the dishevelment has crossed the line of sex and is now a phase of development in girls, too, which causes parents worry!) This type of behavior is easily noted as a repudiation of the parents' earlier insistence on cleanliness and neatness, together with a cynical indifference to the clean-up process that the first faint emergence of a feeling of interest in the opposite sex demands. With the first stirrings of interest in girls comes the associated information and knowledge that girls despise the messiness and uncleanliness of their bratty brothers. It is not unusual, therefore, for the boy to seize upon this as a denial both of parental training and of adolescent growth. The "hate women" stage, the "I'm never going to get married" phase, are the verbal expressions of this denial of desired responses to internal instinctual drives.

Secondly, the repudiation of the feminine rôle by the adolescent daughter finds expression in the phase of tomboyishness, the interest in strenuous athletic activities, even to the extent of an interest in professional sports, and, finally, in extreme cases, to a refusal to eat as an unconscious fear of assuming the adult female form in the physical sense.

At this stage also appear the strong attachments to older men on the part of adolescent boys, or to older women on the part of adolescent girls, with strong desires to emulate them. These older people are usually schoolteachers, club leaders, friends of the father or mother, and I need not tell you that when such an attachment is made by these young adolescents, the opinions and points of view of these older people are, according to the boy or girl, infallible, and they are particularly more valuable and worth while and in accord with the facts—again according to the boy or girl—than are the opinions and ideas of the father or mother. Needless to say, it takes a strong, a tolerant, and a secure parent to take such a devaluation—usually in comparison with someone of whose deficiencies and shortcomings the parent is well aware.

Further devaluation of the parents is seen in the criticism of the parents' home, the home-making qualities of the mother, or even the clothes and jewelry worn by either or both parents. Adolescents become extremely critical of the social and political ideas of their parents and, in fact, take great delight in puncturing, if they can, the most idealistic notions which previously were held as a sacred part of their culture.

Nowhere is the attempted repudiation or devaluation of the parents or the parents' ideas and values seen more clearly in this age group than in relation to the carefully made school plans and vocational choices that parents have determined upon for the child since his or her earliest infancy. If the school is temporarily accepted by the child as a whole, it is certain that the type of course that he has assumed at his parents' direction is probably—according to the youngster—too hard, and surely will, he insists, never be of any use whatsoever to him in later life. There is a suspicion on his part, of course, that the principal and the teachers are in league with the parents to see that such silly school plans are carried out effectively.

Vocational choices change from week to week. They change with new schoolmasters or with the advent of new children in the vicinity. This continuing troubled indecision regarding school plans or vocational plans has led to one of the psychiatrist's happiest phrases— that coined by Kubie, of New York, when he referred to this phase as the phase of the "obsessional indecision of adolescence."

Then there is the secretive, quiet, almost untouchable phase of adolescence, in which the child now looks for confirmation or denial of his ideas and opinions to someone—almost anyone—beyond the home. It is the age of the girl chum or the boy pal, whose knowledge of facts and values and estimates of worth are inevitably truer than ours—the parents! This is the stage of short answers or no answers to questions that have to do with present plans—or with the plans of the evening or the plans of the week-end. Disdainful looks or looks of resigned tolerance greet the parents' genuine concern in what the boy or girl may be doing.

This is the stage when the boy wishes that once and for all his father would give up following the procedure that the textbooks on child guidance have told him is the best for bringing up an adolescent boy—that is, he wishes that his father would give up the feeling that it is necessary to be a pal to Junior. Junior at this stage wants pals, but he does not want a parental pal. Rather he wants pals of his own age, who can share with him his concern and curiosity regarding certain very important problems of growing up, and the parent-pal is certainly of little or no use to him at such grave times. At this stage of his son's adolescence, the wise father will begin to fish and to golf alone again—or with pals of his own age.

Again, finally, there is the strong resistance to early, healthful hours, and even stronger resistance to early coöperative rising in the morning. The former is, of course, a determination to accelerate the move toward maturity and unfortunately, if acquiesced in, results in a pseudo acceleration or a pseudo maturity on all fronts, which none of us care to see in our own or others' children.

I think we can see in these various phases of the adolescent drive for maturity and independence the alternating phases of a need for independence and a need for dependence. Children of this age do not quite dare give up their childhood *in toto,* nor do they quite dare to refuse to grow up. The parents' rôle in all this, it seems to me, is to recognize that there are such conflicts inherent in this bizarre type of behavior, and that beneath the indifference and devaluation there is a strong inner need for parental aid and parental guidance.

Children in the teens do not actually believe that they are capable of controlling all of their inner wishes and demands, nor do they really wish to be asked or allowed to do so completely, because they are not quite sure to what lengths they might allow themselves to go. In addition to recognition of this fear—even when the adolescent expresses the opposite in his bravest moments—and the assumption of an air of tolerance toward the child in his conflicts, the parents must be very, very careful not to answer this aggressive repudiation by the adolescent with parental aggression toward him or her. If this response is elicited from the parents, a vicious cycle immediately is set up—the "either-or" proposition is established, from which unfortunately neither the adolescent nor the parent can withdraw without severe loss of face. I shall return to the rôle of the parent shortly, after we have considered another very important problem of adolescence.

Finally, there is one more task of mental health which has to be dealt with and which developmentally reaches the initial stage of intensity during the years of adolescence, and at that time, in turn, lays the basis for future problems to be solved or for future adult mental health. I refer here to the problems involved in the control and sublimation of the sex instinct.

It is a mistake that many of us make, I think, to assume that the problems of the expression of—or the control of the expression of—the sexual instinct appear newly structured as problems at the time of puberty and only following the physiological maturation of the reproductive system. For in relation to the purely physiological and anatomical aspects of the sexual drive and the expression of the various bodily pleasures associated therewith, the individual in his earlier years has been forced by parental and social dicta to establish controls, and he has been limited to only partial expressions of these drives. These controls by parents and society have been directed at the many varied, diffuse, and infantile—and only partially developed—components of the sexual drive in childhood, as distinguished from the complex sexual instinct as we recognize it later in its more localized, unified, and mature form in adolescence.

Adolescence, then, would seem to be merely a stage —though an extremely important one—in the direction of the instinct as it now has as its object the biological functions of reproduction. In short, adolescence seems to be the stage where the unification of all of the diffuse, pleasurable bodily expressions has to take place if the individual is thereafter to have a normal sexual adjustment.

For example, we sometimes note that some of the controls of the earlier independent segments of this complex drive may have been inadequate and have to be strengthened by inner inhibitions, or some of those types of child behavior that we assume to be more or less normal in earlier life will now in adolescence take on the aspects of atypical or even abnormal sexual behavior. Again, perhaps these controls which the child in his earlier years was able to establish were adequate in those years, but are now seen to be inadequate when the strong heterosexual drive in adolescence supervenes.

Whatever may be the situation, we can be sure that in the interests of mental health and adjustment the adolescent has to establish or reëstablish certain defenses against these inner drives. In most cases this is accomplished without much difficulty. On the other hand, because of the inadequate or too adequate—that is, too rigid—training of the child in early life, the adolescent may establish defenses against sexual expression that by their very extremeness and severity become quite disabling. These defenses of adolescence are commented upon extensively in the literature on child development and are probably well known to you.

Examples of these extreme defenses are tendencies on the part of the adolescent to periods of marked shyness and withdrawal, sometimes in so extensive an area of his daily life as to make the parents and his family physician wonder if he is becoming mentally ill. Usually these worries about the abnormality of this withdrawal are unfounded. They are a phase—a defensive phase—through which the child passes as he builds up within him more adequate controls that will also allow him a normal and acceptable response to his inner drives.

Again, there may be an overreaction against these inner feelings in the sense that he becomes over-conscientious—assumes that everything that has to do with the sexual drive or everything that has to do with the opposite sex is bad, sinful, or evil.

In another phase—usually in later adolescence—he may turn to endless intellectualizations of his problems, with an absorption in some new, radical, or perhaps ultra-conservative type of social order. He is unconsciously absorbed in these new social orders that he constructs as solutions to alleged—or actual—economic and social problems, when in reality the conflict that he is trying to settle is his own emotional conflict relative to the expression or non-expression of certain individual needs and desires in the society in which he finds himself.

At any rate, whatever defense is established, it is extremely important for the parents to recognize what the adolescent is trying to do by such maneuvers and thus, if necessary, be able to help him—that is, to understand that these are the best possible defenses that he can erect at that time to control the increasing power and urgency of his instinctual drive. However, as in the case of all defenses, they themselves may become disabling. We can carry out internal controls and prohibitions to such a degree that the very thing we are trying to insure becomes destroyed in its own defenses.

A second point of importance in relation to these problems is that adolescence is not the only time when these problems will be presented for solution. It is merely that in adolescence the ever-recurring problems relative to this instinctual drive are thrown into relief for initial and sometimes acute and critical solution, but you will note that thereafter not only the instinctual drive itself becomes a problem, but also the multifarious defenses that the child erects to care for it may in themselves constitute problems that call for ever-repeated modification in the light of future development and growth throughout the adult years.

What, then, are the other possible danger signals in these various phases of adolescence, both as regards the desired emancipation and the expression of the sexual instinct, that would indicate to the parent that he or she needs professional help with the adolescent child? Fortunately I think I can assure you that this need does not arise very frequently. It would seem to me that the most useful criterion would be whether or not there is an undue prolonging of the habits and attitudes of childhood into the late teens.

You see, as a psychiatrist, I am much more concerned with lack of development, or refusal to develop, as a phase in adolescence than I am with the attempt on the part of a child to grow up a little bit too fast. I emphasize this undue prolongation of childhood as possibly serious because it itself offers a definite interference to, or a block to, the social and emotional growth that must take place year after year. It points, too, not so much to a problem of the moment usually, but rather to possible unsolved early childhood problems such as we mentioned earlier in our discussion—that is, problems relative to security or passivity or aggression.

There is, again, a necessary concern for the adolescent, I feel, when the parent has strong reason to feel that the educational plans or the vocational aims of the adolescent, both of which may be irreversible decisions, are being neurotically determined. By this phrase, "neurotically determined," I mean determined on the basis of some temporary need of the moment or by some temporary—and, the parent knows, ephemeral —attachment or fixation upon some person in his immediate environment. Such needs and such attachments can for a time upset the whole life plans of the individual, and they should not be accepted by the parents.

Again, occasionally there is a definite destruction of the school situation with deliberate failure in studies that can only be understood as an unconscious aggressive act of the child against the parents—and against hinself also. At such times it might be necessary to seek the help of the professional vocational or educational guidance expert, or here—just as in the previously outlined plans regarding an extension into adolescence of admittedly infantile behavior—it might be necessary to seek the aid of the trained child psychiatrist.

Three things I hope, then, you have received from

this talk on the normal mental health of the adolescent. The first is best called the "genetic point of view,"
by which we mean that the present behavior of a boy
or girl—a cross-sectional segment of it, if you will—can
be understood only in the light of his past experiences
from infancy up—*i.e.*, can be judged only in a longitudinal sense as it, the segment, takes its place in relation
to those responses that have been expressed in earliest
childhood.

The second point of emphasis has been that mental
health is a continuing process that has to be attained
and maintained through an endless number of our responses day after day. In short, the adolescent—and all
of us, too—have to "work at" this problem of mental
health, which in itself is a composite of hundreds of
these momentarily adjusting or momentarily maladjust-
ing bits of behavior.

And, finally, we have stressed the point that adolescents are not a strictly isolatable group with problems
particular to them alone—as a race apart—but rather
that the adolescent is beset by tasks in mental health
strikingly similar to those at all age levels. It is only
that the new demands for final adult status lend to the
trial-and-error aspects—and to the many, varied, but
none the less normal phases—of adolescent behavior its
bizarre, unpredictable and—sometimes to us as parents
—very worrisome characteristics.

My main therapeutic approach to the parents of adolescents—my best treatment advice and prescription to
them in the face of such behavior—is the tried and
true phrase of the men of the ancient church who,
when beset by the unpredictable and the seemingly
uncontrollable, comforted themselves and one another
with the words, "It will pass. It will pass."

The Adolescent, His Conflicts and Possible Methods of Adjustment*

BY *Lydia G. Dawes, M.D.*

It is well known that adolescent conflicts usually center around relationship with parents; love affairs; sexual impulses and how to manage them. Adolescence, one might say, is the halfway point between childhood and maturity. Psychoanalysis, as you already know, made the discovery that during the first five years of a child's life, basic patterns are laid down, characteristic responses and ways of reacting emerge which have far-reaching influence on the later character and mode of reacting that one sees in the adult. Just as earlier, the child's series of naughtiness and unpleasant habits were shown to be no chance happenings, so we know that what, at first glance, looks to be a hopeless jumble of contradictory emotions and attitudes in the adolescent, is actually the repeating of earlier patterns. With the maturation of the reproductive system, a re-grouping

* From *Psychiatry and Religion*, ed. by J. L. Liebman, 1948. Reprinted by courtesy of the author and the publishers, The Beacon Press.

and re-aligning of the instinctual forces also takes place. A silent inner battle begins in which the ego struggles anew for dominance over these fluctuating instinctual forces of which the most powerful is the genital instinct. In adolescence this instinct occupies the center of the stage, surges forward and forces the young person to recognize it and manage it. Old sexual wishes, repressed since early childhood, emerge, usually in the form of daydreams. Most of the difficulties which we observe during this phase of development are due to the fact that the young adult is attempting to gain control and manage this most powerful of all the instinctual urges. In this struggle he often feels completely alone and helpless. He also feels guilty and knows that he somehow must, at all costs, keep his secrets to himself to gain his independence. He senses also that he must detach himself from his earlier childhood dependence on his parents' strength and he must make his own decisions. Earlier parental attitudes have built a barrier which makes it impossible for him to talk freely at home about his feelings. So he begins to act in a bizarre way. Often he will form new attachments to people outside the family circle who, to the parents' consternation, seem to exert a very powerful influence over him. They stand helplessly by, unable to break the attachment. The parents have some cause for worry if the young person makes an attachment to an undesirable person at this time.

The average adolescent is preoccupied with the opposite sex, either openly or in fantasy. In the usual course of development one member of that now mysterious opposite sex seems to be the true embodiment of "everything that is excellent!" Again the parents are alarmed. They are realists and see clearly that the fantasy of the young person has clothed this object with attributes that are not present. The over-evaluation of the chosen object irritates them and they feel often that the boy or girl has picked the wrong type to love. The more they try to dislodge his interest, the harder and faster he holds on to his new choice.

The great upheaval going on within the adolescent, as one may well imagine, exerts in turn a powerful influence on, and provokes a variety of responses from, the parents. On their side, they, too, are going through a very difficult time, because the child they thought they knew so well has suddenly become a most difficult and unpleasant stranger. Gone is the obedient and lovable child of yesterday. In his place is a changeling— an unruly, often cruel and sarcastic, over-critical person, who may be meticulously clean one day and dirty and disorderly the next. He seems to have lost all modesty and sympathy and to have become unfeeling and hateful. "Although too he is capable of great idealism and self sacrifice" (1) and can readily pivot from this behavior to attitudes indicating the egotistical self-interest which is usually uppermost. Whimseys and vagaries are legion. There is so much emotion generated on both sides that the very important problem which confronts the young individual is all but forgotten. One might say that it has been completely overlooked in many instances. But how can anyone think clearly during a bombardment? The adolescent is being shaken within by his urges. He is in conflict and feels guilty and miserable for the aggressive targeting of his parents, which in his heart he realizes is unjust. Yet he stubbornly continues to bother them and blame them for all his troubles and his misery. The parents, in turn, are hard put to it. They feel angry and hurt because all their efforts seem suddenly to have come to naught. Just when they expected to find a companion in the young boy or girl, they have, instead, a scowling, sour, over-critical, know-it-all young person who demands more and more clothes, more and more pocket money, is inconsiderate, who keeps late hours, keeps everyone waiting, who uses the phone or the car without consideration for anyone else, who turns on the parents, and seems, as one mother said, "to hate our guts."

We might pause a moment and ask, "Why does the adolescent use these methods to fight something which is normal and natural and happens in every individual?" We have to recall that, during childhood, he has been busy building and strengthening defenses against all the forbidden instinctual pleasures which suddenly threaten to overwhelm him. The methods used by the mother in curbing these instincts when they first appeared have already laid down definite patterns of response. Now, when the forbidden urges appear again, the young adult becomes able at last to express his negative feelings. These were repressed first during his training period when he was small and helpless. He apparently gave up habits during this time which met with his mother's disapproval either because the wish to keep her love or the fear of her disapproval or punishment made this expedient. When confronted again with the same sort of situations that plagued him earlier, he attempts to free himself once and for all from the highly charged emotionally toned past experiences. For years he has endeavored to comply with the demands made by his parents which concern his instinctual urges. Often he has been unable to do this completely. Now he is again in a difficult position. If he gives in to the urge, he suffers from a guilty conscience. If he attempts to repress the urge and avoid the torment of a guilty conscience, he is in danger of developing crippling hysterical, phobic, or compulsive symptoms. In either case this turmoil makes him difficult to live with. Therefore, all sorts of reactions can be observed if one looks closely at the average adolescent. Usually, the attention of the parents and educators is directed at the symptom in the spotlight, without taking into account the more powerful forces which are behind the scenes. So we find endless variations in the presenting patterns of this age; the shy and timid young people are inclined to daydream a great deal and often present an irritating slowness and lack of coöperation which drives the parents to frenzy. Others are more courageous and begin clumsy flirtations which may have serious consequences. Others proceed to overt sexual acts and make the first steps toward delinquency. The parents are usually unable to handle these problems objectively. No one can hurt or be so harshly cruel in seeing defects in adults as the adolescent. The parents are subject to microscopic examination by their offspring, which, in my experience is so searching that they are unable to stand it without a great deal of counter-affect being mobilized. It is small wonder that even a closely-knit relationship between parent and child, under the severe strain that happens during this period, begins to crack. Painful as it is for the parents, if they can detach themselves from the turmoil, they can recognize it for what it is—a step forward toward maturity. The stronger the attachment was in the first years, the more difficult the child is at this time. He uses every weapon at his disposal to bring his parents into a bad light so that he can hate them—never does the young person feel so alone as at this time—never so friendless nor so frightened. Sometimes the parental figures, more or less sure of themselves through all these years, become panic-stricken. They are afraid of this stranger. Small wonder that they, too, reach for ammunition which will protect them from showing the deep hurts that the children have given them. One woman put it, "I am so angry and so hurt that I come out of myself without knowing why, and behave in a most disgraceful manner." Another woman described beautifully what happens in hundreds of homes in the teen age. She began by saying that she was miserable and guilty and she was "failing her daughter." Her daughter was sixteen and very pretty. This young girl she no longer knew. Her lovable child had disappeared and in her place was an arrogant little hussy whom she felt was a powerful rival, competing for her husband. Daily she was put in the most unflattering light by the girl. No matter how hateful she had been five minutes before, when her father appeared she turned on the charm. The mother was unable to recover so quickly and her bad temper was in evidence. She began to hate the girl because her husband indulged the daughter in every way and always took her part, blaming his wife for lack of understanding. What changed this carefree little girl into a powerful rival for her father's love? What happened that he in turn seemed to be behaving like a man who has suddenly discovered a very charming girl? Is the mother right that there is just a shade of something else appearing in the father-daughter relationship? Why does she show her very worst side? Is she right to worry? We would say that she is right—not because she is witnessing a passing phase of growth in which her daughter practices her new-found charm on a safe admirer, but because of the mother's own response to this natural phenomenon. This mother was unable to step back and watch her daughter with tolerance and even amusement, because she was actually afraid that she was losing the love of her husband. Her irritation with the girl began to widen a breach which might have serious consequences for both, because if home becomes an unpleasant place during these years, the girl may turn to the streets for comfort. The same is true, of course, for the father's relationship with his son.

Let us look at a potentially dangerous situation of this sort: A short time ago I saw a young woman of high intellectual promise who had reached the age of seventeen. After years of studious application with a set of straight A's in college preparatory school and a very good start in one of the Eastern colleges, she suddenly came into the dormitory one night at four A.M. A serious investigation took place and she was suspended. The parents came to me very distraught because their young daughter had been out with a young man until this hour of the morning. They were very puzzled why this supposedly well-integrated girl had done so bizarre and dangerous a thing. In a short time the whole story came out. The mother had been struggling for several years with a difficult adolescent girl who wanted her head but was unable to manage it, so to speak. She had stayed out several nights and there had been scenes at home, with promises "never to do it again," and the father had definitely taken the side of the daughter because he felt that the mother was too strict with her and that if she was reined in too tightly, one day her instinctual forces would cause her to bolt and do something unpredictable. He was frank and open about his own early escapades, which were common knowledge to the girl. The mother, on her part, said that the girl would wall up and refuse to discuss anything with her. She told how many years she had worked to help this girl to get into college. Now her daughter had thrown it all over. She was so bitter, "I hate her," she said. "I can't bear to look at her. I just want her to stay away." Then she cried bitterly. This woman's response was not pathological, but it was unwise, because it further complicated the situation. It is natural, when one has put in a great deal of time and effort, as any mother does in rearing a child, that the time comes when she feels that she has done her work well and she can let the child go. Then when the child disappoints her, as this one did, she has a massive response of which she is very ashamed and guilty and which drives her away from the child at the very moment when that young person needs support, and love, and understanding. It was interesting that the mother had no memory of her own adolescent struggles. After seeing the girl, we (the parents and I) could again meet, and it was possible to bring the girl's problem into focus in an atmosphere where their intellects could function without the emotional bitterness and mutual recriminations that had been obscuring the issue whenever an attempt was made at home to talk things over. The mother's central fear had been that the girl had gotten into some kind of a sexual entanglement with the young man with whom she had been out until four A.M. The father said, "Well, what if she has been? I expect she has to learn just as I did." The girl, on her side had this to say: "I met him, the night was beautiful and warm. I did not know him very well, but he was a very decent fellow. We decided to take a walk and see all the historic points about the city. It was much more fun than going on a sight-seeing bus, and we had a good long time to talk. We walked miles and forgot all about the time. I was more surprised than anyone when I got back to the dormitory and discovered that it was four in the morning." This may sound fantastic but the curious, dream-like quality of this experience was evident as the girl talked.

If we look into the girl's past we see that the mother has no cause for alarm as far as the sexual entanglement goes. The girl was still so naïve and unawakened that she was treading on air as she walked along with the young fellow. Instead of heavy necking and prompt return to the dormitory, which is much more frequent, this girl followed the pattern that had been laid down when she first met the strong instinctual force within herself. Her mother had said, "You must wait until you are grown up." That is what she was doing unwittingly, she was waiting. But there was a note of defiance also, because she felt again that strong instinctual force stirring within and so she took matters into her own hands. That is why the mother's aggressive response is understandable. The mother allowed the girl to come to me and the warm relationship that had originally been directed toward the mother was now very useful in our relationship because I could clear up the girl's tangled ideas on many topics (sex matters included) and help her over a difficult spot. She was reinstated at the college and she said, "Will you tell my mother that I am very sorry to have caused her so much pain. I was silly and I didn't think. Why does growing up have to be so hard? I am the sorriest for her. I can still see her face, all drawn and tired. I really didn't mean to do it; I don't know why I did it, but you can tell her she does not need to worry about me. I won't do anything wrong."

The last report was that these two were getting on quite well. The mother has allowed the girl to take over her own responsibilities. The reality shock that the young girl got when she found the sudden disapproval from an impersonal source seemed to give the last stimulant which was necessary for the girl to make the most important step forward, to realize that she alone, and no one else, is responsible for her conduct; that she must modify her behavior and take reality into consideration or take the consequences of her thoughtless actions.

Now let us look at another typical adolescent problem: Joel, a senior in high school, was sent to me because he was so very rude and overbearing at home that his mother and his young brothers suffered intensely. Also, he was failing in school. His father had died a year earlier and he had been very attached to him. This father had been a very busy, alert, but quick-tempered lawyer. The boy had been interested in law for years and determined to follow in his father's footsteps. The mother, on her own admission, had been extremely jealous of this boy because the father had preferred his company to hers. After the father's death, the boy went through a depression. He was moody, he didn't care to go with his former companions, and his school work began to be poor. Any reminder from his mother that his father would be disappointed brought a snarling retort and impudent rejoinders. The mother told me that if she did not get some relief from this boy she would have to put him out of the house. He watched her comings and goings like a hawk, he catechized her if she came in five minutes late, he accused her of neglecting the family when she went out in the evening, he made scenes at the table—complaining about the food, and in every way making himself obnoxious. The worst scenes occurred when she asked him to look out for the two younger brothers when she went out in the evening. He was usually pacing the floor and when she returned he made caustic comments, saying she was no good. The mother said, "He is so changed that I can't do a thing with him, and my life is one long misery."

The boy came to me over a period of months. He said he hated women, they were no good. (He had been very attached to his mother as a little boy, cried and clung to her at kindergarten age.) He never could see why his father married his mother anyway. If he didn't take over at home, the house would go to pieces, his mother would be out all the time, as a matter of fact. He lit a cigarette with shaking fingers and let his youthful beard grow enough so that he could make a scratching sound with his thumbnail as he talked to me. He was full of great plans for the future. He was a very big fellow. The day he brought a pipe with him and choked trying to light it followed a very bad scene with his mother the night before. When I said I always admired a man who smoked a pipe, he suddenly broke down and cried. He said, "What is the matter with me, Dr. Dawes? I'm terrible to my mother. I don't know what makes me act like that." I said that he couldn't seem to decide whether to be a baby or a grown man. I told him his mother had called today and said she would not pay any more because he was worse than when he started. She said he would not get up, would not pick up any clothes in his room, that he was unbearable in the house, etc. He turned and said, "Will you tell me something, am I crazy?" Then he told me how he had been frightened by his own urges, how he had knotted the sheets in his bed to keep from getting too comfortable and thinking about girls, how frightened he was of his thoughts and feelings, how guilty he felt when he did what he wasn't supposed to do, and so he even dragged up experiences (homosexual, sporadic—when his father died) and what he had done when he was a little boy. I asked what he was going to do about it all. He said, "I feel so much better now that that is off my chest and I'm not crazy, that I don't care if she doesn't pay. I'm going to get a job and come myself."

He did come. He got a job after school. His school work began to pick up, but he was afraid to show his new self to his mother for fear of ridicule. Some weeks later he did not come for his appointment, but his mother telephoned that there had been such a change in the boy that she thought it was a good idea for him to pay for his treatments. As a matter of fact, he had not paid for the last three. He had a better job, but he asked her to say he could not keep his appointments any more. I didn't hear from him again until the Saturday before Mother's Day when he appeared in my office without appointment. He was dressed in his best clothes, was freshly shaven and he handed me $3.00. He said, "I earned it myself, and I have just been to the University to register for next year. My marks are high enough so I will be able to get in. I wanted to get here so you could use this as a present for Mother's Day." I asked what he thought I should buy. He said, something for myself. I suggested a box of candy and he said, "Yes, and you should eat it all yourself and when you eat it, remember that I think of you as my real mother." He got fiery red and dropped his hat. Some months later the mother said that she was ever so grateful, that the boy had steadied down and she wondered if, after his father died, did I think that he might have tried to take his place. "You know, his father was very quick-tempered and he often used to bawl me out when I was out. Anyway, his school work is good and he cleans his room, and is no more trouble at home. Whatever it was, I'm glad it's over."

Some things that would be worthy of consideration at this point are the following: When the child is small, the parent can step in and stop any sort of behavior which seems to be injurious to the child or which is especially distressing to the parents. When that same child reaches puberty, the aggression which has been pushed out of sight through all the difficult first years has been lying more or less dormant and flares into the open, either in outspoken defiance, or passive resistance to the parental suggestions or orders. For example, if the young boy or young girl neglects his person or his room or clothing, he seems to say, "Once you could stop me from being dirty, but now I am big and I will be as dirty as I like and you cannot do anything about it." That is perfectly true. During this stage of development the child's own ego has to take hold of the responsibility of his own actions, and this struggle between the parent and the child which is very frequent gradually diminishes as the child steps further along the road to adulthood. Positions actually seem to be reversed at this stage, because the parents are the helpless ones and the child seems to be the one in control. However, these curious phenomena that are common to all adolescents probably are the outward evidence only of the great upheaval within, and it is as if the parent were used at this point as a target. The "you can't make me, and I'll do it myself" struggle is in direct proportion to the methods used by the parent in

training the child through the successive stages, oral,
anal and genital. The patterns of behavior that cause
the most trouble at this stage are not there by chance,
they are evidence that the struggle was never entirely
mastered by the child in the early years. The length
of the duration of this struggle is in direct proportion
to the methods used in controlling the instinctual force
when it appeared in the first place. The dovetailing of
the parent-child relationship in those early years is still
here, but in a disrupted form, and the parent often
seems to spin with a whirling current of thought and
feeling which surfaces abruptly in the adolescent. He
automatically responds the same way he responded
earlier (in similar situations, e.g., feeding, toilet training, masturbation problem) because these are actually
brief reappearances of earlier conflicts between parent and child. The one great difference in adolescence
now is that this time the parent has to step back from
his controlling rôle and allow the young person to master instinctual desires and forces himself. Parents need
not have so great a worry as they do about the whole
topic of masturbation, because every young person
wants to grow up and in an average case the young
boy or girl gives up this activity because he, too, likes
to grow up, and love for another individual helps him.
Many of the gang activities are the manifestations of the
individual's feeling that he needs support and a chance
to compare himself with other people of his own age
who are struggling through equally difficult times. Probably the new-found urges can better be fought if they
gang up against the common enemy. Therefore, we find
the ardent man and woman haters in the adolescent
groups of boys and girls.

The most difficult part is the parents' rôle in this

stormy time. The more detached and adult the parent
can be, the more objective sympathy and understanding he can offer the young person, and the less he de-
scends to the level of the boy and girl and fights with
him, the more gratifying it will be to him later to find
that all the years of sacrifice and care and love that he
has put into the rearing of the boy or girl will be re-
paid, by seeing that the young individual actually is
able to free himself from his infantile attachments and
enter into a richer, fuller and more mature relationship.

Parents who become bitter, who get angry when
their boy or girl seeks out an older man or an older
woman to whom they can talk and unburden their
souls, should look a little closer. They will usually find
that the person to whom that boy or girl has turned
and begins to copy as a model is no one to be jealous
about, but a reflected image of the child's inner model
who has been there since early childhood and for whom
the original sitter was the parent himself. It seems
strange that the young person fights his inner fears in
this way, but on closer examination one will see that it
is actually so. It is a very painful time too for the
young person. One young boy said, "What good am I
now; I'm too old to sit on my mother's lap and I'm not
old enough to take out a girl, and nobody wants me
around." A young girl said, "Why does my mother yell
at me? Doesn't she know that part of me is still a baby?
I know I have breasts and my period, but I can't grow
up all at once. Big as I am I would like to crawl on her
lap; I feel so funny. And nobody understands me."

If there is too much parental interference in this
stage, the inner conflicts are again suppressed and
the young person does not make the important step

forward but remains dependent and attached to the parents, develops neurotic fears or severe learning inhibitions, work inhibitions. The young people usually feel that the parents have changed, but as they grow up a little bit more they realize it is their own viewpoint which has changed, that these very human beings are full of faults, and if they were not, life modelled on infantile over-evaluation of parental figures, would be very difficult to live up to. As they understand themselves more they become less bitter and less intolerant of their parents.

In closing we should remember that in early life up to adolescence the parent is actually in control and acts as a counterweight in helping the child manage his own instinctual forces, but during adolescence it is necessary that the parent give up this position and that the young person take over completely the control of his own instinctual life. The adolescent has to put his own house in order, so to speak. All the old conflicts which surge up from below have to be mastered. This is a big piece of psychic work and is energy-consuming and difficult. He also has bodily changes, which I have not mentioned and with which you are all familiar. Therefore, we must be patient with him and remember that usually, as the little four-year-old said, "he is able to manage." There is nothing static about the inner world and if the parent could stand back and watch the movement and change taking place before his eyes, and realize that it is a very necessary and important piece of growth, this painful process for both parents and child could be viewed in a more objective fashion. If the work has been done well originally by the parent so that he has given his boy or girl a set of standards of what is decent, he does not need to fear that while nature is busy changing the child's body into an adult's, that the governing part that he has so carefully built into the child will cease to function.

General Discussion

QUESTION: Can't we as parents, adjust our psychological attitudes, our homes and social connections so as not to cause these conflicts in our adolescent boys and girls?

DR. DAWES: In response to this question one might say that we can only approximate such an adjustment because we are dealing with many unknowns, and because we are all human. Probably every conscientious parent strives toward such an ideal picture of himself. If I gave the impression that the parents alone were at fault, I did not mean that, because the adolescents are difficult and I have great sympathy for the parents.

For instance—during the course of an analysis, when the parent is on the couch, one sees all the factors, both past and present, that contribute to his mode of behavior. Sometimes, for instance, his child unconsciously represents to him a rival of some sort. The jealousy then mobilized is not recognized by the parent. Instead, the child is criticized or scolded because of this unconscious feeling. In its place come frustration, hopelessness and disappointment in the child. The parents, unaware of what motivates their own behavior and driven by forces within themselves, are in a state of confusion.

If the relationship between child and parents gets too bad, I suppose the parents usually come to a psychiatrist for help. The parents are then aware that something is wrong. I think it is a healthy sign that they are.

Display of emotion is not to be condemned. However, misdirected emotions are very dangerous. I have seen some homes where every parental emotion is repressed. I don't think that is good, either. One child at the Judge Baker Clinic came from such a home and said, "I wish I lived in South Boston. I know somebody that throws plates when they feel like my mother and father do. Instead of that my mother and father just sit there and give me a fine lecture, and that makes me feel like a worm."

I am not sure that we can completely adjust our psychological attitudes. But we can learn to be critical of our attitudes and our own behavior, as well as the behavior of our children.

QUESTION: You mentioned difficulties of learning as one of the results of adolescent turmoil. Would you care to say something more about this?

DR. DAWES: That is a very large subject and one of the problems that I have been interested in for a good many years.

It would seem to me that learning difficulties are aggravated in adolescence, but that they do not start in adolescence. They originate way back in the child's first years, when his curiosity, which is a very powerful stimulant for learning, is diverted from its original aim. This aim was the acquisition of knowledge concerning the origin of life and the difference between the sexes the answer to such questions as, "Where do I come from?" "Where did you get the baby?" and so on.

If the parents, in attempting to answer the questions, have given the child the impression that one must not talk about such matters, then repressional curiosity occurs with a displacement of the conflict into the "learning field." This means that everything new to be learned is also taboo. In other words, the child tries to comply with the parents' demands, suppressing all curiosity.

I can give you an example. (I don't want anybody to think that I am criticizing any religion, because if I cannot speak freely I am in the position in which parents sometimes are.) I remember a little girl who came to my office. She was eight years old and very intelligent but she was also a daydreamer. She could not read a simple page. So I sat down with her, and we began to look at the words that she couldn't read. She allowed me to have a pencil to take down the words, and I noticed that she made very many mistakes. As I showed her the mistakes, I said, "Why don't we go looking and see what this means—every time you come to 'cat' you read 'kitty.'" She said, "I know what that is." She went on to tell me about her cat at home. The year when this trouble started, she opened the clothespress and found the cat with ten kittens. She tried to find out where the cat got the kittens and so forth, and she couldn't get anywhere. Mother said, "Don't talk about it—it isn't nice," and so on. I said to her, "Where did your mother get the new babies?" She said, "That's all right. They came out of her." "Where do you think the cat got the kittens?" She said, "Out of her, but how could she hold ten?" I said, "In a little while, we'll talk about that." Then she said, "You know, I am not supposed to talk about this because I tried to find out about this before, and Sister says that when I think these thoughts they are not good, and I should think about the shamrock." "About the shamrock? What's the shamrock?" She said, "Father, Son, and Holy Ghost." I said, "But why does she say that?" "I don't know." This child's preoccupation with forbidden topics passed for daydreaming. She restricted herself, following her mother's prohibition, "You cannot learn anything new." Hence her inability to read.

I think this example is similar to difficulties in learning that we find later in college students. The child tries to do what the loved one wants. The child represses one thing and in its place comes an inhibition in the learning field. It is as if the parent still said, "You can talk about anything else, but not this." After a while the connection between the original forbidden curiosity and conscious interest in learning new facts is repressed, so that everything connected with curiosity is taboo.

It is surprising what an amount of knowledge seven- and eight-year-old children have on all these topics, but they hide it in the same way that parents hide knowledge from the children. I very rarely meet a child who is not pretty well versed in most of these subjects. When he is in an atmosphere where he can expand and talk freely, he does so.

Now then, in adolescence the great urge "to know" comes again. Adolescents are curious about the opposite sex and curious about their sexual instincts. They want to know all about intercourse and about all kinds of things, and they have a great deal of knowledge. But if the original repression has done its work well, a "learning inhibition" is the evidence of its existence.

QUESTION: Would you tell us a little about the antagonism between girls and boys in the early teens, and what it means?

DR. DAWES: As we observe it, they seem to be one way or the other—either all for or all against. I suppose that depends on the early training and the strength of the impulses in the child.

You notice it with boys—"Bosh! They don't want anything to do with girls." The girls gang up together in clubs, usually, or groups, and discuss their feelings about the boys and talk about all these mysterious things—each one gathers a little piece and brings it so that they get knowledge that way, you see. The boys are excluded because the talking together is exciting. Anna Freud says that with children, "talking is like doing." That's why I wondered about the advisability of giving lectures on such an explosive topic as sex to children in mixed groups for they are usually struggling to keep this excitement controlled. I think it would be better to give the information to them in separate groups—not to mix the two sexes.

Reference

1. Freud, Anna: *The Ego and the Mechanisms of Defence* (London, 1937), p. 149.

Problems of the Adolescent Girl[*]

BY Phyllis Blanchard, A.M., Ph.D.

[*] From *The Cyclopedia of Medicine Surgery and Specialties,* 1945. Reprinted by courtesy of the author and publishers, F. A. Davis Co., Philadelphia, Pennsylvania.

I. Physiological Changes

Adolescence in girls is usually considered to begin coincidentally with the maturation of sexual functions, as evidenced by menstruation. The age of first menstruation varies among girls of different races and countries. There is also considerable variation as to the age of first menstruation among girls of the same race and living under similar climatic conditions. In the United States, so far as statistical data are available, these indicate that about 50 per cent of white girls begin to menstruate between the ages of 12½ and 14½; about 25 per cent menstruate earlier and about 25 per cent later than these ages. A few girls first menstruate as early as 9 or 10 years of age, a few as late as 19 or 20 years. (1)

The establishment of the menstrual periods is not the only physiological change during adolescence. Growth of the breasts is another characteristic of adolescence for girls, together with an increase in the size of the hips, due to changes in size and angle of the pelvic bone. There is also an acceleration of skeletal and muscular growth, as well as of organs of the body, such as heart, lungs, and digestive organs. For the most part, this growth is rapid during the early teens and becomes slower as it approaches its limits in the late teens and early twenties. Speaking approximately, adolescence in girls is usually considered to include the years from the age of first menstruation up to the time when the growth of bones, muscles, and organs of the body is completed; it is therefore predominantly the age of the teens. (2)

The adolescent maturation of sexual functions and acceleration of physical growth may mean that the girl is subjected to some stress and strain in adjusting and adapting to these changes, both physiologically and mentally. On the physiological side, there may be irregularity of menstruation for a time before the monthly rhythm is established, disturbances of a general health nature, pain and fatigue or other physical reactions at menstrual periods, or disturbances of endocrine functions, perhaps especially of thyroid function. Thus, some girls need medical treatment and supervision at the beginning of the adolescent years.

II. Psychosexual Development and Anxiety over Menstruation

INFLUENCE OF CHILDHOOD IDEAS — On the psychological side, adolescence may or may not be a time of emotional conflict and anxiety, depending to a considerable extent on the girl's earlier emotional development and experiences. The girl whose psychological development has been fairly normal is usually able to accept the sexual maturity which becomes evident through menstruation and the growth of breasts and hips, which give a feminine contour to the figure, as a satisfying proof of her capacity to marry and bear children. But if previous experiences have tended to produce fears of marriage or having children, there may be little satisfaction for the girl in being biologically fitted for these functions in life. Then there may arise conflicts between the natural impulses toward marriage and motherhood which are part of the girl's biological nature and the superimposed fears of fulfilling her biological functions. There are many ways in which such fears can be acquired: A mother may have em-

phasized to a daughter that she found sexual relationships or childbirth unpleasant or painful, so that the
daughter's attitudes are colored by the attitudes of her
mother; or a girl may have witnessed the failure of
marriage for her parents, especially in families where
separation or divorce occurred, and may have been influenced against marriage because of such experiences.
These are but two common ways in which attitudes toward marriage and having children may be influenced
during the childhood years.

III. Unconscious Drives and Conflicts

In order to explain adolescent conflicts and anxieties
more fully, the concept of the *unconscious* must be
introduced into the discussion at this point. In the course
of the personality development during childhood, it is
normal for certain ethical standards to be acquired and
for ideals of the self to be formed. The ego strives to
conform to these standards and ideals, to govern not
only behavior, but also thinking and feeling, in accord
with them. Such thoughts and feelings as are acceptable
to the ego, and to its standards and ideals, are freely
admitted to consciousness, but unacceptable ideas and
feelings are reacted to by the ego with an effort to rid
itself of them. The ego cannot actually eradicate feelings
and impulses which are a part of the personality, or of
the biological, instinctive drives, but it can deny their
existence and refuse to recognize them consciously.
When the ego thus shuts certain thoughts, impulses, or
feelings out of consciousness, it is said that they have
been "repressed" and have become "unconscious." In a
similar fashion, the ego attempts to protect itself against

such early experiences as were unpleasant or painful and caused anxiety by excluding them from the conscious memories, though the memories of these experiences and the affects which accompanied them may still persist in the unconscious.

At adolescence there is normally a tendency for some of these unconscious residues from early childhood to become active once more and to press toward consciousness again. This in itself may operate to revive some of the anxiety which originally surrounded them and caused the ego to enforce their repression. An additional source of anxiety during adolescence is the conflict between the ego's ideals and standards of behavior and the intensified instinctive and emotional drives resulting from the biological sexual maturation. (3)

IV. Fear of Marriage

To return to the conflicting attitudes already mentioned, such as the normal wishes to marry and have children *versus* acquired fears of marriage or childbirth, these are usually unconscious or at least partly unconscious. For example, the girl may be conscious of wishes to marry and have children without knowing that fears inhibit her from carrying out these wishes; or she may recognize only the fears of marriage and childbirth, the wishes being repressed and unconscious. Again, both wishes and fears may not be consciously realized, the conflict between them being a cause of anxiety and tension without the girl having any idea why she is tense and anxious. Or anxiety arising from such unconscious conflicts may be attached to dread of physical pain with menstruation, or ascribed to folklore warnings, such as the superstition that men can tell when a girl is menstruating by her appearance; that to bathe when menstruating is to risk serious illness; that an operation may be necessary if menstruation is not regularly established, etc. There is almost no end to these folklore sayings about menstruation that girls quote as having heard from parents or friends.

V. The Wish to be a Boy

Another barrier to equable acceptance of the adolescent changes which emphasize the girl's femininity is that some girls have never become reconciled to their own sex because of strong unconscious wishes to be a boy. Then the growth of breasts, and especially menstruation, are sources of anxiety and dissatisfaction because they are proofs that the femininity which the girl has unconsciously refused to accept in relation to herself is something which she cannot avoid. The origins of wishes to be a boy and rejection of the feminine rôle in life often are even more complex than fears of marriage and having children, although rejection of the feminine rôle may be another reason for refusing marriage and motherhood.

VI. Fear of Uncleanliness

Sometimes anxiety about menstruation may focus on the question of personal cleanliness. Here, again, this anxiety may have a background in childhood experiences. If a girl was subjected to exceedingly strict toilet training in infancy, with much emphasis on habits of cleanliness, unconscious memories and reactions originally surrounding excretory functions may be revived in the feeling that menstruation is uncleanly and disgusting. Or if a girl suffered from enuresis as a child, menstruation may be associated with the feelings of shame and anxiety which once surrounded this earlier difficulty. Very frequently, memories and feelings originally connected with toilet training or enuresis are repressed and unconscious; the girl has no knowledge that her adolescent attitudes toward menstruation are colored by these old experiences.

It is because so many of the psychological sources of anxiety about menstruation are unconscious that it is useless to question the girl as to whether they exist in any particular case. Indeed, questioning is more likely to lead to intensification of symptomatic complaints, or to complete withdrawal of confidence, than to any other result. It is only in psychotherapeutic work with girls that the connections between experiences in the past and adolescent worries about menstruation can be learned. In such treatment, there is a minimum of questioning; earlier experiences and feelings are gradually recalled as the girl talks more or less uninterrupted by the therapist, until the associations between feelings in regard to other experiences and about menstruation slowly become clear to patient and therapist.

Of course, not all anxiety about menstruation and sexual functions arise from such deep-rooted, unconscious factors as those illustrated above. It is also true that a girl's worries may be due to incorrect information about sexual matters and hygiene. A girl may have lacked any information which prepared her to expect menstruation or to know it to be a normal physiological phenomenon; or she may have been ill-prepared by incorrect information about it. If anxiety is merely due to misinformation or lack of information, correct information should relieve it; if it is on the basis of deeper, unconscious emotional conflicts, giving information is unlikely to afford any relief, or at best only temporary alleviation of anxiety.

VII. The Rôle of Cultural Requirements

Some of the psychological stress of adolescence is probably due to present-day social culture and the demands it makes on the adolescent, which are not always in keeping with biological strivings. Sexual maturation is the biological aspect of adolescence, and a natural part of this sexual maturity is an inclination toward sexual relationships. In primitive societies, mating ordinarily coincides with the age of sexual maturity. In present-day society, marriage is for the most part delayed by educational, economic, and social considerations, sometimes for years beyond the age of sexual maturity. While this has other advantages, it does mean that natural sexual inclinations must be inhibited and controlled; they can only be satisfied by early marriage or by extramarital relationships, and the latter are certainly not productive of satisfaction because they entail shame and guilt or serious social consequences. Sometimes the tension resulting from inhibition and repression of biological sexual strivings may give rise to anxiety or physical symptoms. Some of the symptoms complained of in connection with menstruation, *i.e.*, pains, faintness, nausea, are similar to symptoms which almost any girl has heard of in connection with pregnancy and childbirth. There may be psychogenic factors in the symptom-formation, such as repressed wishes to have children and unconscious pregnancy fantasies, as well as physical factors related to the girl's health condition. At least, clinical cases have been observed in which girls either fear that they are pregnant (sometimes after a sex adventure, sometimes without such inciting cause) or produce even more marked symptoms of pregnancy than nausea and faintness. In present-day society, wishes to have children must be delayed in fulfillment until marriage provides opportunity to satisfy them; thus there is a period in which such normal desires can be gratified only through conscious daydreams of the future or through unconscious fantasies and symptom-formation.

Anxiety which is intense and prolonged and remains unrelieved by information, or physical symptoms for which no organic basis can be found and which do not respond to medical treatment, are examples of adolescent problems for which it might well be felt that psychotherapeutic treatment should be advised. It is not unusual, however, for a girl to resist going to a psychiatrist or psychologist for such help. Many people still believe that anyone who needs psychotherapy must be very abnormal or mentally unbalanced; psychiatry is associated in the lay mind with treatment of mental disease, psychology with mental tests for diagnosis of mental deficiency. It is not as well-known that a large share of psychotherapeutic work is with patients whose problems are within the broad limits of normality. This blocks many people, both adults and adolescents, from seeking help with personal problems when it is needed. Moreover, adolescence is an age when the individual is very reluctant to recognize problems and need for help, lest this imply too much difference from other girls. The adolescent has a great desire to be like others; this wish is apparent on insistence on dressing like other girls, having the same social contacts and privileges, etc. Since friends usually are not going to anyone for psychotherapeutic treatment, the adolescent is unwilling to do so because of reluctance to be different from others. Resistances of this kind often have to be handled, when an adolescent does come to a psychotherapist, before treatment can really go on. And many adolescents, sent to the psychotherapist by parents or by physicians, refuse to accept any plan for treatment because these resistances are so strong.

VIII. Masturbation

Besides such anxieties about menstruation and sexual maturity as have been illustrated, masturbation and worry about it is sometimes an adolescent problem. While this is a less frequent problem for girls than for boys, it is one which does need to be mentioned. The girl who is confronted with this particular problem often finds it aggravated by all the misconceptions which are still current regarding masturbation and which she is very likely to have heard or read. The earlier books on adolescence, and older medical writings, were likely to speak of masturbation as a "degenerate habit" or a "vice," and to warn of it as leading to mental deficiency, insanity, sterility, inability to have normal sexual relationships in marriage, immorality, etc. Many adults believe these old opinions and repeat the warnings to adolescents who question them, in their anxiety about it, thus intensifying the anxiety. Modern psychiatry offers a very different viewpoint on masturbation from that expressed by earlier writers. It is now known that the physical act of masturbation does not cause any of the disasters previously ascribed to it, although the compulsive, excessive type of masturbation may be a *symptom* of neurosis, of sexual maladjustments which would interfere with marital relationships, or other personality difficulties. Besides the anxiety and guilt over masturbation which arise from misconceptions of its nature, there are deeper sources of anxiety and guilt in the unconscious fantasies and emotional conflicts which often form the psychological background for the development of the habit. These psychological factors and the habit of masturbation, which is sometimes associated with them, might be overcome naturally in the process of growth and development, in some instances, but for the misinformation given to the adolescent, which increases the worry over masturbation, keeps it constantly in the mind of the individual and produces despair of being able to control and give up the habit before it has irremediably injured body and mind. The psychotherapist who has worked with adolescents caught in this turmoil over masturbation knows the shame and guilt about it, the heroic struggle to overcome it, the intensity of the anxiety which is undergone. The therapist also knows that before the unconscious fantasies and conflicts which underlie the compulsive type of masturbation can be revealed, much time has to be spent in discussion of all imaginary dangers and punishments which incorrect information has implanted in the patient's mind. Neither threats nor reassurance helps.

IX. Mental Disease in Adolescence

It was once thought that adolescence was an age when mental disease, especially dementia precox, was most likely to claim its victims. While it is true that dementia precox is one of the two most common mental disorders for the adolescent period, statistical studies indicate that mental diseases are more apt to occur during any later decade of adult life than during the adolescent and early adult decade. For example, of the total 28,689 first admissions to institutions for the mentally ill during three years prior to June 30, 1931, only 179 were under 15 years, 3,701 between 15 and 24 years (1,528 girls, 2,173 boys). There were larger numbers of first admissions for each age decade above 24 years. Using the figures for rate per 100,000 of the general population, the rate for first admissions for the ages of 15 to 24 years was 56.1; 25 to 34 was 82.5; 35 to 44 was 101.8. The statistical trend is perhaps even more apparent if the percentage of first admissions to mental hospitals at certain age decades is compared with the percentage of the general population in the same age decades. In 1930, a *greater percentage* of the general population fell in the age-group 10 to 19 years than in any age decade above 19, while the *smallest percentage* of first admissions to mental hospitals in 1933 was for the age decade 10 to 19. Only 5 per cent of hospital admissions were in the 10-to-19-year decade as compared to 19.2 per cent of the general population of that age. In the 20-to-29-year decade, 17.1 per cent of first admissions to mental hospitals compared with 16.9 per cent of the general population of that age. The disproportion between the percentages of mentally ill admitted to hospitals for the first time and percentages of the population in the same age-groups increases with each life decade above 29 years (4, 5).

The types of psychosis vary in frequency of occurrence for different age-groups. Dementia precox and manic-depressive psychoses are the two forms of mental disease most likely to appear during adolescent or young adult life. As reported in one study, these two psychoses accounted for 71.5 per cent of the 3,701 patients who were 15 to 24 years of age. There was a greater prevalence of dementia precox for boys than for girls —57.5 per cent for the former and 38.2 per cent for the latter; but more girls than boys had manic-depressive psychoses—31.8 per cent girls and 15.1 per cent boys suffering from this mental disorder. (5)

It was once considered that the outlook for recovery from dementia precox (schizophrenia) was almost hopeless and while remissions in manic-depressive states were considered probable, the danger of recurrence was emphasized. With better hospital care, the development of the shock therapies, improved psychotherapeutic technics, etc., there is now a far more favorable prognosis for these two mental disorders both as to expectancy of longer periods of remission and of permanent recovery. Delay in securing hospital care and treatment often causes less favorable prognosis. Therefore it is important that hospitalization and treatment be provided as soon as possible at the earliest onset of the illness symptoms. It may be necessary to overcome parents' reluctance to send a young person to a mental hospital, for the lay public still tends to the mistaken concept that the patient may grow worse instead of better in the hospital environment. This idea is contrary to the fact that only hospital care and the therapies offered by it afford the reasonable hope for improvement and recovery in cases of mental illness.

X. Normal Adjustment

So far, the possibilities for difficulties of adjustment during adolescence have been stressed. It should be emphasized, however, that for many girls adolescence is a fairly comfortable period, its changes easily accepted, because emotional development in earlier years has been more or less normal. Another point to be emphasized is that, although adolescence offers a chance that any earlier conflicts and problems will be reactivated, it affords just as much probability that these revived problems will be resolved better than was the case in childhood years, without the aid of either physician or psychotherapist, as that they will require professional intervention.

During the adolescent years, the personality is open to modification, and under favorable life situations, this modification may be in the direction of normality rather than abnormality. Girls who have, in childhood years, been very much attached to the father, for instance, may resolve this so-called Oedipus complex spontaneously during adolescence, turning their affections to boys of their own age. This is not always accomplished without intermediate steps. Sometimes the girl goes through a phase of falling in love with an older, perhaps married, man before she completes the transition from the father to someone nearer her own age. Sometimes, in an effort to break away from a strong tie to a father, she has a temporary period of promiscuous affairs with boys. She may endure considerable suffering in these struggles to leave the father, with intense feelings of shame and guilt over love for a married man or over promiscuous relationships. But often she does come through such strivings to find a normal love relationship and then is able to settle her affections upon a suitable person, whom she can marry with a chance of happiness.

The girl who has rejected the feminine rôle may become more, instead of less, reconciled to it, as an outcome of adolescent experiences. The biological forces of her sexual maturation are in favor of this. Again, if one factor in rejection of femininity chanced to be inability to identify with a mother who was not an acceptable ego-ideal, the girl may find a substitute ideal in some older woman outside the family, during her adolescent years, with whom she can identify herself. All have seen girls change from displaying masculine traits and behavior during the preadolescent and early adolescent years to more gentle, feminine characteristics in later adolescence.

XI. Emancipation from Parental Authority

The adolescent problems which have thus far been mentioned are mostly those related to the girl's psychosexual development. There are also problems centering around the effort at independence from parental authority and control and conflict between the younger and older generations. Much has been written of the rebellious attitude of the girl toward her parents when she becomes adolescent, but less has been said of the guilt and remorse which assail her after her outbursts of defiance and rebellion. Perhaps the tormenting conscience of the adolescent is less apparent to ordinary observation than the defiant and rebellious behavior; the latter is shown openly, the former is endured secretly, in many instances. But anyone who has worked professionally with girls, in a psychotherapeutic situation, has heard not only their descriptions of their behavior toward their parents but also their questions as to whether, after all, the parents may have been "right" and themselves "wrong," and their accounts of remorseful feelings and tears shed in secret after they have disobeyed parents or criticized them.

The conflict between parents and daughters may be over serious or trivial matters. Sometimes it arises because parents are too restricting or too loath to see a child grow up and seemingly break away from family ties. Sometimes it is caused by a characteristic of the adolescent previously mentioned, her desire to be like other girls in her social group; in taking over the standards of her friends, the girl may find herself obliged to reject the standards of her parents. Regardless of how differences of opinion between parents and daughters have come about, and no matter how strong may be the girl's drive to emancipate herself from parental control and become independent, usually she is still bound to the parents by her love for them and is still dependent upon them for approval and affection. Although she may seem to be independent in her speech and behavior, she is far from being so in her emotions and in her own conscience; thus, what appears on the surface as an external conflict between the two generations is really an inner conflict of the girl's besides.

XII. The Adolescent "Crush"

At the same time that the adolescent girl becomes involved in efforts to achieve increasing independence of her family, she is likely to turn to friendships outside the home. Sometimes these friendships, usually with an older woman or another girl, are invested with intense emotions for a time, and take the form of what is designated as a "crush." In some groups, these crushes are regarded with suspicion as having something abnormal about them, perhaps tinged with homosexuality. But, in many instances, the crush serves some temporary emotional need of the girl's. It has already been mentioned that the girl may find a mother substitute in some older woman, and identify herself with this mother ideal to the advantage of her own personality development. If the girl has not found satisfying relationships with her own mother in earlier years, she may try to secure the satisfactions which have hitherto been lacking in demanding a great deal of attention and affection from the object of her adolescent crush, and be as jealous of this person's interest in anyone other than herself as perhaps she was once of the interest shown her brothers and sisters.

Another element in the crush may be that the person on whom the girl has the crush represents her ideal for herself, *i.e.*, the person is loved and admired by the girl because she has qualities of appearance, personality, or accomplishments which the girl would like to possess for herself. The girl, by loving and admiring someone who has these qualifications, compensates for what seems to her lacking in herself, and also she may hope to learn how to develop the same characteristics in herself through association with the other, adopting her style of hairdressing and clothing, her manners, her interests, etc.

Again, the girl who encounters difficulties in meeting boys and making social contacts with them, either because of inhibitions within herself or because of lack of opportunity, may substitute intimate friendships with other girls for the more normal relationships with boys. This type of crush, which grows out of the failure to develop social and affectional relationships with boys, is perhaps more seriously capable of interfering with heterosexual development than those described above. The girl may find sufficient emotional satisfaction in loving other girls, so that she will tend to cling to friendships with her own sex rather than to move on to interest in men and marriage. This is probably the most apt to occur if the original difficulty in forming relationships with boys was due to factors within the girl's own personality rather than to circumstances in her environment.

Very frequently, however, the crush does not carry such dangers with it, but is a stage in the process of the girl's gradual relinquishment of the closer family ties of childhood for a more mature rôle as a member of a larger social group. Normally, in childhood years, the girl has loved and admired her parents and seen in them the ideals of what she would like to be. As adolescence provides an opportunity for wider social relationships, she finds among the parents of her friends, among her teachers, among the leaders in her church or recreational groups, other adults whom she can admire and respect. Thus she can round out her ideals for herself and for her future upon a broader scope than is offered by the family contacts alone. The crush upon some person who at the moment symbolizes these ideals may be but a step in the direction of socialization and personality development. (6)

Perhaps one danger the crush offers is that the person chosen by the girl as the object of her admiration may not be mature enough in her own emotional development to accept it for what it is—a transient stage in the girl's growth. Just as there are parents who are unconsciously reluctant to see their children become adolescent and reach out for wider social experiences outside the family, so there may be persons who find the girl's crush so satisfying to their own emotional needs, so flattering and pleasant, that they may unconsciously wish to prolong it beyond its natural end. Or persons who see in the crush a threat of abnormality and homosexuality may repulse and rebuff the girl, or imply to her that her behavior is pathological, turning what might have been a beneficial experience for the girl into a painful one.

XIII. School Problems

Besides the problems within the family or in her social life, the adolescent girl may meet with others in the school situation. Presumably the percentage of the school population which is definitely mentally deficient will have been placed in special classes or schools (in the larger school systems, at least) before adolescence. But those who have mental ability to complete the first 7 or 8 grades, but who do not have ability for high school work, begin to meet with failure, and must either continue high school work in the face of repeated fail-

ures and continual low marks or transfer to some vocational school. Their situation is difficult because there
are not sufficient vocational schools to take care of the
numbers of students for whom academic or even com-
mercial and other regular high school courses are too
advanced, and also because all too frequently parental
ambitions for a daughter's education are higher than the
girl's native abilities. Real worries are caused by the
girl's feeling, if she is not as intellectual as her parents
have hoped, that she is causing them disappointment in
their ambitions for her education.

Not all the failures in school that begin to crop up in
the junior and senior high school grades are due, however, to lack of intellectual capacity. There may be a
year or two, as a girl undergoes the physiological
changes of adolescence and such emotional tensions accompanying it as those indicated in the earlier pages,
when previously excellent school achievement slumps
badly, to recover its excellence after a period of time.
In psychotherapeutic work, psychiatrists sometimes
have girls brought to them because of trouble with their
work in school, only to find that they are of high intelligence, but so involved in some of the anxieties and
conflicts about themselves, which have been described
previously, that energy and attention were not free for
study. With the relief of their worries and anxieties,
they often resume good achievement in school work.
Presumably, some of those girls who go through a period of trouble with work in school and then become
successful with it again, have lived through a time of
adolescent conflict somehow, without therapeutic help.
It is also likely, however, that some girls grow discouraged when their work becomes bad for no reason that
they can understand, and leave school because they are

hopeless about regaining their lost capacity for good work.

XIV. Adolescent Intensity of Emotion

Another psychological aspect of adolescence should be mentioned, if only briefly, *i.e.*, the richness of the emotional life at this age. This often leads to extreme and seemingly unaccountable changes of mood, with alternations between happiness and unhappiness, between anger and irritability, and gentle, affectionate attitudes. There is the tendency, if the adolescent is sufficiently intelligent and talented, for these surging emotions to find an outlet in creative expression, especially in writing. Interest in writing stories and poetry is characteristic of adolescence as of no other age (except for those who make writing their adult vocation). Appreciation of beauty and nature characterizes some adolescent writings; love themes are indicative of the preoccupation with this emotion during adolescence; moods of depression often appear in poetry. This last phenomenon is not surprising if it is realized that suicides show an increase at adolescence over the earlier childhood years, although adolescents actually commit suicide less frequently than adults, according to statistics. But while suicide itself is not any great probability during adolescence, suicidal reveries and fantasies are not at all uncommon at this time of life. These suicidal thoughts are precipitated by disappointments in love, unconscious identification with a parent who has died, guilt over misconduct of some sort, or spite toward a person whom the adolescent hopes will be grieved and remorseful after the suicide has been accomplished. Perhaps the surprising thing is not that suicide sometimes does occur among adolescents, but that it takes place comparatively rarely in view of the commonness of momentary ideas of self-destruction.

In the past 10 years much has been learned and written about adolescence and about the problems of this age. Even so, probably much less is known about adolescent psychology than is known about the psychology of children or adults. For that matter, the adolescent is less likely to have self-understanding than the child or the adult, althougth there are, of course, exceptions to this generalization. Perhaps it is because adolescence is a period of transition from childhood to maturity that there is more confusion about the self and a need to conceal uncertainty by a pose of self-confidence, with a tendency to minimize worries and problems or to find reassurance in the idea that any immediate difficulties will surely be smoothed out when adult independence is achieved. At least, it often seems harder for an adolescent to admit personal problems, or to talk about them to another person, than for a child or an adult to do so.

References

1. Hollingworth, L. S.: *The Psychology of the Adolescent,* pp. 2–3, D. Appleton and Co., New York, 1928.
2. Cole, Luella: *Psychology of Adolescence,* Chap. II, Farrar and Rinehart, New York, 1936.
3. Freud, Anna: *The Ego and the Mechanisms of Defense,* Hogarth Press, London, 1937.
4. Landis, C. and Page, J. D.: *Modern Society and Mental Disease,* Chap. 4, Farrar and Rinehart, New York, 1938.
5. Malzberg, Benj.: *Ment. Hyg.* 19:449 (July) 1935.
6. Elliott, G. L.: *Understanding the Adolescent Girl,* pp. 65–74, Henry Holt and Co., New York, 1930.

ADULT

The Dynamics of Psychoneuroses*

BY *Edith Weigert, M.D.*

The dynamic point of view was not introduced into psychiatry until the beginning of this century. By uncovering the unconscious mental processes Sigmund Freud outgrew the old psychiatry of description and classification. He taught us to see the mentally ill patient not as a static entity, but in a constant process of adaptation to his environment, in process of integration, disintegration and reintegration. Bridging the gap between biology and psychiatry, Adolf Meyer introduced new concepts and tools for understanding the integrative processes of human beings. William Alanson White opened up a new vista for psychiatry by pointing out that this new understanding of the integrative processes of mentation can be applied not only to mental illness but also to all problems in living in our highly complex society.

Dynamic psychiatry is applicable to all human beings; the borderlines between the various forms of

* Reprinted from *Neuropsychiatry*, Vol. II, No. 3, by courtesy of the author and publishers.

mental illness and so-called normality are fluid. An external disaster can throw any individual into an abnormal state of mind. A shock can produce a disintegrating
panic. The reaction of grief to the loss of a beloved person cannot always be distinguished in its symptoms from
a depression. In our dreams we return to the partially
disintegrated thought processes of a psychosis, which
Freud has taught us to translate into rational language.
The slips and errors of everyday life remind us painfully how easily the comforting emotional equilibrium
that we subjectively experience as "freedom" is jeopardized by unconscious processes beyond our control. External pressure diminishes the security of self control.

It is true that the reactions to external pressure are
far from uniform. We find individuals who stand up
under unbearable hardships with surprising equanimity
and other persons who break down at a minimal provocation. I heard from a Viennese psychiatrist how few
persons he had met who could endure political terror
without distortion of the personality and regression to
an infantile level. There is certainly a constitutional factor that determines the mental resistance to traumatic
experience. We find various degrees of adaptive flexibility. Man is more or less emotionally resistant and adverse to change, particularly to change that implies any
curtailment of satisfaction or security, which are the
pillars of human emotional equilibrium. A sudden
change from wealth to poverty, from recognition to disgrace, from peace to war, may overthrow one's mental
equilibrium. But even the more gradual transition from
protected childhood to responsible adulthood, from full
active life to the limitations of old age, from the freedom of the bachelor to the obligations of marriage and
child-raising may reveal a rigidity, an emotional inertia,

which defeats the necessary adaptation to changed life conditions.

We cannot influence the constitutional factor, but we can gain understanding and influence, in so far as such rigidity, such lag in emotional adaptability, stems from childhood experiences, from the developmental history of the individual.

I shall organize the concepts of psychodynamics under three headings:

1) the importance of the child's developmental history
2) the course of repressions and dissociations, which interfere with this development
3) the chances of transforming these distortions in the experience of analytic treatment.

Man is distinguished from all other animals in that he is born in greater helplessness and must acquire in less than two decades all the tools for dealing with the complexities of human culture in order to be successfully integrated with his fellow men. This process of acculturation is far from being always successful. In particular, emotional maturation frequently cannot keep pace with physiological growth, and failures of adaptation and integration lead to various degrees of dissociation of the personality.

In order to understand the failures of adjustment in the individual the student of dynamic psychiatry must know to what standards and social norms the individual has to adjust. Recent anthropological studies have emphasized how much standards and norms are at variance in different societies and even within the same society. A religious ritual may be carelessly neglected by a nonbeliever, while to the arduous adherent the breaking of a religious tabu may cause endless neurotic scruples. The sense of property varies in different social climates

The respect for the preservation of individual life is not the same in war and in peace, in totalitarian and in democratic societies. Premarital sexual abstinence is highly esteemed in a conservative society, while in the rebellious fringes of this society it may be considered almost as a disgrace. In a cultural milieu in which homosexual behavior is considered as a social disgrace, the dawning awareness of homosexual impulses may produce a panic and paranoid reactions. The potentially homosexual person feels like an outcast from society. We do not expect such fatal reactions to homoerotic impulses in a cultural milieu like ancient Greece, in which homosexual behavior is taken for granted.

Freud located the cultural prohibitions in the dream censor, the Ego ideal or the Superego, concepts that are related to the layman's concept of conscience. Since in the beginning of his career in the Victorian Era sexual impulses were particularly prohibited and hidden in the folds of elaborate hypocrisy, Freud's research interest followed the fate of the subdued sex drive into its repressions, regressions, and disguising transformations. The typical psychoneurotic conflict presented itself to Freud first as an antagonism between sexual drive and drive towards self preservation. In a society where sexual impulses were admitted only if adapted to a most respectable conservative pattern of family integration, all the whims and follies of extramarital sexuality, not to speak of the perversions of extragenital sexuality, were threatening to the self preservation of the individual, to his reputation, his prestige, his standing in the community. Adler's and Horney's concepts were more accessible and acceptable to common sense, but they popularized and diluted Freudian ideas by leaving aside the biological foundations; their psychology was more

an Ego- than an Id-psychology. The Id in Freud's terminology presents the subterraneous roots of the manifold ramifications of Ego development, the reservoir of
libido. Freud has broadened the concept of sexual
libido beyond the usage of this term in biology. Libido
is not only the vital force of sexual attraction; narcissistic libido plays a vital role in individual self preservation. In Freud's later writing the libido concept was
broadened into the Eros concept, Eros being the
integrative principle in individuals as well as suprain-
dividual relations, the life-preserving dialectic counterpart of the death-instinct, which according to Fenichel
might have been more accurately called the destructive
or disintegrative principle. As long as the Eros out-
weighs or neutralizes the death-instinct—Freud calls it
fusion of instincts—the individual is able to integrate his
biological needs, including sex, and his needs for security, that means self-preservation maintained in constructive interpersonal relations. Such integration is
accomplished by the subjective feeling tone of euphoria
or freedom from anxiety, anxiety being a warning signal
of defusion of instincts, a deneutralization of the death-
instinct.

We may also call this integrative ability "love." The
concept love encompasses much more than its biological, libidinal roots; it implies the highly integrated ability to take care of the welfare, that is the satisfactions
and security, of another human being as of one's own.
This is a redefinition of love given by Erich Fromm and
H. S. Sullivan, more practical, less philosophical than
Freud's concept of Eros, but closely akin to it. Fromm
and Sullivan also agree with Freud that the successful
instinct integration or the experience of love appears
relatively late in the process of maturation. Freud has

linked up love with genital maturation. But an individual may have reached full orgastic potency without being well integrated in himself or with others, and vice versa. But all psychoanalysts agree that the child is not yet able to love in a mature sense, but is a needy recipient of love. He is dependent for his satisfactions and his security on his family environment. In the earliest phase of libido development, oral gratification, that means provision of love and tenderness by the parents or their substitutes is necessary for the emotional maturation of the child, deficiencies in this respect retard and misdirect the process of development. Psychoneurotic disorders seem therefore to be inherited from one generation to the other, since the neurotic parent cannot help but give his children an inadequate preparation for life.

Freud has described the early phases of infant and child growth as sadomasochistic stages of sexual development. This implies Freud's view that the death-instinct or the destructive principle has to be contended with and transcended by the life-instinct from the very onset of human development. It is true the survival of the newborn infant would be extremely precarious without mothering care. The revolutionary change from intra- to extrauterine existence produces a state of emergency, a hyperactivity particularly of the body functions innervated by the sympaticus to surmount this state of shock. This state of shock is going to be reproduced in later life by any sudden threat to survival, and then it is experienced as panic.

The tender concern of a well balanced mother or nurse reëstablishes immediately after birth an approximation to the absolute security in the maternal womb. But the propensity towards panic persists due to the helpless dependency of the infant. Grave neglect on the part of the mother threatens the survival of the infant and keeps him on the verge of a panic. The mothering functions are particularly disturbed if the mother herself suffers from severe anxiety. By empathy or intuitively the infant participates, is contaminated by her anxiety. Anxiety disrupts the rapport, the tender coöperation between mother and infant. The infant's needs for food, sleep, comfort are therefore unsatisfactorily taken care of. The growing anxiety of the frustrated infant increases the anxiety and incompetence of the mother in a vicious cycle.

Anxiety stems from the Latin word "angustus"—narrow. The anxious individual is indeed narrowed in his potentialities, hemmed in. The reactions against such a state of helplessness are destructive; in a state of panic the human being manifests sadistic or masochistic impulses in defense. Anger, rage, fury, hatred are means to escape the danger in the direction of sadism; despondency, apathy, exhaustion, stupor evade anxiety in the opposite direction of masochism. But these destructive reactions belong to highly pathological degrees of anxiety, bordering on panic, while in small doses, anxiety has the beneficial function of a warning signal, mobilizing vital energies to master emergency and contributing therewith to the satisfying growth of constructive potentialities.

We have to consider the reactions to severe anxiety later on as main motivation for repression and dissociation. First I will try to outline a relatively healthy development. I do not believe in an innate hostility and do not see the infant as a bundle of unruly, despotic drives which are broken down by the rigid resistances of reality. The wholesome, harmonious relation of mother and infant presents an image of peace and serenity for which human beings are forever striving. The infant's needs are not greedy so long as they are reasonably taken care of by maternal tenderness. The expression of his needs and growing development of his abilities fit into the mother's need for giving tenderness in mutual adaptive coöperation. The sadomasochistic disposition of the infant stems from the manifold miscarriages of this tender coöperation, due to a mother's unfitness to devote herself reasonably to the welfare and development of the child. The hostile, sadistic infant, the angry, raging child is haunted by anxieties, because he is defeated in his need for tenderness. I see the tragedies of psychotic and neurotic distortions arise not from an innate sadomasochistic disposition, but from unmanageable anxieties and failures in early tender coöperation, which may occur because of external hardships, organic or neurotic ill health in the family, and other uncontrollable factors.

In the Freudian psychological system the concept of anxiety underwent several changes. Originally Freud saw in anxiety a transformed product of repressed libido. Later he introduced birth anxiety as the prototype of all anxiety, the physiological response to the threat to survival. If the threat comes from the outside, the accompanying emotion is called fear; if the danger comes from within, the emotion is called anxiety. But even the danger from within originally implies an external danger, namely desertion or loss of love. The child becomes afraid of his own impulses as far as they are in contradiction to parental authority. The anticipated loss of parental love, according to Freud, combined with the threat of punishment by castration, the ultimate destruction of sexual satisfaction, have a determining influence on the child's development. Because of his dependency on parental authority the child incorporates parental prohibitions in his Ego ideal or Superego, and the conflict between impulse and prohibition, between Id and Ego, as Freud has put it, has become internalized.

But on the other hand, anxiety is also an important, positive, formative influence. There is no child-raising without anxiety. Every step forward is accompanied by anxiety, the surmounting of anxiety gives great satisfaction. In the process of transcending anxieties, the child progresses from the automatic adaptation by the pleasure-pain principle to the more and more differentiated adaptation according to the reality principle. The degree or the dosage of anxieties determines whether the influence of anxiety will be constructive or destructive, resulting in success or failure of the child's acculturation.

In a reasonably healthy process of child-raising, the child is constantly guided by small doses of anxiety, which, before the level of verbal communication, arise from mother's forbidding gestures. In the raising of an eyebrow, in a slightly higher pitched voice, a frown that overshadows a former smile, the mother communicates to the child her disapproval of behavior or activities that do not conform to mother's idea of a good child, an idea which is largely dependent on cultural traditions in which mother herself was raised. The baby who is sucking his thumb or playing with feces or making exploratory discoveries in the genital region understands by empathy mother's disapproval, and the shadow of anxiety stirred up by her withdrawal of tenderness forces the dependent baby automatically to conform to mother's idea of the "good child." Such action and reaction, such direction by reward with increased tenderness and punishment with decreased tenderness or heightened anxiety accompany the growing child and channelize his behavior along the lines of parental expectations. Not only the behavior but also the awareness of one's behavior is channelized by the appraisal of the most significant persons of the early environment. The child dares only to get aware of those impulses and habits which are acceptable to parental authority; they form the Superego. Tendencies which have met with disapproval and aroused anxiety are repressed or dissociated. This Superego remains the guardian against anxiety throughout life. It is rather resistive to change.

If parental directions, which determine the Superego, give the child ample room for development of his potentialities, he has a spontaneous feeling of well-being; he feels good, that is, acceptable to his fellow creatures. It is evident that this optimum is hard to reach for at least two reasons. First, the cultural norms and standards in our society are very complex and inconsistent. For instance, how can the individual digest the contradiction of religious ideals and business practices? How can the child reconcile the intolerance against his harmless discoveries in the realm of sex with his observations of adult sexual licentiousness? Second, the mediator who hands the cultural ideals down to the child, the parent, is rarely quite free from crippling distortions of his own personality and on reasonably good terms with his cultural environment to guide the child with a minimal dosage of anxiety into his communal existence and to safeguard his development to the optimum. It is a difficult job to raise a child. Dr. Chisholm has pointed out how badly many people are prepared for parenthood. A young man who wants to raise pigs prepares himself by years of study in an agricultural school. But many prospective parents enter into their jobs as immature amateurs.

Nevertheless, thanks to the indestructible trends towards mental health, quite a lot of people reach maturity with a steady self, broad enough to permit free development of their natural assets and flexible enough to adapt to the vicissitudes of fate. I refer to Strecker's and Appel's definition of maturity: "The mature person is flexible, can defer to time, persons and circumstances; he can show tolerance, he can be patient, and above all he has the qualities of adaptability and compromise." This person has a solid self-esteem and to the degree that he respects himself, he is also able to respect others. He discriminates intelligently between constructive and destructive tendencies in his relations to others. The imitative, automatically conforming coöperation of the dependent child gradually grows into the capacity to collaborate with self-reliance and mutual respect. The most broadening experience in adolescence or preadolescence is the experience of love. Full maturity permits the integration of this experience of love with the vital need for sexual gratification.

Let me return from this outline of successful acculturation to the child whose development is seriously hampered by lack of security in early relations. Most psychiatrists agree that the earlier the traumatic experiences which interfere with the process of emotional development, the graver must be the mental disorder resulting from them. The child who in early infancy was exposed to an unusual degree of deprivations in his need for tenderness is basically hampered in his relations to people. Even if he accepts an external acculturation, he remains fundamentally lonely, and he is threatened by a psychotic break under stress and strain.

It looks as if in the gravely neglected child the need for tenderness, which was too frequently met by painful frustration and anxiety, had gone underground. What Freud has called the pleasure-pain principle, which implies an automatic avoidance of all too painful experience, has led to a repression or dissociation of the need for tenderness. Where in the growing child you would expect the expression of a longing for tenderness, you meet with anxiety, or more often, since anxiety is a painful experience too, a defense against anxiety: rage, anger, defiance as an active, expansive defense reaction, or indifference, boredom, apathy, in the passively despondent child. Rage is particularly frequent in children exposed to irritably punishing parents who restrain the child in his freedom, while the passive forms of despondency develop more often in children continuously starved in their need for affection or intimidated by parental overprotectiveness.

There are various degrees of failure in tender parental coöperation with the child; they may be due to a variety of intrafamily conflicts or hardships and pressures from the outside. In many a psychoneurotic life history we hear that the patient had the tragic experience of being an unwanted child. The lack of welcome to the child may not be frankly expressed, not even admitted to conscious awareness. An immature adult may have a fundamentally unwanted child because of extraneous motivations. The prospective parent has reached the age where society expects him to raise children; it adds to his prestige. A couple may want to patch up a disharmonious marriage by a child. They may expect to be saved from feelings of loneliness and inadequacy. Unfortunately, even physicians sometimes recommend conception as a cure for neurotic dissatisfaction. But if the child fails to fulfill these hopes, if he turns out to be an additional unbearable burden, then open anxieties may disrupt the tender coöperation between parent and child, or the hostility engendered by such anxieties makes the parent feel guilty. Guilt has a disrupting effect on tender coöperation similar to anxiety. Due to the close empathic link between parent and child, the child cannot be fooled by a display of unspontaneous, fabricated tenderness. Oversolicitude, overprotectiveness interfere with his need for growth and development. His dependency becomes overextended and his fears of desertion intensified or prolonged. Inconsistencies are bewildering for the child and contradictions between the parents throw the child into anxiety-arousing conflicts of loyalty.

An overload of disapproval and criticizing punishment creates a very narrow framework for the child's development. He may adapt to this narrow frame and dissociate much of his spontaneity, become for instance a goody-goody in the sense of parental expectations, but then he will later on not gain the approval of his contemporaries, who call him a sissy. There are constant collisions between his various needs for approval and his needs for expansion of his too narrow frame.

We have recognized that the dependency on approval which dissociates anxiety-arousing experiences from awareness does not only split off destructive impulses that are generally considered bad, but also dissociates constructive impulses, for instance the child's longing for tenderness, which has too frequently received a painfully negative response. The overprotected child dissociates more or less the belief in his growing abilities.

We have seen that the anxious child tries to get rid of his anxiety by anger, rage, or temper tantrums. But such frankly hostile behavior is not likely to meet approval either. This disapproval forces the child into further repression and dissociation. The repressed anger is transformed into smouldering resentment. Swallowed hostilities overload the organism with indigestible tensions. Freud has called the phenomenon of transformation of psychological tensions into physiological disorders "conversion." If the repression of resentment leads to disturbances of digestion, circulation, respiration or other physiological functions, we are confronted with psychosomatic disorders, which are frequent in unhappy, bitter children.

Feeding problems are a typical bone of contention in a disturbed mother-child relationship. Numerous conflicts are centered around the education toward cleanliness. If the mother is not in rapport with the child's growing abilities, she may hurry or delay the child unduly in the process of teaching him mastery of the excretory functions. If the tender coöperation fails, conflicts and anxieties arise which prevent the child from learning according to his growing abilities. Irregularities of bowel function or enuresis may result.

If the child feels doomed to failure, the learning of other functions may become seriously impeded. Speech disorders like stammering and stuttering betray a highly negativistic resistance to interpersonal communication. Later school progress can be blocked emotionally to a degree that defects in intelligence are incorrectly assumed.

If the child has once accepted it as a fact that he is incorrigibly bad, his lowered self-respect seeks relief in tearing down others in defiance. The child becomes a bully or he specializes in mischievousness in order to get attention which he cannot gain in any other way. The experience of tyrannical power is substituted for the dissociated need for tender coöperation. In his need for despotic power the more or less isolated child tries to get rid of the unbearable helplessness which accompanies his repressed anxieties. Despotic power is an unsatisfactory substitute for tenderness. It never fills the bill. Therefore the need for such power is characterized by insatiability and compulsion.

Tenderness is, in Freud's terminology, the expression of aim-inhibited libido or Eros. The aim of sexual lust already exists in childhood, age three to seven, in budding forms expressed by curiosity, voyeur wishes, exhibitionistic and masturbatory activities which are harmless if not frowned upon by the adults, but they become conflict-laden and compulsive if the child suffers under the lack of tender gratifications and from insecurity in his most vital relations to his environment. If the child is not inhibited in his emotional development, feels secure in the tenderness of parental love, it is not difficult to tame his awakening sexual impulses and the accompanying experiences of rivalry, envy and jealousy, to tune down these passions without serious upheaval of the family harmony.

You remember that Oedipus of the Greek tragedy had been a rejected child; his parents got rid of him in infancy on the basis of a prophecy which threatened to interfere with their own selfish interests. Freud used the Greek tragedy as a symbol for the conflicts that are implied in the child's sexual and aggressive impulses which endanger his adaptation to the family and later socialization. These incestuous impulses toward a parent or sibling, as well as death wishes against the rival, are intensified in an anxious child, in a child who is irresponsibly seduced, used for more or less veiled selfish gratification of an elder or deprived of the security of tender coöperation. Under such circumstances sexual lust and murderous impulses can become compulsive and insatiable. These compulsive preoccupations are threatened by intense disapproval and therefore they have to be repressed and dissociated.

The child who cannot trust parental tenderness feels, of course, particularly threatened by the arrival of a sibling rival. The adaptation to the growing family is complicated by envious competition. The greater the anxiety, the more impetuous is the claim for exclusive possession. The self-defeating bid for despotic power gains in importance in proportion as the reliance on friendly sharing and participation fails.

The child with a cruel Superego or a lowered self-esteem is often insecure about his fitness for his sexual role. The boy may be doubtful whether he is a real boy. He feels he is a sissy, later he calls himself effeminate. Even if he overcompensates by pretended toughness, the doubt about his manliness may accompany him far into adulthood. Likewise the girl who distrusts her future value as a woman, her capacity to win a male partner, to bear and rear children, may evade such painful doubts by playing the role of the tomboy, but without finding real comfort in such a substitution. Freud has named these manifestations of lowered self-esteem "penis envy" and "castration fear" respectively. Their intensity is correlated to the cruelty of the Superego and the desperate need for punishment.

The world of the "as if," of phantasies and daydreams, is a natural playground of the child's testing and probing imagination, as long as the horizon of his real environment is limited to nursery and home. If the growing child does not dare to branch out, to widen his horizon, due to arresting anxiety and diffidence, this world of imagination becomes an isolating refuge. Daydreams of a superman's perfection, of heroic achievements, of perfect love are substituted for real experiments in living and gains in the process of coöperative adaptation to others. The child remains self-centered and lonely. The more he approaches adulthood, the greater the discrepancy becomes between the inexpensive victories of his autistic phantasies and the defeats in real living with others. He does not dare to expose his pretentious ambitions to honest competition with his compeers; he cannot take the chance of losing, or of revealing real incompetence. Since he finds that his self-centered ambitious claims antagonize others, he may learn to outwit and cheat, to win by hook or by crook. But such anxiety-ridden secretiveness does not increase self-respect. A fundamentally lonely existence becomes more barren, dull and boring, the more the aspirations of phantasy are spent in pretense. The secluded daydreamer fails to learn that which makes life really meaningful, namely spontaneous participation and devotion to someone or something outside of himself.

Deceit, like hostility, is not an innate vice, but a kind of magic which by wishful thinking averts anxiety. It stems from the conflict of the helpless child with the powerful parental authority. The child, and later the child in the adult, attempts to ward off nightmarish dangers by prayer or other propitiating gestures. If the closed room or the open street have become invested with uncanny imaginary threats, the helpless child conjures up imaginary powers to protect himself. A handwashing ritual has to atone for secret dangerous sins. Threatening black magic is fought off by protective white magic. We recognize in the imaginary dangers the symbol of the bad, hateful, punishing parent, while the protective, comforting power presents the good, approving and rewarding parent. If the hope for genuine trust in the child-parent relationship has become more or less dissociated, given up in despair, the child, particularly if he is intelligent, substitutes for trust the magic weapon of deceit to transform the dangerous, punishing parent into the good one. The parent can be outwitted and placated by "as if" performances, apologetic gestures, going through the motions. The child learns the art of hypocrisy; he gets away with murder, he pursues selfish, not permissible purposes secretively, avoiding parental disapproval. He appears good, obedient, and often reaches a pseudo-peace with the powerful authority. By such defiant obedience, the child perpetuates the conflict between obedience and rebellion in relation to authority. Though he appears good, he does not feel good deep down. The longing for real peace and reconciliation, which is repressed, out of reach, keeps him restless and unsatisfied. Various degrees of hypocritical adaptation are prescribed not only by the home, but by many larger cultural institutions.

To a greater or lesser degree the child is deceived by his own deceitful manipulations of the authority. He learns to fortify the weakness of his position by rationalizing argumentation. In the stubborn insistence on self-justification lie the roots of a paranoid development. The child becomes identified with the role that he plays. He gradually believes in his hypocritical goodness, his self-righteousness, or even his saintliness. But this form of hypocritically conforming adaptation absorbs an enormous amount of energy and separates him further from spontaneous exhange with others.

The obsessional adult remains preoccupied with the

elaboration of the most complicated devices to gain rewards and to avoid punishment. But deceived by his own deceit he cannot see through his complex maneuvers, which do not make sense on the surface level of consciousness. Spontaneity is very restricted by defensive substitutions, and the system of unspontaneous adaptation is fraught with anxiety.

This precarious equilibrium may break down under pressure with neurotic symptoms, such as depression and free floating anxiety. The patient suffers intensely and yet there are signs of dramatization of his misery. By self-accusation and self-condemnation he takes the wind out of the sails of a disapproving authority; he begs for contradiction, reassurance, which is of no avail. By self-punishment he tries to bribe parental approval. We miss an honest regret about that which separates him from his fellow creatures, namely the lack of his own spontaneous coöperation. He has remained in infantile parasitic dependency. This fundamental handicap is farthest removed from his awareness and grasp, because of very early and deep repression and dissociation.

Up to now I have attempted to present the two main points of my program: 1) the developmental history; 2) the role and the results of repression and dissociation. I will devote the rest of my time to some remarks on psychoanalytic treatment. As I have tried to convey, psychoneurotic suffering is due to arrested emotional development in childhood. The psychoneurotic adult is bound to repeat the original conflicts which arrested his development in all subsequent interpersonal relations. This repetition tends to maintain the old dissociations and the habitual patterns of substitution. This form of repetition compulsion has been called transference by Freud, parataxic distortion by Sullivan. We also see on all levels of development a spontaneous tendency towards recovery which breaks the compulsive patterns of defense and permits new and broadening spontaneous experience.

How can the psychotherapeutic process approximate and accelerate such spontaneous recovery? If the psychoneurotic patient seeks help from a doctor, we cannot offer any simple relief of his symptoms, which are deeply embedded in his character. He needs an overhauling of his character structure in order to introduce profitable change and to open the floodgates of arrested maturation. The important lever is the transference, the tendency of the neurotic to carry over the crippling conflicts with significant persons of his childhood into the relation to the doctor who offers to help him.

The psychoneurotic has only a limited and distorted knowledge of himself. This is due to early adaptation patterns, a restrictive Superego which excludes from awareness impulses and tendencies which caused disapproval by authority and therewith anxiety. He expects the same disapproval on the part of the doctor and he meets him with the old weapons of defense. The more intelligent the patient, the subtler are his defenses. The patient fights to preserve his comforting daydreams, illusions of grandeur, claims and titles of childhood, which shield him from frightening new experience. The patient tries ardently to seduce the doctor into a conspiracy of repetition; he prompts him to provide the same substitute satisfactions which he got as a child from the outwitted parent. The patient tries to manipulate the doctor, to involve him in a power struggle, to repeat with him the never ending conflict of obedience and rebellion. The patient expects magical help and if frustrated in his infantile demands he may break out into anger or rage, by which he tries to intimidate the doctor and to circumvent the reliving of painful, old anxieties, or he may withdraw into passivity, apathy or despondency. The distortions that the drive towards repetition of old conflicts carries into the doctor-patient relationship are often phantastic. A patient who came to an interview with me in a drunken state had the illusion of seeing me in mother's evening dress, with a hat on my head with old-fashioned hatpins, which in his infantile rage he wanted to screw into the skull of his mother.

The great opportunity for profitable change in analysis is given by the fact that the doctor is *not* father or mother or any other anxiety arousing authority of the past, that he does *not* get involved in transference repetition, but remains outside in benevolent neutrality. Therewith he gives the patient an opportunity to relive the old anxieties and to find a more constructive way out of them. The patient has to test the doctor out, and it is too bad if the doctor is pretentious, condescending or artificial, for he loses his usefulness for the patient, even if the patient does not become aware of it. Only genuine respect for the patient can dispel his fears of being rejected, forsaken, overpowered, or exploited. Only in an atmosphere free of fear and passionate involvements can the patient catch up with his retarded and misdirected development. The tragedies of childhood thus relived need no longer bog him down in anxious helplessness. He can get hold of his dissociated impulses and rechannelize them towards constructive goals.

For this process of reëducation the doctor needs a lot of information, accurate facts and data to reconstruct the patient's development, its stagnations and aberrations. In the beginning of analysis the life history of the patient presents itself in a more or less legendary form. Because of the falsifying influence of the habitual self-deception, there are many gaps and omissions of memory to be filled in and falsifications to be corrected. The most painstakingly honest report of the neurotic patient is filled with contradictions and incompatibilities. Particularly the image of the early significant persons is often distorted in one way or other, by a sentimental whitewash or the tendency to see the authority all over black, overlooking whatever was good and constructive in the early relationship.

In order to overcome the forces of repression, dissociation and substitution, Freud had introduced the method of free association and dream interpretation after having dropped the exploration by hypnosis. But the patient may still mislead the doctor by endlessly rambling associations, and the need for approval or defiant obedience may influence even his dreams.

Thus the psychoanalyst needs a lot of life experience to see through the patient's intricate network of illusions, self-deceptions and distortions, by which he maintains his precarious equilibrium. You will understand how important it is that the analyst before he starts in his difficult work undergo a successful analysis of himself, with repetition if he gets stale, to discover his blind spots, to free his potentialities from repression and compulsion. He must gain the maturity, the spontaneity, the objectivity and the tolerance which encourage the patient to give up his childhood ties, to dare to experiment, and to share in the relation, freed from transference repetition, the broadening experience of spontaneous collaboration.

Physical Complaints of Neurotic Origin[*]

BY *Frederick A. Weiss, M.D.*

Physical complaints can be of neurotic origin; they are bodily expressions of psychological conflict. Our term, "psychosomatic medicine," now used to describe such symptoms, is recent; but our knowledge that the *psyche* —the mind—can affect the *soma*—the body—is of considerable antiquity. Two-and-a-half thousand years ago Socrates stated: "The body cannot be cured without the mind." Observation since that time has piled up a steadily increasing confirmation of Socrates' opinion, and the experience of [the Second World] War shows once more the enormous importance of the problem.

Between 4 and 5 million men in the war were rejected or discharged as unfit for service; more than a third of the rejections, and over 40 per cent of the medical discharges have been for neuropsychiatric reasons. Among the leading psychosomatic disorders involved

[*] This is a summary of a lecture delivered on April 5, 1945 before the Auxiliary Council to the Association for the Advancement of Psychoanalysis; reprinted by courtesy of the author and the Auxiliary Council.

are: asthma, peptic ulcer, gastrointestinal disturbances, and neurocirculatory asthenia—a condition formerly described as "effort syndrome," or disordered action of the heart.

In the last fifty years medicine has made gigantic strides. X-ray and electrocardiogram, bacteriology, and blood chemistry, enable the physician of today to treat many diseases much more successfully than in the past. Medicine has reached its machine age. Every organ of the body can be investigated after death, each cell examined under the microscope; new and better weapons are constantly being invented to enable the doctor to look deeply into all parts of the living body also.

But, unfortunately, this great mechanical progress all too often causes the physician to forget that behind the cells and organs exists the individual as a whole, in whom mind and body form an inseparable unit. Before each opening of the body stands a specialist ready to diagnose the most minute physical changes with gastroscope, bronchoscope, cystoscope, or rectoscope; but the most observant specialist may nevertheless fail to realize that he is looking, not merely at a stomach or a bronchus, but at the stomach or bronchus of a specific individual who is living in a specific total life situation.

Any doctor's office will provide endless examples of the person who brings physical symptoms that can be relieved only through an understanding of the patient's total situation.

There is, for example, the excited woman of 50 who comes to have her blood pressure checked. It is above 200, and she naturally thinks of heart trouble, and fears a stroke. But the very first interview reveals a cause for the high pressure: the woman's son has recently married, and his mother-in-law now tries to influence him to regard his parents as people of a lower social level. His mother feels both deserted and enraged, but she represses her anger and hurt, and says nothing; instead, her blood pressure speaks for her, a very clear language.

Following the first visit, weekly readings of the blood pressure were taken, and at such times the woman was given an opportunity to talk. We describe such talks as "cathartic" for they allow a person to express his grievances fully. In about six weeks the blood pressure was down to 120, and the grateful patient remarked: "Doctor, could you not continue treatment with this wonderful apparatus? It has helped me so much." The "wonderful apparatus" was, of course, the manometer, which did nothing but register the pressure.

Another example is the diabetic shopkeeper; variations in the amount of sugar in his urine reflect almost exactly the weekly state of his business, but reflect it in reverse—a high tide in his sugar excretion indicating a low tide in his income.

Then there is the down-trodden husband whose stomach ulcer invariably speaks whenever he would like to "speak up" to his wife, but dares not. And there is the patient with asthma; he goes away to a health resort to escape the pollens to which he is allergic at home, but he nevertheless comes down with a severe attack of asthma after receiving a letter from his mother. His specialist has carefully eliminated all sources of allergy, but has failed to consider the possibility that his patient is allergic to—his almost sadistically dominating mother.

These instances are, of course, still very simple examples of psychosomatic action. But they illustrate the importance of viewing the disturbed function of a bodily organ as part of the disturbed function of the whole body-mind unit; and of viewing the patient as part of a still greater social unit of interpersonal relations.

TRANSMITTING EMOTIONAL TENSION: During the past twenty years we have learned to understand the vital function of the so-called autonomous nervous system— "autonomous" because it is not dependent on our conscious will, nor controlled by it. This vital system has well been named "the nerves of life." By means of its two antagonistic branches it reaches and controls all organs of the body from the hair on top of the head to the sweat glands on the soles of the feet. It regulates the action of heart and blood-vessels, and the whole process of circulation, the function of the bronchi and the process of respiration, the function of stomach and intestines and the process of digestion and, in addition, all other viscera such as liver, kidneys and bladder, and particularly the hormone glands such as the thyroid, the pituitary in the brain, the sex glands, and the adrenals above the kidneys.

The extensive network of the autonomous nervous system acts as a kind of keyboard; on it the emotions play and through it neurotic conflicts, and strong emotions such as hostility and anxiety, are under certain conditions *converted* into bodily symptoms.

A great variety of single tones and mighty chords can be sounded on this keyboard, but the loudest discords are produced by the powerful emotions of fear, rage, anxiety, and hostility. Under their stimulus the respiration deepens, the heart beats more rapidly, the blood pressure rises, the function of stomach and intestines becomes intensely disturbed; sugar is shifted from its storage room, the liver, into the blood; the spleen contracts and sends its blood reserve into the body like a powerful blood transfusion; sweat may be poured out on the body surface.

Such an extreme total response of the whole organism was interpreted by Dr. Walter B. Cannon as the body's original reaction to vital danger—a preparation for life-saving fight or flight.

"The forces of the organism," Dr. Cannon says, "are put upon a war footing. But if there is no war to be waged, if the emotion has its natural mobilizing effects on the viscera when there is nothing to be done . . . obviously this very mechanism will upset the whole organism. It is not surprising, therefore, that fear and worry and hate can lead to harmful and profoundly disturbing consequences."

ANXIETY, CONFLICT, AND PHYSICAL SYMPTOMS: What fear and external danger mean to primitive man, anxiety and internal danger mean to us who live in the present. In order to explain what anxiety and internal danger are, psychiatry had to develop beyond its earlier and limited approach, which confined it to a mere classification of the end results of emotional conflicts—the psychoses. It had to follow each step in the development *from* the so-called normal *to* the psychotic, and include in its investigation the large neglected field of neurotic disturbances, which for centuries had been regarded as only meaningless deviations from normal behavior. To find the meaning of neurotic symptoms the static system of psychiatry had to be changed to the dynamic method of psychoanalysis.

We owe it to the genius of Sigmund Freud that today

we are closer to the answer of this problem. Freud discovered that disturbances of our psychological as well as our physiological functions could be caused by anxiety or an unconscious conflict. Many of Freud's basic discoveries remain valid; but considered from the viewpoint which emphasizes the character as a whole, his concept of anxiety appears limited.

Freud's concept of the role of conflict in neurosis, though very constructive in itself, is also limited because of his introduction of congenital instincts as the main factor in this fight, a fight which is understood by him as a struggle between the instinctual impulses of the Id, and the relentless coercive demands of the Superego— with the Ego the victim of the insoluble conflict.

Conflicts do play a decisive role in the structure of neurosis, but they are *human* conflicts caused by the clash between contradictory neurotic trends which had been formed as safety devices during an insecure childhood. The compulsive need for affection may clash, for example, with the compulsive need for power.

Any vital threat to the safety of the individual may set in motion the whole powerful response of the autonomous nervous system. Safety, to the neurotic, is based on the satisfaction of his neurotic needs. His safety also depends on preserving intact the ideal image he has formed of himself—an image composed of the less questionable aspects of his conflicting trends so unified that contradictions are hidden and appear as part of a "superior" or "unique" personality.

This image is essential to his feeling of safety, for it enables him to harbor and protect in himself completely conflicting trends. The strongest threat to a neurotic individual is the breakdown of this image, for it faces him with full awareness of his conflict. But any frustration of his neurotic needs is also felt as danger. Anxiety and hostility result.

Such is Dr. Karen Horney's creative concept of anxiety, and it enables us to use Dr. Cannon's viewpoint for an understanding of psychosomatic medicine.

FUNCTIONS AND MEANINGS OF PHYSICAL SYMPTOMS: The neurotic tries to escape anxiety. Four ways are open to him: 1) he may *rationalize* it—turn anxiety into a seemingly rational fear; 2) he may *deny* it—exclude it from consciousness; 3) he may *narcoticize* it—drown it in alcohol, drugs, work, sex, or sleep; and finally, 4) he may *avoid* all situations, thoughts, or feelings which arouse anxiety. When this last mechanism is well-established and operates automatically we have the phenomenon known as *inhibition*.

It happens with particular frequency on escape roads 2 and 4 that the partial or total dissociation of anxiety from consciousness leads to the formation of physical symptoms. Sometimes a person banishes the whole existence of neurotic conflict from his mind; but more often he represses only one of the conflicting trends. Any drive, need, feeling can be repressed if it endangers another drive, need, feeling, which for the individual is of vital importance.

On road 2 anxiety is merely denied, and nothing else is done about it. All that shows is the physical accompaniment of anxiety such as shivering, sweating, accelerated heart beat, choking sensations, frequent urge to urinate, diarrhea, vomiting, and in the mental sphere a feeling of restlessness, of being rushed or paralyzed. We may experience these same feelings and sensations when we are afraid and know that we are afraid. When we are afraid and do not know it, then the feelings and sensations are the only expression of repressed anxiety, and in that case *all that the individual knows* about his condition is this outward evidence of disturbance—symptoms with no apparent physical cause.

On road 4 a person escapes anxiety because the mechanism of inhibition takes away his ability to do, think or feel, anything that might produce anxiety. He is usually unaware of feeling any anxiety, and has no capacity for overcoming inhibition by conscious effort. We meet the most extreme physical symptoms resulting from this mechanism in the various so-called *hysterical* losses of body function.

"Hysteria" is derived from *hystera,* the Greek word for womb, but the condition it describes is no longer connected specifically with the womb, or other sex organs, and its occurrence is just as frequent in men as in the owners of the womb—women. The neurotic personality in which we are most likely to find this condition is that characterized by excessive needs for affection and approval. Hysterical symptoms—such as hysterical blindness or deafness—have a double meaning, and the individual experiencing them is unaware of either meaning: they protect him from the perception of an unacceptable reality, and they bring him special attention and affection. Hysterical speechlessness may represent an attempted solution of two conflicting drives: the desire to express hostility openly, and the conflicting need to preserve a relationship of dependency toward the object of one's hostility. In a similar way the paralysis of a leg allows a patient to avoid taking certain necessary "steps" in the direction of a possibly dangerous decision.

We can easily observe such visible psychosomatic reactions as blushing or trembling, but we have only limited opportunity to see psychosomatic changes *within* the body. We can follow the reactions of internal organs to emotional conflict with such instruments as the fluoroscope, and see that position, shape, and movement of stomach and intestine change completely if, under hypnosis, emotional conflicts are produced and released. A stomach may be found several inches lower than usual under emotional tension, and the contour of the bowels —usually rather smooth—may look so ragged that a specialist in such matters can easily diagnose repressed rage from this picture. Or—to take another example—the gall bladder contracts visibly in emotional tension, so that less and thicker, darker bile is secreted. Some kind of intuition must have enabled the Greeks to guess at this phenomenon, for their word *melancholia* means "black bile."

A nine-year-old boy once burned his esophagus with hot clam chowder, but this tragic accident allowed medical science really to observe what happens in the stomach of a person in a state of anxiety or rage. Through the permanent opening into his stomach which had to be created to feed him we have seen that when he represses hostility—due to inner conflict—his stomach becomes dark red, and blushes like his face; the glands also produce excessive hydrochloric acid, and the stomach's motility increases. It is well known that these conditions, occurring together, will lead to severe inflammation of the stomach wall and, if they continue over a long period, to the formation of a gastric ulcer. In this particular patient the most extreme gastric reactions occurred whenever anything threatened his idealized image of himself as a very special and privileged person, or whenever he had to repress a need toward aggression, or toward fighting back.

War experience has confirmed on a great scale the importance of repressed hostility as a cause for ulcers, and other psychosomatic disorders. In a large percentage of cases it was not those at the front who developed ulcers, but those who experienced bombings without being able to fight back. In Leningrad many people developed a disease named "sequel of bombing"—a specific kind of high blood pressure that ends in ruptured blood vessels and cerebral hemorrhage.

We can now interpret the exact function in the neurotic conflict of some symptoms, but others do not yet permit such specific interpretation. We can say, however, that they are the expression of emotional tension produced by repressed anxiety or conflict.

Some of this "language of the body" is astonishingly well described in popular phrases. We speak, for example, of not being able to "swallow" an insult or belittling remark; we have a "load on our chest" when worried or depressed; we "breathe more easily" after an anxiety state is over; we warn our neighbor against anger with—"Don't get your blood pressure up!" People may indeed have difficulty in swallowing when confronted with unwelcome life situations, and vomiting may express the rejection not only of food but of some unacceptable fact—Napoleon vomited when told that he must go to St. Helena.

It is often the chronic repetition of relatively slight traumatic experiences which lead to functional disturbance, and finally to organic change.

CHOICE OF ORGAN: We cannot yet answer in all cases why a given organ becomes the seat of neurotic disturbance; but we do know some of the factors that determine the choice:

1) The choice may be what we describe as *symbolic:* that is, the symptom may play a symbolic role in the unconscious attempt at a solution of conflict. For example, the paralysis of an arm may be the neurotic solution of a conflict between a desire to express hostility by physical action, and the opposed desire to preserve the ideal picture of a good relationship.

2) *The medical history of the patient* may play a significant role; the neurotic mechanism may occasionally select and use a biologically inferior organ, but it is more apt to follow the way prepared by an earlier organic disease. A neurotic may develop, for example, a swollen wrist, which symptom the body had "learned" during a previous attack of rheumatic arthritis; or asthma may first show during a severe bronchitis, but reappear later under emotional tension.

3) *Identification* represents another mechanism that may influence the choice. If, for instance, a domineering mother has heart trouble, migraine, or asthma, her dependent daughter may unconsciously respond to conflict situations with the same symptoms; or a girl who has a repressed wish for pregnancy may imitate a pregnant friend's "morning sickness."

4) Finally a kind of *conditioned reflex* may operate —as in the famous case reported by the French Dr. Trousseau, in which a woman who was sensitive to roses had an asthmatic attack when she saw an artificial rose in Trousseau's buttonhole.

SEXUAL SYMPTOMS OF NEUROTIC ORIGIN: Since the neuroses affect interpersonal relationships, it is not surprising that we meet a great many neurotic disturbances in the field of sex—the closest interpersonal relation. Partial or total impotence and premature ejaculation in the man, partial or total frigidity and vaginal spasms in the woman, are all definitely neurotic symptoms. Conflicts between a need for affection and a need for domination are frequently found as a background for such disturbances.

To relieve the symptoms the conflicts have to be analyzed and resolved, instead of the medieval treatments of prostate massage in the male, or stretching the vagina in the woman. Frigidity, the passive resistance, and vaginal spasm, the active resistance against the full acceptance of the relationship, cannot be cured with instruments, nor can they be analyzed as isolated symptoms. Sterility, which seems so far removed from psychoanalytic considerations, also belongs to our subject. Not only is a woman who has no orgasm less likely to conceive, but emotional conflict may prevent ovulation —the formation and expulsion of the egg—and may cause spastic contraction of the tube and block the passage of the egg. Menstrual disorders too, irregularities, absence or increase of menstruation, and particularly premenstrual pain, may have their function in the subconscious mechanism of the conflict.

SECONDARY GAINS: In addition to its main function of protecting the neurotic from the full impact of anxiety and hostility, and from the full awareness of his basic conflict, the psychosomatic symptom provides him with several important secondary gains: his symptoms may gain him special consideration from friends and relatives, or special public esteem, and may provide him with an escape from difficult tasks or responsibilities, and particularly from those situations that endanger his idealized image, that involve competition or risk, or that simply entail his growing up emotionally.

These secondary gains are NOT the cause of the neurosis, but represent an added "bonus" derived from it, and the fear of losing this seeming advantage can increase the patient's resistance during analysis.

Finally, the psychosomatic symptom has a special value in one type of neurotic—or pseudo—solution: a mechanism we name "externalization," whereby internal difficulties are projected onto the external world. As a neurotic will invariably prefer to blame his condition on others, or on external circumstances, so he will usually prefer the *somatic* interpretation of his symptoms to the psychoanalytic one. He correctly regards it as much easier to change his diet or climate, or even to undergo one or more operations, than to change his personality.

PHYSICAL SYMPTOMS AND PSYCHOANALYSIS: From the viewpoint of psychoanalysis, we have always to keep in mind that psychosomatic disturbances are only *symptoms* of neurotic conflict. In the course of an analysis, physical symptoms often go through three more or less distinct phases. During the *first* period, simple symptoms like sweating or vomiting may disappear rather quickly, due not to the analytic process itself, but to the general feeling of support, and the relief of tension produced by the "catharsis" of being able to express oneself freely. During the *second* period symptoms may reappear at moments when the neurotic trends are threatened by increase of insight, or by the breakdown of defense mechanisms. Such an increase in symptoms may therefore be a sign of progress, as it may show that the neurotic pseudoequilibrium is shaking, and the conflict entering awareness.

Only in the *final* period of analysis—when the neurotic trends are no longer needed to give a false sense of security—will the psychosomatic symptoms really disappear. An analysis should approach the awareness of conflict with full consideration for the patient's psychological tolerance. When the timing is carefully handled, the patient will be able to recognize his conflicting needs—as for example, needs for dependency and aggression; his real security will grow until he becomes strong enough to do without his ideal image, to *accept* reality or *change* it.

NEUROTIC CONFLICTS AND PHYSICAL ILLNESS: During the last three decades such scourges as tuberculosis, diphtheria, scarlet fever and typhoid have greatly diminished, but circulatory and digestive diseases, asthma and goitre, have tremendously increased; angina pectoris has nearly trebled. The increase is in just those diseases which are typical results of psychosomatic action, and due to inner conflict.

Which conflict? There are, of course, many, but one in particular has become the basic conflict of the neurotic of our time: that between the neurotic need for dependency and for competitive aggression. Elements in our present society tend to foster this conflict.

The development of our mechanized and specialized system is characterized by a growing interdependence. More and more of us—bookkeepers, clerks, accountants, factory hands—are confined to a routine of fixed hours and often montonous tasks, and become entangled in a great web of dependency. But at the same time we are forced to compete and be aggressive in a steadily increasing degree. In this social *compression chamber* the neurotic individual is much more apt to be confronted with a sudden awareness of his inner conflict. He resents the dependency, and feels hostility coming up; but this hostility is repressed, not only for reasons of external security, but because it contradicts his ideal image of himself as a good, socially minded citizen. So he swallows his resentment, and this swallowing is more important in the causation of gastric ulcers than the swallowing of rough or hard food.

The word "anxiety" has the same root as has the Latin word *angina*, which means narrowness, a narrow pass. The neurotic feels hopelessly caught in the narrow pass between his conflicting trends. Only a successful analysis can resolve his conflict.

Obesity*

BY *William Parson, M.D.*

AND *K. R. Crispell, M.D.*

Obesity should be regarded by every practicing physician as a symptom, a problem and a challenge. We have come to regard obesity as a "disturbance in homeostasis" due to varied causes, the main one being psychologic in nature. We will attempt to develop this theme in this presentation.

Bruch (1) has defined obesity as "a variation of body build which is characterized by excessive growth in volume." Regardless of definition it is an extremely common and serious symptom—how common we do not actually know. Patients do not usually consult a physician because of obesity but rather because of associated symptoms. The seriousness of obesity is well known and is borne out by medical statistics. Newburgh (2) has stated that between the ages of 45 and 50 years 25 pounds (11.3 kg.) of excess weight result in an increase in 25 per cent in mortality. Obesity (3) has

* From *The Medical Clinics of North America*, March 1952, Volume 36, Number 2. Reprinted by courtesy of the authors and the publishers, W. B. Saunders and Company.

been found to be associated with an increased incidence of diabetes, hypertension, atherosclerosis, varicose veins and toxemia of pregnancy. For these reasons it seems of importance to reëmphasize the dangers and to "rechallenge" all physicians to renew their interest in obesity.

Etiology

The etiology of obesity is simple and yet it is exceedingly complex. It is simple in that it follows a thermodynamic principle relating to energy which states that energy can neither be created nor destroyed. In other words, in health, the caloric intake equals the energy output and a constant weight is maintained. It may be expressed as follows:

Caloric Intake = Energy Output = Constant Weight

This is an example of homeostasis or "wisdom of the body" which is truly amazing. We may attend a banquet and perhaps consume five to six thousand calories which is perhaps three thousand more than usual. How many of us consciously regulate our diet so that over the next few days we take in three thousand less calories? Probably none and yet in health one maintains a constant weight regardless of the irregularity of caloric intake or energy output.

When a patient becomes obese, we assume that something has happened to this homeostatic mechanism which controls caloric intake. The controlling factors are poorly, if at all, understood. Terms such as hunger, appetite and satiety which are thought of as controlling factors are hard to define. Janowitz (4) has defined appetite as simply the desire to eat and hunger as a complex constellation of sensations both gastric and extragastric which give rise to the desire to eat. A standard dictionary defines satiety as a state of being satisfied fully or gratified to repletion. It is of interest that glut is listed as a synonym for satiate and is defined as greediness or overloading, sometimes with repletion before greed is satisfied. It seems that the first definition of satiety applies in health, while the synonym glut applies to the patient who overeats. The factors regulating satiety are exceedingly complex and need much more investigation. The role of the distention of the gut, blood sugar level and amino acid level has been investigated and found not to be the critical factor. Strang (5) has recently put forth the interesting concept that the rate of mass exchange may be a component of the sensation of satiety. In other words, a person tends to have a daily intake of food which bears a constant relationship to body mass. It is an interesting observation and should stimulate investigation along this line.

Many factors other than physiological also influence caloric intake. These include cultural, social, economic and psychologic factors. Many examples could be quoted for each, but one needs to think only of the frequent invitations to dinner, the banquet circuit and the cocktail party to realize that most of our social activities are integrated with "caloric intake." The psychologic factors will be discussed in detail later.

In discussing etiology we have purposely avoided mentioning endocrine disorders and decreased energy output as important factors in weight gain. As for endocrine disorders it seems to suffice to say that people with endocrine abnormalities may have obesity as one of the symptoms but an extremely small percentage of people with obesity have an endocrine abnormality. There is evidence that hormones play a part in the distribution of fat as exemplified by the difference between normal male and female, and by an abnormal condition such as Cushing's syndrome with its "pot belly," "moon face" and "Buffalo hump." However, there is no evidence at the present time that hormones per se are a key factor in the regulation of caloric intake.

Young (6) has postulated that during the period of growth it is possible that growth hormone which causes a retention of nitrogenous material for tissue anabolism may indirectly bring about an increased caloric intake. The increased appetite and sense of well-being resulting from administration of androgenic steroids is probably a similar mechanism. There is no evidence that growth hormone or androgenic steroids play any part in obesity. Nor would one expect it as both are concerned primarily with protein metabolism and not with the accumulation of fat.

The role of exercise, or rather the lack of it, in producing obesity is not the key factor. The patient in whom the homeostatic mechanism for maintaining constant weight is intact will reduce the caloric intake when energy output is decreased. For example, we see many patients with myxedema who do not gain weight. They are tremendously "slowed up" but their weight has remained constant because almost "automatically" their caloric intake has decreased.

Working Hypothesis

It seems reasonable to use as a working hypothesis that in the process of getting fat the homeostatic control of Caloric Intake = Energy Output = Constant Weight has been disturbed due to psychologic factors. Evidence to support this hypothesis has been obtained from the brilliant observations by Bruch (7) in children, experimental work in animals and from some personal observations in dealing with patients with obesity.

The studies by Bruch (8) of obese children and the family frame of such children have shown that typically the family is of small size. The mother is dominant and has a particularly close hold on the potentially obese child. These mothers are "overaffectionate," and express this affection by overfeeding the child. Mixed with this "overaffectionate" attitude is an underlying hostility which causes her to nag and criticize the child. However, in order to retain his affection and loyalty, food is used as bribe to keep him close and dependent. As a result the obese child grows up with a feeling of insecurity and helplessness, and food becomes his only known source of comfort and satisfaction. Bruch (7) states further that "many obese adults, like fat children, are emotionally immature, passively dependent and helpless in meeting the exigencies of life. They seek comfort in overeating in the face of failure and of frustrating experiences."

There are numerous psychologic factors which may cause a person to overeat. To the patient with obesity, food has an exaggerated value above that of its caloric value. It represents love, security and satisfaction, and provides an apparently simple means of relieving the ever present nervous tension. Freed (9) has reported that of 500 obese patients who were asked the question "When you are nervous or worried, do you eat more or less?" 375 patients replied that they ate larger meals

or ate more frequently, 95 of the remaining 130 ate
more when they were idle, bored or tired. It is well to
remember that the desire to eat in most obese patients
is an unconscious drive and is as impossible to control
in the obese patient as is diarrhea in the patient with
mucous colitis or the intake of alcohol by the chronic
alcoholic. The intensity of this drive to overeat is recognized by all of us when an intelligent patient, after
having been presented with mortality and morbidity
statistics, is unable to follow a reduction diet.

The work of Brobeck (10) in which hyperphagia and
resulting obesity may be produced in the rat by specific lesions in the hypothalamus has given us a lead that
the central nervous system is involved in the homeostatic mechanisms involved in satiety and maintenance
of constant weight. The drive to eat is so strong in these
hypothalamic operated animals that they attempt to eat
before they are completely recovered from the anesthesia. As a result food must be withheld during the recovery stage so that they do not develop aspiration
pneumonia by attempting to eat while still partly anes-
thetized. These animals if allowed access to unlimited
amounts of food become tremendously obese. Brobeck
(10) has shown very clearly that the mechanism is one
of hyperphagia, as the operated animals maintain the
same weight as the controls if their food intake is restricted to the amount consumed by the controls. It
would appear that this area in the hypothalamus is a
"link in homeostatic chain" controlling food intake.
Anand and Brobeck (11) have recently described an exciting new piece of evidence which demonstrates that
there may also be an "antiphagic" center in the hypothalamus. They have been able to produce lesions in

particular area of the hypothalamus which cause the rats to stop eating, and they will actually die if not maintained by tube feedings.

At the present time we have no recognized clinical counterpart in humans as regards specific hypothalamic lesions. The hypothalamus is now thought to be an integral part of the mechanism by which we react to stress. At least it has been shown experimentally in dogs by Hume (12) that the pituitary adrenal axis can be activated by stimulating the hypothalamus. It is interesting to speculate as to what part the hypothalamus may play in homeostasis, especially in the control of food intake. This question cannot be answered until we have better "tools to measure hypothalamic function" and more adequate cytologic and histochemical technics for studying the hypothalamus.

Our own experience with obese patients would agree with the observation of Bruch that psychologic factors may be the most important part of this complex mechanism of satiety. The following case report seems typical of many patients who are seen in every doctor's office.

CASE REPORT.   Mrs. L. T., a 35-year-old white woman, was admitted to the University of Virginia Hospital on May 24, 1951 with the chief complaint: "I can't lose weight."

A routine history revealed that she had been obese for at least twenty-five years. During this time she had consulted at least ten physicians, a chiropractor and an osteopath. She had been given a diet by each physician and would lose 10 to 15 pounds each time she was given a new diet. She would become discouraged after two months of dieting and fail to make return visits. She had been told by her last physician that she had "glandular trouble" so was referred to our service.

Physical examination was unremarkable except for a weight of 290 pounds. Routine laboratory studies were all within normal limits.

Our first two interviews with this patient were carried out on the ward, and she told us that she was happy, she enjoyed her family, and knew of no reason why she should be tense or anxious. She was then interviewed in our office on five separate occasions. The following facts from her life situation seemed important. She was the oldest of five children and stated, "I have been fat as long as I can remember. Daddy was a wonderful man but Mother ran the family." She remembers being encouraged to eat at each meal and at age 10 her father spoke about her to their guests as "his big fat baby." Mother was extremely strict and did not allow her to date or have anything to do with boys. She remembered "getting something to eat" when her mother refused to let her have a date. All decisions were made by her mother as to her activities, clothes, time of sleep and the like. She married at the age of 19 a man she had known only a short time. She became pregnant soon after marriage, but her husband demanded that she have an abortion which she did with a marked feeling of guilt. Following the abortion she gained from 135 pounds to 210 pounds in a six-month period.

The patient is constantly worried that she will hurt people, that her husband will lose his job, that "I will do something to hurt Mama." She admits that at these times when she is upset and anxious she "feels better for awhile" after she eats. As a result she often has "a little sandwich and a glass of milk" every two or three hours. It also became quite obvious as the discussions continued that she was not too much con-

cerned about her overweight. Her main concern at
this time were periods of marked depression in which
she cried a great deal and was unable to carry on her
usual household duties.

COMMENT. This patient presents many of the features
that have been emphasized as being of importance in
the development and maintenance of obesity. She is
immature, passively dependent, insecure, and almost
helpless in meeting everyday problems. Food to her has
taken on a special value in that she feels "better for
awhile" after she eats and at the present time it offers
a way to relieve anxiety and tension.

Treatment

From our working hypothesis that there is a disturbance in homeostasis due to psychologic factors comes
the approach to the obese patient.

In the experience of most of us the mere handing out
of a reduction diet has not been successful. To attempt
to alarm patients by quoting mortality and morbidity
statistics often serves to increase their anxiety and actually may cause them to eat more. It is apparent that
no patient wishes to be told that the cause of his difficulty is that he eats too much. He prefers to be told
that he has a "glandular difficulty" and receive some
"reducing pills." It must always be kept in mind that
few patients consult a physician because they are overweight. The usual procedure is for the physician to
recommend a reduction in weight rather than for the
patient to ask for help in reducing. As a matter of fact,
it has been our experience that if a patient asks for help

in weight reduction, his prognosis is far better than for the patient to whom we suggest that he lose some weight.

What constitutes a positive approach to the obese patient if one believes that psychologic factors are of major importance?

First of all, as with any problem in medicine, one must obtain an adequate history which includes his early development, relationship to parents and friends, sexual and social adjustment, reaction to stress situations, and other factors which seem important either to the physician or the patient in his personality development. As always, one should remember that this takes time and may require several office visits.

After a careful history is obtained, the next step is to try to judge the seriousness of the emotional problem. It may vary from a rather simple situational problem which may easily be handled to one in which the patient must be referred to a psychiatrist because the obesity is only one symptom of a serious emotional illness. This is usually no more difficult to decide in patients with obesity than with any other psychosomatic problem.

The main role to follow in handling these people is not to take away food unless something else is substituted which they can use to relieve their anxiety and provide security. This "something" usually consists of support, reassurance, interpretation, and an attempt to help them in the resolution of their anxieties.

The amount of food restriction depends again upon the personality of the patient. Some of the patients are rigid, ritualistic and perfectionistic and will do best if they are placed on a rigid diet. In others we have found that they do much better if they are allowed to choose their own diet and are given only reassurance and support.

We have not found thyroid or amphetamine to be of value in the long-time management. Amphetamine and similar drugs produce a temporary anorexia but the effect is usually not maintained. They have no effect on the basic psychologic difficulties and may actually produce harm if the patient becomes dependent upon them because of their stimulative properties.

Results of Treatment

The results of treatment have at best been very poor. The statistics which are available are scant and difficult to evaluate mainly because many studies cover only a short period of time. The results of short-term studies are usually good with any type of diet or diet plus anorexogenic drugs. Therefore, in evaluating the results of any treatment for obesity one must always separate the short-term from the long-range results.

Danowski and Winkler (13), reporting on the long-term treatment of obesity by diets alone, have found approximately 80 per cent failures. Adlersberg and Mayer (14) have shown that long-term results with diet alone compare favorably with those obtained with diet plus amphetamine. They do not report their data from the standpoint of total failures. Nicholson (15) has compared the results of psychotherapy without the use of calculated diets, calculated diets only, and calculated diets plus amphetamine or thyroid. Psychotherapy alone resulted in a higher percentage of successful results than the other methods studied.

From our experience we agree with Nicholson that

calculated diets by themselves are unsatisfactory and that psychotherapy, mainly in the form of reassurance and interpretation, offers the best opportunity for the reëstablishment of proper dietary habits.

Summary

1. Obesity represents a disturbance in homeostasis which may be initiated and maintained by psychologic factors.
2. Food to the obese patient has an exaggerated value above that of its caloric value.
3. For effective treatment the psychologic problems must be evaluated and their solution, if possible, substituted for food.

References

1. Bruch, Hilde: "Obesity in Childhood and Personality Development." *Am. J. Orthopsychiat.* 11: 467, 1941.
2. Newburgh, L. H.: "Obesity." *Arch. Int. Med.* 70: 1033, 1942.
3. Dublin, L. I.: "Influence of Weight on Certain Causes of Death." *Human Biol.* 2: 159, 1930.
4. Janowitz, Henry D., and Grossman, M. I.: "Gusto-Olfactory Thresholds in Relation to Appetite and Hunger Sensations." *J. Applied Physiol.* 2 (4): 217, 1949.
5. Strang, James A.: "Satiety as a Factor in Nutrition States: Observations on Mass Exchange." *Am. J. M. Sc* 221: 537, 1951.
6. Young, F. G.: "Growth Hormone and Experimental Diabetes." *J. Clin. Endocrinol.* 2 (5): 531, 1951.
7. Bruch, Hilde: "Psychological Aspects of Obesity." *Bull. New York Acad. Med.* 24 (2): 73, 1948.
8. Bruch, Hilde, and Touraine, Grace: "Obesity in Child-

hood: V. The Family Frame of Obese Children." *Psychosomatic Med.* 2 (2): 141, 1940.

9. Freed, S. Charles: "Psychic Factors in the Development and Treatment of Obesity." *J.A.M.A.* 133: 369, 1947.

10. Brobeck, J. R., Tepperman, J., and Long, C. N. H.: "Experimental Hypothalamic Hyperphagia in the Albino Rat." *Yale J. Biol. & Med.* 15: 831, 1943.

11. Anand, B., and Brobeck, J. R.: "Localization of a Feeding Center in the Hypothalamus of the Rat." *Proc. Soc. Exper. Biol. & Med.* 77: 323, 1951.

12. Hume, David M., and Wittenstein, George J.: "The Relationship of the Hypothalamus to Pituitary Adrenocortical Function." *Proc. First Clinical ACTH Conference,* edited by John R. Mote, Philadelphia, The Blakiston Company, 1950.

13. Danowski, T. S., and Winkler, A. W.: "Obesity As a Clinical Problem." *Am. J. Med. Sc.* 208: 622, 1944.

14. Adlersberg, David, and Mayer, Martin E.: "Results of Prolonged Medical Treatment of Obesity with Diet Alone, Diet and Thyroid Preparations and Diet and Amphetamine." *J. Clinical Endrocrinol.* 9 (3): 275, 1949.

15. Nicholson, William M.: "Emotional Factors in Obesity." *Am. J. M. Sc.* 211: 443, 1946.

The Addictive Drinker*

BY *Giorgio Lolli, M.D.*

Unhappiness stems from the inability of the individual to avail himself of what the environment offers, from the failure of the environment to provide what the individual needs, or, more often than not, from a combination of both. The individual for whom alcohol represents the main answer to unhappiness—the most cherished source of pleasure and the surest means of dulling pain—is usually carrying the load of deviant personality traits and fostering resentments against an increasingly hostile world. He is the addictive drinker. He is the one who, despite advancing years, remains infantile in many of his drives and in the ways he finds of satisfying them. The word "addictive" suggests the irresistible urge—and also the inevitable frustration growing out of the inadequacy of the agent used to satisfy the urge.

Alcohol, as an agent, performs its role through its immediate effect upon bodily functions, especially those

* Reprinted from *Quarterly Journal of Studies on Alcohol*, Vol. 10, 1949, New Haven, Connecticut, by courtesy of the publishers and author.

of the central nervous system. Its pharmacological properties explain the dramatic psychological changes which it produces—changes which, however short-lived and subjective, allow the individual momentarily to re-interpret himself and his environment in a more satis-factory light.

Addiction to alcohol is an expression of lopsided growth; infantile traits in one part of the personality co-exist with mature traits in another. But because of the interdependence of mental functions, those which are stunted often affect adversely the functions which have developed normally. The factors responsible for this un-even development are the same which operate in all human behavior—heredity and the early and late rela-tionships of the individual to his environment.

The etiological emphasis which is usually given to environmental factors is justified by the impressive evi-dence of childhood and adult difficulties antedating the onset of addiction. The fact that these difficulties are sometimes observed in individuals who are not ad-dicted to alcohol suggests the necessary, although minor, role played by heredity, which now can be inter-preted only as a genetic transmission of an ill-defined susceptibility to difficult life experiences. The respective impacts of heredity and environment may vary greatly from person to person, with a probable preponderance of "nurture" over "nature" in all cases.

An appraisal of "nurture" necessitates a distinction be-tween early and late experiences. Despite marked vari-ations in their respective significance, the former usually play a more important role than the latter; witness the fact that addiction to alcohol often develops in individ-uals whose adult lives have been relatively untroubled but whose problems are largely determined by the perpetuation of infantile neuroticism.

In rare cases when addiction sets in as the sequel of overwhelming new problems in individuals previously well adjusted, quiescent but unsolved childhood difficulties can almost always be uncovered. Once they are reignited, their explosive contribution to the development of addiction is just as significant as in the more numerous instances when their operation was obvious throughout.

The importance of the childhood background is confirmed by clinical experience. From this emerges a concept of alcohol addiction which maximizes the role played by the prealcoholic personality at the expense of the role played by alcohol. The quality which characterizes the addict is his "disposition" to react to the effects of alcohol in such a way that some of his anomalous and pressing needs are satisfied, albeit briefly and inadequately.

The dominant physiological connotations of this disposition are instability and a limited capacity for enduring stress. Prerequisite to normality and efficiency is the ability of the living organism to maintain a constant physiological equilibrium in the presence of conditions which might prove disturbing. This constancy is not stillness, but rather the expression of continuous, well-regulated readjustments.

The addictive drinker seems to display unsteadiness in some of his biological constants as evidenced, for instance, by wider than average fluctuations in the values of blood pressure and of blood sugar concentrations, and in the emptying time of the stomach. This unsteadiness is probably related to the low stress tolerance of the addict, to his limited ability to withstand physical and mental pain, with the consequence that unusual physiological deviations occur whenever stimuli cannot be discharged as soon as they arise.

The initial pangs of physiological hunger, for instance, are poorly tolerated by the addictive drinker and felt as keen pain earlier than by the average man. Hence the impulsive search for food and satiation, lest unbearable tension arise. Similar reactions are observed in the presence of stimuli arising within (as urination, evacuation) or without the organism. These deviant physiological regulations may be determined, in part, by dysfunctions of the pituitary-adrenal cortex system whose thorough investigation in addictive drinkers is long overdue.

More obvious than the physiological, however, are the psychological connotations of the prealcoholic personality. The latter seem to be caused to a great extent by anomalous family constellations which created serious difficulties in childhood. The fixations and regressions growing out of such experiences can be interpreted by means of widely accepted principles of dynamic psychology which apply to both normal and deviant mental development.

The critical phases of human life—early infancy included—are highlighted by pleasurable and painful experiences. A normal proportion of both generally results in a satisfactory adult adjustment. An excess of either kind, however, tends to halt the individual at that particular phase of his emotional development at which the excess is felt—as though in one case he hated to relinquish what was so gratifying, or in the other case he hoped eventually to discover the gratifications thus far denied to him (fixation).

He who pauses thus along the road may or may not be able to recover from the experience and to reach an adequate adjustment to adult life. In any event he is more susceptible than the average person to the impact of later difficulties. He may react to these just as he did during that earlier period of his life when pleasure or pain was unusually predominant (regression).

The addictive drinker, as has been noted, is an impulsive person who faces great difficulty in resisting his instinctual drives. Impulsiveness dominated his psychological as well as physiological behavior long before he first resorted to alcohol—indeed, throughout his life—and is only a perpetuation of behavior patterns which are normal in the infant. A baby experiences hunger as unbearable tension and at the same time as a dreadful threat to his existence. The acuity of his discomfort motivates the "impulsive" (and, in him, entirely normal) search for satiation, which for him represents supreme pleasure inextricably united with the feeling of unchallenged security.

With sharp contrasts between states of pain and pleasure, with swift, reversible shifts from one to the other, physiological and psychological phenomena are inseparable in the life of the infant. He experiences that unity of body and mind from which the maturing individual progressively and painfully disengages himself as a result of the eversharpening differentiations of growth.

Unlike the well-adjusted adult, the addictive drinker is still chained to this unity when he suffers from the intolerable pressure of his unconscious (and, to a certain extent, conscious) longings for physical warmth, pleasurable skin sensations, maternal coddling, liquid and warm filling of his stomach. For him these are undifferentiated from longings for security, assurance, self-respect, independence, omnipotence, and total oblivion. In contrast to the infant, the addictive drinker is denied in real life the experience of undifferentiated pleasure for which he is hopelessly yearning as a compensation for his unblended pleasure of body and mind, and at the same time to satisfy most of his specific longings, marks the beginning of addiction. The satisfaction, however, is temporary and incomplete. Because of its chemical action on the central nervous system, with related psychological repercussions, alcohol only magnifies the addict's infantile longings, rendering attempts at their gratification increasingly unsuccessful.

Thus the life of the addictive drinker is governed by a vicious circle: real failures are compensated for by illusory alcoholic "successes." If not broken, this circle ultimately leads to alternations of ever-lengthening euphoric stupors and ever-shortening periods of painful awareness of reality. As the addiction progresses, these alternations resemble more and more the rhythm of hunger and sleep at the very dawn of the infant's life until they are concluded by the irreversible stillness of death.

The persistence of infantile psychological traits is, of course, common to all human beings in varying degrees, contributing in an exaggerated form to the maladjusted behavior of many a neurotic who will never become an addict. What characterizes the addictive drinker is not the survival of these drives but rather their peculiar grouping, their intensity (which is sustained and even aggravated by alcohol itself), and—preëminently—the fact that alcohol satisfies these strivings in a *unitary* way.

Milk, which quenches the infant's thirst, satisfies his

hunger, gives him the security and power of mother's love, and eventually leads to the oblivion of sleep, causes predominantly alimentary reactions in the adult and satisfies predominantly physiological needs. In the irrationally controlled life of the infant, milk and the emotional feeling attached to it are one and the same thing; but in the life of reason of the ego-governed adult the reality of an object is quite distinct from its symbolic significance: milk mainly means milk, not supreme pleasure or eternal glory. Not even for the individual with excessively persistent infantile strivings do the psychological outweigh the physiological connotations. In the same way the psychological needs of the reality-adjusted adult are mainly satisfied by psychological means whose physiological overtones are minor though present occasionally. Honors which may come to him through achievement, power stemming from financial success, the love of another individual, the consolations of religion—these cannot supply pleasurable skin sensations or the soothing feeling of an adequately replenished bowel.

The physiological and psychological realms begin to merge when the adult bears the lineaments of an addictive drinker. Then some of his tensions no longer respond to purely psychological or purely physiological gratification. It is alcohol alone which can facilitate a simultaneous psycho-physiological fulfillment of his innermost urges. Under its influence the addictive drinker first disregards and finally denies the reality of the world he lives in. Under its influence he eventually unmasks and upholds the reality of his unconscious so that he himself becomes witness to the dialectical identity of opposite drives: dependence, independence; love, hate; self-depreciation, self-aggrandizement.

To unmask and to uphold the reality of his unconscious versus the reality of the world in which he
lives means that the unitary fulfillment of his infantile
promptings is reached through the detour of an alcohol-
induced severe mental disorder—a real, though brief,
psychosis. This fulfillment, found in the episode of acute
intoxication, is seldom consciously sought in the prein-
toxication period. The causes precipitating a drinking
episode are more likely to be derivative: perhaps conflicts with the environment arising from primitive impulses, physiological deviations which are sources of
pain, or any neurotic reaction pattern (unrelated to
addiction) which might lead to complications with the
environment. In short, either mental or physical discomfort, rather than addictive conflicts themselves, usually
impels the desire for alcohol, for its anesthetic more
than for its euphoric properties. This assertion is valid
if by discomfort we mean any sudden or slow accumulation of tension. The latter is early felt as pain by the
addict because of his limited capacity for enduring
stress.

Seldom does the addictive drinker plan a long spree.
Like any other individual he decides to have a drink or
two and, surprisingly enough, is sometimes able to stop
there, although for him occasions of controlled drinking
are infrequent. The addictive drinker can stop only if
the amount of alcohol ingested and the conditions under
which it is taken (full stomach, fractioned ingestion)
do not allow the alcohol concentration in his blood
to reach the minimum level requisite for psycho-
physiological unity; or, in rare instances, if repressions
are operating to such an extent that the urge for such
unity goes unfelt. In either case the margin of safety is
so narrow that inevitably the controlled phase ter-

minates in new episodes of acute intoxication. The explosiveness of the situation is enhanced by the fact that the controlled phase magnifies the addictive drinker's grandiose confidence, encourages him to test himself anew against increasing amounts of alcohol, until the relapse occurs.

If addiction is a striving for psychosomatic unity, and if this striving is fulfilled in alcohol, it is understandable why the nonaddictive drinker is able to stop with a moderate amount of alcohol, or rather is hardly ever able to ingest an immoderate amount. More often than not, the infantile type of gratification offered by immoderate amounts of alcohol has no appeal for the well-adjusted or for the nonaddictive neurotic person. Even if he occasionally enjoys this type of regression, the pleasure involved is brief and constantly threatened by those distortions of external and internal perceptions which the reality-adjusted adult abhors. The adequate individual interrupts his drinking in good time because its disadvantages tip the scale. In the addictive drinker, however, disadvantages do not outweigh advantages until much later.

Having once achieved a state of psychosomatic unity, usually early in the spree, the addict's personality favors his clinging to this infantile regression, unlike the well-adjusted individual who tends to pull out of it once the stress is over. Maturity does not mean denial to the individual of infantile gratification, but rather the ability not to over-indulge, so that temporary and normal retreats can be followed by further advances.

The addict's rigidity fosters a continuing retreat. His goal is to maintain his blood alcohol concentration at a point where this unity will not be disturbed—a well-nigh impossible task. In most episodes of acute intoxication the psychosomatic unity is lost and regained countless times. Yet this elusive pleasure is still the crucial phase of the drinking pattern, the one that makes for its perpetuation. The end of a spree does not come until the unity is broken beyond repair, whether by dwindling supplies of liquor or serious miscalculation of the amount needed.

The psychological phase of this unity is characterized by the paradoxical satisfaction of contradictory emotions which, against the rules of reason, are tolerated and enjoyed despite—perhaps because of—diametrically opposite connotations. For example, the addictive drinker, who is torn between his longings for passive dependence and equally strong cravings for rebellious independence, cannot in his sober moments satisfy either drive without experiencing a frustrating and painful magnification of its opposite. But with the optimal blood alcohol concentration he can simultaneously gratify both and be witness to the fact that in a fleeting phase of his intoxication opposites are the same, just as they are all the time in one's unconscious life.

It thus appears that in this pleasurable, if short and illusory, synthesis of opposite pairs of emotions, *combined with physiological gratification*, is the basic difference between addictive and nonaddictive drinkers. In the example of the conflict between dependent versus independent drives, for instance, the peculiarity is not its presence (shared by all human beings), nor its abnormal pressure (shared by many nonaddictive neurotics), but rather the way it is unrealistically solved by means of alcohol. To hurt and to be hurt, to be secure and to be in danger, to be great and to be meek, to be generous and to be stingy, to reject and to be rejected, to be masculine and to be feminine, to be a child and to be an adult—all these and other pairs of opposites, unreconciled in sobriety, contributing to the mounting tension of the addict, find expression and gratification in one phase of intoxication.

The fleeting instants of unified and unadulterated pleasure are overshadowed during the episode of intoxication by longer phases when pain predominates and the over-all simplification of mental processes induced by alcohol is most obvious. The highest brain centers, whose normal operation underlies the intricacies of adult mental life, are the first to be affected by alcohol; then, with mounting concentration in the blood, its sedative action spreads downward to progressively lower nervous centers. As a result of this chemically induced, impermanent return to a simpler functioning of the central nervous system, the intoxicated person is enabled to interpret himself and his world with a clarity which, although false, is often more appealing than the real complications of sobriety. The bold relief of primitive drives, keenly felt inside and freely expressed outside, takes the place of subtleties and differentiations, so that the issues of man with himself and his environment become clear-cut.

Even more than in the solitary drinker this process of simplification is obvious in the actions and reactions of groups of drinkers, addictive or otherwise. Their attitudes and patterns of behavior bear striking resemblance to those observed in groups of children—in the elementary emotions displayed, in extremes of friendliness and hostility, in monotonous repetitions, and in the fact that the game is never up until exhaustion sets in or forces outside the group intervene.

In this sense alcohol is a real social lubricant whose operation in some ways resembles the socializing effects of art.

The free expression of elementary—and often objectionable—emotions shared by individuals drinking in groups invites mutual repulsion but also, and more often, mutual understandings which would be difficult to achieve when sober (and hence more complex) personalities meet. Underlying this process is an alcohol-induced suspension of those critical functions with which the individual discriminates between reality and fantasy, guilty and guiltless behavior.

In art also—especially tragedy—there is a communion of emotions shared by the artist and his audience. All those participating, however, are aware of the unreality of the experience. Knowing that they live momentarily in a world of fantasy, they can tolerate, share, release guilt-laden emotions. The plots of Oedipus or Hamlet will be eternally "socializing" because they make mankind aware of one basic truth, the universality of guilt.

Alike in their ability to release shared emotions, art experiences and intoxication are nevertheless poles apart. The distinction between reality and fantasy is upheld in art, denied in intoxication. And art boldly faces morality; "guiltless," or rather amoral, the opaque emotional release in intoxication is infinitely removed from the elevating catharsis of great art.

Behavior during the non-unitary phases of intoxication, although tending always toward a simpler, more primitive level, varies greatly because of the endless possibilities resulting from the interaction of at least three factors: the amount of alcohol acting on the central nervous system, the impact of the environment during intoxication, and the addict's total personality which affects his reactions to alcohol. This last factor, which largely determines the first two, casts light on the apparent paradox of addiction: the individual resorts to alcohol because of his nonaddictive rather than his addictive traits. The latter perpetuate but do not precipitate the drinking episode.

There is practically no case of alcohol addiction isolated from other neurotic disorders or body illnesses. Alcohol addiction can be set apart from an intricate personality frame for descriptive purposes only and because an understanding of what is and what is not addictive is prerequisite to prognosis and treatment. This knowledge permits an evaluation, in a given patient, of how addictive and other neurotic reaction patterns interact. The fact that deviations other than addiction usually operate in the direction of precipitating or prolonging an addictive pattern of drinking has led to the dubious conclusion that excessive and uncontrolled drinking may be only the "symptom" of an unspecific variety of mental and physical deviations, from latent homosexuality to manic-depressive disorders, from so-called spontaneous hypoglycemia to the hormonal disorders of menopause.

If the definition of a symptom as "a phenomenon which arises from and accompanies a particular disease or disorder and serves as an indication of it," * is accepted, the conclusion emerges that the condition dealt with is addiction itself, whose physiognomy colors the individual's sobriety as well as his drinking behavior with "addictive" traits. Moreover, what distinguishes addictive drinking from most symptoms is the fact that,

* The American College Dictionary, Random House, New York.

308 AN OUTLINE OF ABNORMAL PSYCHOLOGY

although indicating an underlying disorder, the "symptom" in this case magnifies the disorder which leads, in turn, to a magnification of the "symptom."

That conditions other than addiction are not the ultimate cause of uncontrolled drinking, but only factors which precipitate or perpetuate it, can be illustrated. There is little doubt, for example, that the incidence of latent homosexual trends is high in addictive drinkers of both sexes and that what is latent in sobriety becomes, in many instances, patent in intoxication. The fact that an addictive pattern of drinking may be precipitated by mounting homosexual tensions and that the tensions, in turn, can be enhanced by drinking, contributing thus to its perpetuation, can hardly be challenged. This fact does not explain, however, why so many individuals suffering from homosexual anxieties do not resort to alcohol or are controlled drinkers. Only those homosexuals who exhibit addictive traits resort to an addictive pattern of drinking. Evidence that successful therapy aimed mostly at the homosexual anxieties may lead to an interruption of the drinking pattern proves only that to free emotional energies which were tied to the homosexual conflicts makes those energies available again for holding in check the addictive urge to drink.

In the field of physiopathology it has been observed that a limited number of women develop an addictive pattern of drinking after the onset of menopause. The link between hormonal changes, depression, and the addictive use of alcohol as a weapon against depression, is clear. Here again medication combined with psychotherapy aiming mostly at the menopausal syndrome may lead to sobriety. Here again it is noteworthy that only a few women in the throes of a menopausal upheaval resort to alcohol in an addictive way—only those whose histories have betrayed addictive-impulsive traits. In these cases a stormy menopause precipitates but does not cause the addiction, which otherwise might not have developed. Once brought into operation, however, the addiction unfavorably affects the menopausal syndrome. The same principles apply to a variety of disorders whose enumeration would cover the whole field of medicine with all its branches.

Although alike in the stage of unitary pleasure, the latent homosexual and the menopausal woman differ widely during other phases of intoxication. Alcohol offers to the former the possibility of expressing his anomalous drives without guilt; to the latter it gives a rosier vision of the present and the future. Infinite variations in the physiognomy, length, depth and frequency of the episodes of intoxication correspond to the infinite shades of human personality. The hysterical girl for whom sex is "guilt" in sobriety can turn promiscuous when intoxicated, while the girl who is promiscuous in sobriety, and so "suffers" in order to atone for her ill-repressed aggression, may reject and beat the male when intoxicated, thus fulfilling some of her deepest desires. Similar examples could be multiplied; they would only corroborate the fact that alcohol tips the emotional balance of the individual in directions favoring the expression of drives which are more or less controlled during sobriety. The nature and pressure of these drives vary from person to person and at different times in a given individual. These variations, together with variations in the amount of alcohol ingested and in the reactions of the environment, account for the physiognomy of the episode of intoxication.

Alcohol, then, favors a return of the repressed. A study

of the individual when intoxicated gives clues to a better understanding of his sober personality. It is this return of the repressed, the release of primitive drives, which sets the addictive drinker at odds with the world. If the workings of civilization consist in taming the beast in man, the workings of addictive drinking are characterized by the reverse process with resulting asocial or antisocial behavior.

More is unknown than is known about the addictive drinker. What is already known breeds a more tolerant attitude toward him and favors a shift of attention from his objectionable deeds to those unfortunate experiences that determined them. The moral issue is not denied but reinterpreted in the light of medical, psychiatric and sociological facts. This reinterpretation helps considerably in efforts to free the addict from his ties to alcohol.

Because the addictive drinker cannot revert to controlled drinking, his goal must be permanent abstinence; this is prerequisite to and at the same time the outcome of favorable changes within the individual and in his relations to his environment. While therapeutic successes are highly rewarding, failures should not be considered fruitless efforts. They still add to the moral values of a civilized society earnestly striving for improvement.

Psychological Factors
in Epilepsy*

BY *Cary Suter, M.D.*

I. Introduction

Since ancient times psychological and religious factors have often been accorded a large or even a supreme

* From *Neuropsychiatry*, Vol. 3, No. 3. By courtesy of the author and publishers.

place as a cause of epilepsy. Progress in the understanding and treatment of epilepsy has been largely a matter of disproving these psychological or religious theories and proving that epilepsy is a symptom of an organic disorder. As early as 400 B.C. Hippocrates wrote a book to disprove the then current idea that epilepsy was due to possession by either a god or a demon. He contended that epilepsy was no more divine than other diseases and that it must not be treated by magic but by diet and drugs.[1] His writings were either not known or not accepted and it was not until the latter part of the nineteenth century, through the writings and teachings of Hughlings Jackson,[2] that an organic theory of epilepsy really began to gain wide acceptance. Only during the past twenty years has absolute proof of the organic or physiological cause of epilepsy been made possible by the perfection and use of the electroencephalograph.

Even now it is not unusual to see articles attributing epilepsy to various psychic causes such as an unconscious desire to return to the womb, repressed aggression or sexual urges, or passive oral dependency. It is characteristic of such reports that EEG findings are not presented in detail. As recently as 1950 one such article[3] stated that "EEG tracings show no correlation with the absence or presence of convulsive disorders," a statement which is completely contrary to fact. Concerning such opinions about the psychic etiology and

[1] *The Falling Sickness,* by Owsei Temkin, M.D. The Johns Hopkins Press, 1945.
[2] *Selected Writings of John Hughlings Jackson,* ed. J. Taylor. 2 Vols. London: Hodder and Stoughton, 1931–1932.
[3] "Psychodynamic Aspects of Epilepsy" by Gert Heibrunn. *The Psychoanalytic Quarterly,* 19: 145–157, 1950 (No. 2).

treatment of epilepsy, Lennox,[4] one of the most outstanding authorities in the field, recently said, "We believe this view is erroneous and that the practice of psychoanalysis, sans medicine, for the person with uncomplicated epilepsy is malpractice."

Nevertheless there are many psychological factors which must be considered in any complete study of epilepsy or more correctly in the complete study and treatment of the person who suffers from epilepsy. Lest these factors be made to seem more important than they are it seems best to first consider the question—what is epilepsy?

II. What is Epilepsy?

The word epilepsy is Greek and means "a seizure." If we make a habit of using the terms seizure or seizure state we can better escape the strictures which the past connotations of the word epilepsy impose upon our thinking.

Epilepsy (a seizure) is a symptom and not a disease. It is a symptom of disturbed or pathological brain cell metabolism. It is always associated with an abnormal electrical discharge. This abnormal discharge tends to occur in bursts and hence epilepsy has been defined as "a paroxysmal cerebral dysrhythmia."[5] Clinical seizures do not necessarily, or even often, accompany each abnormal burst but some electrical abnormality does ac-

[4] "The Sociopsychological Treatment of Epilepsy," by W. G. Lennox and C. H. Markham. *J. A. M. A.*, 152: 1690–1694, August 29, 1953.
[5] "Epilepsy, a paroxysmal cerebral dysrhythmia," by F. A. Gibbs, E. L. Gibbs, and W. G. Lennox. *Brain*, 60: 377–388, 1937.

company every seizure. These bursts may occur almost continuously or they may occur hours or even weeks apart. Therefore while some abnormalities usually show up during the course of an electroencephalographic (EEG) tracing (30 minutes to 1 hour) on a person subject to seizures, it is possible to obtain repeated normal EEGs on a person who is known to have typical seizures. If, however, while an EEG tracing is being made a patient has a spell or attack and no electrical abnormality occurs then that person is most likely suffering from hysteria or some other condition and not epilepsy.

Since a seizure is a symptom it may take on a great variety of forms according to the location and extent of the brain tissue involved and the type, strength, and spread of the electrical abnormality produced. Sudden loss of consciousness with or without convulsive or automatic movements is the most characteristic manifestation of a seizure. However, abdominal pain, bright lights before the eyes, a strong unpleasant odor, brief loss of speech, or jerking or numbness in a hand may represent a focal type of seizure. If such experiences as these precede a more severe seizure they are referred to as an aura and constitute an important clue as to the location from which the seizure discharge begins.[6]

The nature of the disturbed brain metabolism which results in an abnormal electrical discharge and at times in a seizure is not yet known. It seems certain, however, that a great many different agents or conditions can produce this abnormal state and it seems likely that several factors usually combine to produce a seizure

[6] *Epilepsy and the Functional Anatomy of the Human Brain,* Wilder Penfield and Herbert Jasper, Little, Brown and Company, 1954.

state in any one individual. The most common "causes"
of seizures are listed below.

1. Hereditary tendency.

2. Congenital deformity or disorder.

3. Birth trauma.
   a. prolonged or difficulty delivery.
   b. intracranial hemorrhage.
   c. anoxia.

4. Head trauma.
   a. concussion.
   b. penetrating wounds of the brain.

5. Toxins and drugs.
   a. alcohol.
   b. uremia.
   c. metrazol.
   d. high fever.
   e. hypoglycemia, etc.

6. Infection.
   a. encephalitis.
   b. meningitis.
   c. brain abscess.
   d. syphilis.

7. Vascular.
   a. aneurysms.
   b. thrombosis.
   c. hemorrhage.
   d. vasospasm.

8. Tumors.

In the past, cases of epilepsy have usually been classified as secondary or as idiopathic. "Idiopathic epilepsy" was considered a disease entity associated with various stigmata of physical and mental degeneracy and was thought to be largely inherited. With the use of the EEG many cases of "idiopathic epilepsy" were shown to be due to focal lesions, but a number remained which showed generalized dysrhythmia, and this was taken as evidence of the all-pervasive nature of the disorder. Studies by Jasper [7] have indicated, however, that focal stimulation of the diencephalon can cause generalized cerebral dysrhythmia and it now seems possible that "idiopathic" seizures are due to focal disturbance in the upper brain stem which may be caused by a variety of factors, only one of which is heredity. As cases of epilepsy are investigated more thoroughly with better histories, better EEGs and other studies, less and less have to be labeled "idiopathic" and it may be that we can soon dispense with this term altogether.

For practical purposes seizures can best be classified on the basis of the clinical picture presented. The main clinical types of seizures are as follows:

GRAND MAL. A grand mal seizure consists primarily of a generalized convulsion associated with unconsciousness. The seizure is preceded by an aura in about 30 per cent of cases. Often there is a sudden turning of the head to one side, at times a cry, and then the person falls. A tonic and then tonic-clonic contraction of the muscles follows which usually lasts only one to three minutes, but which may be repeated several times. The

[7] Jasper, H. H., and Droogleever-Fortuyn, J., "Experimental studies on the functional anatomy of petit mal epilepsy." *A. Res. Nerv. and Ment. Dis. Proc.*, 26: 272–298. 1947.

person often bites his tongue. Cyanosis develops due to the absent or irregular breathing and saliva may flow from the mouth due to the inability to swallow. After the convulsion the person can usually be aroused in a few minutes but often passes into a more or less natural sleep for 20 minutes to an hour. After this most persons can return to their usual work or schooling that same day.

Grand mal seizures occur at one time or another in a large percentage of persons with a seizure state and are the only form of seizure in about 45 per cent. When the person has only grand mal seizures the interseizure EEG is often normal and complete control of seizures by anticonvulsive drugs is usually possible.

PETIT MAL. The typical petit mal seizure lasts only a few seconds and consists primarily of a loss of consciousness. This is best decribed as a "stop and stare" after which the patient continues whatever he was doing or saying as if nothing had happened. The lapse of consciousness may be longer and may be associated with some movements of the face and even at times the hands. In a few cases there is a brief loss of muscular tone so that the person falls or almost falls suddenly but regains his posture just as suddenly. These are called *akinetic* seizures.

In general petit mal seizures begin early in life (4 to 8 years) and decrease with age. When they occur alone in typical form they are almost invariably associated with EEG changes consisting of bursts of three per second spike and dome waves but there is seldom any evidence of severe brain damage or mental change. When associated with other forms of seizures the picture is not so clear, the prognosis for control or sponta‑

neous recovery is worse, and evidence of organic brain damage is more frequent.

Decreased CO_2 content of the blood, alcalosis and hypoglycemia tend to bring on the attacks while acidosis seems to protect against them. Actually petit mal seizures alone are not very common and only make up 8 to 10 per cent of cases with seizures. Confusion as to the incidence of petit mal exists because many observers call any brief or mild seizure petit mal when more exact observation and EEG records prove these to be psychomotor or cortical focal seizures of some kind.

PSYCHOMOTOR SEIZURES. This group covers a great variety of forms but characteristically consists of a seizure in which a person while unconscious or in a trance-like state carries out some fairly complicated behavior. The person may undress, may seek to climb upon a table or chair, may seem frightened and run or seek to hide, or may rummage through his pockets or about the room as if he had lost something. If interfered with he may become violent and destructive. In some cases the seizures consist mainly of peculiar dreamlike psychic states with little or no motor activity. Psychomotor behavior usually occurs alone but may precede or follow a generalized convulsion. In any one person the same or a similar pattern of behavior is repeated with each seizure.

Psychomotor seizures often present difficult diagnostic problems and are often mistaken for psychotic, psychoneurotic and at times even criminal behavior. In general, control of psychomotor seizures by drugs has been less effective than other types of seizures and in many ways this is often the most difficult type of seizure problem the physician encounters.

Many persons with psychomotor seizures show a typical focus on the EEG in the region of the anterior temporal lobe.[8] This shows up in more cases if the EEG is done while the patient is asleep. Penfield and his associates[9] have demonstrated various kinds of lesions in the anterior temporal lobe at operation and in a number of individuals removal of this portion of the brain has resulted in marked improvement or even complete cure. Beginning in 1953 focal surgery for temporal lobe seizures is being made the subject of extensive study at the new Clinical Center of the National Institutes of Health at Bethesda, Maryland, and much more should be learned about psychomotor seizures by the operations and other investigation being carried on there.

JACKSONIAN (FOCAL MOTOR CORTICAL SEIZURE). This is the entity first described by Hughlings Jackson[2] and consists of a motor seizure involving first one part of one side of the body (usually the face or arm) and then spreading to the entire side and often to the other side and thus ending in a generalized convulsion. The spread of the seizure represents the spread of abnormal electrical discharge over the motor cortex and follows the known representation of motor control in this area. Consciousness is not usually lost unless the seizure becomes generalized and speech may or may not be involved depending on the extent of the seizure and whether or not it begins in the side of the brain which controls speech.

SENSORY SEIZURE (FOCAL CORTICAL SENSORY SEIZURE). Just as a focus in the motor cortex can result in a motor

[8] Gibbs, E. L., Gibbs, F. A., and Fuster, B. "Psychomotor epilepsy." *Arch. Neurol. and Psychiat.*, 60: 331–339, 1948.
[9] Penfield, W., and Flanigin, H. "Surgical therapy of temporal lobe seizures." *Arch. Neurol. and Psychiat.*, 64: 491–500, 1950.

seizure, so a focus in the sensory areas can give rise to sensory seizures alone. These often spread and result in loss of consciousness and motor seizures as well. The most typical sensory seizure is the so-called "uncinate fit" characterized by the subjective experiencing of a very strong unpleasant odor.

MYOCLONIC SEIZURES.   This condition consists of frequent sudden jerkings of the muscles of the face and extremities usually without loss of consciousness. It is rather rare and is thought to be due to a degenerative lesion in the brain stem.

STATUS EPILEPTICUS.   This is the name given to the state where a person is having one seizure after another so that there is little or no clear interval between. This usually refers to grand mal type seizures and represents a medical emergency.

III. Psychological Factors in Epilepsy

1. Personality

Many writers, [10, 11, 12] especially before the present-day perfection of the electroencephalogram and psychological tests, have contended that persons with epilepsy have a definite personality type. Different authors list different traits as being characteristic of "the epileptic"

[10] Clark, L. P. "A personality study of the epileptic constitution." Amer. J. Med. Sci., 148: 729–738, 1914.
[11] Doolittle, G. J. "The epileptic personality." Psychiat. Quart., 6: 89–96, 1932.
[12] Sjobring, Henrik—as quoted by Alstrom, C. H., in "A study of epilepsy." Acta Psychiatrica et Neurologica. Supp., 63, 1950.

but they all agree in one respect; all the traits listed are undesirable. The traits most often mentioned are egocentricity, emotional poverty, rigidity, supersensitiveness, irritability, stubbornness, hostility, aggressiveness, paranoid tendencies, and stereotyped manners and speech. Traits listed by one writer are often just the opposite extreme of those given by another. Stauder[13] even claims that there is a typical Rorschach test response found in epileptics consisting primarily of perseveration but also including retardation, stickiness, circumstantiality, poverty of content in thinking, and evidence of explosiveness and irritability in action. He admits the same responses are found in normal persons on large doses of phenobarbital. As Harrower-Erickson[14] has aptly pointed out, Stauder's patients were of the severe institutionalized type and his findings are typical of severe organic brain damage whether associated with seizures or not.

Just like Stauder's Rorschach studies most of the other studies which support the idea of an "epileptic personality" were done on groups of institutionalized patients and while they may reflect the effect of institutionalization and of severe brain damage they are certainly not representative of the 95 per cent of persons with seizures who are not in institutions. More recent studies[14, 15], many of which were done on patients seen in the office or clinic have largely disproved the whole idea of

[13] Stauder, K. H. *Konstitution und Wesenänderung der Epileptiker*. Georg Thieme, Leipzig, 1939.
[14] Harrower-Erickson, M. R. "Psychological studies of patients with epileptic seizures." In Penfield and Erickson, T. C. *Epilepsy and cerebral localization*, pp. 546–574. Springfield, Ill., Thomas, 1941.
[15] Kogan, K. L. "The personality reaction pattern of children with epilepsy, with special reference to the Rorschach method." *Assoc. for Research in Nerv. and Ment. Dis.*, 26: 616–630, 1947.

a typical personality type in epilepsy. Lennox[16] is of the opinion that a majority of patients with seizures show no more peculiarity of personality than any other sample of the general population. Where changes in personality exist he feels they are most often due to associated brain damage, the action of drugs, the effects of ostracism, or to mental deterioration. Harrower-Erickson[14] both from clinical observation and the results of Rorschach and other psychological tests concludes that no typical "epileptic personality" exists. From his intensive study of 897 patients in Sweden, Alstrom[17] concludes that no typical personality type exists but rather that there are as many personality types as patients. Taking the particular trait of "perseveration and adhesiveness of thoughts and affect" which is supposed to be typical of idiopathic epilepsy, he found that it occurred most often in that group of patients with seizures due to a known or suspected cause (usually head trauma) and could not be found in any large number of patients with "idiopathic epilepsy."

Gibbs and Gibbs[18] state that the "epileptic personality" is rare in persons with petit mal or ground mal seizures but common in those with psychomotor seizures. Actually what their statistics show is that 40 to 50 per cent of persons with psychomotor seizures have some form of psychiatric disturbance of which they list 40 varieties but not a typical personality. The same statistics show that only about 10 per cent of patients with

[16] Lennox, W. G. *Seizure States in Personality and the Behavior Disorders*, Vol. II, pp. 938–967. J. McV. Hunt, Ed. The Ronald Press, New York, 1944.

[17] Alstrom, C. H. "A study of epilepsy in its clinical, social and genetic aspects." *Acta Psychiatrica et Neurologica. Supp.*, 63, 1950.

[18] Gibbs, F. A., and Gibbs, E. L. *Atlas of Electroencephalography*, Vol. II. Addison Wesley Press, Inc., Cambridge, Mass., 1952.

all other forms of seizures have any of these psychiatric disturbances.

When one considers the multiplicity of seizure patterns and the many different causes of seizure states it should be obvious that logically no such entity as an epileptic personality can exist. This has been confirmed by the author's experience with a large group of patients seen in the office and clinic. Many of these patients have personality changes and emotional problems but this is true of any segment of the population if it is subjected to careful scrutiny. Furthermore, the personality problems of patients with seizures are more often due to the fear, superstition, feelings of guilt, over-protection and other products of misinformation by which their communities and families surround them than to any other cause. When these conditions are changed as they often can be by simple factual education, the particular personality reaction often disappears.

There are some patients in which personality and intellectual changes seem directly related to known brain damage according to its location and extent. There are also patients in which unusual behavior seems to actually be a seizure and others in which particular anticonvulsive drugs produce undesirable changes in behavior or mood.

Something should also be said about the good and admirable personality traits seen in many persons with seizures. For some reason children with petit mal seizures alone often seem unusually bright intellectually and of pleasant personal appearance. Most patients with seizures bear their difficulty with unusual courage. Very few of them become seriously depressed. Most persons with seizures are anxious to work and do work well if given the opportunity. Far from being dull and without imagination or all alike, patients with seizures as much as any group (unless it be psychiatric problems) present a varied cross-section of interests, moods, philosophies of life, and ways of reaction to life's vicissitudes.

2. Intelligence

It is one of the tragedies of the person's life who develops seizures that his family and associates often believe this means that his intelligence either has been or will be seriously impaired. This is not true. Naturally if a person suffers severe brain damage as a child mental retardation often results and the same person may have seizures as another symptom of this brain damage. In cases of seizures with mild brain damage and in those where no evidence of brain damage exists there is little indication that seizures themselves affect intelligence unless they are unusually frequent and severe. Here again studies on institutional populations done in the past have been quoted to show that persons with seizures have low intelligence.

In 1941 Lennox[19] in a study of 1640 clinic and private patients found 67 per cent mentally normal, 23 per cent slightly subnormal, 9 per cent deteriorated, and 1 per cent markedly deteriorated.

Collins and Lennox[20] however, in a study of 300 private office patients reported in 1947, found that this group had better than average intelligence. The average I. Q. for this group was 109. The I. Q. of those with

[19] Lennox, W. G. *Science and Seizures*, Harper, New York, 1941
[20] Collins, A. L., and Lennox, W. G. "The Intelligence of 300 private epileptic patients." *Assoc. for Research in Nerv. and Ment. Dis.*, 26, pp. 586–603, 1947.

known brain damage was 10 points lower than those with no evidence of damage. Patients with petit mal showed the highest I. Q. while those with both grand mal and psychomotor showed the lowest. The highest I. Q.s also were found in those with little or no EEG abnormalities between seizures. If the seizures had begun very early in life there was less chance of normal intelligence.

This indicates that intelligence is more closely related to brain damage than to the presence or frequency of seizures.

One very interesting condition is seen in children who appear to be very much retarded, at times not even speaking or walking. A few such children have been found to be having almost continuous seizure discharges of the petit mal type and if these are suppressed by anticonvulsive medicine the child may then go on and develop normally or nearly so. This indicates that at least one EEG record is justified on any child with mental retardation.

Intelligence tests must be given with care because many patients lack some formal schooling and many of them are sensitive about having missed school. For these reasons test scores often seem lower than the clinical picture and actual performance indicate.

3. Behavior Disorders

Rather severe behavior disorders are often seen in children following encephalitis and, at times, after head trauma. Overactive, impulsive, and often destructive behavior is the usual picture. Even though intelligence may remain normal the short attention span makes

learning difficult. Some of these children also have seizures and most of them have a definitely abnormal
electroencephalogram. Often a seizure will be the first
evidence that organic factors, in addition to emotional
factors, are present. This group of patients presents good
proof that difficulties in behavior in epileptics are more
directly correlated with the type and extent of brain
damage than with the seizure state and many of the
worst behavior problems have few seizures or none at
all.

In these children the proof of organic as well as emotional factors will help in planning their treatment. This
proof is best obtained from the EEG tracings and from
psychological tests for organicity.

Medication with anticonvulsive drugs will result in a
definite change for the better in behavior in some
cases. In general dilantin or one of the stimulants such
as dexedrine or benzedrine will give the best results.
Barbiturates often make the behavior worse though
now and then phenobarbital is very effective.

These cases with fairly severe brain damage, behavior
disorder, and seizures demand a multi-disciplined approach consisting of psychological tests, psychotherapy
with child and parents, special schooling, and medical
evaluation and management of drug therapy.

A separate group of behavior disorders such as
enuresis, sleepwalking, spells of extreme irritability or
anger, or periods of inattentiveness, which occur only
as episodes in an otherwise normal child may be actual
seizures and deserve the benefit of consultation with a
neurologist, one electroencephalogram and often a
therapeutic trial on anticonvulsive drugs, as well as
psychiatric evaluation.

4. Hysteria

The misdiagnosis of a seizure state as hysteria or psychoneurosis is a common error made by physicians and laymen alike. Also the use of the term "hysterical seizures" contradicts itself. There is no evidence that the author can find to support the idea that hysteria can cause real seizures. A person either has hysterical attacks or he has seizures, or has both as separate conditions. The real proof comes from the electroencephalogram though this may be difficult to obtain. If an attack can be observed or produced while the EEG is being recorded and no EEG change occurs, then the condition is almost certainly not a seizure. With a seizure some electrical abnormality will result and with up-to-date machines they can usually be recorded.

Hysterical attacks can usually be differentiated from seizures on a clinical basis alone. The person with hysteria seldom if ever bites his tongue, seldom has attacks during sleep, and seldom can really duplicate a true seizure so it cannot be differentiated by a trained observer. Also during and after a seizure neurological changes such as the Babinski reflex can be obtained while this never happens in a case of hysteria.

If doubt still remains as to the nature of attacks, various procedures calculated to precipitate attacks or EEG change can be tried. These include excessive hydration and also injection of metrazol. Therapeutic trial of drugs is also indicated. Hysteria is seldom changed, much less controlled, by anticonvulsive drugs while they often have a dramatic effect on seizure states.

Hypnosis has been advocated as a means of differentiating seizures from hysteria and has been used with one large group of service men. However, in civilian practice not nearly so many cases of hysteria or malingering are seen and in a large clinic we have not found the use of this technique necessary.[21]

5. Psychic Seizures

Reference has already been made under the description of psychomotor seizures to the fact that many bizarre forms of behavior can actually be seizures. In addition to peculiar behavior all types of queer subjective states and sensations can occur as a result of a seizure discharge. So-called dreamy states occur, often with the same mental content. Also feelings of sudden fear can be a seizure. Running fits have been described and it has been shown that in these the nature of the behavior during a seizure (such as running) is psychologically determined and can be treated by psychotherapy. Whereas the seizures will continue, they will not have the same content.

It has long been noted that mood changes may occur a day or hours before a seizure. Also some persons with seizures develop peculiar mental symptoms if their seizures are controlled either spontaneously or by medicine. When a seizure does occur, they feel a definite release.

With direct cerebral stimulation at operation, Penfield[6] has been able to produce psychic seizures and has found that stimulation in exactly the same area carried out repeatedly will each time result in the same sub-

[21] Hypnosis in Differentiation of Epileptic from Convulsive-Like Seizures," John W. Summer, Jr., Richard R. Cameron, and Donald B. Peterson. *Neurology*, Vol. 2, No. 5, pp. 395–402.

jective experience, such as a tune, a vision, or a certain emotional feeling.

6. Psychic Stress

It has been demonstrated repeatedly that undue psychic stress can increase the frequency and severity of seizures in a person with a seizure state. At times the onset of seizures is associated directly with some emotional upheaval, but when this occurs evidence indicates that a lowered seizure threshold as proved by EEG already existed beforehand.

Just how psychic stress increases seizures is not known but the vascular changes, irregularity of food and fluid intake, loss of sleep, hyperventilation and fatigue, all follow emotional episodes and would seem sufficient to upset a precarious cerebral metabolic adjustment. The main point is that these things activate an already existing condition but do not cause the seizure state. Emotional states alone seem to have little effect on the EEG and the minor changes that do occur are nonspecific and not like those seen in epilepsy.

7. Psychoses

It has been the clinical impression of persons working in psychiatry that psychotic states are rare in persons with epilepsy. Alstrom[17] in his study of 897 cases of seizures found the same instance of psychoses in that group as in the general population. Studies of EEG records on a series of hospitalized psychotic patients have failed to reveal any unusual EEG findings. However, a series of EEG records on patients with episodic psychotic behavior revealed a fair number with temporal lobe foci.

Psychotic behavior when it does occur directly related to seizures usually follows a particularly severe seizure or several of them. It may last only a few hours or may go on a few days. On the other hand, more prolonged psychotic reactions often occur in persons who have their seizures controlled by some drug, but the drug seems to be toxic in the sense of creating mental disturbance. This has caused Gibbs to express the opinion that seizure activity and psychotic activity both seem related to temporal lobe lesions but the one seems to be antagonistic to the other.

Milder disturbed mental states[22] often occur when a person's seizures are controlled and a seizure seems to "clear the air."

8. School

Most persons with seizures can attend regular school classes since their intelligence is not impaired. Attendance in ordinary public school classes should be advised even though some seizures occur in school. There is no basis for the feeling that other children should be "protected" from seeing a seizure and if the situation is explained the other children will usually accept the situation easily. The difficulty comes from parents who still associate epilepsy with various mental and moral stigmata.

Participation in school often helps a great deal to reduce seizures because it lessens feelings of inferiority and makes life more routine. In this situation complete reports from both a psychologist and a physician to the

---

[22] "Occurrence of 'Continuous Symptoms' in Epilepsy Patients," John S. Scott, M. B., and Richard L. Masland, M.D. *Neurology*, Vol. 3, No. 4, pp. 297–301.

teacher can do much to help the teacher understand and be sympathetic to the problem.

9. Marriage and Family

In the past much psychological damage has been done because persons with seizures were usually advised not to marry or have children. Though Lennox believes that a hereditary factor does exist in epilepsy, he does not believe that it is great enough a factor to make one advise against marriage in most cases.[4] He states that when one parent has seizures one child out of 30 may have seizures but only in half of these will seizures be repeated often enough to be a problem. Hence the chances are actually one in 60. Since in the general population one child in 200 has seizures this is not a very serious matter.

When seizures are due to a known injury or infection and there is no family history of seizures then it would seem safe to assume that no hereditary factor will be operative. Determining this in a child may be important to the parents in the event they desire other children.

Being able to marry and have a family completes the striving to be "normal" which most patients have and certainly this door should not be closed except to those with very severe brain damage or with some other definitely hereditary condition.

10. Rehabilitation

It has been estimated that 80 per cent of persons with seizures can be rehabilitated if given the opportunity. Actually only about 30 per cent are self-sustaining on a permanent basis. This leaves a large group that needs help with special training and job placement. Not only does such rehabilitation relieve the family or the community of the economic care of the patient but it can have a very beneficial effect on the seizure state itself. Here again the best rule is that work and training must be a part of treatment and not wait until seizures are largely or completely controlled. Regularity of work and training and the hope of eventual economic independence help the person take medications more regularly and in general stay in better health.

If rehabilitation is to really be effective then the whole community, including employers, must be educated as to the nature of seizures, and collaboration between physician, social worker, psychologist, and various social agencies is essential in this field. Advances in the treatment of seizures have been dramatic in the past fifteen years. From a practically hopeless outlook we have arrived at the place where seizures can be completely controlled in 50 per cent of cases by drugs and reduced a great deal in another 30 per cent. This has been due mainly to the development of a number of drugs such as dilantin, mesantoin, tridione, paradione, mebaral, gemonil, hibicon and dexedrine, and to the increased experience on the part of physicians in using these drugs. Not only can seizures be treated more effectively but the "whole person" can now be treated and the attainment of a "normal" existence including school, work, marriage and family reasonably set as a goal in most cases.

The "Phantom Anesthetist" of Mattoon: A Field Study of Mass Hysteria*

BY Donald M. Johnson, Ph.D.

The story of the "phantom anesthetist" begins in Mattoon, Illinois, on the first night of September, 1944, when a woman reported to the police that someone had opened her bedroom window and sprayed her with a sickish sweet-smelling gas which partially paralyzed her legs and made her ill. Soon other cases with similar symptoms were reported, and the police organized a full-scale effort to catch the elusive "gasser." Some of the Mattoon citizens armed themselves with shotguns and sat on their doorsteps to wait for him; some even claimed that they caught a glimpse of him and heard him pumping his spray gun. As the number of cases increased—as many as seven in one night—and the facilities of the local police seemed inadequate to the size of the task, the state police with radio-equipped squad

* From *The Journal of Abnormal and Social Psychology*, Volume 40, No. 2, April, 1945. Reprinted by courtesy of the author and publishers, The American Psychological Association, Inc.

cars were called in, and scientific crime detection experts went to work, analyzing stray rags for gaseous chemicals and checking the records of patients recently released from state institutions. Before long the "phantom anesthetist" of Mattoon had appeared in newspapers all over the United States, and Mattoon service men in New Guinea and India were writing home anxiously inquiring about their wives and mothers. After ten days of such excitement, when all victims had recovered and no substantial clues had been found, the police began to talk of "imagination" and some of the newspapers ran columns on "mass hysteria"; the episode of the "phantom anesthetist" was over.

Journalistically the story died in a few weeks. In the police records the last attack was reported on September 12. Scientifically, however, the episode demands attention as a fascinating psychological phenomenon. Only one case of a "mental epidemic" has been reported in recent years: an outburst of hysterical twitching in a Louisiana high school was described by Schuler and Parenton (7). They were unable to find any reference in the standard sources to hysterical epidemics in the United States for over forty years, and they raise the question whether these phenomena are disappearing. The writer, therefore, undertook an investigation of the Mattoon case, with two general aims: (1) to preserve, for the sake of the record, an accurate account of the events, and (2) to attempt an analysis of the psychological factors involved in these events. The investigation consisted chiefly of an analysis of the records in the Police Department and interviews with those who reported physical symptoms from the gas. The study was begun in the middle of September and continued until the end of the year, but most of the interviewing was done in October. All the work was done by the writer, who assumes responsibility for this report.

The Facts of the Case

Mattoon is a small Illinois city, located about 50 miles southeast of the center of the state. The population, according to the 1940 census, was 15,827, of which 98 per cent were native-born white. It is surrounded by rather prosperous farm land, and its economy is largely determined by this fact. In addition, it is a junction for the Illinois Central and the New York Central railroads, both of which maintain repair shops at this point. There are a few small industries, a shoe factory, a furniture factory, Diesel engine works, a foundry, and the like. All in all it is a fairly typical midwestern city. As a result of the war it has enjoyed a mild boom, but not an upsetting one.

The outlines of the story can be quickly set down as a background for discussion of specific questions. On September 1 about midnight Mrs. A had a friend telephone the police that she and her daughter had been gassed. The police found no signs of an intruder, but Mr. A reported that, when he came home about two hours later, he saw a man run from the window. The police were called again, and again they found nothing. The next evening the Mattoon *Daily Journal-Gazette* carried a front-page story on the "gas attack" and a headline: "ANESTHETIC PROWLER ON LOOSE."

On the following day, Sunday the third, Mr. B reported to the police that he and his wife had had a similar occurrence. In the middle of the night of August

31—the night before Mrs. A's attack—he woke up sick, and retched, and asked his wife if the gas had been left on. When she woke up she was unable to walk. At first they had attributed these symptoms to hot dogs eaten the evening before. About the same time Mr. C, who works nights, told the press that his wife and daughter had likewise been attacked. The daughter woke up coughing and, when Mrs. C got up to take care of her, she could hardly walk. They did not suspect gas until they read the papers next day. These two accounts appeared in the Mattoon paper on September 5, since no paper was printed on Sunday the third or Labor Day the fourth.

On the evening of September 5 two new attacks were recorded. Mrs. D came home with her husband about 10:30, picked up a cloth from the porch, smelled it, and reported that the fumes burned her mouth and lips so badly that they bled. Mr. E, who works nights, reported that his wife heard someone at the bedroom window, smelled gas, and was partially paralyzed by it.

On the sixth three more cases occurred, according to the police records. On the seventh, none; on the eighth, four; on the ninth, five; and on the tenth, seven. This apparently was the climax of the affair, for no cases were reported on the eleventh, only one on the twelfth, and none thereafter.

The symptoms reported were nausea and vomiting, palpitations, paralysis of the legs, dryness of the mouth and throat and, in one case at least, burns about the mouth. All cases recovered rapidly, hence there was little possibility for outside check on the symptoms. Four cases were seen by physicians, who diagnosed all cases as hysteria.

In at least three cases, so the testimony goes, the

family dog "must have been gassed also" since he did not bark at the intruder.

Those who reported smelling the gas described it as "a musty smell," "sickish," "like gardenias," or "like cheap perfume." In some cases, though symptoms were reported, the gas was not smelled.

Police activity took several directions. Most important, probably, was the attempt to catch the "mad gasser" *in flagrante delicto.* The police answered all telephone calls as soon as possible and, when the state police came into the picture with modern radio equipment, were often able to surround a house, in the words of the Commissioner of Police, "before the phone was back on the hook." Despite all this and despite the amateur efforts of an excited citizenry no one was ever apprehended "in the act." Less direct procedures revolved around examination of a few objects found near houses where attacks had been reported, particularly chemical analysis of the cloth found by Mrs. D, and the usual round-up of suspicious characters. The results of these attempts were also negative. On the eleventh the Commissioner of Police put a note in the paper requesting that "roving bands of men and boys should disband," and that guns be put away "because some innocent person may get killed." About the same time the police adopted the policy of having the victims sent to a hospital for examination.

Gas or Hysteria?

Obviously something extraordinary took place in Mattoon, and for its explanation two hypotheses have been advanced. The "gasser" hypothesis asserts that the symptoms were produced by a gas which was sprayed on the victims by some ingenious fiend who has been able to elude the police. This explanation was disseminated by newspapers throughout the country, at the beginning of the episode at least, and it is widely believed in Mattoon at present. The alternative hypothesis is that the symptoms were due to hysteria.

The evidence for the "gasser" hypothesis comes from the reports of the victims concerning their symptoms, reports which are notoriously difficult to check. The fact that vomiting did occur was authenticated in a few cases by outside testimony but, since vomiting could be produced by gas or hysteria or dietary indiscretions, this fact is not crucial. There is plenty of evidence from the police and other observers that the victims were emotionally upset by their experiences, but this too is not a crucial point.

Another difficulty with the "gasser" hypothesis is the self-contradictory demands it makes on the gas. In order to produce effects of the kind reported when sprayed through a window it would have to be a very potent stable anesthetic with rapid action, and at the same time so unstable that it would not affect others in the same room. It would have to be strong enough to produce vomiting and paralysis, and yet leave no observable after-effects. Study of a standard source on anesthetics and war gases (3) and consultation with medical and chemical colleagues at the University of Illinois indicates that the existence of such a gas is highly improbable. Chemists are extremely skeptical of the possibility that such an extraordinary gas could be produced by some "mad genius" working in a basement.

Several people reported seeing a prowler who might

be the "anesthetist." This too is not an important matter since prowlers have been reported to the police in Mattoon once or twice a week for several years. And, of course, prowlers do not produce paralysis or dry throats.

A minor weakness in the gas hypothesis is the lack of a motive. No money was stolen, and the circumstances were such that there would be little gratification for a peeper.

The best evidence for the hysteria hypothesis is the nature of the symptoms and the fact that those cases seen by physicians—though there were only four—were diagnosed as hysteria. All symptoms reported are common in hysteria and can be found in the medical literature for many years back. For example, here is a description of a mild hysterical attack dated about a hundred years ago. Janet (4) quotes it from Briquet:

> I choose, for an example, what happens to a woman somewhat impressionable who experiences a quick and lively emotion. She instantly feels a constriction at the epigastrium; experiences oppression, her heart palpitates, something rises in her throat and chokes her; in short, she feels in all her limbs a discomfort which causes them in a way to drop; or else it is an agitation, a necessity for movement, which causes a contraction of the muscles. This is indeed the exact model of the most common hysterical accident, of the most ordinary hysterical spasm.

The hypothesis of hysteria accounts for the rapid recovery of all victims and the lack of after-effects. It explains why no "gasser" was found in spite of mobilization of local and state police and volunteers. It accounts for the fact that nothing was stolen and that dogs did not bark. The objections to the hypothesis of hysteria come from the victims themselves—quite naturally—and from others who do not realize the intensity and variety of effects which are produced by psychological forces.

Some who like compromises may argue that these two explanations are not exclusive, that there may have been a "gasser" at first even though the later spread of the symptoms was a hysterical phenomenon. The "anesthetist" soon became scared and ceased his fiendish activities. We may grant the charm of compromise as a general thing but insist that the above arguments still hold—for the first part of the episode as well as the last. The hypothesis of hysteria fits all the evidence, without remainder.

Quantitative Data on Chronology

If we consider the whole affair as a psychogenic one, as a "mental epidemic" due chiefly to suggestion, the sequence of events takes on a particular significance, and fortunately a more-or-less objective chronology of the case is furnished by records of telephone calls to the Police Department. In the Mattoon Police Department the desk sergeant regularly records the date and time of all calls and a brief note of the nature of the call and subsequent police action. From these records calls specifically reporting a "gassing" were easily segregated. Another category of calls, usually designated as "prowler calls" by the police, was found to be useful. This designation means that someone phoned and reported that a man was acting strangely on the street, or that noises were heard on the back porch, and that, when the police answered the call, they could find no evidence of any damage or break-in. The records were broken down in this way for the period of the excitement and a few weeks before and after.* Figure I shows the trends which appear when these data are grouped into weekly intervals.

The "gasser" curve starts from zero, reaches a peak rapidly, and rapidly returns to the baseline, as one would expect. (The decline is actually quite sharp, as noted earlier, though in the figure it appears more gradual than the rise because of the grouping into weekly intervals.) The "prowler" curve rises and falls with the "gasser" curve, a parallel which cannot be merely coincidental. Since the police do not list a call as a "prowler" call if they find evidence of damage or entry, it is likely that these calls result, in many cases at least, from psychological causes operating in a vague or ambiguous perceptual situation. Thus, during a period of great excitement like a manhunt, when anticipation is intense, the number of "prowler" calls would increase. Similarly, as the excitement subsides, the number of such calls would subside.

The most striking fact is that there were so few "prowler" calls in the last part of September and none whatever in October until just before Hallowe'en. This is very unusual, according to the police, and a check of the records for the same months in 1943 discloses no similar fluctuations. The only plausible explanation is that the lack of "prowler" calls results from the development of contra-suggestibility. After hearing of the "phantom anesthetist" and then of "imagination" and "hysteria," the people who ordinarily would have called the police when they heard a suspicious noise became critical and inhibited their "imagination."

* The writer is very grateful to Sgt. Edward Davidson for carrying out a day-by-day analysis of these records.

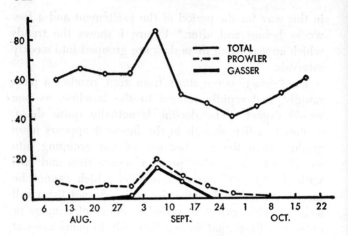

FIG. 1. ANALYSIS OF RECORDS OF TELEPHONE CALLS TO THE MATTOON POLICE DEPARTMENT

Gasser calls begin on September 2, increase rapidly, and decrease rapidly to zero. Prowler calls, which develop out of an unstructured situation, begin in this graph at their average level, rise with the excitement of the gasser episode, and fall to zero as contra-suggestibility develops. Total calls at the police station begin at the average level, rise with the increase in gasser activities, decline as contra-suggestibility develops, then return to the average level.

The curve for total calls is similar. Police business in general increased sharply during the "gasser" episode, then declined for a few weeks before coming back to normal.

In the light of the evidence presented thus far it seems proper to speak of a wave of excitement or a "mental epidemic" sweeping through Mattoon. The people who succumbed to the epidemic can be grouped into three classes according to the intensity of their response. In the first class are those who merely put off their evening stroll and locked their windows more carefully than usual. Such conduct would of course be called "sensible" and hardly requires any explanation, but it must be remembered that there were many in Mattoon—perhaps a majority—who completely ignored the incident. In the second class are those who reported to the police that they saw or heard a prowler. A report of this kind indicates a higher level of susceptibility since it means that suggestion enters into and complicates perception. The third class is made up of those who reported physical symptoms from "gassing." The occurrence of the physical symptoms indicates a high degree of suggestibility, on the average at least, and perhaps some constitutional predisposition to physical complaints as well.

Agencies of Communication

How was the suggestion carried to all these people so quickly and uniformly? There are three possibilities: direct face-to-face contact between victims, indirect conversation or gossip, and the newspapers. In talking to the victims the investigator attempted to determine when and how each had first heard of the "phantom anesthetist." The replies gave very little evidence of face-to-face contact. With the exception of four cases in which two people lived together and were "attacked" at the same time it seems that the victims were practically unknown to each other. The possibility of indirect contact through neighborhood chatting is a more likely one, and one which is difficult to check. The chief argument against this avenue of communication is that it takes time, and the "epidemic" spread rapidly. The cases were widely scattered throughout the town, and, as we shall see later, only about a third of the victims had telephones.

As a means of communication the newspaper is, of course, the most effective. According to 1941 figures (9) 97 per cent of Mattoon families read the Mattoon *Daily Journal-Gazette* every evening except Sunday. This is the only paper with a large circulation in Mattoon, and obviously it is the source to which most residents would turn for information in a case of this kind. It is necessary, therefore, to examine the *Journal-Gazette's* treatment of the story and to analyze its psychological influence.

The Mattoon *Daily Journal-Gazette,* which usually runs to about eight pages, resembles other small newspapers both in size and in editorial policy. In general its treatment of the news is conservative, and one would expect that its readers have confidence in its reliability. No one would consider it a "sensational" paper. When a headline, "ANESTHETIC PROWLER ON LOOSE," appeared, therefore—as it did Saturday evening, September 2—it was no doubt taken at face value. The story which ran on the front page in a full column headed "Mrs. (A) and Daughter First Victims," was written as a straightforward news item. Including the headline it covered 47 square inches.* In retrospect it makes rather interesting reading. The careful reader's eye is caught particularly by the word "First" in the heading, since only the one case is mentioned. Whether this was an instance of prophetic insight or merely an error is not

---

* Measurement of newspaper space, as for our purposes, is not well standardized. In the present analysis the square inch is used, and the figures given include headlines and photographs as well as text. Those who like to think in terms of the column inch can halve these figures and get the length of *a standard two-inch* column which would contain the material.

known, but the word does now, and probably did then, arouse a tingle of anticipation.

On the next two days, Sunday and Labor Day, no paper was printed, but on Tuesday, the fifth, 26 square inches appeared on page six. On the sixth there were 40 square inches, including a headline, on the front page. On the seventh 29 square inches were used, including a headline, "MAD ANESTHETIST STRIKES AGAIN." No headline was used on the eighth and only 28 square inches of space. Objectively and in terms of newspaper space the excitement seemed to be dying down. But note the first paragraph:

> Mattoon's "mad anesthetist" apparently took a respite from his maniacal forays Thursday night and while many terror stricken people were somewhat relieved they were inclined to hold their breath and wonder when and where he might strike next.

Several attacks were reported that night, and on the evening of the ninth a three-quarter-inch headline was used, crowding the war news to a secondary position. In all, the story took up 51 square inches of space. Evidently the climax is approaching. Up to this point the reader is treated to an absorbing horror story—with a mysterious marauder whose "maniacal forays" increase in a fantastic crescendo, a frightful new scientific device for gassing the victims, and a succession of tantalizing clues. His interest may be aroused to the point where he participates in the manhunt—vicariously, through reading about the scientific investigations of the state crime-detection experts or trying out his own hunches, or actually, by following the police cars or patrolling the streets. In other cases it was not the thrill of the chase which was aroused but apprehension and fear. It was in these people that the hysterical symptoms appeared.

On the eleventh (the tenth was Sunday) the tone of the story changes. Although 62 square inches were given to the story, the headline contained the phrase "few real" and the treatment is critical. No headline was used on the twelfth and the keynote phrase was "hysteria abates"; the story took up 28 square inches. The next evening a comical twist is given to the affair, expanding it to 59 square inches about two false alarms which turned out to be a black cat and a doctor trying to break into his own office after he had forgotten his keys. On the fourteenth the account falls to 19 square inches, and next evening it is put back on page six with only 14 square inches, although a box of 10 square inches appeared on the front page telling how widely the story had been circulated.

The *Journal-Gazette* dropped the affair from this point to the twentieth, when an editorial was printed, apparently in reply to some ribbing by a Decatur paper. The editorial asserted that, although much of the excitement may have been due to hysteria, there really had been some odors in Mattoon—perhaps blown up from Decatur. With this epilogue the drama takes its leave from the columns of the Mattoon *Daily Journal-Gazette*.

Of the out-of-town newspapers the *Chicago Daily Tribune* and the *Chicago Daily News* have the largest circulations in Mattoon, with coverages of 24 per cent and 20 per cent respectively (9). The *Tribune* started the story on the sixth with 10 square inches each day thereafter until the fifteenth. The editorial viewpoint of the story became skeptical about the twelfth. The *Daily News'* treatment was similar except that it ran photographs and did not question the authenticity of the "anesthetist." These papers have enough circulation in Mattoon to have an important influence but, since they came in late and since their readers read the local paper also, their influence was probably merely one of emphasis and reinforcement.

The *Chicago Herald-American*, though its coverage in Mattoon is only about 5 per cent (9), handled the story most thoroughly and most sensationally. Its text and photographs were often cited to the investigator. It started late—on the eighth—with 41 square inches, including a photograph. The opening paragraphs of the front-page story which appeared on the tenth are worth quoting:

> Groggy as Londoners under protracted aerial blitzing, this town's bewildered citizens reeled today under repeated attacks of a mad anesthetist who has sprayed a deadly nerve gas into 13 homes and has knocked out 27 victims.
>
> Seventy others dashing to the area in response to the alarm, fell under the influence of the gas last night.
>
> All skepticism has vanished and Mattoon grimly concedes it must fight haphazardly against a demented phantom adversary who has been seen only fleetingly and so far has evaded traps laid by city and state police and posses of townsmen.

By the eleventh the story was up to 71 square inches, including a 1½-inch headline: "STATE HUNTS GAS MADMAN." On the twelfth it was given 95 square inches, with pictures of crying babies on the front page. After that the account becomes somewhat critical but continues to carry hints that the "gasser" may be a woman, or an apeman, and the like. On Sunday, the seventeenth, however, after the other papers had dropped the story, the *Herald-American* printed a long interview with a psychiatrist, Dr. Harold Hulburt, beginning at the top of the front page above the headline, and covering 196 square inches, with several photographs. This article discusses the dynamics of hysteria in general and includes some sympathetic conjectures regarding unconscious motives of Mrs. A. Further articles resulting from the interview with the psychiatrist appeared on the eighteenth and the twentieth. On December 3 *The American Weekly,* a Sunday supplement of the *Herald-American,* carried a full-page article by Donald Laird entitled "The Manhunt for Mr. Nobody."

The story was carried by the press services and was used or ignored by newspapers throughout the country according to their editorial policies. The *New York Times,* for instance, did not refer to it, while *PM* had 12 square inches on the seventh and 5 on the twelfth. The *Stars & Stripes* (London Edition) carried 7 square inches on the eleventh. Among the weeklies, *Newsweek* for September 18 carried 20 square inches, while *Time* for the same date carried 26. Both of these accounts were skeptical—*Time* was even sarcastic—but neither dared come to any definite conclusions. *Time* elevated the number of cases at the peak from seven to seventeen. *Dispatch,* a weekly of the Persian Gulf Command, gave it 13 square inches on the eighteenth.[*]

Striking evidence of the interest aroused by these accounts comes from the large number of letters and telegrams—estimated at about 300—which were received by

[*] Radio treatment of the story was not considered important enough to warrant study. There is no radio station at Mattoon, and no one in Mattoon or elsewhere mentioned a radio account to the investigator. In general, radio editors treat these stories conservatively.

Mattoon officials from all over the United States. The writer examined a sample of 30 of these and found half of them more-or-less sensible, though ill-informed, containing suggestions for capturing the "menace." The other half could be judged psychopathic—on the basis of ideas of self-reference, intensity of affect, and the combination of poor judgment with good vocabulary and expression. Paranoid trends were common.

Characteristics of the Susceptible

SAMPLE: Thus far in our investigation we have treated the Mattoon affair as a social phenomenon. The next question, and perhaps the most important, concerns the individuals in the affair. Why were some people susceptible while their next-door neighbors were not? Phrased in more workable form the question becomes one of finding differences between the susceptible sample and the rest of the population of Mattoon. The experimental literature on suggestibility and the clinical literature on hysteria offered several attractive hypotheses for check, but the nature of the case put a distinct limitation on the methods which could be used. It was apparent from the first few interviews that the victims, while they would talk about the "gassing," and their symptoms, and similar superficial matters, would not be willing to coöperate in any inquiry directed toward, for example, unconscious motivation. They had been victimized twice: once by the concatenation of factors, environmental and personal, which produced the symptoms, and later by publicity and gossip, which carried the implication that people who have hysterical attacks are more peculiar, or less sincere, than their neighbors. For these reasons the best one could hope for was a description of the sample in respect of a few objective characteristics.

The 1940 Census Reports (8) give data on a number of characteristics of the Mattoon population; getting the same data for our sample would permit a comparison in these respects. Those characteristics were selected which seemed easy to verify and of possible significance for the present problem: age, sex, schooling, economic level, and occupation. Age was estimated and, in doubtful cases, checked by the estimates of acquaintances. To get a picture of the economic level of the sample four conveniences were used as indices: radio, mechanical refrigerator, electricity, and telephone. Percentages for the first three are given in the Census Reports. The number of residential telephones in Mattoon was kindly furnished by the manager of the local telephone agency, and the percentage computed in reference to the number of occupied dwelling units given in the Census Reports. The Census Bureau's descriptions of their occupational categories were studied before the interviewing began so that the necessary data could be obtained. For example, the Reports state specifically that railway brakemen are classed as "Operatives" while locomotive engineers and firemen are classed as "Craftsmen, Foremen and Kindred Workers." Furthermore in a small town like Mattoon the variety of jobs is limited and cross-checking is relatively easy. Hence placing the occupations of the sample into the Census Bureau's categories offered less difficulty than might be expected. A woman's occupation was used if she worked, otherwise her husband's. (Only two women had husbands in military service. One of these worked, hence her own occupation was used. In the other case the husband had been inducted only recently so his civilian occupation was used.) All these data are brought together in Table I for comparison with similar data for the total population of Mattoon.

Statistically speaking, the sample is small; the number of cases on which the percentages in Table I are based varies from 14 for schooling to 29 for sex. The table includes, however, nearly all the cases in which physical symptoms were reported. The investigator checked police records and newspaper accounts for names and found a few others while interviewing. Two people could not be found at home despite repeated calls. Three had left town. One would not talk to the investigator. Some of the data on these were obtained from acquaintances. Table I gives us at least a partial description of the people who were most intensely affected by the excitement.

To begin with, the sample has a much greater proportion of women than the general population of the city. This is in agreement with the laboratory studies on suggestibility (1) and the clinical reports on hysteria (5, 6). All of the cases have been married but one, who was about twenty years old. As to the age data a word of explanation is necessary. In three cases mothers reported that their children had been "gassed." Since the investigator did not talk to the children apart from their mothers, these cases were eliminated. In two of these cases the mothers reported symptoms for themselves also, hence it is only the age data which are affected. Aside from the absence of children the most noticeable difference between the sample and the population is the surplus in the age group 20 to 29. The significance of this, if it is not accidental, is not obvious.

Since children are more suggestible than adults (1),

TABLE I.   THE SAMPLE OF "GASSER" VICTIMS COMPARED
WITH THE TOTAL POPULATION OF MATTOON IN RESPECT
TO CERTAIN OBJECTIVE CHARACTERISTICS

	PERCENTAGE OF SAMPLE	PERCENTAGE OF POPULATION
SEX		
Women	93	52
AGE		
Below 10	0	14
10–19	0	18
20–29	37	17
30–39	16	15
40–49	21	13
50–59	16	10
60–69	10	7
Over 70	0	6
EDUCATION		
Grade school only	71	58
Some high school	29	32
Some college	0	10
INDICES OF ECONOMIC LEVEL		
Electricity	80	95
Radio	80	91
Mechanical refrigerator	28	46
Telephone	33	60
OCCUPATIONAL CATEGORIES		
Professional and semi-professional	0	7
Proprietors, managers, and officials	16	13
Clerical, sales, and kindred workers	32	21
Craftsmen, foremen, and kindred workers	5	16
Operatives	37	24
Laborers, farm laborers, and farm foremen	10	5
Domestic service workers	0	5
Service workers, except domestic	0	9

why were there not more children in the sample? Many children probably did accept the suggestion in the sense that they reported to their parents that they saw the "gasser" or smelled gas. While the dynamics of symptom-formation are not well understood and may be different in each case, it does seem likely that adults would be more inclined to the withdrawing, incapacitating sort of symptoms which appeared in this "epidemic" than children. In the case reported by Schuler and Parenton (7) among high-school children the symptoms were of a more positive, lively nature.

In education the sample is below the total population. This too might have been predicted from the literature on suggestibility.

From the economic indices it seems clear that the sample is less prosperous than the population at large, at least in respect to these four conveniences. The investigator also classified the sample into the economic groups A, B, C, and D, according to a widely used scheme based on the location and appearance of the home, occupation, conveniences, and the like. (The investigator has had some experience in using this scheme in consumer research for the Psychological Corporation. In terms of these categories the sample was about equally divided between the C and D groups. There were two cases which could possibly have been put into the B group. It is noteworthy that no attacks occurred in either of Mattoon's two high-income areas.

Our sample, then, is characterized by low educational and economic level. These two characteristics go together in our culture. In a study similar in some respects to the present study Cantril (2) found that those people who were most strongly influenced by the Orson Welles 1938 broadcast, "War of the Worlds," were likewise of low educational and economic level. No doubt it is education which is more directly related to suggestibility. Cantril found that the better educated were more critical in that they made more and better outside checks on the authenticity of the broadcast and thus were less frequently panicked.

The data on occupation are not clear-cut since the categories used by the Census Bureau were not constructed for studies of this kind. As the number of cases on which good occupational data were available was only 19, the number in some categories was small, and some rearrangement was advisable. The category "Farmers and farm managers" was eliminated as there were none in the sample and less than 1 per cent in the general population. Professional and semi-professional classes were combined. "Laborers, except farm" was combined with "farm laborers and farm foremen." The category "Proprietors, managers, and officials" is a broad one which could include a wide variety of people, hence it is of little use to us. The proprietors in our sample were proprietors of small shops and rooming houses.

As it stands Table I shows a lack of any professional or semi-professional people, which agrees with the data on educational level. A fairly clear-cut vertical comparison can be made if we consider the craftsmen and foremen as skilled workers, the operatives as semi-skilled, and the laborers as unskilled. The proportion of the sample in these three group decreases—in comparison with the proportion in the population at large—as the amount of skill increases.

It is hard to account for the lack of service workers and domestic service workers in the sample. The susceptibility of domestics might be influenced by their living arrangements and by contact with their employers, who in general are in the educated, high-income group. As to the other service workers, one explanation is that police, firemen, and hospital workers were in a sense "on the inside." Also, it is known that, while there has been little change in the Mattoon population in general since 1940, jobs connected with the servicing of automobiles have decreased considerably. But none of these "explanations" is very convincing.

The interviews, one can easily realize, were conducted under rather unfavorable conditions. It was not possible to get any insight into personality makeup of the victims except in a very superficial way. But it was possible usually for the investigator to work in a few general questions about the victim's health. In only fourteen cases was any information obtained in this way, but, of these, eight, or over half, replied with such phrases as "always been nervous," "never sleep much," and "doctoring for nerves." We have no control data for the total population, but the percentage does seem extraordinarily high. The interview data do not go far, but they reinforce the diagnosis of hysteria and show, as far as they go, that, extraordinary as the Mattoon affair may be on the surface, psychologically it follows a familiar pattern.

CONCLUSIONS: Analysis of records available at Mattoon together with the results of interviews with most of the victims leads to the conclusion that the case of the "phantom anesthetist" was entirely psychogenic. There is always the possibility of a prowler, of course, and it is quite likely that some sort of gas could be smelled at various times in Mattoon. But these things do not cause paralysis and palpitations. Hysteria does. The hypoth-

esis of a marauder cannot be supported by any veri-
fiable evidence. The hypothesis of hysteria, on the
other hand, accounts for all the facts.

What, then, produced this mass hysteria? There are
some gaps in the story, to be sure, but a fairly clear
picture can now be drawn. Mrs. A had a mild hysterical
attack, an event which is not at all uncommon, which is,
on the contrary, familiar to most physicians. The crucial
point is that her interpretation of her symptoms was
rather dramatic—a quick look through any textbook
(e.g., 5, 6) will convince any reader that hysterical symptoms usually are dramatic—arousing the interest of the
press, with the result that an exciting uncritical story of
the case appeared in the evening paper. As the news
spread, other people reported similar symptoms, more
exciting stories were written, and so the affair snow-
balled.

But such acute outbursts are necessarily self-limiting.
The bizarre details which captured the public imagination at the beginning of the episode became rather
ridiculous when studied more leisurely. The drama of
the story lost its tang with time and the absurdities
showed through. For example, the volatility of the gas,
which was such an asset in penetrating physical barriers, became a liability when anyone tried to capture
the gas and examine it. The facts seemed to evaporate
as rapidly as the agent which produced them. At last
the failure of the police and volunteers to find anyone
or anything tangible (the best the news photographers
could do was to pose women pointing at windows,
babies crying, and men holding shotguns) combined
with the statements of city officials in the paper produced a more critical public attitude. The attacks
ceased. The critical attitude increased and spread, how-

ever; police business struck a new low. It is proper to say that the wave of suggestibility in Mattoon left a wave of contra-suggestibility in its wake. Objective records document this generalization.

Naturally the more suggestible people accepted the story at face value. Of these only a small percentage reported physical symptoms from "gassing," presumably because of some personal motivation toward, or gratification from, such symptoms. As might be predicted from psychological and psychiatric literature, those who succumbed to the "mental epidemic" were mostly women and were, on the average, below the general population in educational and economic level. This supports the above analysis and puts the "phantom anesthetist" of Mattoon, in some aspects at least, into a familiar psychological pattern.

References

1. Bird, C. *Social Psychology*. New York: Appleton-Century, 1940.
2. Cantril, H. *The Invasion from Mars*. Princeton, N. J.: Princeton Univ. Press, 1940.
3. Goodman, L., and Gilman, A. *The Pharmacological Basis of Therapeutics*. New York: Macmillan, 1940.
4. Janet, P. *The Mental State of Hystericals*. New York: Putnam's, 1901.
5. Rosanoff, A. J. (Ed.) *Manual of Psychiatry*. New York: Wiley, 1920.
6. Sadler, W. S. *Theory and Practice of Psychiatry*. St. Louis: Mosby, 1936.
7. Schuler, E. A., and Parenton, V. J. "A recent epidemic of hysteria in a Louisiana high school." *J. Soc. Psychol.* 17, 221–235, 1943.

8. U. S. Bureau of the Census, *16th Census of the United States*. Washington, D. C.: U. S. Govt. Printing Office, 1942.
9. Illinois Daily Newspaper Markets. Paul L. Gorham, Leland Bldg., Springfield, Ill.

Schizophrenic Disorders[*]

BY *James C. Coleman, Ph.D.*

General Dynamics

Despite a tremendous amount of research the dynamics underlying the development of schizophrenic reactions are still not completely clear. In fact, there is some question as to whether we are not dealing with such a diversity of reaction patterns that any general dynamic formulation would be of limited value in a particular case of schizophrenia. However, a brief consideration of the contemporary status of the problem will aid us in understanding these reactions.

Biological Factors

Responsibility for schizophrenic development has been attributed at one time or another to numerous biological factors, among them heredity, endocrine and other physiological dysfunctioning, constitution, and cerebral birth trauma.

1. HEREDITY.   It is hardly surprising that so many early
and contemporary investigators should have emphasized the importance of heredity in schizophrenia, in
view of the disproportionate incidence of schizophrenia
and other mental disorders in the family background of
schizophrenic patients. Kraepelin found an incidence of
53.8 per cent of mental disorders in the families of 1054
schizophrenic patients (Lewis 60), and later studies
have reported similar findings (Barahal 3).

Kallmann (44) has summarized the statistical evidence for a genetic theory of schizophrenia by pointing
out that an individual's average expectancy of becoming
schizophrenic varies directly with the closeness of his
blood relationship to a schizophrenic patient. The children of one schizophrenic parent have a probability of
developing this disorder which is 19 times that of the
general population, and the grandchildren, nephews,
and nieces are about 5 times more likely to show an
outcropping of schizophrenia than the average person.
When both parents are schizophrenic the average expectancy rate for their children is 80 times normal. Kallmann, who has long championed the cause of heredity
in psychopathology, concludes that "this distribution of
schizophrenic rates indicates clearly that the chance of
developing a schizophrenic psychosis increases in direct
proportion to the degree of blood relationship to a schizophrenic index case*—a conclusive proof of the operation of heredity."

Neither Kallmann nor most other contemporary investigators, however, assume that schizophrenia is inherited directly, but hold rather that it is transmitted

---

* A known case of schizophrenia in a family is called an "index
case" in family studies of this type.

by recessive genes in the form of "predisposition." The theory is that individuals with this predisposition will develop schizophrenia when placed under severe stress, whereas other persons will develop some other defensive pattern. If the individual is never placed under excessive stress, there is no reason to believe that a schizophrenic reaction will ever appear.

Many investigators are inclined to minimize the concept of a hereditary predisposition to schizophrenia. They point out that the life situation of an individual with a family background of schizophrenia or other serious mental disorder is usually characterized by considerable stress as well as undesirable parental example. Certainly we would expect a much higher incidence of mental illness among children reared in families with a schizophrenic parent.

However, the most telling blow to Kallmann's conclusions concerning the role of heredity in schizophrenia has come from Pastore's (82) critical evaluation of Kallmann's experimental methods and procedures. Pastore found so many weaknesses here that he concluded that "the genetics of schizophrenia is still an open question." As Pastore further points out, this conclusion is not intended to minimize the importance of hereditary factors in the etiology of schizophrenia, but merely to emphasize that their specific role is at present unknown.

2. CONSTITUTION. Since Kretschmer's (58) contention that schizophrenics tend to be of asthenic (slender) physique, considerable effort has been directed toward the importance of constitutional factors in the etiological pattern. The results of later investigators, such as Sheldon (92), have tended to confirm Kretschmer's findings,

indicating that about two thirds of all schizophrenic patients do have an asthenic build. Among the remainder all types of body builds are found.

The relation of physique to schizophrenia, however, is difficult to evaluate. For one thing, schizophrenia occurs among a younger age group than is characteristic of other psychotic disorders—a group generally more slender than older age groups. Second, schizophrenics often reveal a long history of gradual, increasing withdrawal and introversion, a type of background that would not be conducive to muscular development. Of course, it is possible that their slender builds led to a withdrawal from the rough and tumble contacts of childhood and to the development of introversive tendencies. In any event we are dealing with an interaction of factors whose specific importance is not clear, but it seems doubtful that physique in and of itself is of great etiological importance.

The study of Escalona (27) on psychotic children . . . provides the most convincing evidence for the importance of constitutional factors in the development of psychotic reactions, but . . . the specific constitutional factors and their exact roles remain as yet to be delineated. In addition, of course, her findings on such seriously deviant psychotic children may not apply to schizophrenics or other psychotics in general.

3. ORGANIC PATHOLOGY. Many investigators following the early leads of Kraeplin (56) and Bleuler (7) have attempted to establish an organic basis for schizophrenia. Despite a tremendous amount of research in neuropathology, endocrine pathology, and general bodily biochemistry, however, all attempts in this direction

have so far been unsuccessful. Nevertheless, these researches have been of value in demonstrating positive correlations between schizophrenic disorders and numerous physiological conditions. For example, Elliot (26) found a greater number of symptoms of autonomic imbalance in a group of 100 schizophrenic women than in a control group of 100 nonpsychotic women, leading to the conclusion that the soma does not function so efficiently in schizophrenic women as in normals. Numerous investigators have pointed out that in many cases of schizophrenia the heart is small and the vascular apparatus inadequate, and there is a deficient functioning of the thyroid glands. This has led some to believe that schizophrenia is related to lower energy levels, involving a deficit in metabolic functioning which decreases the functional potential of the cortex and other bodily systems (Hecker 38). Campbell (17) specifically suggests that this lowered level of physiological functioning is evidence of a constitutional defect of vitality of the organism which predisposes it to schizophrenic reactions when placed under excessive stress.

However, we find ourselves faced again with the problem of the degree to which this correlated organic pathology is a cause of mental illness and how much it is a result or accompaniment of the individual's general adjustive approach to his problems. For example, a psychological withdrawal and preoccupation with a fantasy world might be accompanied physiologically by a general diminution and underactivity in bodily metabolism, in reactions to stimuli, and in other bodily functions. The patient reacts psychobiologically to any stress and we should not be surprised to find both psychological and biological withdrawal. This would probably tend, in turn, to a vicious interactional circle: the lowered bodily energy and vitality would further encourage effortless fantasy rather than more vigorous attempts to make a more successful adjustment.

More recently, attention has turned to the role of the pituitary gland, which secretes a hormone called corticotrophin when the organism is under extreme stress—whether it is some outside poison, great physical exertion, or emotional stress. This in turn causes the adrenal glands to increase their flow of corticoid hormones. When the stress is of short duration these hormones help the body to meet the emergency. But when the stresses are prolonged and severe, a vicious circle presumably develops in which the emotional changes lead to actual tissue injury—the inner walls of the blood vessels become injured, an excessive load is placed upon the kidneys, and minute hemorrhages may occur within the heart or brain. More important, the adrenal glands apparently break down under the strain and fail to put out the hormones which are so essential to the organism in meeting stressful situations (Maisel 64). Although of great theoretical interest, there is not yet adequate clinical evidence for this point of view to justify its immediate application to the understanding and treatment of schizophrenia.

Winkelman and Book (107) made an intensive clinical and post-mortem study of 10 schizophrenics with special emphasis upon possible brain pathology. Although the gross appearance of the brain was not at all distinctive, microscopic findings did indicate focal and general loss of nerve cells and other pathological brain changes. Their findings, together with other related studies in the field, led the authors to suggest that schizophrenia should be included among the "organic" psychoses. It may be noted, however, that the patients may have been schizophrenic for many years before the autopsy and in addition to inadequate dietary and other habits, may have undergone various illnesses and even senile brain changes before death. Again the sequence of cause and effect is difficult to evaluate. Also, the findings of other competent clinicians have revealed no such obvious brain pathology in schizophrenia—either in terms of electroencephalographic or of anatomical criteria.

Other lines of organic evidence are worthy of mention. Katz (53) has concluded from his investigations that injury to the brain during and after birth has been an important factor in certain cases of schizophrenia, although he concludes that ordinarily a number of causative factors are at work, including emotional conflicts. Finally, Herman and his colleagues (39) report 12 cases of catatonia in patients with syphilis of the nervous system, epilepsy, head trauma, and toxic psychoses. They therefore conclude that catatonic reactions can be grouped into three categories: those in which cortical damage predominates, those with marked hypothalamic involvement, and those in which psychological factors predominate.

Such evidence tends to support the conclusion that schizophrenia is not a disease entity but a syndrome or a reaction type in which either psychogenic or organic factors may predominate (Bellak 5). Or, stated differently, individuals of a certain constitutional and psychological make-up may react to excessive stress with a schizophrenic adjustive reaction whether the stress is organic or psychological or both.

Psychological Factors

Despite their fundamental organic bias, both Kraepelin and Bleuler believed in the importance of certain psychological processes in the development of schizophrenia (Katzenelbogen 54). Bleuler in particular emphasized the role of frustration and conflict, concluding that there was a splitting of personality, determined by complexes. Other psychological factors, too, will claim our attention.

1. FRUSTRATION AND CONFLICT. Since the time of Bleuler there has been increasing agreement among psychiatrists and psychologists that schizophrenia is primarily the result of faulty responses to frustration and conflict. In the face of stress which the individual feels inadequate to cope with, he resorts to the extreme use of rationalization, projection, emotional insulation, fantasy, and other ego defensive measures. Below is a summary of Adolf Meyer's conclusions concerning the development of this pattern (Christian 19, Meyer 70, 71, 72, 73):

> In the process of personality development, the individual learns various methods of coping with his problems. Some of these methods involve dealing directly with life's problems and making the most effective adjustment to them that is possible. However, other adjustive reactions are in the nature of evasive substitutions—utilizing rationalization, projection, fantasy satisfactions, and emotional withdrawal and insulation. These evasive reactions inevitably lead to failure and self-devaluation which in turn makes their use even more necessary. Thus vicious habits of response become established which

lead to a complete miscarriage of ego defenses—instead of helping the individual to adjust successfully, they actually make such an adjustment impossible.

The individual who later develops schizophrenia usually manifests an early withdrawal from a world he interprets as frustrating and hostile. This withdrawal is often concealed behind what seems to be an exemplary childhood, but which on closer examination reveals adherence to meekness and formally good behavior in order to avoid frights and struggles. Instead of participating in an active and healthy way in the activities of childhood, the individual withdraws behind a façade of goodness and meekness. This withdrawal, of course, inevitably leads to failures and disappointments which in turn serve to encourage further withdrawal from the world of reality and foster the use of fantasy satisfactions to compensate for real life failures.

As this "good" child enters the adolescent period, he tends to be overly serious, painfully self-conscious, inhibited, and prone to prefer his own company. Often he is unduly preoccupied with various religious and philosophical issues. Normal interest in the opposite sex is lacking, and vivid ideas of the evilness of sexual behavior are usually only too apparent. As the adolescent enters the period of adulthood, with its demands for independency, responsibility, and family relationships, the youth's lack of adequate socialization and preparation for meeting these problems proves fatal. Instead of increased effort and a vigorous attack on the problems associated with the assumption of adult status, the youth finds the world unbearably hurtful and turns progressively inward to fantasy satisfactions.

It is out of this type of background that schizophrenic reactions develop. These reactions may be precipitated by the increased stress placed on the individual during the period of puberty and young adulthood, or by stresses occurring later in life. However, it is particularly in coping with the ordinary adolescent and young adult conflicts centering around dependency-independency problems and the handling of hostility and sexual drives that the insecure, withdrawn personality seems to get into serious difficulty. It is usually difficult for such an individual to enter into vigorous social competition for jobs and adult status. Rather he tends to find the competitive aspects of adult life terrifying and disillusioning; it seems much safer to maintain his childhood position of dependency upon the family. His whole problem is often complicated too by unrealistic levels of aspiration and altruistic ethical ideals to which he expects others to conform. Such a psychologically vulnerable individual is of course easily hurt by the inevitable setbacks and frustrations of adult life.

In the sexual sphere, his problems are usually complicated by his highly moralistic attitude toward sex and his failure to develop to a normal heterosexual level of adjustment. In general, his sexual behavior is relatively immature and undifferentiated. Usually he has had few if any sexual contacts with the other sex (it is not unusual to find schizophrenics over 30 years of age who have never even had a date). Even if he has been married and so has had what appear to be more adequate sexual patterns, these are usually found on closer examination to have been hopelessly unsatisfactory and conducive to feelings of repugnance and guilt. As a result of his sexual immaturity, his sexual fantasies, like those of the early adolescent, may include a wide range of sexual objects, including members of the same sex. Since even heterosexual fantasies are considered immoral and unacceptable, it is not surprising that homosexual fantasies often lead to severe personality conflicts, to self-devaluation, and in some instances, as in paranoid schizophrenia, to the use of projection and other defense mechanisms for protecting the "self" against these immoral inner desires.

Homosexual fantasies, as well as overt homosexual behavior, involve far more males than is ordinarily realized, and need not lead to schizophrenia. They have a part in schizophrenia only in cases where the individual is predisposed to evaluate them as horribly immoral and repugnant, and it is the resulting conflict and self-devaluation, rather than the homosexual fantasies or behavior, which leads to mental illness. In a similar way, the handling of hostility is a particularly stressful problem for such an individual, because he usually considers it completely immoral and terribly dangerous. The hostility generated by his feelings of hurt and frustration is often more than he can bear, yet as a consequence of his withdrawal from normal social participation, he typically lacks any adequate comprehension of the role of hostility in normal everyday social relations. He does not know how to express it in socially acceptable ways and he is completely upset when he is the object of other people's hostility. Consequently he usually tries to repress his hostility and to deny even to himself that he is the kind of person who has such unacceptable impulses. The author is reminded here of a schizophrenic patient whose adjustment difficulties centered in part around his complete inability to express hostility. After several group therapy sessions, this patient proudly related to the group how for the first time in his life he had actually told a fellow who shoved in front of him in the cafeteria line to wait his turn.

As in the case of the neurotic, the schizophrenic's conflicts get him into a vicious circle. He withdraws from social participation because he is hurt and scared. But this withdrawal does not necessarily reduce his need or desire for social approval, status, and love. However, it does materially reduce his chances of gratifying these desires by removing him from the normal stream of social development and preventing him from acquiring the necessary attitudes and skills requisite to the attainment of his desires. Thus it can readily be seen that individuals who are severely sensitized to the hurts and frustrations of social relations and who are handicapped by their subsequent withdrawal from the educative effects of normal social give and take, find the stresses of young adulthood too much to handle.

2. EARLY PSYCHIC TRAUMA.   This general developmental picture of schizophrenia as a failure in socialization, and the gradual accumulation of faulty attitudes and habits of response, is supplemented by the increasing clinical evidence of early psychic trauma in schizophrenia. As Menninger (67) points out, "There is much proof that the injuries suffered by those individuals who later become schizophrenic occur very early in infancy." These injuries may take many forms, such as neglect and rejection by the mother, death of a parent, or other severe frustrations or disappointments. Many of these wounds take place in what seem to be exceptionally good homes, and often the parents are quite unaware of any trauma to the child. In a study of the parent-child relations in childhood schizophrenia, Kanner (45) found that many of the parents were prominent and respected citizens in the community, but that toward their children they were undemonstrative and showed a mechani-

zation of human relationships with an almost complete
lack of any real warmth and affection. According to
Kanner, the resulting apathy, seclusiveness, and irritability of the children seemed to be an act of turning
away to seek protection and comfort in solitude. These
early wounds will be reinforced by any subsequent
events which lead to feelings of inferiority and self-
devaluation or to the perception of the world as a hostile
and dangerous place.

Menninger (67) describes it this way:

Children injured in this way are apt to develop
certain defenses. They cover up, as the slang expression puts it. They deny the injury which they have
experienced or the pain which they are suffering. They
erect a façade or front, "All's well with me," they seem
to say. "I am one of the fellows; I am just like everybody else. I am a normal person." And indeed they
act like normal persons, as much as they can. They
go to the same schools, they complete the same work,
they seek the same goals, they do the same things that
all the rest of us do. Often they are noticeable only
for a certain reticence, shyness, perhaps slight eccen-
tricity. Just as often, they are not conspicuous at
all . . .

What is underneath that front? One might say that
the same sort of thing goes on in the emotional life
that goes on when an abscess slowly develops beneath
the surface of the body, for example in the lungs or
in the liver. There has been an injury, an infection.
Counteracting processes have been set up so that
tenseness and pressure and potential pain are gathering. But all of this is concealed from the outsider.
There is intense conflict and tension and anxiety and
strong feelings of bitterness, resentment and hate
toward those very people with whom the external

relationships may be so perfectly normal. "I hate them! They don't treat me right. They will never love me and I will never love them. I hate them and I could kill them all! But I must not let them know all this. I must cover it up, because they might read my thoughts and then they woudn't like me and wouldn't be nice to me."

All this is covered up as long as possible—by trivial conversation, pleasant greetings, chat about the movies or the picnic and the next date, and the rest of the ordinary things of adolescent or early adult life. For the chief problem in the person who is going to develop what we call schizophrenia is, "How can I control the bitterness and hatred I feel because of the unendurable sorrow and disappointment that life has brought to me?" His efforts to control it often show themselves in various kinds of withdrawal, lone-wolfishness, seclusiveness, even mild suspiciousness, or just a quiet going of one's own way with disinterest in active social participation.

. . . And as in the case of coronary sclerosis and diabetes, the regimen under which they live has much to do with their successful adaptation. Given certain new stresses, the façade may break down and the underlying bitterness and conflict may break through. The patient may suddenly begin to hear voices talking about him, saying that he is mean, that he is hateful. Or he may begin to detect the hostility of other people in a far larger measure than could possibly be true. He may begin to consider himself persecuted.

Or the break-through may be like this: A little girl who was one of the most popular members of her community, president of her high school class and prominent in her Sunday school, calmly walked into her father's bedroom one night and shot him with a revolver. The following day she was the same "sweet, pleasant, demure but somewhat shy girl" that she had always been. No one could believe, at first, that she had really committed the murder. Nor could anyone believe, either, among those who knew and loved her, that she had schizophrenia. But the psychological test showed it very clearly. . . .

The most important cases of overt schizophrenia are not those in which the break-through appears in such aggressive and violent direct action as I have described. In fact, most cases of schizophrenia are not dangerous. The commonest type of "break-through" . . . is that in which the conflict appears in the form of physical symptoms. These physical symptoms usually appear as chronic pains in the abdomen or in the back or in the head.

The descriptions of both Meyer and Menninger afford an excellent clinical picture of the development of schizophrenic reactions. The individual's gradual withdrawal into his own self-limited, self-ruled, and self-defined world can be understood as a repudiation of a world of reality which is interpreted as unbearably hurtful and dangerous. And it would be impossible for an individual to repudiate reality in favor of his own self-created world without considerable emotional blunting and distortion relative to events in the world of reality. His loss of interest and emotional insulation then serve as a protection from further hurt and from the necessity of further striving.

3. LACK OF REALITY CHECKS. Many schizophrenics are handicapped in their social development by oversolicitous and overprotective mothers (Duval and Hoffman 25; Wittman and Huffman 108). This, together with their early social withdrawal, has a variety of effects which are of developmental significance. Perhaps most impor-

tant, these factors tend to cut him off from the normal activities of social reality testing—from social give and take—so that he tends to be passive and protected and fails to develop the necessary skills and emotional attitudes for healthy social participation. For example, in the matter of role playing, the schizophrenic is handicapped by a lack of social experience. We all model our behavior after that of others and attempt many roles which we test out in the group and either adopt as successful or discard. Since this eliminative process does not take place in the schizophrenic's social development, he may have very unrealistic ideas of the types of social roles that are open to him, and it may be easy to fantasy himself as a great religious savior or some other remarkable or unusual person.

Our self-evaluation is to a large extent determined by the way other people react to us. We gradually learn to see ourselves somewhat as others see us and to evaluate ourselves accordingly. However, the schizophrenic is handicapped by a lack of ability to see himself from the perspective of others; consequently his attitudes toward himself are apt to be fantasy-ridden and distorted. The same point holds, of course, for his environmental attitudes, which suffer from the rigidity and lack of perspective of his own limited viewpoint, uncorrected by social experience.

Thus it is the lack of reality checks, rather than the fantasy preoccupation in itself, which is so devastating to personality development. As the schizophrenic's language and thought processes are not subject to normal reality checks, they become progressively more individualistic. Such a lack of constant reality checks in the development of environmental and self-evaluations would in itself make for an ever-widening breach between the schizophrenic and other people.

4. REGRESSION. Considerable interest has been shown in the dynamics underlying the disorganization or disintegration of thought processes in schizophrenic. Kasanin (52), Goldstein (32), and others (Levy 59) have advanced the belief that in schizophrenia there is a reduction from conceptual thinking to a more primitive "concrete" thinking in which the individual is dominated by the external and internal stimuli acting upon him at the moment and reacts to parts of the perceptual field as if they were wholes. As a result of this "concrete" approach, the patient loses the normal demarcations between himself and the world, his words lose their usual representative character, and his perceptions no longer show the expected relation of parts to a whole. Kasanin attributes this concretization or fragmentation of thought processes to extreme regression to immature and childish levels of thinking.

Here Kasanin points out that the child lives in a world which is partly real and partly magic, and that he forms all sorts of fantastic notions and ideas about the things around him. He tends to personify and vitalize inanimate objects and to endow them with various powers. He may also tend to feel that he is the center of the universe and to develop ideas of his own omnipotence. Also commonly found, according to Kasanin, is the belief that adults can read his thoughts.

Kasanin then attempts to relate many of the odd and bizarre delusions of schizophrenics to the magical thinking and other characteristics of children's thinking. For example, he points out that most schizophrenics at one time or another express ideas of omnipotence. This may be expressed by the patient who sits quietly in his chair with his index finger flexed in a certain way, afraid to change its position because the world would suddenly be destroyed if he moved. Similarly, many schizophrenics are convinced that other people can read their minds and know their thoughts. Everyone knows what they are thinking about, and when questioned by the psychiatrist, they may look at him in amusement and consider the whole thing a farce since he obviously knows their thoughts already without being told.

According to Kasanin, the schizophrenic's deterioration in personal and ethical habits is also part of this general picture of regression. In extreme form this regression presumably is manifested by the catatonic patient who assumes a fetal position, apparently symbolizing his desire to return to a helpless, irresponsible, dependent level. In this connection Arieti (2) has pointed out that in advanced cases, patients frequently collect apparently useless objects with which they later decorate themselves. Arieti considers both habits to be evidences of regression to more primitive levels of response.

In a similar vein, the parallels between schizophrenic thinking and the thinking of primitive peoples have been emphasized by Boisen (9, 11). In primitive religions and even in those which are not so primitive, there are ideas of rebirth and previous reincarnation, divine intervention, and salvation through sacrifice. Commonly found also are ideas of taboo and magic, and the tendency to believe in mysterious supernatural forces and in possession by good and evil spirits.

Regression has been accepted by a number of psychoanalysts as the basic mechanism underlying schizo-

phrenic reactions. A general picture of this viewpoint
can be obtianed from Brown (15):

> Schizophrenia represents a deep libidinal and ego
> regression. . . . The hallucinated voices and figures
> represent projection of the previously introjected
> parental images. His schizophrenic gesturings and
> postures represent normally unconscious ideas to
> which his weakened ego allows expression. His de-
> lusions can almost always be shown to come from
> unconscious wishes which are not controlled by the
> reality principle. The schizophrenic splitting repre-
> sents the return to the early level where effect and
> cognition were not yet differentiated.*

There is some contradiction, however, both in findings and in interpretation. Despert (22), Cameron (16),
and other investigators (Boas 8; Yerbury and Newell
109) find no such close resemblance between schizophrenic thinking and characteristics inherent in the
thinking of either children or primitives. Cameron, in a
study of deteriorated schizophrenic and senile patients,
concluded from his studies that schizophrenic thinking
was characterized by over-inclusion and an inability to
organize and subordinate the events occurring simultaneously in the environment rather than by a regression to
childish modes of thought. Boas (8) too states: "The
comparison of forms of psychoses and primitive life
seems still more unfortunate. The manifestation of mental disturbances must necessarily depend upon the culture in which people live and it must be of great value
to the psychiatrist to study the expression of forms of

* By permission from *Psychodynamics of Abnormal Behavior*, by
Junius F. Brown. Copyright, 1940, McGraw-Hill Book Company,
Inc.

psychoses in different cultures, but an attempt to parallel forms of healthy primitive life and those of disturbances in our civilization is not based on any tangible
analogy." Although there are certain common elements
in and obvious resemblances between the thinking and
fantasy of children, primitives, and schizophrenics, it
would appear in the light of Cameron's and Boas' findings that basically these thought processes are not the
same. The child can distinguish adequately between
his fantasies and the world of reality; likewise the primitive, however much in error his concepts may be, is
not out of contact with his social and physical environment.

Thought disturbances quite similar to those in schizophrenia are found also in most other psychotic reactions, and are considered by many investigators to be
more in the nature of ego disintegration or disorganization than of regression to more primitive levels. As a
result of this ego decompensation, the patient seems no
longer able to maintain the habitual responses which
marked his training in thinking and behavior. This involves a lowering of reality and ethical controls which
has been likened to the thought processes in dreams.
There would appear to be many resemblances between
schizophrenic ideation and dreams in terms of bizarre
content, the splitting of affect and thought, and the
gratification of fantasy wishes. It does not appear contradictory to assume that regression also plays an important role in this entire process.

Related to the problem of schizophrenic decompensation is the question of whether or not a permanent irreversible loss or deterioration takes place in so-called
"deteriorated" schizophrenics. In general this question
has been answered in the negative. Kant (48) examined

under sodium amytal 100 unselected male schizophrenics with an illness duration of at least ten years, with the object of determining the degree of deterioration. He found that although apparent extreme disorganization was always present in cases presenting pronounced withdrawal symptoms, even the very disorganized patients could generalize and conceptualize rather freely when adequate rapport and coöperation had been established.

5. EGO DEFENSIVE VALUES OF SYMPTOMS. As we have noted, the emotional blunting and distortion in schizophrenic reactions protect the individual from the hurt of disappointment and frustration. Regression enables him to lower his level of aspiration and to accept a position of dependency. Projection helps him to maintain some semblance of ego integrity by placing the blame for his difficulties on others and attributing his own unacceptable desires to them. Wish-fulfilling fantasy enables him to achieve some measure of compensation for his feelings of inferiority and self-devaluation. In various combinations and degrees, these mechanisms seem to constitute the basic defensive framework of schizophrenic reactions.

In the exaggerated use of fantasy and projection, we find the two mechanisms which are most apt to lead to the development of delusions and hallucinations with their many ego defensive values. Delusions of influence enable the patient to blame others for causing his own inadmissible thoughts and behavior. Fantasies of being the focus of widespread interest and attention help the patient to compensate for feelings of isolation and lack of social recognition and status. Delusions of persecution explain away the patient's failure to achieve a satisfactory adjustment in the real world by placing the blame on his enemies. Delusions of grandeur and omnipotence may grow out of simple wishful thinking and may help to counteract feelings of inferiority and inadequacy by a sense of great personal worth and power.

Hallucinations in functional psychoses are interrelated with delusions and have similar dynamic functions. They are closely related to wishful thinking, the projection of unacceptable desires and impulses, feelings of unbearable guilt, and so on. Schizophrenic patients may speak to God and hear him confer great powers upon them and assign them the mission of saving the world. Or the patient with guilt feelings over homosexual thoughts may hear voices which accuse him of being a homosexual or of being guilty of other sexual misdeeds. Occasionally patients hallucinate sexual relations.

Of course, it may be noted that acutely disturbed patients may be so upset by their emotional conflicts that almost a delirious ideation occurs; here the delusions and hallucinations are part of a picture of acute mental turmoil in which their ego defensive value is greatly reduced or comes to be nonexistent.

Finally, the stereotypies and other symbolic behavior of the schizophrenic can also be understood in terms of the patient's mental processes and general reactive pattern. Thus the patient who thinks he is Christ may prostrate himself on the floor with his arms spread at right angles to form a cross, or dangerous obsessive desires may be counteracted by various magical rituals. Often the symbolism is by no means easy to fathom, but the study of it may be of value in furthering an understanding of apparently meaningless behavioral symptoms.

Psychodynamic Differences between the Types

How do the dynamics in hebephrenic reactions differ from those in paranoid or catatonic reactions? The work of Boisen (10), a psychiatrically trained chaplain who himself suffered an acute episode of catatonic schizophrenia, has been of great value here.

In terms of general personality organization, Boisen points out that the schizophrenic is characteristically a "good" boy. This means that he has accepted for himself the role his parents and teachers have chosen for him—that is, he has internalized the ethical and moral values of society and has judged himself in accordance with these standards. This moral and ethical personality dimension or *superego* Boisen refers to as the "generalized other." In this the schizophrenic differs sharply from the delinquent, who usually has not accepted the authority or standards of his parents and teachers, and also from the mature adult who has evaluated these standards and modified them in his own behavior rather than accepting them blindly.

The schizophrenic, having accepted his social role, now finds himself unable to achieve a sufficient degree of personality unification on the basis of this role. He suffers from various unresolved internal conflicts centering around feelings of failure, unacceptable sexual and hostile desires, and so on. This results in intense inner turmoil, self-condemnation, and anxiety, the net result being an anxiety-ridden and intolerable self-devaluation. There are several different ways in which he may attempt to cope with his mounting feelings of personal failure and conflict.

In latent schizophrenic reactions the individual is

forced to only a mild use of the various schizophrenic defenses in order to handle his inner needs and to cope with reality. He manages to maintain his general reality orientation and to stabilize his defenses on a marginal level of adjustment. If the stress were to increase, he would decompensate further.

In simple schizophrenic reactions the individual withdraws from the struggle of life, becomes disinterested and emotionally apathetic, and gives up the fight to achieve social status and esteem. Although the price of this withdrawal in terms of self-devaluation may occasionally be reflected in episodes of mental turmoil or impulsive behavior, the emotional insulation is generally effective, with slow but gradual personality disintegration. Of course, in simple schizophrenic reactions this decompensatory process may be stabilized, so that the individual becomes an apathetic drifter or remains a dependent, noncontributing member of the family without decompensating further to the point where hospitalization would be required.

In hebephrenic reactions, the emotional withdrawal and personality disintegration reach their ultimate in degree. The individual gives up all claim to social approval and status and under the pressure of his conflicts seems to egress and disintegrate at the same time. The word-hash, silliness, regression, and other evidences of severe personality deterioration are considered part of this general hebephrenic fragmentation or disintegration, growing out of the patient's discouragement, his loss of faith in himself, and his withdrawal from social contacts and reality.

In catatonic reactions, according to Boisen, the patient is engaged in a desperate struggle and is stirred to the bottommost depths of his mental life in his attempt to solve his difficulties and maintain his ego integrity. Thus Boisen regards the catatonic excitement as a frenzied attempt to deal with the threats to the ego, and catatonic stupor as a retreat during which the individual strives desperately to find some philosophy of life, some system of beliefs, some faith in himself and the world on which to build. Here malignant reactions have not become established as yet and the individual, though panic-stricken, is still fighting desperately to save himself and resist personality disintegration.

In the paranoid reaction, the patient tries to maintain feelings of personal worth and respect by misinterpreting the facts: he simply projects the blame for his difficulties upon others. Now it is all the other fellow's fault. He likes them but they don't like him. They are interfering with him and persecuting him. As we have noted, it is only another step to explain all the attention others are paying him by means of delusions of grandeur in which he is indeed a remarkable person with great abilities. We shall presently see that in so-called paranoia proper such delusional defenses hold up so well that the rest of the patient's personality remains relatively intact. However, in paranoid schizophrenia the patient is so overwhelmed by both inner and outer demands that even with the aid of these psychotic defenses he undergoes severe personality disorganization.

Finally, in unclassified schizophrenic reactions we may be dealing with almost any possible combination of the dynamics of the other types, as well as with very acute psychotic episodes which reach a high level of intensity and then subside rather rapidly, much like the psychotic reactions . . . in connection with combat exhaustion.

Thus of the six schizophrenic reaction types, only the

catatonic and the acute unclassified reactions hold any material possibility of spontaneous ego reorganization and remission to a more healthy adjustment level. The others involve more serious and chronic ego disorganization and require extensive, long-term psychotherapy.

Sociological Factors

The role of sociological factors in the development of schizophrenia is poorly understood. We have seen in our previous discussion that there is more schizophrenia in our culture than in certain primitive cultures, and that within our own culture there is a higher incidence in the poorer areas of our large cities. Faris (29) concludes that the social disorganization in these poorer areas intensifies the personal problems of the individual and also provides a social environment in which no satisfactory conventional solutions are available. Malzberg (65) suggests that the increased stress and strain and lesser security of the larger cities are responsible for the higher incidence in urban areas than in rural ones.

Schizophrenia has also shown a relatively high incidence among certain sub-groups within our society. For example, the rate is particularly high among nuns. Apparently, however, it is not that the actual way of life produces disorders so much as that individuals with schizophrenic trends are often attracted to a life of meditation withdrawn from everyday hustle and strife (Jahrrciss 42).

Therapy and Prognosis

The prognosis in schizophrenic reactions has been traditionally unfavorable. Under the routine hospital treatment prevalent before the introduction of modern shock and psychotherapeutic procedures, the rate of discharge approximated about 30 per cent. But only a small percentage of these patients could be considered fully recovered, and even here the recovery was due not so much to the hospital treatment as to the patient's spontaneous recovery by restructuralization of his own ego defenses. Hospital treatment did serve, however, to reduce the number of deaths due to infectious diseases such as tuberculosis and pneumonia, which at one time were of common occurrence among physically debilitated schizophrenics.

With the introduction of new forms of therapy the general prognosis in most cases of schizophrenia has become much more favorable. These newer therapies are still in experimental stages and the results vary considerably from one investigator to another. Insulin therapy has proved to be the most effective medical therapy, showing recovery or marked improvement in some 40 to 60 per cent of all cases. In a follow-up study Ross (90) and his colleagues found that 57 per cent of a large series of insulin-treated patients were still in the hospital at the end of two years, and 37 per cent were making a successful adjustment in the community. At the end of five to ten years Rupp and Fletcher (91) found that 53.5 per cent of 641 schizophrenics were still in mental hospitals and 27.5 per cent in the community. (13.9 per cent were dead and for the remaining 5.1 per cent no adequate follow-up was available.) The combination of insulin shock with electro-shock has often proved more effective than insulin alone, particularly with cases of long duration. Taylor (98) reports that 438 out of 782 (64 per cent) schizophrenic patients so treated recovered sufficiently to be released from the

hospital. Even more encouraging results are reported
by Veit (103), who found that 78 per cent of a series
of 158 schizophrenic patients receiving insulin and/or
combined shock treatment were able to leave the hospital.

But shock methods alone are inadequate in terms of
long-range results, all indications being that most patients so treated tend to relapse over a period of time.
For the best long-range results, the combination of psychotherapy with shock therapy is most effective. Shock
therapy may hasten the recovery of a patient who might
have been able to restructure his defenses and make a
reasonably good recovery anyway. Its greatest value,
however, probably lies in the fact that it does result
in a temporary alleviation of symptoms, enabling the
therapist to get through to the patient with psychotherapy designed to help him gain insight into his illness
and achieve more adequate techniques of adjustment.
Various therapeutic aids, such as recreational and occupational therapy, are also helpful in schizophrenia;
they give the patient pleasant contact with reality and
acceptable outlets for emotional drives.

Two other treatment procedures for schizophrenics
deserve special mention, namely psychosurgery and
group psychotherapy. Prefrontal lobotomies and other
psychosurgical procedures have been used on chronic
cases which have not responded to less drastic methods of treatment. Although there are many favorable
reports on results, there is still need of further experimental evaluation before we shall be able to evaluate accurately the long-term results and range of effectiveness
of psychosurgical procedures. Group psychotherapy has
been increasingly used in the treatment of psychotic patients and seems to offer a therapeutic approach of

great value, particularly in providing the schizophrenic patient with a safe social environment for reality testing and for the development of understanding and skill in interpersonal relations. Although there is convincing evidence that group psychotherapy is the most effective medium for the socialization of withdrawn schizophrenic patients, this method of therapy too is still undergoing experimental evaluations designed to increase its effectiveness and range of application.

The prognosis is not the same for all cases of schizophrenia. The following conditions generally indicate a short duration of disorder: (1) early treatment—before eighteen months, (2) onset acute (as in the catatonic type) rather than gradual and insidious, (3) known precipitating conditions—environmental setbacks, such as severe financial losses and the death of loved ones,* (4) a catatonic reaction pattern or one showing evidence of manic-depressive symptoms, (5) insight—the greater the patient's insight into his illness, the more favorable the prognosis, and (6) a favorable and understanding environment to which the patient can be returned (Kant 49; Rennie 87).

Although these conditions make cure more hopeful, there is no substitute for early detection and prevention in schizophrenia (Menninger and Rapaport 68). In this respect it may be of value to note some of the early personality trends often found in the background of patients who later develop schizophrenic reactions (Bradley and Bowen 13, Dunham 24, Gottlieb 34, Sherman and Jost 94, Yerbury and Newell 109). These include: (1) seclusiveness—introverted preoccupation

---

* Kant (46) found that severe precipitating stresses in the life situation of the patient were five times as frequent in those schizophrenics who recovered as in those who deteriorated.

with their thoughts, (2) social withdrawal, together with a lack of good social attitudes—such children are often meek and formally good and do not enter into social activities with healthy enthusiasm, (3) rigid personality—this often involves narrow interests, (4) emotional ambivalence and apathy—such children may alternate between intense affection, hate, and apathy toward loved ones, (5) over-sensitivity to criticism and environmental change, (6) self-consciousness and shyness, and (7) obsessive-compulsive or hypochondriacal patterns.

Although none of these trends necessarily insures the later development of schizophrenic reactions, they are all socially handicapping, and their early detection and correction are vital for healthy personality development.

The value of diagnostic tests in the early detection and prevention of schizophrenic reactions has been emphasized by Menninger and Rapaport (68), and many other investigators. By means of the Make A Picture Story Test, the Rorschach, the Thematic Apperception Test, and other diagnostic instruments, dangerous trends can be detected and steps taken to correct undesirable techniques of adjustment before they become well established.

References

2. Arieti, Silvano: "Primitive Habits in the Preterminal Stage of Schizophrenia; With Particular Reference to the Hoarding and Self-Decorating Habits." *Journal of Nervous and Mental Disease,* CII (1945), 367–375.
3. Barahal, Hyman S.: "Is Dementia Praecox Hereditary?" *Psychiatric Quarterly,* XIX (1945), 478–502.

5. Bellak, Leopold: "The Concept of Projection." *Psychiatry*, VII (1944), 353–370.

7. Bleuler, Eugen: *The Theory of Schizophrenic Negativism* (trans. by William A. White). Washington, D. C.: Nervous and Mental Disease Publishing Co.

8. Boas, Franz: *The Mind of Primitive Man* (rev. ed.). New York: Macmillan, 1938.

9. Boisen, A. T.: *Exploration of the Inner World*. Chicago: Willett Clark, 1937.

10. ———: "Onset in Acute Schizophrenia." *Psychiatry*, X (1947), 159–166.

11. ———: "The Form and Content of Schizophrenic Thinking." *Psychiatry*, V (1942), 23–33.

13. Bradley, Charles and Bowen, Margaret: "Behavior Characteristics of Schizophrenic Children." *Psychiatric Quarterly*, XV (1941), 296–315.

15. Brown, Junius F.: *Psychodynamics of Abnormal Behavior*. New York: McGraw-Hill, 1940.

16. Cameron, Norman: "Deterioration and Regression in Schizophrenic Thinking." *Journal of Abnormal and Social Psychology*, XXXIV (1939), 265–270.

17. Campbell, C. M.: "Clinical Studies in Schizophrenia." *American Journal of Psychiatry*, XCIX (1943), 475–483.

19. Christian, H. A.: *Psychiatry for Practitioners*. New York: Oxford University Press, 1936.

22. Despert, J. Louise: "A Comparative Study in Thinking in Schizophrenic Children and in Children of Pre-School Age." *American Journal of Psychiatry*, XCVII (1940–1941), 189–213.

24. Dunham, H. Warren: "The Social Personality of the Catatonic-Schizophrene." *American Journal of Sociology*, XLIX (1944), 508–518.

25. Duval, Addison M. and Hoffman, Jay L.: "Dementia Praecox in Military Life as Compared with Dementia Praecox in Civil Life." *War Medicine*, I (1941), 854–862.

26. Elliot, Helen E.: "Comparison of Non-Psychotic Women

with Schizophrenics, with Respect to Body Type, Signs of Autonomic Imbalance and Menstrual History." *Psychiatric Quarterly*, XV (1941), 17–22.

27. Escalona, Sibylle: "Some Considerations Regarding Psychotherapy with Psychotic Children." *Bulletin of the Menninger Clinic*, XII, No. 4 (1948), 127–134. Reprinted by permission of the author and the *Bulletin of the Menninger Clinic*.

29. Faris, Robert E. L.: "Reflections of Social Disorganization in the Behavior of a Schizophrenic Patient." *American Journal of Sociology*, L (1944), 134–141.

32. Goldstein, Kurt: "The Significance of Psychological Research in Schizophrenia." *Journal of Nervous and Mental Disease*, XCVII (1943), 261–279.

34. Gottlieb, Bernhardt S.: "Prognostic Criteria in Hebephrenia; The Importance of Age, Sex, Constitution and Marital Status." *American Journal of Psychiatry*, XCVII (1940), 332–341.

38. Hecker, A. O.: "Schizophrenia: A Neurobiologic Approach." *Annals of Internal Medicine*, XV (1941), 678–699.

39. Herman, Morris, Harpham, Dorothy, and Rosenblum, Marcus: "Non-schizophrenic Catatonic States." *New York State Journal of Medicine*, XLII (1942), 624–627.

42. Jahrreiss, Walter O.: "Some Influences of Catholic Education and Creed Upon Psychotic Reactions." *Diseases of the Nervous System*, III (1942), 377–381.

44. Kallmann, Franz: "Modern Concepts of Genetics in Relation to Mental Health and Abnormal Personality Development." *Psychiatric Quarterly*, XXI (1947), 535–553.

45. Kanner, Leo: "Frosted Children." *Time*, April 26, 1948, pp. 77–78.

46. Kant, Otto: "Study of a Group of Recovered Schizophrenic Patients." *Psychiatric Quarterly*, XV (1941), 262–283.

48. ———: "Clinical Analysis of Schizophrenic Deterioration." *Psychiatric Quarterly*, XVII (1943), 426–445.

49. ———: "The Evaluation of Prognostic Criteria in Schizophrenia." *Journal of Nervous and Mental Disease*, C (1944), 598–605.

52. Kasanin, J. S.: "Developmental Roots of Schizophrenia." *American Journal of Psychiatry*, CI (1945), 770–776.

53. Katz, B.: *The Etiology of the Deteriorating Psychoses of Adolescence and Early Adult Life*. Doctoral Dissertation, University of Southern California, 1939.

54. Katzenelbogen, S.: "Dementia Praecox: Formulation by Kraepelin, Bleuler and Meyer." *Psychiatric Quarterly*, XVI (1942), 439–453.

56. Kraepelin, Emil: *Clinical Psychiatry* (trans. by A. Ross Diefendorf). New York: Macmillan, 1937.

58. Kretschmer, Ernst: *Physique and Character*. New York: Harcourt, Brace, 1925.

59. Levy, Erwin: "Some Aspects of the Schizophrenic Formal Disturbance of Thought." *Psychiatry*, VI (1943), 55–69.

60. Lewis, Nolan Don C.: *Research in Dementia Praecox*. New York: The National Committee for Mental Hygiene, 1936.

64. Maisel, Albert Q.: "Hope for Millions." *McCall's*, September 1949.

65. Malzberg, Benjamin: *Social and Biological Aspects of Mental Disease*. Utica, New York: New York State Hospitals Press, 1940.

67. Menninger, Karl: "Diagnosis and Treatment of Schizophrenia." *Bulletin of the Menninger Clinic*, XII (1948), 96–106. Reprinted by permission of the author and *Bulletin of the Menninger Clinic*.

68. Menninger, Karl and Rapaport, David: "Schizophrenia." *American Journal of Psychiatry*, CIII (1947).

70. Meyer, Adolf: "Fundamental Conceptions of Dementia Praecox." *Journal of Nervous and Mental Disease*, XXXIV (1906), 331–336.

71. ———: "The Dynamic Interpretation of Dementia Praecox." *American Journal of Psychology*, XXI (1910), 385–403.

72. ———: "Fundamental Conceptions of Dementia Praecox." *British Medical Journal*, II (1906), 757–760.

73. ———: "The Nature and Conception of Dementia Praecox." *Journal of Abnormal Psychology*, V (1910), 274–285.

82. Pastore, Nicholas: "The Genetics of Schizophrenia." *Psychological Bulletin*, XLVI (1949), 285–302.

87. Rennie, Thomas A. C.: "Analysis of One Hundred Cases of Schizophrenia with Recovery." *Archives of Neurology and Psychiatry*, XLVI (1941), 197–229. Reprinted by permission of the American Medical Association and Dr. Rennie.

90. Ross, John R. *et al.*: "The Pharmacological Shock Treatment of Schizophrenia." *American Journal of Psychiatry*, XCVII (1941), 1,007–1,023.

91. Rupp, Charles and Fletcher, Elizabeth: "A Five to Ten Year Follow-up Study of 641 Schizophrenic Cases." *American Journal of Psychiatry*, XCVII (1941), 1,007–1,023.

92. Sheldon, William H.: *The Varieties of Temperament*. New York: Harper, 1942.

94. Sherman, M. and Jost, H.: "Qualifications of Psychophysiological Measures." *Psychosomatic Medicine*, VII (1945), 215–219.

98. Taylor, John H.: "A Further Report on the Use of Shock Therapy: Results in 1,302 Cases." *Diseases of the Nervous System*, V (1944), 56.

103. Veit, Henry: "Insulin Therapy at Colorado Psychopathic Hospital." *Diseases of the Nervous System*, VIII (1947), 320–323.

107. Winkelman, N. W. and Book, M. H.: "Observations on the Histopathology of Schizophrenia." *American Journal of Psychiatry*, CV (1949), 889–896.

108. Wittman, Mary P. and Huffman, Arthur V.: "A Com-

parative Study of Developmental, Adjustment and Personality Characteristics of Psychotic, Psychoneurotic, Delinquent and 'Normally' Adjusted Teen-aged Youths." *Elgin State Hospital Papers*, V (1944), 228–237.

109. Yerbury, Edgar C. and Newell, Nancy: "Genetic and Environmental Factors in Psychoses of Children." *American Journal of Psychiatry*, C (1943), 599–605.

[This reference list is part of a larger one appearing in Dr. Coleman's book. Only the references which appear in the section of the work used have been listed, with original reference numbers.]

Some Psychological Features of Schizophrenia*

BY *David Shakow, Ph.D.*

I should like to discuss some aspects of the psychological findings deriving from a systematic interdisciplinary investigation of schizophrenia at the Worcester State Hospital (5), a project which extended over many years.

Perhaps I should first present the *context* in which I shall consider the various aberrancies in schizophrenic behavior which our psychological, and to some extent our physiological, studies have turned up. It involves a simple formulation, and one to which most of you, I believe, will raise little objection. Assuming that the fundamental needs of the human being are, have been, or are potentially present in the schizophrenic—and it is difficult for me to see how we can assume otherwise—then the difficulty which he has in achieving the satisfaction of these needs in the normal manner may be due to either of these two kinds of defects: (1) actually low

* By permission from *Feelings and Emotions, The Mooseheart Symposium* (Ed. by Martin L. Reyment). Copyright, 1950, McGraw-Hill Book Company, Inc.

capacity; or (2) an inability to perform at the essentially normal capacity level which he has.

If low capacity is the cause then schizophrenics are below par in potentialities. They start, relatively, with a primary handicap in intellectual, affective, or motor functions which they presumably can never overcome, even under optimum conditions.

If it is rather the inability to achieve normal capacity level that is basic—and the evidence seems to point in this direction (13)—then despite the presence of approximately the normal range of capacities, something prevents schizophrenics from reaching capacity level. This defect must, by definition, be secondary. It may be due either to (1) *immaturity* or (2) *lack of integration*, or to both. (These may be present independently or together, but it must be emphasized that the terms are *not* synonymous.)

If we say that inability to achieve at his capacity level is a result of *immaturity*, we mean that the subject is unable to react to situations consistently at a level of development to be expected from him insofar as he is a normal "ideal" person of that chronological (and mental) age. This immature response may be due either to *retardation* or *fixation* in the process of personality development, or to *regression*. What we mean by the former is clear. By the latter we mean the reversion to a channel of expression belonging to a phase of personal development earlier than that indicated by the chronological and/or mental age of the person.

If the inability to achieve capacity performance is due to lack of integration, what is involved is a condition of inharmonious working of the organism, in which there is a lack of coördination and organization as a totality. This disorganization may manifest itself in a

variety of ways; for example, in tendencies toward segmentalization or in unequal development between habit
systems and needs. We are concerned, of course, not
only with the *quality* but also with the *stability* of the
integration.

In this context, so barely delineated here, let us examine the major kinds of disturbances that we have found
in schizophrenia. These disturbances must, of course, be
understood to represent *characteristic* rather than invar-
iable patterns of behavior. The difference between
schizophrenic and normal persons lies in their differing
prevalent behaviors. We must recognize that the schizophrenic makes sporadic or even persistent attempts at
using normal devices, but usually, with successive failures, these efforts become less and less frequent.

At certain levels of psychological function, disturbance does not apparently occur or is at least minimal.
We might give these some consideration as an introduction to the discussion of disturbed behavior. In our own
experiments, we found that simple, noncentral processes, where the voluntary factor is at a minimum, are
least or not at all affected. These include, besides certain
autonomic functions such as galvanic skin response and
insensible perspiration, and some simple cerebrospinal
system and sensory functions such as patellar reflex latency time (7) and direct current threshold (6), some
aspects of motor response (16, 17) in which the time
factor is permitted to operate or in which the coöperation factor is eliminated. These undisturbed functions
are relatively few in number.

The *affected levels of response*, those in which there
are significant statistical differences between schizophrenic and normal subjects are many more.

An examination of these varieties of conduct reveals

that in one respect they appear to involve one or another aspect of expression of a single but complex type of difficulty, namely, *the inability to keep a major set* (14). By this I mean the inability to maintain a state of readiness to respond to a coming stimulus, a state which facilitates the particular type of activity called for. Sometimes this requires a readiness to respond to a specific stimulus, sometimes a readiness to respond to a generalization from a group of stimuli. Sometimes it requires a readiness to respond to the final one of a series of stimuli, *i.e.*, to organize one's self in time, whether in a matter of milliseconds, or more extended periods. Whatever the situation, there is one major set involved and many possible minor sets that may enter. It would appear that the schizophrenic difficulty lies in not being able to keep the major set. We shall take up the more general aspects of this fundamental characteristic later. For the present I wish to consider the three main ways in which this difficulty is dealt with by the schizophrenic. These ways are (1) withdrawal, (2) simplification, and (3) unsuccessful handling of the complicated situation.

By the first, *withdrawal*, I mean the type of reaction which some patients show, that of withdrawing from the experimental situation to which it is necessary to react and thus avoiding the difficulty altogether. This may come about through total lack of coöperation or through partial unresponsiveness to stimulation. Our psychological data are full of instances of disturbed functions clearly related to degree of coöperation. In its clinical aspects the phenomenon is well known to you in the so-called withdrawal of the schizophrenic. A paper by Angyal, Freeman, and Hoskins (1) has described a physiological analogue in the hyporeactivity of schizophrenics to a variety of stimulating agents. Such metabolic stimulants as thyroid and dinitrophenol evoked much smaller responses from schizophrenic than from normal subjects. The autonomic nervous system in schizophrenics seems to be much less affected by epinephrine and by the forced breathing of hot moist oxygen (4). Central nervous system reactions such as the nystagmic response to vestibular stimulation, both rotatory and caloric, are also considerably reduced in the schizophrenic (2).

By the second way, *simplification*, I mean the kinds of reaction which on occasions the schizophrenic shows when he appears to simplify the experimental situation in one of a number of ways. This may possibly be the result of a conscious or unconscious recognition that his reaction to the complicated situation he has to meet is not adequate. Whatever the case, we have instances in which he becomes only superficially involved in the experimental situation. Thus, in an experiment directed at determining his accessibility to environmental stimulation in an entirely free setting, he may superficially play with the objects about him but not become deeply involved (11). Or in an aspiration experiment he may set rigid and unchangeable goals (9). Or in a play experiment he may organize the material at a simple functional level, *e.g.*, place all furniture together in a row, all the dolls together, etc., rather than follow the instructions to construct a family scene (18). Or in a tachistoscopic experiment he may take great care not to make errors, even if in this way he reduces his score considerably (3). In the types of activity here described, the patient has considerable freedom in structuring the situation, but he insists on organizing it in a highly simplified manner.

In the next group, where there is an *unsuccessful handling of a complicated situation,* the patient does enter into the task, frequently because the situation is one to which he *must* react, since it does not lend itself easily to avoidance or simplification. A few examples will illustrate what I mean. The schizophrenic's difficulty with "conceptual thinking" and his frequent preference for "concrete" thinking can be appreciated in the scheme of major and minor sets which I have presented. The behavior of the schizophrenic in a stress learning situation is another instance. When stresses such as distracting noises, lights, etc., are introduced into a pursuitmeter learning situation, the normal subject's learning curve is disturbed only during the stress trials (12). Neither the interspersed non-stress trials nor the post-stress period trials are affected. In the schizophrenic, the effect on the interspersed non-stress trials is about as much as on the stress trials, and the post-stress effect is even greater; the curve of learning takes on a U shape. This may be viewed as a type of set difficulty. Apparently what happens is that the schizophrenic does not keep the disturbing factors in their place but carries them over to situations in which they do not exist. The major set, resulting from the instructions to follow the airplane image with the stick and foot pedals, becomes largely replaced by a perseverative minor set—a continuing reaction to a stimulus which is no longer present in reality.

I have discussed certain unaffected levels of response and a larger group of situations which are significantly affected in the schizophrenic. Some of the latter, under certain conditions, become *normalized* or at least are affected in the direction of normality. It is important to consider these, since they have important implications for the problems of fundamental capacity and deterioration.

These normalizing factors I have characterized as *temporary* because as they have turned up in our experiments and other studies they appear mainly to be effective in relation to the specific situation involved. They do not seem to be permanent characteristics that are carried over to other settings.

The first of these factors, *time for preparation*, is involved in a situation such as exists in the tapping experiment (16). This task, though more complicated than a reaction-time task, gave mean rates not significantly different from the normal for those patients whose coöperation seemed up to the level of the normal subjects. In reaction time the patients remained consistently much poorer than the normal subjects. We could account for this only on the basis of the difference in the conditions of the two experiments. Whereas in the reaction-time setting the experimenter determines when the stimulus is to come and the subject is expected to respond to it at that time, in the tapping situation the subject is permitted to prepare himself and to commence tapping when he himself has determined that he is ready.

Mere *lapse of time* also seems to have some normalizing effects in schizophrenia. In a learning experiment, using the prodmeter, when periods of 3 months intervened between tests, it was found that additional learning, rather than forgetting, as in normal subjects, occurred (15). This presumably was the result of the dropping out of the inordinately numerous interfering factors which had prevailed during the original learning.

Repetition may result in the schizophrenic's reaching

a normal level. This was found in the direct-current threshold experiment (6) where, on the first day of experimentation, the threshold to electrical shock was higher in schizophrenic than in normal subjects, but on the second day it reached the normal level which had remained constant.

Social pressure such as is found in a competitive situation tends to normalize schizophrenic achievement. For example in a learning experiment, the amount of learning was markedly affected in the direction of the normal level by the introduction of individual and group competition.

In some situations, usually those of a simple type, a high level of *coöperation* is the factor which seems to be important in eliminating the differences which exist between the schizophrenic and normal levels. A study of steadiness function brought this out (17).

Stress introduced into experimental situations sometimes results in changing activity in the normal direction. Thus in an experiment on the effect of frustration on the themes in Thematic Apperception Test stories, we have on occasion found that after frustration the patient changes from relatively disorganized stories to better structured ones—stories showing much less evidence of confusion and disconnection.

I have talked about the "inability to keep a major set" as a prominent characteristic, perhaps *the* most prominent formal psychological characteristic, of schizophrenia. I have considered "set" as a state of "readiness to respond" to discrete, continuous, or serial stimulation. It may be voluntary or involuntary, verbalized or unverbalized, conscious or unconscious, temporary or permanent.

I have said that the schizophrenic falls down in this

very important aspect of adaptation. Actually, this inability to keep a major set is, I believe, a secondary result of a positive characteristic, a primary *need to establish minor sets*, to segmentalize both the external and the internal environments. If I may become speculative at this point and go much beyond the data I can here make available, I believe he does this in order to discover the answer to, and attain the satisfaction of, fundamental unsatisfied needs which have never been satisfied in the ordinary course of events as they have been in the normal person. And these needs have to express themselves through a developed body and a nervous system which have continued their normal growth. Schizophrenc behavior reminds one in this respect of Santayana's characterization of the nineteenth century, which, he says, ". . . yearned with Rousseau or speculated with Kant, while it moved with Darwin, Bismarck and Nietzsche."

This is one kind of segmentalization—between the "archaic" need and the "modern" means available for gratification. Another is the segmentalization of the process of attaining the satisfaction of the need. If there is any creature who can be accused of not seeing the forest for the trees, it is the schizophrenic. If he is of the paranoid persuasion, he sticks even more closely than the normal person to the path through the forest, but examines each tree along the path (sometimes even each tree's leaves) with meticulous care. (Is this possibly a reaction formation to the underlying fundamental schizophrenic trend toward segmentalization?) If he follows the hebephrenic pattern then there are no paths; he strays off the obvious path entirely and examines, not only visually, but olfactorily and gustatorily, any and all trees and even the undergrowth and floor of the forest in a superficial flitting way, forgetting altogether about the place he wants to get to. In both groups almost every step of what is essentially an impersonal process appears to become personalized, invested with affect, deeply or superficially (depending upon the type).

Many psychiatric observers have been struck by some aspect of this characteristic, which they have variously called intrapsychic incoördination, disintegration, intrapsychic ataxia, splitting, etc.; but nowhere that I know of has the all-pervasiveness and the apparently common basis for this characteristic been sufficiently emphasized. It is in the lack of integration of the organism at all levels, but especially at its higher levels, that we see this tendency toward segmentalization which is probably the fundamental formal characteristic of the disease group.

On the *psychological* side we can see certain overlappings and certain analogies with the physiological, but at the present stage of our knowledge it is, of course, difficult to correlate these aspects too closely. The hypotheses of Cannon and Coghill are of distinct relevance here, however. What we seem to have psychologically are archaic needs which have to be satisfied by a functioning organism which has outgrown them through the process of automatic physical and intellectual maturation that comes with age. This is even more complicated by the fact that the organism finds itself in an environment which also grows in the sense of providing fewer and fewer infantile outlets and is therefore not organized to satisfy needs of this kind. These segmental cravings cannot be satisfied while integrated control, the channel which is indispensable to the maintenance of major sets, is effective. There is then a perverted use of the automatically matured devices to satisfy these needs, and we see a preoccupation with bodily processes, with the mechanics of processes rather than with ends, the use of thinking in peculiar ways, etc., the great variety of schizophrenic symptoms which can be viewed as different types of individuation or segmentalization. There is an increasing awareness of and preoccupation with the ordinarily disregarded details of existence, the details which normal people sweat so valiantly over the years to forget. When a patient develops a persisting aversion to food because the cafeteria menu lists a common item which we read as "soup" but which he can only see in its excretory significance as "so-u-p," we realize how very many of the details of daily existence get by us poor normals! The schizophrenic's activity might justifiably be called "centipedal" activity, for, as in the case of the well-known centipede of the fable, he is so deeply concerned about the way his feet move that he gets all tangled up about where they are going.

Man has been called a "time binder" and in a sense this is true. The normal human being acts generally in a present grounded on the past to satisfy present, but predominantly future, needs. He does this most effectively when he is mature—free of what has been called "narcissism." The schizophrenic, on the contrary, appears to act in the present to satisfy some present urgent needs, but predominantly to satisfy past needs; he gives the impression of not even having any real future needs. To attain his goal it seems necessary to segmentalize both himself and his environment.

Perhaps I can sum up best what I have been trying to say in this way: As grown-up human beings we have a job to do and we get on with it more or less directly and effectively. The schizophrenic does not. In fact, sometimes we get impatient with him for the devious manner in which he goes about doing his *schizophrenic job*. We see so many ways in which he could accomplish this so much more quickly and efficiently! Can it be that this he really knows better and that our attitude merely reveals how little we know about schizophrenia?

Bibliography

1. Angyal, A., Freeman, H., and Hoskins, R. G.: "Physiologic aspects of schizophrenic withdrawal." *Arch. Neurol. Psychiat.*, Chicago, 1940, 44, 621–626.

2. Angyal, A., and Sherman, M. A.: "Postural reactions to vestibular stimulation in schizophrenic and normal subjects." *Amer. J. Psychiat.*, 1942, 98, 857–862.

3. Angyal, A. F.: "The diagnosis of neurotic traits by means of a new perceptual test." *J. Psychol.*, 1948, 25, 105–135.

4. Freeman, H., and Rodnick, E. H.: "Autonomic and respiratory responses to changes of intra-pulmonary atmosphere." *Psychosom. Med.*, 1940, 2, 101–109.

5. Hoskins, R. G., Sleeper, F. H., Shakow, D., Jellinek, E. M., Looney, J. M., and Erickson, M. H.: "A cooperative research in schizophrenia." *Arch. Neurol. Psychiat.*, Chicago, 1933, 30, 388–401.

6. Huston, P. E.: "Sensory threshold to direct current stimulation in schizophrenic and in normal subjects." *Arch. Neurol. Psychiat.*, Chicago, 1934, 31, 590–596.

7. ————: "The reflex time of the patellar tendon reflex in normal and schizophrenic subjects." *J. Gen. Psychol.*, 1935, 13, 3–41.

8. ————, Shakow, D., and Riggs, L. A.: "Studies of motor function in schizophrenia: II. Reaction time." *J. Gen. Psychol.*, 1937, 16. 39–82.

9. Radlo, G., and Shakow, D.: "Aspiration level in schizophrenia." Unpublished.

10. ————: "The effect of group competition on performance in schizophrenic subjects." Unpublished.

11. Rickers-Ovsiankina, M.: "Studies on the personality structure of schizophrenic individuals: I. The accessibility of schizophrenics to environmental influences." *J. Gen. Psychol.*, 1937, 16, 153–178.

12. Rodnick, E. H.: "Set in the schizophrenic." Unpublished.

13. Roe, A., and Shakow, D.: "Intelligence in mental disorder." *Ann. N. Y. Acad. Sci.*, 1942, 42, 361–490.

14. Shakow, D.: "The nature of deterioration in schizophrenic conditions." *Nerv. Ment. Dis. Monogr.*, 1946, 7, No. 70.

15. Shakow, D., and Huston, P. E.: "Learning capacity in schizophrenia: with special reference to the concept of deterioration." *Amer. J. Psychiat.*, 1949, 105, 881–888.

16. ————: "Studies of motor function in schizophrenia: I. Speed of tapping." *J. Gen. Psychol.*, 1936, 15, 63–106.

17. ————: "Studies of motor function in schizophrenia. III. Steadiness. *J. Gen. Psychol.*, 1946, 34, 119–126.

18. Shakow, D., and Rosenzweig, S.: "Play technique in schizophrenia: II. An experimental study of schizophrenic constructions with play materials." *Amer. J. Orthopsychiat.*, 1937, 7, 36–47.

Paranoid Disorders*

BY *Norman Cameron, M.D., Ph.D.*

The term paranoia was current in ancient Greece and
Rome up to about the second century A.D., but it seems
to have been used more or less indiscriminately in a
sense equivalent to that of our modern catch-all, *insanity*. It was revived for a brief period in the eighteenth
century and again in the nineteenth, since when it has
remained permanently in the literature but with widely
varying meanings. Paranoia received its present rather
precise formulation under the influence of Kraepelin,
who reserved the name for cases of chronic, highly systematized delusions without personality deterioration.

The Kraepelinian conception of paranoia, however,
has turned out to be so restricted in scope that only the
rare case of systematized delusion can qualify under
it. On the other hand, paranoia-like cases are not at
all uncommon in office, clinic and hospital practice.
These do not quite correspond to Kraepelin's formulation of paranoia, being less often chronic and having delusions that are less systematized, but they still show

* From *The Psychology of Behavior Disorders—A Biosocial Interpretation*, 1947. Reprinted by courtesy of the author and
publishers, Houghton Mifflin Company.

neither serious disorganization nor serious deterioration. Such cases have for many years been called paranoia-like or *paranoid*. A growing recognition of the relatively greater importance of these paranoid disorders has finally led to the inclusion of paranoia under them as merely a rare variant (1). It should be noted that in contemporary usage the word *paranoid* is equivalent to *delusional,* and the once prevalent term *paranoid delusion* has thus been reduced to tautology.

By *paranoid disorders* we mean *behavior which is dominated by more or less systematized delusional reactions, but which shows little or no tendency toward disorganization or deterioration, is not incidental to mania or depression, and lacks an adequate basis in organ or tissue pathology.* Of the delusions already discussed, only two kinds appear prominently in paranoid disorders, those of persecution and those of grandeur, and delusions of persecution are by far the commoner of these two. The greater prevalence of persecutory paranoid disorders is undoubtedly related to the fact that our culture provides an abundance of fear, hatred, guilt and insecurity excitants for everyone, while it offers comparatively little support to persistent self-reactions of personal grandeur. Because the persecutory variety is the prevalent form of paranoid disorder, we shall use it in what follows as our principal example.

Development of Paranoid Disorders

Delusional behavior, we have said, is common among normal individuals and most common under conditions of special need or anxiety. Thus, in everyday life we find that expectant or emotional attitudes and reactions of

PARANOID DISORDERS 409

personal insecurity tend to favor delusional development by making one reaction-sensitive to whatever
arouses them, while detached or relatively unemo-
tional attitudes and reactions of personal security tend
to avert delusional development (2). Delusional incidents are of frequent occurrence also, because everyone
must be continually acting on the basis of incomplete
and uncertain data. Indeed, to proceed only on the
basis of completeness and certainty would be to accomplish virtually nothing, since almost nothing is finished and sure. Those exceptional individuals whose
need or anxiety compels them to seek absolute certainty,
as for example, in the compulsive disorders, are by that
very fact rendered susceptible to the development of
serious behavior pathology.

The normal person has neither the opportunity nor
the time, nor for that matter even the inclination, to
check rigorously on everything he does, sees, hears or
thinks. It is therefore inevitable that he should make
frequent mistakes in his everyday interpretations, inferences and conclusions. Many of these mistakes are never
corrected, and in the great majority of instances no harm
results. But every now and then a misunderstanding
has important personal consequences that call for a
reconsideration, if trouble is to be averted.

To be successful in correcting the important mistakes
in interpretation, inference and conclusion, and thus
to eliminate the possibility of a paranoid disorder, a
person must have adequate skill in taking roles and shifting his perspectives under stress, and his need or anxiety
must be neither excessive nor everlasting. For we know
that ease in shifting perspective in a crisis—from that
of participant, for example, to that of disinterested observer—is the basis upon which the average person is

enabled to correct in one role what he may have mis-understood in another. If, instead, an individual must depend upon rumination, solitary observation and un-shared surmise in personally vital matters, there is little to prevent his delusional convictions from growing into paranoid disorders.

Contrary to popular belief, paranoid disorders end as a rule in recovery and rarely develop the elaborate, log-ically systematized organization of classical paranoia. The rarity of rigid logical systematization in paranoid disorders should not surprise anyone, since it is excep-tional, even among highly intelligent and well-trained normal persons, for matters of deep personal and emo-tional significance to be settled by operations of strict verbal logic (3). Moreover, as we have already pointed out, different kinds of human behavior show different degrees of social maturity in the same individual; and it is the unshared, personally important emotional behav-ior which in all of us is most likely to include am-biguities, self-contradictions, ambivalences and other logical violations in its organization. Thus, we find, in intelligent or highly trained persons as well as in the unintelligent or untrained, that delusional convictions often develop into paranoid disorders on grounds which seem almost incredibly absurd to a dispassionate ob-server. We shall see most of these fundamental facts illustrated in the two following cases.

A thirty-nine-year-old successful lawyer consulted an internist, complaining of sleeplessness, tension, headaches and loss of appetite. The internist, finding no adequate basis for the complaints in organ or tissue pathology, referred him to a psychiatrist. In the course of several consultations with the psychia-trist, the patient gave no important evidence of personal difficulties excepting his repeated, unsolicited insistence that his sex life had nothing to do with his symptoms. "I know what you doctors think," he kept saying. Eventually, however, it came out that for several months he had been tormented day and night by the conviction that he was the victim of a conspiracy between his wife and her physician, and that her family knew of the conspiracy and condoned it.

According to the patient, he had become suspicious when his wife, who was of Italian extraction, had insisted upon going to an Italian obstetrician, the friend of her parents. This was her second pregnancy, and in her first she had been content with the care of a general practitioner whom none of them had previously known. The patient's distrust was heightened by the fact that his wife seemed pleased with the frequency and regularity of her visits to the obstetrician and praised the kindness and consideration with which he treated her. Finally, suspicion of her conduct was transformed into certainty that she had been unfaithful to him when, following his wife's delivery, the patient received a bill far smaller than he had expected. He was convinced that the child was not his but the obstetrician's, and that this explained his wife's choice of physician, her failure to complain of the tedium of repeated examinations, the small amount charged for professional services, and even his wife's delight in her baby and her decreased attention to her first child.

The novice, hearing this succession of unwarranted inferences and their outcome in delusional conviction, may easily be himself misled into concluding unjustifiably that the patient must be incapable of reasoning or must have a "diseased mind." He can avoid committing such an error if, instead of being preoccupied with questions of mere verbal logic, he attempts to understand the biosocial background of the delusional development. Our patient, first of all, was a proud man, proud partly because he was chronically insecure, but both proud and insecure also because his parents had consistently overcompensated for their own humble origins by stressing always the importance of status and the high virtue of conformity. He was trained to look out continually for the approval of his neighbors, and to consider appearances before everything else.

The patient left home for good when he was twenty-four, and at the age of thirty-one moved to a metropolis where he was thrown in with persons of widely different backgrounds. It was under these circumstances that he met and fell in love with a girl of Italian parentage. In spite of secret misgivings and the warnings he received from his own parents, he allowed himself finally to marry into a family for which he had neither liking nor respect. When he entered marriage, the patient did so also with the realization that his premarital sex pace had always been considerably below the level claimed by his companions. He feared that he might be unable to come up to the sexual expectations which, with no basis other than his own prejudices, he attributed to his wife becuase of the nationality of her parents.

Because of his social prejudices and his doubts concerning his sexual adequacy, the patient found that his marriage meant a reduction in personal security and status, whereas what he needed was an increase in both. His wife's first pregnancy raised no major problems for him, but during the second one he involved himself in an extramarital sex adventure which was in part a spite reaction to his wife's supposed attachment to the obstetrician, and in part an attempt at reassuring himself as to his own adequacy. This adventure unexpectedly aroused in him considerable guilt, self-condemnation and fear of discovery, which was augmented by the unwillingness of his partner in it to terminate the affair.

From this brief sketch of the patient's background, it is clear that his paranoid disorder arose, not because of some primary defect in reasoning, as behavior pathologists would have assumed fifty years ago, but because of selective reaction-sensitivity which was in turn determined by the patient's life history. This insecure, conventionally reared man married into a cultural in-group from which his own prejudices excluded him in his self-reactions. He could not accept his wife's relatives and friends because he felt different in kind from them as well as superior. The sexual characteristics which he attributed to his wife, at first solely on the basis of prejudice and insecurity, became reinforced in his thinking as one result of his own sex misbehavior (*assimilative projection*).

Out of an actual in-group of Italian-Americans, and the interactions of its members, the patient organized in his own thinking a *pseudocommunity* made up of the interrelationships he believed to exist between his wife, her physician and her family. They all differed from him and agreed among themselves in cultural background, national derivation, childhood tongue and anatomical appearance. The second baby when it came looked, he said, like a little foreigner. It seemed to belong to this in-group from which he had by his own reactions excluded himself, and he could therefore not accept it as his child. Thus, the baby's advent, instead of bringing pride and increased confidence to the patient, had only confirmed his conviction and increased his isolation. Under prolonged motivational analysis this man succeeded in working out the origins and implications of his emotional attitudes sufficiently to overcome his paranoid disorder.

We have said that it is exceptional for the uncomplicated paranoid disorder to persist indefinitely. Nevertheless, the accumulated total of those cases that do become chronic constitutes a grave social problem, for the community at large as well as for institutional psychiatry. It is therefore of importance to the average citizen, as it is also to the behavior pathologist, to understand the background of persistent and cumulative delusional convictions.

For delusions of persecution to develop into a chronic paranoid disorder several conditions must be present. There must be something of importance to which the patient is strongly reaction-sensitive, something that arouses insecurity, guilt, fear, humiliation, resentment or a sense of isolation and inadequacy. The patient must be one who builds up cumulative or persistent tensions easily, so that he tends to be habitually anxious, but at the same time intolerant of suspense. He must have well-established habits of dealing with personal problems in solitude, by brooding, puzzling and ruminating, and poorly developed habits of shifting perspectives and taking successively different roles under stress. As a result of this one-sided development, such an individual lacks skill in the techniques of analyzing or retesting situations that make him uneasy; and because he cannot adequately share his attitudes in personal matters with others, he has no way of objectively validating his conclusions in these areas.

Cumulative and persistent paranoid disorders develop chiefly in persons who for some reason have failed to acquire adequate role-taking skills and have

not learned habits of free discussion and interchange
of attitude with others, excepting in impersonal matters
and at a relatively superficial level. When such an individual arrives at a conclusion, he cannot shift to another
point of view, and therefore this conclusion remains the
only possible one. Starting afresh with his conclusion,
he proceeds with the same inadequate techniques and
the same single perspective to make further inferences
and arrive at similar conclusions, until finally he builds
up a more or less consistent delusional organization.
The patient's progressive reaction-sensitivity determines
his selection and interpretation of new incidents which
fit into his growing paranoid system. In his ruminations
the patient reshapes what he recalls—a procedure that
is common also in normal remembering (4)—and
includes this distorted product as confirmatory and
supporting evidence for his delusional convictions (*retrospective falsification*).

Once an insecure, socially unskilled person becomes
suspicious, it is never difficult for him to find apparent
grounds for his distrust. His long-established habits of
ruminating over personal difficulties without sharing
them, and his relative ineffectuality in testing social interrelationships, make it easy for him to build up elaborate structures of interpretation out of flimsy evidence.
At every choice point such a person, because of his selective reaction-sensitivity, toes in the direction of prevailing fear, suspicion, resentment or guilt. He looks about
him for confirmatory signs and finds them. Like a man
who is actually wanted by the police, he watches everything and suspects everyone. The little movements, gestures, looks and signs that are always going on around
us become to the reaction-sensitive, suspicious patient
indications of a concerted plot of which he seems to be

the object. Out of these selected fragments of behavior he organizes the paranoid *pseudocommunity* whose members seem united against him. In the following case we shall see how childhood determinants, vocational peculiarities, unfortunate incidents and lifelong habits of social isolation are interwoven in the development of a paranoid disorder (5).

The patient, an unmarried man of forty-nine, was brought to the hospital by relatives with the complaint that he believed himself pursued by gangsters who intended to capture, torture and then kill him. According to the patient, his difficulties had arisen suddenly the day after a quarrel over a small racing bet which he had placed with bookies. It is of some importance to note that the patient, who had a steady income from previous business ventures, had not been working at all for several years prior to the onset of his paranoid disorder. He lived alone in a cheap hotel and spent his entire time in sitting around idly, reading the papers, thinking, conversing, playing cards, placing around a dozen small bets daily on the ponies, and occasionally looking into business prospects without finding anything he wanted. It was in this setting of idleness, fantasy and small talk that his illness developed. There was, as we shall see, also a background of guilt, suspicion and resentment to help account for the patient's reaction-sensitivity to signs of punishment and persecution.

The quarrel which seems to have precipitated the disorder grew out of the patient's attempt to collect on a winning horse when the bookies insisted that he had put his money on a different horse. The patient, after fortifying himself with a few drinks, returned and noisily demanded the pay-off, shouting insults at the bookies, threatening them with prosecution and inviting them out on the street to fight. Eventually he cooled off and returned to his hotel, where he began thinking over what he had done. He remembered hearing stories of national gangster protection given to bookies. The more he thought about it, the more dangerous his threatening and insulting them seemed to him.

Next day the patient noticed some strangers in the lobby, "rough-looking characters," and they seemed to him to be looking at him intently and to be signaling to each other. During the morning an automobile full of men stopped in front of the hotel door and the patient was convinced that he was about to be kidnapped, tortured and killed for the trouble he had been making. He began to notice strangers and loiterers everywhere he went, and they all seemed to be watching or shadowing him. He felt that he was a marked man, and barricaded himself in his room. From there he communicated by telephone with a relative, who was thoroughly convinced at the time that the patient was in deadly peril. They arranged to leave town next morning on a long automobile trip. However, the patient decided during the night that his telephone message must have been tapped by the gangsters, so he skipped town before morning, alone in his car, and headed for the home of another relative a thousand miles away.

As the patient drove on, it became apparent to him that he was being trailed. In one city, for example, he saw a policeman examining his auto license; this meant to him that the police were in league with the gangsters and were tipping them off. Once, in a shoeshining parlor, the attendant eyed him narrowly; this was a sign that "the grapevine system was catching up." He was determined not to be caught alive, so he concealed razor blades about his person, carried a bottle of lysol in his pocket and sealed a lethal dose of sed-

atives in a chewing-gum package. When he reached
his relatives, it was evident to them that the patient
was ill, they got wind of his suicidal intent, and, on
the advice of a general practitioner, took the patient
by air to the hospital.

In the hospital the patient felt for some time contented and secure. He was well-oriented, his talk was
circumstantial but clear and sequential, there were no
signs of behavior disorganization and, while he obviously preferred his own company, he was pleasant
and courteous to others. In conferences with his psychiatrist he made frequent allusions to things in his
past that he would like to get cleared up; but although
given many opportunities to go into them, he could
bring himself only to recount some unethical business
dealings. When a shift in the medical staff was made,
the patient persuaded the new physician to let him
telephone a local pastor to come and visit him in the
clinic. To the pastor he told the story of his recent
difficulties and, without consulting the physician, the
two arranged for another visit at which, the patient
intimated, he would go into other matters.

After the pastor had gone, the patient began pon-
dering over the visit in his usual way, and the more
he thought about it, the more he suspected that he had
been unwise to confide so much to a stranger. He recalled that the pastor was somewhat dark-skinned and
foreign-looking, and he suddenly realized that his
telephone call had probably been intercepted by the
gangsters, who had sent around a confederate to pose
as a minister of the gospel. He suffered a violent
resurgence of fear and, although under expert surveil-
lance, made a serious but unsuccessful suicidal attempt. Following this incident, the patient no longer
felt safe in the hospital. He was unable to entertain
any interpretation of the pastor's visit other than the
once which fitted into his delusional system. He

wished, he said, that he could be in a hospital that was in the middle of an army encampment. Failing this, he insisted upon being transferred to a government hospital.

Because of the patient's inability to establish an adequate communicative relationship with his psychiatrists, there remain serious gaps in what is known of his personal history, particularly in relation to his sex behavior and interests. Nevertheless, even his relatively superficial account gives us important clues to the origins of his selective reaction-sensitivity and of his lack of the social skills he needed to protect him from paranoid developments. The patient's childhood was motherless and he was shifted about among various relatives, "from farm to farm and from state to state," now with siblings and now separated from them. He never had the feeling that he had a settled place to live in. He grew up a lonely, insecure, brooding child who got along well in casual contacts, but lacked close friends with whom he could share confidences and exchange perspectives. He had always felt the need to confide and confess, he said, but he had never been able to do either.

Early in adulthood the patient drifted into vocations that permitted him to continue in the pattern of living he had acquired during childhood. As a salesman he worked alone and on his own schedule, leading a restless, unsatisfying, roving life, moving his headquarters innumerable times and changing from one job to another. In spite of these shifts, and in spite of never liking his work, the patient achieved substantial financial success. By the time he had reached his middle forties, he was able to live on a modest scale without working. He never gained personal security and he never succeeded in identifying himself emotionally with the firms that employed him. The patient felt that his employers underrated him and discriminated against him; they seemed always suspicious of him as he was of them. In view of the fact that spotters were regularly employed to check up on salesmen, it is difficult to decide how much of this was projection on the patient's part and how much was justified by what he knew. For a time he was himself employed as a spotter, checking secretly on the activities of other field representatives. This work, he said, heightened his distrust, but it made him better able to recognize "what was going on."

After his return to selling, the patient believed that the operatives of his employers and competitors were continually watching and trailing him, a belief that may not have been wholly unfounded. His habitual insecurity at this time was increased by guilt over some business dealings outside of his agreements. Whenever he became convinced, on the basis of rumination and circumstantial evidence, that he was being persistently trailed, his reaction was to make a sudden change in his headquarters without consulting anyone. He had never seriously doubted the validity of these convictions. It is obvious that the socially inadequate techniques by means of which the patient, under stress of fearful fantasy, built up a *pseudocommunity* of homicidal gangsters were the same techniques which had kept him perpetually insecure in his work. It is also clear that the patient's lack of skill in role-taking and in shifting perspective stood in the way of his recovery.

The Paranoid Pseudocommunity (6)

Both of the cases cited above illustrate well the development and operation of the paranoid pseudocommunity, which is a product of reaction-sensitivity and projection . . . The patient, like the normal person, reacts selectively to his environment on the basis of dominant attitudes which facilitate certain responses and inhibit others. When he thinks he is under suspicion or scrutiny, he may proceed to watch and listen, as indeed anyone else might, and to ponder over what he sees and hears. However, as we know, skill in interpreting the attitudes and intents of another person depends chiefly upon skill in role-taking, since it is only by taking a person's role that we can gain his perspective and see things approximately as he sees them. The person who is relatively incompetent in this maneuver lacks one of the most important social techniques for the prevention and correction of delusional developments. In the extreme case, as we have pointed out, the patient has but one perspective in personally important matters, and he can therefore arrive at only one kind of conclusion which, for him, is inescapable fact.

The average person, when his observations, hypotheses and role-taking maneuvers only increase his insecurity or perplexity, usually turns to someone he trusts and shares his difficulties. This procedure objectifies the situation by making it something discussed in terms of social communication, instead of something only brooded over in private fantasy. It gives the frightened or perplexed individual the comfort of sharing his anxiety, and it brings the role-taking resources of another person to bear upon the now mutual problem. The patient who, like our salesman, has never succeeded in developing habits of confiding and sharing, lives in a world of strangers with whom he cannot communicate in personal matters and from whom he can get neither comfort nor support when he feels discriminated against or threatened.

The frightened solitary patient who seriously lacks the requisite skills with which to carry out shared social operations is like an unskilled and inexperienced man who finds himself lost at night in a jungle, and seems suddenly to become the focus of a hostile, living environment which is at first obscure and unintelligible. Every shadow, every sound and movement seems to threaten him personally. His fear binds together trivial and unrelated incidents around him into a great net from which he can see no escape. Likewise, the anxious patient, inept in social skills, attributes harmful intent to the trivial and unrelated responses of persons in his environment and of other persons whose existence he imagines or infers. He unintentionally organizes these individuals through his own reactions of fear and projection into an apparent community; in his interpretations their responses, attitudes and plans seem unified and all directed toward him. The organization of this pseudocommunity does not, of course, comfort and reassure the paranoid patient, but it does satisfy his immediate pressing need for an explanation of what is going on. It brings the kind of relief from doubt and suspense that expected bad news brings when it finally comes.

The community which paranoid patients thus build up fails to correspond, of course, to any shared organization of interpersonal behavior. Moreover, the attitudes and intentions ascribed by the patient to those individuals whom he identifies as members of the community are not actually maintained by them, and they are not united in any common undertaking against him. In other words, what he takes to be a functionally integrated social group is only a pseudocommunity, an organization of his own reactions into a structure without social validity. We may define this *pseudocommunity* as *an organization of a patient's reactions to the observed or inferred behavior of actual and imagined persons, on the basis of delusional conviction, which makes the patient seem to himself a focus or a significant part of some concerted action, malignant or benign.* The patient's conviction often comes suddenly, as closure or *sudden clarification*, with the familiar statement, "It has all become clear to me."

Unfortunately, the organization of a pseudocommunity in a patient's reactions usually adds impetus to the whole delusional development, much as a new integrating scientific hypothesis may suddenly speed up research. The pseudocommunity, once organized and formulated, tends to expand through progressive reaction-sensitization to include new activities and new personnel until the patient finally considers it a grave threat to his security. It is at this point that the paranoid patient bursts into defensive or vengeful activity in the field of social operations against his pseudocommunity. The social community, which usually cannot share in his attitudes any more than he shares in the community's, meets his aggression with counteraggression, and this seems to the patient final evidence that his fears and suspicions have been fully justified.

The best-organized pseudocommunities are to be found among the paranoid disorders, but they are by no means restricted to this group. For example, in the delusional behavior of schizophrenic patients we find disorganized but often richly fantastic pseudocommunities. Manic and depressed persons also frequently develop this kind of delusional organization, although with them it is usually a by-product of the mood disorder which tends to disappear without special attention as the illness subsides.

Determinants of Paranoid Disorders

It has been obvious throughout the preceding discussion that paranoid disorders are most likely to develop in those individuals who cannot readily seek counsel, who habitually work out their difficulties in solitary brooding, and who lack skill in the techniques of role-taking and in shifting their perspectives under conditions of personal stress. Many such individuals, by the time adolescence is reached, already have well-established attitudes of suspicion, criticism and resentment toward others, expect and demand special consideration of everyone, or show marked concern over the opinions others have of them, while lacking the necessary skills for sampling those opinions. We shall turn briefly to a discussion of some of the childhood influences that help to develop these predisposing behavior trends.

Childhood Influences

Any child, in adopting the prevailing attitudes of his early environment, is likely to develop habitual suspicion, resentment, pride and overconcern regarding his neighbors' opinions of him, if these are the habitual attitudes of his elders. For example, in an isolated mountaineer community where strangers are always treated as suspect and unwelcome, the average child will exhibit an attitude of suspicion and hostility toward strangers that would be considered pathological in the child of an ordinary rural or urban community. However, there are always individual families within the ordinary rural and urban community whose elders, for personal rather than general cultural reasons, are habitually dominated by attitudes favoring delusional developments and tend to train their offspring in similar attitudes (7).

Children reared in a domestic or general cultural atmosphere where such attitudes prevail must be regarded as more susceptible than the average to paranoid disorders in middle life. Their dominant attitude organization tends to make them chronically insecure in personal interrelationships, interferes with their acquisition of social techniques and serviceable self-reactions, and so leaves them in a crisis with fewer behavior resources than they need to deal successfully with later biosocial problems. Of course, by no means all individuals with this childhood background become paranoid. . . . Adult personality organization is not usually determined by the characteristics of one parent or the effects of one personal trauma. There are two parents interacting with each other to help determine a child's attitudes, there are siblings, a neighborhood with other children and other influential elders, and, sometimes most important of all, the peer culture at every age level from childhood through adolescence and adulthood.

The social inadequacies that favor paranoid disorders may be the result, not of adopting a prevailing pattern, but of failure to find opportunities for developing social skills. . . . The prime requisites for the development of

adequate role-taking in childhood are parental acceptance, a secure home, freedom to explore the neighborhood at an early age and to engage in associative and
coöperative play with other children. The child who,
through neglect, denial, rejection or inhibitory supervision, is denied the security or opportunity he needs for
the practice of social skills may be unable in later adult
life to avoid paranoid disorder under personal stress.
The same is true of the child whose elders lead him to
develop self-attitudes of inferiority or guilt through their
habitual reactions to what he says and does, or through
the implications of what they do for him *(indulgent
overprotection)* or to him *(domineering overprotection)*.

Parental attitudes such as these sometimes lay the
ground in a child's self-reactions for the development in
later life of paranoid grandiosity. The grandiose paranoid disorder may be a direct reaction against paren-
tally induced self-reactions of inferiority or guilt. It may
also be an outgrowth of fantasied achievements with
which the adult has learned to console himself for his
failure to accomplish what parental overevaluation in
childhood had led him to expect.

Age and Paranoid Disorders

It is undoubtedly significant that the great majority
of paranoid disorders develop between the thirty-fifth
and fifty-fifth years (8). Two plausible explanations
for this age-range present themselves. In the first place,
the paranoid disorder is arbitrarily limited by definition
to delusional developments which are more or less systematized and show no serious tendencies toward behavior disorganization. These specifications eliminate the

delusions characteristic of the schizophrenic disorders which usually begin fifteen or twenty years earlier. From this it can be inferred that the socially inept person who undergoes maximal stress during adolescence or early adulthood suffers behavior disorganization because he is at the time relatively immature. His social techniques are not yet well established at the level of adolescent or adult life and, like any other complex behavior that is still imperfectly learned, are more easily disintegrated by emotional disturbance, failure or conflict. To such a result we give the name *schizophrenic disorder*.

The socially inept individual who manages to get through adolescence and early adult life without developing severe behavior disorder, but who undergoes maximal stress after a decade or two of adult life, does not easily develop disorganization as a reaction to severe emotional disturbance, conflict or failure. His social techniques, although still relatively inadequate, are sufficiently established as habitual operations to preserve the patient's general personality organization in spite of delusional distortion. To such an outcome we give the name *paranoid disorder*. We shall return to this hypothesis when we consider the schizophrenic disorders.

Another possible explanation for the age-range in paranoid disorders may supplement the one suggested above. We know that between the thirty-fifth and fifty-fifth years there are many occasions for new and increased personal insecurity. Each adult, as his youth recedes, must one day recognize what growing older means for him. For some the most impressive thing seems to be a sudden realization that one's life-span is limited, for others it is the growing certainty that lifelong goals will never be attained. Waning or lost youth means to many the loss of abilities, attractiveness and status.

Among the varied reactions to the increased need or anxiety which ageing fosters are those of attempting to preserve one's self-respect by blaming others for one's difficulties, and of seeking aggressively to overcome obstacles and frustration by greater effort. Either technique in the hands of the socially inept may lead to paranoid disorder. The first is, of course, one of the commonest precursors of delusional organization. The second, the aggressive increase in effort, will only hasten a showdown if the individual is unsuccessful, thus adding to the conditions responsible for the original aggression. Moreover, the aggressive use of unskillful social techniques is likely to stimulate counteraggressions in other persons and thus open the way for the patient to develop in his own reactions an organized paranoid pseudocommunity.

The importance of sex need, frustration and conflict in paranoid disorders, which Freud was the first to recognize, is now a generally accepted fact. However, the original formulation, which ascribed all persecutory delusions to narcism and latent homosexuality, has turned out to be unnecessarily restrictive (9). It has been found, for example, that paranoid disorders appear in women with well-established heterosexual interests, either because marital opportunities have dwindled or because forbidden heterosexual attachments have developed which arouse anxiety and guilt (10). Men whose sex code has been unusually rigid sometimes develop paranoid disorder under comparable circumstances. It is always possible, of course, to argue that these are all cases of latent homosexuality with a heterosexual

façade, but this claim needs more than logical plausibil-
ity to support it. Moreover . . . no matter how important sex factors may be in behavior pathology, they are
always part of a more inclusive personality organization
and can be understood only within their biosocial
framework (11).

Paranoid Disorders as Adjustive Techniques

Persecutory paranoid disorders, since usually they increase anxiety by amplifying and crystallizing the apparent threats to a person's security, are of relatively little
use as adjustive techniques. However, we sometimes find
the paranoid patient utilizing delusional accusations,
in which he himself, of course, believes, as *aggressive*
weapons for the control and manipulation of situations
for his own benefit. Paranoid disorders, whether persecutory or grandiose, may sometimes function as
identification. The patient, in organizing his pseudocommunity, may develop the conviction that he is being
persecuted or honored because he is thought to belong
to an actual or fantasied group—religious, societal, national or racial—which arouses these reactions in others. Sometimes a paranoid person concludes, from the
attitudes he seems to find in others, that he must really
belong to such a group, or that he must be the reincarnation or representative of a persecuted or honored per-
sonage.

Paranoid disorders are frequently *compensatory*.
Compensation is obvious, for example, when a woman
substitutes the conviction that she is being pursued by
a would-be lover or assailant for her previously unsatisfied need to be desired and overcome. Both persecutory
and grandiose paranoid disorders are known to origi-

nate often as attempts to gain status—for example, as an important victim, leader or criminal—as a substitute for satisfactions which the patient has failed to gain for his other needs, including the sexual. Sometimes the delusional system, after it has been developed, is used as *insulation* or *negativism* which enables the patient to escape participation in unwelcome duties or hazardous competition.

Paranoid Disorders in Relation to Other Behavior Disorders

The wide distribution of delusions throughout the behavior disorders is responsible for the exclusive character of the definition of paranoid disorders. We bar those cases in which the delusions are a by-product of mood disorder, and we specify that neither serious disorganization nor serious deterioration must be present. In spite of these exclusions, however, the task of differentiating paranoid from other behavior disorders is often an exceedingly difficult one.

Hypochondriacal overconcern is a common complication of paranoid disorders. Indeed, chronic body complaints frequently dominate the clinical picture before paranoid developments are evident, and sometimes a fixed hypochondriacal preoccupation becomes the foundation for an organized delusional system. This close relationship between paranoid and hypochondriacal disorders is not surprising in view of the fact that both are so often outgrowths of compensatory and rationalizing techniques, and the incidence of both is high in the same period of life (12). A similar close relationship can be demonstrated between fatigue syndromes and paranoid disorders. The differentiation between paranoid disorders, on the one hand, and hypochondriacal disorders and fatigue syndromes, on the other, is made chiefly on the basis of whether or not the patient has developed organized delusions.

Anxiety is almost always present in paranoid disorders at some stage of development or recession, while fleeting delusions are characteristic of many cases of anxiety disorder. The distinction is made on the basis of the degree to which delusions are systematized and dominate the clinical picture. Acute anxiety and panic reactions are by no means uncommon in cases of paranoid disorder, and occasionally what begins as panic reaction may terminate in paranoid disorder. There is seldom serious difficulty in distinguishing paranoid from *hysterical disorders* on the basis of dominant symptomatology. Both frequently involve disowning reactions, but whereas in hysteria this results in autonomy or inactivation, in paranoid disorders it leads characteristically to the organization in the patient's reactions of the paranoid pseudocommunity. Hysterical symptoms may appear in what is predominantly a paranoid disorder, while a certain degree of delusional organization is sometimes incidental to hysterical inactivation and autonomy.

The distinction between paranoid disorders and *mania* or *depression* is made on the basis of whether or not the delusions are incidental to a mood disorder; if the delusions are not incidental, we speak of paranoid disorder. In practice this differentiation is frequently difficult and occasionally impossible to make. The same difficulties arise in relation to *brain damage*. A patient with unquestionable brain damage may nevertheless develop a delusional system on the basis, not of his deficit but of his reaction to the fact that he has suffered injury or has been made to feel inferior and underrated.

The most difficult distinction of all is that between paranoid disorders and *schizophrenia*. Indeed, there is a considerable area of overlap between the definitions of paranoid disorder and paranoid schizophrenia, since perfect organization is exceedingly rare in the former and severe disorganization frequently absent from the latter. The most helpful attitude to take in relation to these syndromes is that paranoia lies at one extreme of the scale of an organization continuum, while at the other extreme lies the severely disorganized schizophrenic. The less completely systematized paranoid disorders extend from paranoia toward paranoid schizophrenia with which they overlap; while paranoid schizophrenia extends from this area of overlap down toward the more disorganized varieties of schizophrenic disorder.

References

1. *United States Army Technical Medical Bulletin* No. 203 (Washington, D. C.: United States Government Printing Office, October 19, 1945), Section 18. Also reprinted in *Jour. Ment. Science*, 1946, vol. 92, pp. 425–441, and in *Ment. Hyg.*, 1946, vol. 30, pp. 456–476.

2. See, for example, the study of reactions to a radio broadcast of the fictitious account of a Martian invasion of the United States. H. Cantril: *The Invasion from Mars*. Princeton, N. J.: Princeton University Press, 1940.

3. J. Morgan and J. Morton: "The distortion of syllogistic reasoning produced by personal convictions," *Jour. Soc. Psychol.*, 1944, vol. 20, pp. 39–59.

4. See for example F. Bartlett: *Remembering, A Study in*

Experimental and Social Psychology. Cambridge, England: Cambridge University Press, 1932.

5. N. Cameron: "The development of paranoic thinking," *Psychol. Rev.*, 1943, vol. 50, pp. 219–233.

6. N. Cameron: "The paranoid pseudocommunity," *Amer. Jour. Soc.*, 1943, vol. 49, pp. 32–38.

7. If a child or an adult is directly indoctrinated in some specific delusional behavior by a dominant paranoid person, it is customary to speak of *induced paranoid disorder* or *folie à deux*. See the article and bibliography by A. Gralnick, "Folie à deux: the psychosis of association; a review of 103 cases and the entire English literature with case presentations," *Psychiat. Quart.*, 1942, vol. 16, pp. 230–263 and 491–520.

8. N. Dayton: *New Facts on Mental Disorders; Study of 89,190 Cases* (Springfield, Ill.: Thomas, 1940), pp. 308–318; *United States Army Technical Medical Bulletin* No. 203 (Washington, D. C.: United States Government Printing Office, October 19, 1945), Section 18. In a study confined to a university population, T. Raphael and L. Himler found that the mean age of persons developing paranoid disorders was 11.6 years older and the median age 13.0 years older than that of persons developing schizophrenic disorders. "Schizophrenia and paranoid psychoses among college students," *Amer. Jour. Psychiat.*, 1944, vol. 100, pp. 443–451.

9. J. Page and J. Warkentin: "Masculinity and paranoia," *Jour. Abnorm. Soc. Psychol.*, 1938, vol. 33, pp. 527–531; R. Knight: "The relationship of homosexuality to the mechanism of paranoid delusions," *Bull. Menninger Clinic*, 1940, vol. 4, pp. 149–159.

10. F. Curran, in a study of acute alcoholism, found that women patients commonly hallucinated voices accusing them of sexual inferiority and prostitution, but were less troubled by hallucinated homosexual self-accusations than were similar male patients. "Personality studies in

alcoholic women," *Jour. Nerv. Ment. Dis.*, 1937, vol. 86, pp. 645–667.

11. Compare C. Miller: "The paranoid syndrome," *Arch. Neurol. Psychiat.*, 1941, vol. 45, pp. 953–963.

12. E. Billings: *Elementary Handbook of Psychobiology and Psychiatry* (New York: Macmillan, 1939), p. 126.

Experimental Approaches to Psychodynamic Problems[*]

BY *Jules H. Masserman, M.D.*

Historical Review

Until recently, psychiatry in general and psychoanalysis in particular were usually defined as "sciences devoted to the study and treatment of diseases of the mind." Currently, however, many pragmatically minded thinkers and investigators are questioning this glib definition somewhat more closely. What, to begin with, *is* "the mind"? Is it the supraorganic expression of some ineffable "soul" vouchsafed only to human beings? Is it a composite of "faculties," of psychological abstractions vaguely named "instincts," "emotions" and cognitions, or of topographic subdivisions called, "id," "ego," "superego," etc.? Or is the mind, after all, only a categorical term used to summarize the totality of a person's ob-

[*] Reprinted from *Journal of the Mount Sinai Hospital,* New York, Vol. XIX, No. 5, January–February 1953, by courtesy of the author and publishers.

servable visceral and neuromuscular *behavior?* But if
the last definition comes closest to being operationally
meaningful, how can we speak of the mind as being
"diseased"—or do we mean by "mental disease" merely
that one person judges whatever he can observe of the
behavior of another to be grossly inappropriate for the
contingencies of time, place and culture? And even so,
why did the subject behave—and the observer judge—
as they did?

Mysticism and Magic

Questions such as these must have troubled men long
before they were able to approximate them in words; at
any rate, our ancestors seem to have reiterated the same
blind, groping and self-delusive answers to them down
the ages. Primitive man, fearfully close to the stark realities of helplessness, loneliness and the ever-present
threat of suffering and death, developed perhaps man's
most deeply rooted defenses against these anxieties:
first, the cherished premise of his own invulnerability
and immortality; second, a glorification of sexuality as
affording him enraptured moments of trustful reunion
with another human being in the quasi-deistic act of
procreation; and third, the wishful belief that he could
likewise, through magic thoughts, words and rituals, as-
sert his omnipotence over the very Gods of the Universe
themselves. So basic are these fundamental self-
delusions of humanity that they are immanent in nearly
all of our customs, our cultures, our religions—and our
philosophic and psychologic rationalizations about our
own behavior. First, perhaps, came the rites for controlling the Givers of Food and Shelter, such as totemiza-

tion of game-animals and the worship of primal mother symbols (incidentally, we still put cocks on our spires, and arch our doorways or tack horseshoes above them to honor the cornucopic womb of Isis). Almost immediately, too, there developed both the sacred and profane adulation of the sexual orgasm and of the powers of parenthood—man's only thaumaturgy potent enough to deny suffering through ecstasy and to conquer death by engendering life anew. And certain it is that at the very dawn of recorded fantasy man was also creating gods who, in the image of glorified and all-powerful parents, would protect, cherish and serve him as he wished.

And here also, as man's imagery grew, were ready-made "explanations" of his own behavior. Obviously, he both controlled *and was controlled by* various categories of gods: those of bodily lust (Dionysos, Loki, Ahriman, Siva and all the other dark and cloven-hoofed ancestors of our Devil); those of reason, compassion and light (Apollo, Thor, Ahura-Mazda, Brahma and other gentle demi-gods who lived in the guise of men and helped them deal with the realities of this world as well as the putative next) and finally, the supreme and sublimely indifferent Givers of Universal Law: Zeus, Wotan, Yahweh and their imperious ilk. These seemed to play with men as pawns, but, even so, indomitable Man could alter his fate by threatening, cajoling or bribing the very divinities he created in heaven and himself represented here on earth.

Diagnostics and Dynamics

These, then, were man's first wishful rationalizations of his own conduct. But, as August Comte pointed out,

though all sciences begin with mysticism, they generally
develop through two other theoretical phases, namely:
the taxonomic and, finally, the dynamic. Psychiatry,
about two centuries ago began to concentrate on the
second of these phases through the observation and
classification of human behavior. Of course, man's first
observations of the complexities of his own conduct
were predictably biased and inaccurate, and his clas-
sifications often arbitrary and dogmatic; indeed, even today we are prone to survey each other with a defensive
clinical stare and the covert appraisal: Compared to
me, thou art a "narcissist," a "neurotic," a "cyclothyme"
or some other deviate with an even more resoundingly
condescending appellation.

It would be tempting to round out this fragmentary
introduction by assuming that in modern times psychiatry has at last left such rubrics behind and is now a
truly scientific discipline devoted to a dynamic understanding of man and the application of rational methods for readjusting unhappy deviations from the golden
norm. As psychiatrists we wish this were completely
true, and yet we must admit that all about us are residues of mysticism and irrational dogmatisms in our
field. Without adequate diagnosis or rationale, too many
patients are still being partially burned or suffocated to
cure their "mental illness" (*ex* evilness)—a source of
future regret even though the electrical *auto-da-fe* is
now confined to the brain under the guise of "shock
therapy," whereas the Inquisitorial suffocation is scientifically yclept "carbon dioxide inhalation treatment."
And even in the relatively enlightened spheres of psychiatry there are relics of mystical thinking: *vide* the
misinterpretation of Freud's teaching by some disciples
who equate his concepts of "Id," "Ego" and "Super-

ego" for the triple oligarchies of gods that were once thought to control man's "psyche," or the misuse of selected Hellenic myths (Narcissus, Oedipus) not as expressive topical allegories but as supposed "proofs" of man's universal motivations.

Fortunately, this recidivism even in modern psychiatry is far outweighed by recent advances. Thus, in the fields of neurophysiology and psychosomatics psychiatry is reëstablishing a scientific liaison with biology and medicine; in the modern developments of psychoanalysis (Fromm-Reichmann, Kubie, French, *et al.*) it has achieved a sounder and more comprehensively dynamic rationale, and in some of its group applications (e.g., mental hygiene, orthopsychiatry, group therapy, etc.) it has become better correlated with anthropology, sociology, political science and such other broad disciplines. Moreover, it has relatively recently begun to derive support from another heuristic source in which it had been conspicuously lacking: namely, validation of its data, hypotheses and methods by laboratory experimentation.

Experimental versus Clinical Data

In all fairness, it must be noted that the clinical psychiatrist might take exception to the validity or relative importance of experimental data. He might insist, for instance, that every human being, in Adolf Meyer's words, is *ipso facto* an "experiment of nature," ready-performed and with results open to inspection. In effect, each person's inborn energies, potentialities and propensities have already been utilized in and influenced by his special familial, educational, social, sexual and other experiences, and in this manner molded into the complex configuration of traits and action-patterns that we call his personality. This in turn is open to retrospective and reconstructive analysis, provided only that our psychologic and psychiatric methods are made sufficiently discerning and penetrating.

Taken at face value, this argument sounds attractive, although one almost immediately wonders why it is not taken as seriously in other fields of medicine in which conclusions derived from clinical histories and observations alone are checked whenever possible by laboratory research. Further appraisal, however, leads to the recognition that *sole* reliance on clinical studies may be especially misleading in psychiatry for many reasons. Three of the most important of these may be outlined as follows.

Complexity and Multidimensionality of the Data

Human behavior is, perhaps, the most protean and variable of all phenomena. What observer, then— indeed, what combination of mortals—can possibly catalogue all of its facets, changes and expressions: anatomic, chemical, physiologic, pathologic, motivational, perceptual, conceptual, expressive, social, cultural, and others? And if the totality of behavior can never really be observed, let alone comprehended, in even a single individual, how can we really speak (as so many psychiatrists pretentiously do) of "the person as a whole" while at the same time myopically investigating his conduct by some narrowly constricted technique (e.g., a "psychiatric history," a neurological examination, or a Szondi test) picked on limited and sometimes purely arbitrary assumptions? In short, even though we are given two billion "experiments of nature," we do not necessarily know what particular phenomena to endow with what special significance for our field of interest.

LIMITATIONS OF DESCRIPTION: But even when we have selected our data, another difficulty arises: how shall we record them? Is any verbal language capable of describing the infinitely variable nuances of human conduct? And are not vaguenesses and confusions multiplied when we attempt to "define" even first-order psychologic abstractions i.e., categories of "motivation," "emotion," "intellect" and so on? What, for instance, are the palpable distinctions among "instincts," "unconditioned reflexes," "id-tendencies," "latent impulses," "goal-directed strivings" and other such postulates as to the basic motivations of conduct? Or, at the level of symbolic evaluation, who is to say whether some pattern of observed conduct arises from "inference," "intuition," "prejudice" or "delusion?" In short, we not only do not know what to look for in the welter of human conduct, but our descriptions of artificially isolated phenomena are often inexact, presumptive and judgmental.

COMPLEXITY OF ANALYSIS: Further, our semantic difficulties seem to mushroom incredibly when we attempt to progress from the recording of human behavior to its formulation in generic and causative (etiologic) terms. Here, unfortunately, is where some psychiatrists departed furthest from the rules which govern sound scientific theory: operational definition of terms, parsimony of premise, clarity and coherence of formulation, specificity of application and validation by unprejudiced test. Indeed, until recently it seemed that the wilder or more fantastic the speculation the more it fascinated certain writers in the field. For instance, only two decades ago self-styled "depth metapsychologists" were still promulgating oracular vacuities about "death-instincts," the "racial unconscious," the "birth trauma," "organ inferiority," and so on while their organic-minded psychiatric colleagues were proposing "constitutional inferiority," "stigmata of degeneration," "neurasthenic diatheses," and other sententious but equally baseless etiologic postulates for deviations in behavior they could not understand. All in all, psychiatry (if I, too, may indulge momentarily in the logical sin of animism) even now seems like a child emerging from its private world of uncontrolled fantasy into the less dramatic but more substantial and orderly universe of operational reality.

As has been indicated, however, many influences have stimulated recent progress in the field, not the least of which has been the pressure from psychiatrists themselves for better clinical and experimental validation of psychiatric theses and methods. Indeed, the studies of N. Tinbergen, W. Grey Walter, Horsley Gantt, H. A. Liddell, J. Hunt, David Levy, J. Finesinger, Curt Richter, and many others have indicated that certain basic tenets on which much of modern dynamic psychiatry implicitly rests are demonstrable in nearly all behavior—animal (or even "inanimate") as well as human, and "normal" as well as "abnormal."

Let us, then proceed to state these tenets—herein called "biodynamic principles"—and in the remainder of this article describe how they are illustrated by typical experiments in animal as well as human behavior.

Principles of Biodynamics

These may be condensed into four relatively simple statements relative to motivation, reaction patterns, substitutive behavior and "neurosis" formation as follows:

Motivation: All behavior is actuated by the current physical needs of the organism in the process of survival, growth and procreation.

Thus, even as the reader peruses this a physiologic want for fluids, or for warmth, or even for relief from bladder tension would, if sufficiently urgent, take precedence over his current interests or more complexly derived "instincts" (e.g., sex or "aggression") considered basic in some systems of psychology.

Reaction Formations: Behavior is adaptive to the "external" environment not in any "realistic" sense, but according to the organism's special interpretations (concepts) of its milieu in terms of its own perceptive-integrative-response capacities ("intelligence") and its unique concatenations of experience.

In the human being these interpretations and reactions become exceedingly elaborate; nevertheless, despite superficial cultural uniformity, each person's concepts of, and reactions to his universe are individually determined. To a literal minded farm laborer, a hammer and sickle are merely the tools of his trade; to a Communist they herald a fanciful Utopia; to an anti-Communist, the same insignium may represent the threat of barbarism and tyranny.

Behavior Substitution: When accustomed methods of achieving a goal are frustrated, behavior becomes de-

*viated into substitutive techniques or orientated toward
ancillary goals.*

Thus, if a man's methods of wooing a girl meet with
rebuff, he tries (a) other methods, (b) another girl or
(c) another goal, e.g., achieving success as a religious
prophet, a jazz drummer or perhaps as a clinical psychologist.

*Neurotic Deviations: When two or more accustomed
modes of response become mutually incompatible and
conflictual, physiologic tension ("psychosomatic anxiety") becomes manifest and behavior becomes vacillat-
ing, inefficient and unadaptive ("neurotic") or excessively substitutive, erratic and regressive ("psychotic").*

This principle of inner conflict is expressed or implied
by almost every theory of neurosis, albeit the elements
supposedly in conflict vary widely in the different contexts: e.g., animal *versus* rational soul (Plato), excitation
vs. inhibition of conditioned reflexes (Pavlov) or Id
vs. Ego *vs.* Superego (Freud). However, when formulated in biodynamic terms, this theory of conflict is
amenable to more direct clinical and, as will be seen, experimental demonstration. There now remains the task
of describing as briefly as possible the actual experiments from which the generalized biodynamic principles were derived.

Experiments in Biodynamics

Animal Subjects

Any animal with sufficiently high perceptive-
integrative-reactive capacities may be utilized: rat, dog,
cat, or monkey. The cat, an animal with easily isolated

motivations and relatively high intelligence, was employed in most of the experiments described below.

MOTIVATIONS: Any relatively strong physiologic want may be evoked: asphyxia, thirst, cold, escape from pressure or pain, erotic excitement, etc.—all have been tested and employed to motivate specific behavior patterns. However, we have found that hunger for food, though a relatively complex need, is most easily worked with for a number of reasons: it is easily renewable, is satiable in easy stages, and is neither as climactic nor potentially traumatic as are sexuality, cold, pain or other physiologic tensions.

NORMAL ADAPTIVE BEHAVIOR: In a typical experiment, a cat was deprived of food for a day, then placed in a glass-enclosed experimental cage at one end of which was a food box with a hinged lid partially open. The animal, of course, readily learned to secure pellets of food from this box by prying the lid farther open so as to make the food available. The animal was then taught (a) to wait for various combinations of sound and light signals before attempting to feed (conditional responses), (b) to manipulate various electrical switches so as to actuate these signals for itself (manipulative skills) and (c) to close two or more switches a given number of times in definite sequence (space and number categories) or in response to interposed cues (behavioral contingencies). If the training of the animal was too rapid for its age and capacities—and cats seemed to vary in relative intelligence as much as humans—the animal sometimes became recalcitrant, inept and resistive. If, however, the pedagogic process was adjusted to the individual cat, the behavior of the latter continued to be efficient, well-integrated and successful; indeed, pussy—as indicated by her eagerness to enter the laboratory, her avidity ("love") for the experimenter and the food switch, and her *legato sostenuto* purring while she worked for her rewards—presented the appearance of a "happy" animal, contented in an environment she had sufficiently mastered.

RANGE OF NORMAL ADAPTATIONS: Such control experiments presented an opportunity to investigate whether certain variations in individual and social behavior parallel to those seen in human beings could also be reproduced under laboratory conditions. Some of these studies deserve brief mention.

HABIT IDIOSYNCRASIES: If an animal was thoroughly trained to depress a disc-switch to secure food and then the switch was disconnected for several days so that its manipulation produced little or no reward, the animal would develop a marked tendency to push down upon other objects in its environment: saucers, loops, boxes or even other cats. This obsessive manipulative activity took many forms: sitting on the switch or on similar small platforms rather than in more comfortable places, prying into the experimenter's clothes instead of into the food box, etc.

MASOCHISM: Even greater deviations in symbol-values and goal-mediation could be produced, including conduct patterns which, when seen in human beings, have been somewhat misleadingly called "self-punitive" or "masochistic." Thus, a cat was first trained to accept a mild electric shock as a signal for feeding, and then taught to press a switch and administer the shock to itself in order to secure the food reward. The intensity of the shock was then gradually increased to as much as 5000 v. of a pulsating 15 ma. condenser discharge, yet the animal continued to work the switch avidly for the food. The food reward was then given only rarely or even discontinued for long periods; nevertheless, in the interim the animal persisted in its accustomed patterns of depressing the switch, apparently solely for the substitutive experience of a "painful" electric shock. Such observations suggest that, contrary to the biologically paradoxical postulate of a death-instinct, "masochistic" behavior is not basically "self-punitive" or destructive, but rather a seeking for survival by patterns of evaluation and response that seem awry only to an observer unacquainted with the special experiences of the subject. Clinically, we can understand why a woman may enjoy only certain "painful" forms of sexual intercourse when we learn that she reached her first orgasm while being beaten or raped, and that thereafter she valued all aspects of the erotic associations including those considered by others as "painful." Similarly, we can cease to wonder why a man marries a succession of shrewish wives if we determine under deeper analysis that what appears to his friends to be their nagging and persecution simply represents to him the security he had once experienced with his tyrannical but devoted mother.

SOCIAL DOMINANCE OR SUBMISSION: "Social" interactions can also appear in animal groups with revealing clarity. Thus, if after a given signal two cats compete for a single food-reward they may, at first, scuffle a bit at the food box. Soon, however, all external evidences of competition abate and only one of the animals—usually the more alert and intelligent—responds to the signal while its partner, though hungry, waits patiently until the "dominant" animal is either satiated or removed from the cage. Stable hierarchies of "privilege" can be produced in groups of four or more animals, although in the same group the animals may range themselves in a different order with regard to precedence in playing with parts of the apparatus or chasing a mechanical mouse. In short, a stratified "society" with fixed rankings in various activities evolved under the conditions described.

One variant of these experiments was particularly enlightening, since it seemed to reproduce in cats paradigms of "worker-parasite relationships" usually seen only in more elaborate forms of social organization. In these experiments two cats, each of which had been trained to manipulate a switch to secure food, were placed in the cage together. This time, however, a partition was so arranged that the animal which essayed to work the switch was delayed in returning to the food box for its reward until its less enterprising partner had eaten the pellet. Under these circumstances some pairs of cats evolved a form of coöperative effort in which, for a day or so, they alternately worked the switch to feed each other. This coöperation, however, lasted no longer among cats than it does among men: one animal sooner or later showed tendencies toward "parasitism" in that it ate the pellets produced by its partner's efforts but refused to leave the food to manipulate the switch. The worker animal, finding its own "coöperative" behavior completely unrewarding, in turn ceased to produce food, so that both animals, the parasite usually near the food box and the worker near the switch, lolled about the cage for hours or days in a travesty of a sit-down strike. But as hunger increased—generally most urgently in the relatively undernourished worker—the latter, in attempting to break the impasse, would discover that if the switch were depressed 6 or 8 times in rapid succession so that as many pellets were deposited into the food box, he could traverse the barrier and get the last one or two before the parasitic partner had time to gulp them all. In most experiments the end result was that the "worker" animal labored hard and eagerly for a meager living while supporting its parasitic partner in leisure—a form of relationship apparently accepted by both animals. However, two workers out of some 14 studied solved the situation with a flash of technological genius not anticipated by the experimenter: *viz.*, they learned to wedge the switch into a recess in the cage so that, with its electrical circuit closed and the mechanical feeder operating continuously, both animals could feed without further effort by either.

SOCIAL AGGRESSION: It may have been noted in the experiments described thus far that each animal pursued its own goals with its own initiative and techniques, without necessarily becoming hostile or combative toward others even in circumstances of direct rivalry. Indeed, so infrequently did overtly aggressive behavior occur that special experiments had to be devised to determine the specific circumstances under which such behavior could be elicited. In general, these studies demonstrated that animals became overtly belligerent under two sets of conditions: (a) when they were displaced from a position of social dominance to which they had become thoroughly accustomed or (b) when their goal-seeking activities were internally inhibited by neurotic conflicts. The first of these contingencies may be illustrated in a typical series of experiments as follows:

Let four cats compete for food under controlled conditions in Group A until Cat A1 emerges dominant, with A2, A3 and A4 in the hierarchy of precedence below him. Let Cats B1, B2, B3 and B4 range themselves correspondingly in Group B. If A1 is now paired with B4 the latter, accustomed to permit all other animals to feed before him, will offer no competition and the new pair remains peaceful. The same interactions of course occur when B1 is paired with A4. But if A1 and B1 are paired after each had been accustomed for weeks or months to dominance in its respective group, a new contest of speed and skill in securing the food on signal occurs. As before, each animal at first strives for the reward directly and deviates none of his energies into physical attacks on the other. Once again, of course, one animal emerges dominant—say B1—and thenceforward secures the food pellet after each signal. A1 now gives up his own efforts to obtain the food reward as long as B1 is in the cage. Instead, between signals A1 may sit on the food box menacing B1 with tooth and claw or may even attack him viciously, yet at no time does A1 utilize such physical attacks as a means of securing the food-pellet himself. Other pairings (A2-B3, B2-A3, etc.) evoke less definitive reactions ranging modally between the extremes of peace or hostility here described.

As indicated previously, aggressivity also appears when a well-patterned goal-directed striving in an animal is strongly inhibited by an adverse experience. For instance, if in Group B the dominant animal is made fearful of feeding on signal he will abandon this learned response and permit the subdominant B2 to feed instead —yet attack the latter animal between feedings. The induction of such "neurotic" deviations of energy will be more fully described below; however, it may be emphasized here that hostility and aggression appeared in our experiments only under conditions of external frustration or internal inhibition. These biodynamic observations therefore support the clinical and sociologic conclusions of Dollard, Horney, the author and others that hostilities among human beings also spring from the frustrations of their unconquered environment and the anxiety-ridden inhibitions imposed by their persistently barbarian culture—and not, as some would have it, from an inborn homo-suicidal "death instinct." Nor, as the author recently pointed out in an article on the social implications of biodynamics, is this point purely of academic interest. If aggression is merely a blindly exaggerated reaction-formation to perceived or conceived threat, then the hope of humanity lies in the abolition of tragic want and raging despair. If, however, aggression is the inevitable expression of a primeval and implacable "instinct" of destruction then we must indeed resign ourselves to the impending self-destruction of mankind. But in the latter case, why bother to think, write, or treat in the face of the holocaust?

The Production of Experimental Neuroses *

Perhaps the portion of our work most relevant to clinical psychiatry (in its older definition as a study not of the totality, but of the "abnormalities" of behavior) has been concerned with (a) the production of experimental neuroses in animals and (b) a study of the methods for restoring the behavior of such animals to "normal." This

* Grateful acknowledgment is made to the U. S. Public Health Service for grants-in-aid that made these research studies possible.

section of the present report must of necessity be even more greatly condensed than the preceding, but possibly the following brief description of the rationale, techniques and results of the experiments will indicate their main significance.

RATIONALE: As previously indicated, many theories as to the causes of neurotic aberrations converge on the concept of "conflict," whether this conflict is conceived to be between disparate "humors of the body" (Galen), "inhibition *vs.* excitation" (Gantt), "love against hate" (Karl Menninger) or other such noumena. In biodynamics this field theory is somewhat clarified by defining the conflict as occurring between or among patterns of behavior rendered mutually exclusive because (a) they arise from incompatible needs, or (b) they cannot co-exist in space and time. This general statement can be exemplified by a relatively simple method of producing an experimental neurosis in animals.

TECHNIQUE: A cat was trained to manipulate an electric device which, in the order named, flashed a light, rang a bell and deposited a pellet of breaded salmon in a food box. The animal was permitted over a period of months to become thoroughly accustomed to this routine of working for the food. One day, however, just as the animal was about to consume its reward for honest labor it was subjected to a physically harmless but "psychically traumatic" stimulus, e.g., a mild air-blast across its snout or a pulsating condenser shock through its paws. The animal, of course, dropped the food, beat a startled retreat from the food box and began to show hesitation and indecision about again manipulating the switch or approaching the box. When it did so, it was permitted to feed several times but then subjected once more to the disruptive blast or shock. After from two to seven repetitions in as many days of such conflict-inducing "neurotigenic" experiences, the animal began to develop aberrant patterns of conduct so markedly like those in human neuroses that the two may be described in the same terms. Examples are the following:

PHYSIOLOGIC ANXIETY: This was manifested by a rapid heart, full pulse, catchy breathing, raised blood pressure, sweating, trembling, erection of hair and other evidences of pervasive physiologic tension.

HYPERSENSITIVITIES AND PHOBIAS: The animal showed extreme startle reactions to minor stimuli, and became "irrationally" fearful not only of physically harmless light or sound stimuli, but also of closed spaces, air currents, vibrations, food pellets (or all food), caged mice and many other stimuli directly or remotely associated with its conflictful experiences. Odors welcomed in the normal state became particularly disturbing to the neurotic animal until, in further control observations, they were neutralized by a chlorophyll-containing deodorant placed in the apparatus.*

PSYCHOSOMATIC DYSFUNCTIONS: Neurotic animals developed gastro-intestinal disorders, recurrent asthma, persistent salivation or diuresis, sexual impotence, epileptiform seizures or muscular rigidities resembling those in human hysteria or catatonia.

MOTOR CHANGES: Peculiar stereotypes of behavior ("compulsions") emerged, such as restless, elliptical

* The studies of normal and neurotic olfactory behavior were supported by a special grant-in-aid from the Airkem Corporation.

pacing or repetitive gestures and mannerisms. One neurotic dog could never approach his food until he had circled it three times to the left and bowed his head before it.

SOCIAL ALTERATIONS: Neurotic animals lost their group dominance and, as indicated, became reactively aggressive under frustration. In other relationships they regressed to excessive dependence or various forms of kittenish helplessness.

Experiments with Monkeys

It may be added here that in more recent experiments with various species of monkeys not only has it been possible to establish and study highly complex response patterns (for example, "reading" behavior, time-perception, etc.) but also to use completely "symbolic" traumata (e.g., the exhibition of a toy rubber snake when food was anticipated) as means of precipitating an experimental neurosis. As might be expected, the neurotic behavior of the monkey was then even more closely similar to that of the human in a variety of ways. Psychosomatically, individual monkeys developed asthma, functional colitis, tics, "hysterical" paralyses and other organic or neuromuscular disturbances; sexually, homoerotism or persistent masturbation and autofellatio was substituted for previously normal heterosexual conduct; whereas socially, complex dominance relationships, defensive "friendships," or generalized aggressions occurred in patterns quite parallel to those observable in groups of neurotic or psychotic children and human adults.

Experimental Psychotherapy

In nearly every case the neurotic patterns described above rapidly permeated the entire life of the animal and persisted indefinitely unless "treated" by special procedures. These, too, were worked out in experiments too numerous and varied to be recounted here in detail; however, the techniques found to be most effective experimentally were so significantly similar to those used in the treatment of human neuroses that again the two may be outlined in parallel order. As nearly as they could be isolated, the methods were as follows:

CHANGE OF MILIEU: A neurotic animal given a prolonged rest (three to twelve months) in a favorable home environment nearly always showed a diminution in anxiety, tension, and in phobic-compulsive and regressive behavior. However, these neurotic patterns were prone to reappear when the animal was returned to the laboratory even though it was not subjected to a direct repetition of the conflictual experiences. To draw a human analogy, a soldier with severe "combat neurosis" may appear "recovered" after a restful sojourn in a base hospital, but unless his unconscious attitudes are altered his reactions to latent anxiety recur cumulatively when he is returned to the locale of his adaptive conflicts.

SATIATION OF A CONFLICTFUL NEED: If a neurotically self-starved animal which had refused food for two days was forcibly tube-fed so that its hunger was mitigated its neurotic manifestations correspondingly decreased. Hippocrates is reported by Soranus (perhaps apocryphally) to have utilized a parallel method in human psychotherapy. Hippocrates, it seems, was called into consultation to treat a strange convulsive malady which was keeping a recent bride virginal. Discerning, after a private interview, that she was torn between strong sexual desires neatly balanced by fear of injury, Hippocrates advised the husband "to light the torch of Hymen" with or without the patient's consent. The results of the therapy are not recorded, but Soranus parenthetically comments that, in general, it is only of temporary advantage "to substitute one Fury for another."

FORCED SOLUTION: A hungry neurotic cat was prevented from escaping from the apparatus and instead was brought mechanically closer and closer to the feeder until its head was almost in contact with a profusion of delectable pellets. Under such circumstances some animals, despite their fears, suddenly lunge for the food; thereafter, they need lesser degrees of mechanical "persuasion" until their feeding-inhibition disappears altogether carrying other neurotic generalizations with it. This method is a variation of the Hippocratic one mentioned above, but entails a greater degree of activity on the part of the patient. In some ways, the "therapy" is akin to pushing a boy afraid of water into a shallow pool. Depending on his capacities for reintegrating his experiences (in analytic terms, his "Ego strength"), he may find that there was, after all, no reason for fear—or he may go into a state of abject terror and thereafter hate not only water, but pools, swimming—and all future therapists. Because of the latter eventuality ruthless force is generally considered a dangerous method in dealing with neurotic anxieties.

EXAMPLE OF NORMAL BEHAVIOR: An inhibited, phobic animal paired for several weeks with one who responds normally in the experimental situation will show some diminution in its neurotic patterns, although never to the degree of complete "recovery." In like manner problem children do better when they have an opportunity to live with normal youngsters in an environment that favors normality—although more specific individual therapy is nearly always necessary to complete the "cure."

REËDUCATION BY A TRUSTED MENTOR: As noted, a neurotic animal, perhaps by the very virtue of its regression to earlier patterns of relationship, becomes exceedingly dependent upon the experimenter for protection and care. If this trust is not violated the latter may then retrain the animal by gentle steps: first, to take food from his hand, next to accept food in the apparatus; then to open the box while the experimenter merely hovers protectively, and finally to work the switch and feed as formerly without further "support" from the therapists. During its "rehabilitation" the animal not only reëxplores and resolves its hunger-fear conflicts but also masters and dissipates the symbolic generalizations that spring from this nuclear "complex": i.e., its inhibitions, phobias, compulsions and other neurotic reactions. This, indeed, may be the paradigm for the basic processes in much clinical psychotherapy. The neurotic patient channelizes his needs for help toward a therapist upon whom he transfers his dependence and other relationships. The therapist then utilizes this "transference" with optimal patience and wisdom to guide and support the patient as the latter reëxamines his conflictful desires and fears, recognizes his previous misinterpretations of reality and essays new ways of living until he is sufficiently successful and confident to proceed on his own. Whether this be called reëducation, retraining, rehabilitation or psychoanalysis depends more on the context of the problem, the necessity for thoroughness in anamnestic review and symbolic analysis and the form of utilization of the interpersonal relationships involved than on any fundamental differences in the essential dynamics of the respective procedures.

PHYSIO-PHARMACOLOGIC METHODS: As the experiments described thus far have indicated, many of the vectorial processes of so-called functional psychotherapy can be isolated in principle and demonstrated in operation. There remains, however, the fact that various physical methods such as the use of drugs, electroshock, etc., have also proved clinically useful in the treatment of behavior disorders. Space now remains only for the most cursory review of specific further experiments dealing with this subject.

ACTION OF VARIOUS DRUGS: Preliminary tests of the effects of various sedative and narcotic drugs on normal animals showed that, in general, such drugs disorganized complex behavior patterns while leaving relatively simple ones intact. Thus, in one series of experiments an animal was taught in successive stages (1) to open a food box, (2) to respond to food-signals, including signs reading FOOD or NO FOOD, (3) to operate the signal-switch, (4) to work two switches in a given order, and finally (5) to traverse a difficult maze to reach one of the switches. If the animal was then drugged with a small dose of barbital, morphine or alcohol, it would become incapable of solving the maze but would still work the food-switches properly; with larger doses, it could "remember" how to work only one switch; with still larger doses, earlier stages of learning would also be disintegrated until finally it lost even the simple skill required to open the food-box. Conversely, as the animal recovered from its intoxication its learned responses were reconstituted in their original order. If now the animal was made neurotic by an adaptational conflict, it developed a new set of highly intricate and elaborate reactions; i.e., inhibitions, phobias, compulsions, etc., as previously described. *These, too, proved relatively more vulnerable to disintegration by the sedative drugs than the simpler, pre-neurotic behavior patterns*, so that if a neurotic animal was given barbital or morphine its anxiety reactions and inhibitions were significantly relieved. In effect, instead of crouching tense and immobile in a far corner or showing panic at the feeding signals, it could respond to the latter by opening the box and feeding (in a somewhat groggy but comparatively effective manner) as though, for the time being, its doubts and fears were wraiths forgotten.

DRUG ADDICTION: In one variant of these studies in which alcohol was used as the nepenthic drug the animals which experienced relief from neurotic tensions while partly intoxicated were later given an opportunity to choose between alcoholic and non-alcoholic drinks. To our surprise (and, it must be confessed, subdued delight) about half the neurotic animals in these experiments began to develop a quite unfeline preference for alcohol; moreover in most cases the preference was sufficiently insistent and prolonged to warrant the term "addiction." In further proof of its neurotic basis the induced dipsomania generally lasted until the animal's underlying neurosis was relieved by the dynamic methods of therapy described above. It seems redundant to discuss the human analogues to these experimental observations.

TENSION-RELIEVING EFFECTS: In still another series of experiments we observed that the administration of hypnotic drugs (including alcohol) so dulled the perceptive and mnemonic capacities of animals that they were, while thus inebriated, relatively immune to the neurosis-producing effects of traumatic experiences. In this connection it may be recalled that many a human being long ere this has been tempted, through subversive experience, to take a "bracer" before bearding the boss, getting married, flying a combat mission or facing other presumed dangers.

EFFECTS OF CEREBRAL ELECTROSHOCK: In view of the widely broadcast and as yet scientifically questionable claims made for the efficacy of various forms of "shock therapy" for all forms of behavior disorders, we also investigated the effects of cerebral electroshock on our neurotic animals. In briefest summary, we found that when the ordinary 60-cycle current usually employed clinically was passed through the brain of the animal, the resultant shock acted like an intoxicant drug to disintegrate complex and recently acquired patterns of behavior, whether these were "normal" or "neurotic." Unlike most drugs, however, electroshock produced *perma-*

nent impairment, however subtle, of future behavioral efficiency, even though this could not be correlated with pathological changes in the brain detectable by present methods. Weaker or modified currents now being tested clinically (i.e., the direct square-wave Leduc type) produced lesser degrees of deterioration in our animals, but also had less effect on their neurotic behavior. All in all, these experiments supported the growing conviction among psychiatrists that electroshock and other drastic therapies may be useful in certain relatively recent and acute psychoses, but that the cerebral damage they produce makes their indiscriminate use replete with potential tragedy. More recent experiments in our laboratory indicate that this is probably true also for the operations of lobotomy, lobectomy and thalamotomy.

Significance of the Work

This, then, is a summary—possibly condensed beyond the limits of lucidity—of a long series of experiments designed to analyze the biodynamics of behavior and to discern principles that would apply alike to "normal" and "abnormal" conduct, to animal and human subjects, and to experimental and clinical therapy. The gap between the responses of cats, dogs or monkeys in cages and the conduct of man in society is undeniably wide; certainly man, of all creatures, has developed the greatest facility in experiential association and integration, the highest capacity for symbolic, verbal and other imagery, and the most elaborate repertoire of "normal," "neurotic" and "psychotic" behavior patterns in a constantly changing social and cultural milieu. And yet, as elsewhere in medicine, the best way to unravel an especially complex problem is to take it into the laboratory as well as the clinic, investigate it by specially designed experiments, check their results with a rigid self-discipline that eliminates subtle errors and cherished preconceptions, and so advance bit by bit toward clearer formulations of general principles and more pertinent applications of them. In psychiatry, such experimental and operational approaches, when correlated with clinical practice, may not only dissolve the verbal barriers among the various schools and methods but may also foster a needed rapprochement between psychiatry on one hand and scientific medicine and the humanities on the other.

References

(The following contributions by the author will serve as an introduction to the hundred or so technical reports on which the above article was based.)

Masserman, Jules H.: *Behavior and Neurosis*. University of Chicago Press, 1943.

———: *Principles of Dynamic Psychiatry*. Philadelphia, W. B. Saunders Co., 1946.

———: "Motion Pictures on Animal Behavior." *Psychological Cinema Register*, State College, Pa., 1936 to 1950.

———: "Psychological Medicine and World Affairs." *Modern Trends in Psychological Medicine*, London, Butterworth and Co., 1948.

———: "Some Current Concepts of Sexual Behavior." *Psychiatry J. for the Study of Interpersonal Processes*, 14; 67, 1951.

———: "Psychoanalysis and Biodynamics." *Int. J. Psychoanalysis*, 34, 1953.

Rorschach Variables in Relation to ESP Scores*†

BY *Gertrude R. Schmeidler, Ph.D.*

EDITOR'S NOTE:‡ *In the field of "psychical research" or "parapsychology"—the study of alleged paranormal abilities of man, to make contact with his environment through some means other than those now recognized by physics and physiology—two great movements have characterized the present era. One is the steady improvement of experimental and quantitative methods for analyzing the conditions under which extrasensory*

* From *The Journal of the American Society for Psychical Research*, Vol. XLI, No. 2, April 1947, by permission of the author and the American Society for Psychical Research.
† Dr. Gardner Murphy, Chairman of the A.S.P.R. Research Committee, has discussed with me every step of this procedure; and I should like to acknowledge here both my gratitude to him for his kindness and my great debt for his wise advice. The research reported here was begun in October 1945, and has continued until the time of writing (February 1947). Gathering, analyzing and interpreting this material comprised the greatest part of my work when Research Officer (Jan. 1946 to Feb. 1947) of this Society.
‡ From Introduction to Schmeidler, Gertrude, "Personality Dynamics and Psychical Research," *Bulletin of Menninger Clinic*, 18:1, 1954. Reproduced by courtesy of the author and publishers. Copyright, 1954, The Menninger Foundation.

perception (ESP) is carried out. This field of study is associated with the names of S. G. Soal and Whateley Carington, in England, J. B. Rhine, J. G. Pratt, Charles Stuart, Dorothy Martin, and others in the United States. The work, now domiciled in a number of university laboratories and other research centers, undertakes to ascertain the effects of various motivating conditions, such as competition, and various physiological factors, such as drugs and fatigue, upon the capacity of individuals to "see" concealed materials to a degree significantly beyond the degree to which such material could be "guessed."

In all work which is to be taken seriously, conditions are so arranged that the experimental subject can have no normal source of sensory contact with the material; typically, the material is concealed in opaque containers or behind a wooden screen or in another room at a distance from the subject. Noting the amount of agreement to be expected by chance between the guesses made and the materials concealed, and expressing the results in terms of the probability (P) that such and such a deviation above the expected amount would occur by chance alone, the experimenter seeks to ascertain the most favorable working conditions, and to study the individual gift or idiosyncrasy for this sort of thing. Most evidence has shown that the scoring levels of ordinary unselected subjects (not the so-called "gifted" subject) typically run only slightly ahead of chance expectation. If the amount were great, it could hardly remain undetected in daily life. But, any con-

sistent and cumulative effect must, according to the canons of science, be studied.

The hypothesis to be studied and tested is that there is an extrasensory process at work. In addition, there are numerous definite psychological hypotheses about the conditions most favorable for this process, and systematic and repeated experimental testing to ascertain whether these hypotheses are correct. Some of these hypotheses relate to the kinds of materials (letters, colors, pictures, playing cards, etc.) which can be most successfully guessed; some to the distance between subject and material; some relate to the tempo of guessing; some to the novelty or familiarity of the task; some, like those to be described here, relate to the personality of the subject.

In such experimental studies, the work of Dr. Gertrude R. Schmeidler has been one of the great inspirations of my scientific life in the last dozen years. Her own experimental work can speak for itself.

G.M.

ABSTRACT: Nine ESP runs were conducted in college classrooms, by a group method, with each of 250 subjects. The Rorschach method of personality diagnosis, in the form of a group test, was administered to the same subjects. Using the Munroe Inspection Record as a criterion of adjustment, it was found that the well-adjusted tended to score above chance if they believed in the theoretical possibility of ESP, and below chance if they rejected this possibility, while the poorly adjusted, in both of these categories, scored about at chance.

Finer analysis of Rorschach records found more specific indices of adjustment factors related to scoring success.

Introduction

When I conducted group ESP experiments with students whom I had been teaching for several months, there were many whose ESP scores seemed to reflect their personalities; who seemed to handle the ESP situation in the same way that they handled the affairs of everyday life. It therefore appeared worth while to begin a large-scale study of the relationship between personality factors and paranormal ability.

The question then arose of how to bring the problem from a vague personal hunch to the scientific domain of demonstrable fact. We should have to have two objective tests: one of personality, and one of paranormal ability. If we administered these tests to large groups of subjects and found consistent, repeatable relationships between them, we should be on solid ground.

What tests should be made? Here there was real difficulty. What we wanted was clear enough; a good test should: (1) be easy to administer, so that we could collect enough cases to give a sound basis for generalization; (2) permit easy and objective scoring so that we could be sure of our data; (3) give a fair statement of what it aims to test (not like the earlier "personality tests," which actually showed, in many cases, only the subject's ability to outguess the examiner); (4) give more information about the problem than was needed for the particular point of inquiry, so that when we completed the research, we could have a broader perspective than when we began it.

It will hardly be necessary to say that the perfect test

for either personality or paranormal ability has not yet been devised; that in evaluating tests for use in this research, it was necessary to balance weakness in some of these criteria against strength in others. Whenever time allowed, I have tried to give a "battery" of tests instead of a single one. But since there are good tests, even if not perfect ones, for both personality traits and paranormal ability, it seemed wiser to go ahead with the research than to wait for perfection.

The test for the paranormal which was used was the familiar one of guessing ESP symbols. This is not difficult to administer in a classroom; and scoring is objective. The question whether an ESP score affords a fair measure of a subject's telepathic or clairvoyant or precognitive ability is harder to answer. Perhaps no test can. Sometimes a striking report of a spontaneous case comes from a mature person who says that he has never had a similar experience; and subjects who make high scores in one experiment may make low scores in the next. Although such observations raise the problem whether any single test of paranormal ability will be valid, two factors argue in favor of continued use of ESP runs. The first is that various subjects have been reported who maintained high ESP scores for long periods of time, and also showed other signs of paranormal ability (2, 6, 7, 12); apparently for these subjects, ESP guesses are a valid test. In the second place, it was from experiments with ESP cards that this investigation emerged; and it seemed logical to continue with the same method.

Can we get any information from an ESP test in addition to the single figure representing a subject's total score? Other possibilities are present but limited, for the rich opportunities for symbolism or qualitative accuracy which other tests offer are almost entirely lacking. But we may look for displacement, as in the case of B. S., the subject who so often seemed to be guessing one ahead of his target (12), and the variation in score from one run (or one part of a run) to the next may be studied. Thus, while a series of ESP runs is not to be considered a completely satisfactory test of paranormal ability, it probably offers, by and large, the best possible test we can use, since its excellence in the first two test criteria overshadows its comparative weakness in the latter two.

In evaluating personality tests, the Rorschach (1, see also discussion in 5) seemed the best for our purpose. Running through the four criteria listed above, we find:

(1) There is an accepted, standard procedure for group administration. And though this procedure is time-consuming, taking about an hour, it is easy to find subjects for it because of widespread interest in the test.

(2) Scoring methods are probably the Rorschach's weakest point, because the scoring is slow, and depends to some (not completely determined) extent on the judgment of the examiner. We felt, however, that the scoring categories were sufficiently objective to make the test usable, especially with the safeguard against bias provided by the rule that scoring a subject's Rorschach must always be completed without knowledge of his ESP scores.

(3) The Rorschach is one of the best tests of personality, as evidenced by its increasingly wide use in clinic and college, and in the armed forces during the war, and by the growing number of psychologists who employ it. It compares favorably with such other valid tests as the Thematic Apperception Test, and is at present far more objective in its scoring.

(4) It essays to show the basic organization of the subject's personality structure, and thus gives extremely rich material for personality research. One of its outstanding characteristics is that there are no "right" or "wrong" answers. Each subject can make of his responses the unique pattern which represents himself alone; and thus the data are not forced into predetermined and limiting patterns.

The problem of where to find subjects offered little choice. Ideally, we should have chosen two groups to be studied and contrasted: those who show much paranormal ability, and for a control, those who show little. But if we had tried to put this plan into practice, it would have taken many months to find enough subjects who think they have paranormal ability and who would be willing to take part in such an experiment; and then we should have had to take even more time to weed out of this group the ones who deceived themselves into claiming more of such ability than they had. A more practical approach was to make a random selection of subjects who were readily available, on the assumption that some would show considerable paranormal ability.

My own classes were always eager to take part in the experiment, and acted willingly as subjects. The plan of the research helped in enlisting other classes: several instructors in psychology felt that their students would gain enough from taking the Rorschach and having it interpreted to them, to justify the use of class time for research in parapsychology.* The number of subjects

* I am grateful to Mr. William Triebel for helping make the arrangements, and to Dr. Rudolf Ekstein, Dr. Genevieve Chase, Miss Edith Wladkowsky, Dr. Eugene Hartley, Miss Ruth Berenda and Miss Virginia Staudt, who coöperated so generously by giving me from two to five hours of their classes' time for this research.

was limited only by my own capacity for giving these tests, since each Rorschach protocol took, on the average, about half an hour to score.

Procedure

The data to be reported here were obtained in eleven group experiments, which gave a total of 303 usable records. One of these experiments was conducted by Gardner Murphy, using the members of his own class as subjects; three were performed by myself on my classes; and I conducted the remaining seven on classes borrowed for the occasion. All subjects were students in psychology in the New York City colleges. All experiments followed the same basic procedure and gave approximately similar results. They will be presented as a unit since it would serve no useful purpose to present them separately.

The procedure of these group experiments was parallel to the method that I have used with individual subjects and have already reported in this JOURNAL (8, 9). Lists of 25 ESP symbols were made by an assistant, the order of the symbols being obtained by a random method of selection. These lists, used as targets by the subjects, were not known to me until after the guessing was completed. The person who made the lists, who alone had seen the order of the symbols, was never present at the experiment. The lists were concealed from the subjects until their guesses had been made. With all these precautions, there was no possibility of sensory cues to guide the correct guesses. The average number of correct guesses to be expected from each run was five.

The basic procedure, which all the separate experiments had in common, consisted of distribution of record sheets to the members of the class, and of a few introductory comments by the experimenter. The subjects were then told about the nature of the symbols, the number of guesses in a run, and the fact that three runs (75 guesses) should be taken as a unit. We emphasized the impossibility of "figuring out" the correct symbol by any intelligent method. Subjects were told to make guesses in sequence, rather than by skipping; and they were warned against changing a symbol once they had written it.

When they understood what was expected of them, each subject was asked, as in the earlier experiments, to characterize himself as a "sheep" or a "goat." A sheep was defined as a person who thought there might be some possibility of guessing the symbols with better than chance success; the goats were those who were convinced that any relationship between targets and guesses was coincidental. I made it a practice to draw a line on the blackboard, representing the continuum from *belief* that there would be a correspondence between guesses and targets, to *disbelief* in it. Labelling the center with a question mark, as shown below, I went on to say (in effect)

belief————?————disbelief

that of course the subjects to the left of the question mark should be called sheep. But by my definition, the subjects at the center, and even the ones toward the right of the continuum, were also sheep. It was only those *at the extreme right*, who had no reservation, and no shadow of doubt in their minds, who were goats.

For one class, I omitted to draw this continuum,

and to give these final instructions. Such an extraordinarily large proportion of these subjects wrote "goat" at the top of the record sheet that I reëxamined the procedure, remembered the omission, and in the next class period told them about it. Several of the "goats" said that they would have called themselves sheep under the full instructions. It therefore seemed best to discard all the "goat" records from this class.

Once the subjects had written either "sheep" or "goat" after their names on the record sheets, they began their ESP guesses. When all had completed the first three runs, the envelope containing the target lists for these runs was opened, and the lists were read to the class. The subjects then guessed the fourth, fifth and sixth runs; and again when they were finished, the targets were read to them. We followed the same procedure for the seventh, eighth and ninth runs; and this completed the ESP experiment proper.

A group Rorschach Test was given (sometimes before, sometimes after, administration of the ESP test) to all these classes by projecting upon a screen ten slides corresponding in order to the ten cards used in the individual test. A booklet was provided each subject to record what he saw in the slides. In addition, various minor tests were given or questions asked of the students. It was hoped that these supplementary tests would serve two purposes: by such slight changes of procedure from one group to the next, the experiment would not become too much a matter of routine; and in addition, the tests might suggest hints about new directions for research. None of these supplementary tests have given sufficient data to justify a report, but some are promising enough to make me expect to continue using them.

All the Rorschach records of the subjects reported here were scored without knowledge of the results of the ESP runs, so that any bias of the experimenter cannot have affected the data. All ESP scores have been double-checked.

Results

The first question we put to the data was whether they confirmed our previous hypothesis about sheep and goats. We may call this:

Hypothesis I: Sheep will tend to make ESP scores above chance, and goats will tend to make ESP scores below chance.

This hypothesis has been fully discussed in previous articles (8, 9, 10, 11). Six experiments with individual subjects and one group experiment had already been performed and all had tended to confirm it. It is based on four premises: (1) that ESP occurs; (2) that a subject's attitude toward the ESP task (whether it be conscious or unconscious) will affect his scores; (3) that, by and large, subjects who believe that ESP may occur would like to make good scores in an ESP experiment; (4) that subjects who commit themselves before the experiment to the unqualified conviction that the idea of the experiment is nonsensical, will, by and large, hope to disprove the ESP hypothesis by their data, and will thus unconsciously aim at making incorrect guesses. (More sophisticated subjects, of course, would aim at the "chance" score of five successes in twenty-five guesses.)

Table I summarizes the data of all the students who

participated in the current experiments, and who classified themselves as either sheep or goats. It shows a small difference in the predicted direction. The difference is marginally significant, and tends, as did all our previous research, to confirm the first hypothesis. We may speculate that these deviations are so much smaller than in the individual experiments because of the more impersonal atmosphere of the classroom, which—especially with a visiting experimenter—might make the students feel more remote from the situation; thus motivation for either high or low scores would be lessened, and the average would be nearer chance.

TABLE I

	SHEEP			GOATS		
	Subjects with no Rorschach	Subjects with Rorschach	Total	Subjects with no Rorschach	Subjects with Rorschach	Total
Number of Subjects	29	117	146	24	133	157
Number of Runs*	255	1049	1304	217	1197	1414
Deviation	+9	+111	+120	−21	−127	−148
Mean	5.04	5.11	5.09	4.90	4.89	4.90

When we come to analysis of the Rorschach records, the richness of the material creates difficulties. One conventional method of listing the scoring categories for

* Although all subjects were asked to complete nine runs, there were a few who did not. Their records have been included, and thus the number of runs is not always nine times the number of subjects.

the Rorschach gives 66 items (1); and even this has been criticized for omitting some of the most important scores. It has seemed to me that it would be absurd to try to use so many categories when working with hundreds of records; and I have in general followed the much simpler scheme proposed by Dr. Ruth Munroe, which she calls the Rorschach Inspection Record (3).

But in addition to the mechanical listing of high and low scores for various categories, it is possible to approach the Rorschach from a more directed point of view: to put specific questions to a record, such as, "How well-adjusted is this subject?" or, "Does he respond freely to new situations, or does he look for security by restricting himself to a narrowly conventional, 'correct' approach?"

This is, in part, what I have done. On the basis of each group of experiments, new hypotheses presented themselves as to conditions for high or low ESP scores. Subsequent experiments would give an opportunity to test each such theory; and they in turn would give rise to new ones. The Rorschach material will therefore be presented from two points of view: whether it confirms an impression that grew out of previous work (Tables II and III) and whether the cruder listing of items brings new points into prominence (Tables IV and V).

The reader may remember that some of the subjects described earlier in this report were students in my classes. These classes, tested in the spring of 1945, were all given Rorschachs as well as ESP tests, and it was from comparison of these records that our second hypothesis arose. (The data are not cited here because I had seen the ESP scores of the students before scoring the Rorschachs, and there might, therefore, have been bias in the Rorschach scoring.) It seemed to me that many of the badly adjusted students made extremely poor ESP scores (*i.e.*, near chance expectation), while most of the well-adjusted youngsters did nicely (*i.e.*, the sheep scored above chance and the goats scored below chance) in the ESP tests. The second hypothesis, therefore, is:

Hypothesis II: Sheep who are well-adjusted will, on the average, make higher ESP scores than sheep who are not; and goats who are well-adjusted will have lower ESP scores than the other goats.

It is fortunate that a single Rorschach score for good or poor adjustment has recently been devised by Dr. Munroe (3, 4). It is derived, essentially, by listing some twenty significant Rorschach categories, and giving one or more checks to each, whenever a subject deviates from "normal" in that category. Adding up a subject's checks gives a summary statement of how deviant he is in these more diagnostic categories; and thus the total of checks is probably as good an indicator of his adjustment as any one figure, obtained from a single test, could be.

But where does good adjustment stop, and bad adjustment begin? Any such boundary is arbitrary and subject to considerable error; but I have set it (following certain implications of Dr. Munroe's discussion) at a point which divides the group into approximately a ratio of 5.3 for well-adjusted in relation to poorly adjusted.* This may seem rather severe to our college population, and, of course, does not imply that the Ror-

* The criterion actually used was ten checks or less for good adjustment, and eleven checks or more for poor adjustment. This number was determined on the basis of the subjects from the spring of 1945, and we may therefore take the entire current series of data as a test of the second hypothesis.

schach predicts that three out of eight students will be sent to prison or a mental hospital, or otherwise come to a bad end. But perhaps it is not too far out of line to say that at least a third of the students are so mixed up in their own problems that they are likely to approach a new, non-compelling situation like a class ESP experiment from a highly personal point of view. Thus we could not expect them to accept without reservation the simple motivation of the experimenter's "Now try to guess the list!" nor even the implied motivation of "Now prove by your failure that the experiment is a lot of nonsense!" And if the subjects who are preoccupied with their own difficulties do not accept such motivation, we get a clearer differentiation between sheep and goats when those cases are omitted.

TABLE II. *Summary of ESP scores according to Hypothesis II: that well-adjusted sheep will make higher ESP scores than poorly adjusted sheep, and that well-adjusted goats will make lower ESP scores than poorly adjusted goats.*

	SHEEP		GOATS	
	Well-adjusted	Poorly adjusted	Well-adjusted	Poorly adjusted
Number of Subjects	74	43	83	50
Number of Runs	665	384	746	451
Deviation	+108	+3	−159	+32
Mean	5.16	5.01	4.79	5.07

When scores of well-adjusted sheep and well-adjusted goats are compared, C.R. diff = 3.55; P = .0002.

This in fact occurs. Table II shows the ESP scores of well-adjusted and poorly adjusted sheep and goats. Poorly adjusted sheep scored almost exactly at chance (Mean = 5.01); poorly adjusted goats were slightly above chance (Mean = 5.07). Thus the entire negative deviation of the goats of Table I, and virtually the entire positive deviation of the sheep, was contributed by the well-adjusted subjects. The difference between the well-adjusted sheep and the well-adjusted goats is highly significant statistically.

Although it is always gratifying to have an experiment come out as predicted, these data offered no temptation to look at Hypothesis II as a final statement of the problem of ESP. There was a staggering number of individuals whose scores did not follow the general trend. This would, I think, have been predicted by anyone who had studied psychical phenomena. We might say about a sensitive that no one could expect her to give a good sitting during a certain period because at that time she was so disturbed by her personal worries (and this would correspond to the poor ESP scores of the subjects whose Rorschachs showed personality difficulties). But no one would suggest that good psychiatric adjustment should be the crucial test of a successful psychic, and just as surely our data do not mean that all subjects who are well-adjusted will score better than chance at ESP and that all maladjusted subjects must score badly.

I suggest, therefore, that we interpret Hypothesis II with due caution, and with proper reservations. We are entitled to say that evidence from a fairly large number of cases suggests that well-adjusted subjects tend to get good (*i.e.,* non-chance) ESP scores. But then we should add that this rule applies to groups, and does not predict that each individual well-adjusted subject will score well. In addition, there is the difficulty that "good adjustment" refers to a complex pattern of behavior which is not easy to define, and which will vary from one situation to the next. Perhaps certain aspects of good adjustment are significant for us, and others are irrelevant. In other words, this hypothesis offers, at best, only a first approximation to a theory of personality in relation to the paranormal.

As for the second aspect of these same data: the average ESP score of the subjects with poor adjustment was not far from chance. Does this mean that subjects with poor personality adjustment show no paranormal ability? Or does it imply that some will do well and others will do badly, making it impossible to predict about the group as a whole?

My own impression is that the latter alternative comes closer to the truth; and that we should be able to separate high-scorers from low-scorers in the poorly adjusted group when we know more about them. Two contrasting cases come to mind to support this point, both relating to subjects who, at the time of the experiment, were college sophomores with severe personality problems.

The one with poor ESP scores was a very quiet youngster, whose voice seldom rose above a whisper and whose handwriting was tiny and cramped. He dressed neatly; he came to class on time; his grades were good; and his surface adjustment was adequate. But he was an unhappy, dissatisfied boy, unsure of his ability or his choice of a career, whose self-restraint was so excessive that it seemed to hamper him at every turn. Perhaps it would not be too far from the truth if we guessed that the factors of restraint related to his maladjustment, also kept him from the paranormal contacts required for success in ESP.

The other boy was as untidy as the first was neat. He was considered brilliant, and had a talent for poetry that won the respect of his professors. But he seemed at the mercy of his impulses, doing such unpredictable things as emptying a glass of water over a girl who made a joke that annoyed him, or leaving college for a week while classes were in session because he wanted to see an art exhibit in another city. The freedom with which he flung himself into activity, and with which he gave scope to his creative powers, was extraordinary; was it also a condition for the release of paranormal ability? Whatever the reason, in spite of his undoubted poor adjustment, his ESP scores were high and he reported spontaneous telepathic experiences.

But to return to our Rorschach. As the first batch of data was being tabulated, it seemed to me that there was a very large number of exceptions to the rule that good adjustment was tied with good ESP scores; and also that a particularly large number of these exceptions had the personality trait that psychologists call "constriction." This might show itself in a variety of ways, through all of which runs a common thread of extreme self-control; a constricted person might have a colorless personality, or a highly conventional, over-correct approach to problems, or he might be inflexible. Constriction is defined in the Rorschach in terms of an unusually high percentage of responses that rely exclusively on the formal aspects of the material; the usual formula is to say that a record which contains half, or more than half, of such "F" responses is constrictive ($F\% \geq 50\%$).

This impression of the frequency of poor ESP scores

among constricted subjects led to the formulation of a refinement of the previous theory, namely:

Hypothesis III: Well-adjusted and non-constricted sheep will tend to have higher ESP scores than sheep who are poorly adjusted or constricted; and well-adjusted, non-constricted goats will tend to have lower ESP scores than goats who are poorly adjusted or constricted.

This hypothesis is based on the data collected before May, 1946. Table III will present separately the cases obtained before and after the theory was stated.

Only ten of the subjects of the July group were both constricted and well-adjusted; and, of course, this number is too small to offer an adequate test of the relation of constriction to ESP success. Out of the ten subjects, the five sheep scored exactly at chance, but the five goats scored below chance (Dev. = —21; M = 4.76). These first data must, therefore, be considered ambiguous in respect to constriction, although they tend to confirm Hypothesis III as it was stated.

There were indications in the July records that the third hypothesis had been stated too narrowly and that two additional factors should be included as contra-indicators for ESP. One of these factors implies a rigidity or self-restraint in the subject's use of his own creative ability. This score is given if more than half of the M (human movement) responses are like the frozen movement of a statue, or the tensed position of a person who is poised but motionless. Munroe indicates the score as "Mr" where "r" stands for "rigid."

The other factor which seemed prominent in these records was the "quantity ambition" or intellectual ambition of many of the subjects who had low ESP scores.

TABLE III. *Summary of ESP scores according to Hypothesis III: that well-adjusted and non-constricted sheep will tend to have higher ESP scores than sheep who are poorly adjusted or constricted; and that well-adjusted, non-constricted goats will tend to have lower ESP scores than goats who are poorly adjusted or constricted.*

A. SHEEP

Date of Expt.	WELL-ADJUSTED AND NON-CONSTRICTED			POORLY ADJUSTED AND/OR CONSTRICTED		
	Oct. '45 to Apr. '46	July '46	Total	Oct. '45 to Apr. '46	July '46	Total
No. of S's	29	29	58	40	19	59
No. of Runs	261	260	521	357	171	528
Dev.	+102	+52	+154	−23	−20	−43
Mean	5.39	5.20	5.30	4.94	4.88	4.92

B. GOATS

Date of Expt.	WELL-ADJUSTED AND NON-CONSTRICTED			POORLY ADJUSTED AND/OR CONSTRICTED		
	Oct. '45 to Apr. '46	July '46	Total	Oct. '45 to Apr. '46	July '46	Total
No. of S's	25	49	74	33	26	59
No. of Runs	224	441	665	298	234	532
Dev.	−69	−90	−159	+33	−1	+32
Mean	4.69	4.80	4.76	5.11	5.00	5.06

When ESP scores of the well-adjusted, non-constricted sheep and goats of the July, 1946 series, are compared, C.R. diff = 3.33; P = .0004.

This refers, not to ambition as such, but to *intellectual* ambition, a kind of showing-off, or forcing one's ideas forward. It is indicated by a large number of responses, and I have set the criterion number at 30 or higher in the group record (where time of administration is limited) and at 50 or higher in the individually administered protocol.

When so many factors appeared, in a cursory examination of the Rorschach scores, to have a possible relation to ESP success, it was obvious that a more systematic examination would be needed. I therefore made a table which is summarized in Appendix I,* listing each of the Rorschach scores and the ESP score for each of the 250 subjects described in this report. The summary table gives the ESP average and certain other data for the various Rorschach scores.

Glancing down the right-hand column (ESP Mean) in this Appendix table, it is obvious that there is a hodgepodge of high and low ESP scores in which it is difficult to see a pattern. I have attempted to find some order in this confusion by pulling out of the table the subjects whom we expect to have poor scores. In a first attempt, for example, all cases which showed poor adjustment or constriction were excluded, and the table was reconstructed with the records of the remaining subjects. The poor ESP scores of the subjects whose Rorschachs showed either $R \geq 30$ (thirty or more responses) or Mr (rigid movement) then suggested another reconstruction of the table. I drew it up again with those cases omitted. After several such jugglings, in which

---

* The detailed Appendixes mentioned here and throughout this article were considered of interest primarily to the specialist and have therefore not been reprinted here. Readers wishing to study them are referred to the original article.

various categories were taken out or put back in, the table presented in Appendix II emerged. This table represents my final attempt until more data are available. None of the intermediate forms are presented here.

In this final listing, seven categories have been selected as showing an association with poor ESP scores. They include the three described above, two others which may have a logical association with them, and a pair which seem to represent a contrasting personality pattern. The four new items are:

Total Movement $\geqq$ 60%, *i.e.*, an extremely large percentage of responses describing movement. Such a score is taken to mean an extremely active "inner life." It may carry something of the same significance for our purposes as "quantity ambition." Both have the connotation that a subject may force himself to have ideas even in situations where it would be better for him to be relaxed instead of working so hard.

Absence of both color shock and shading shock (evidence of emotional shock when confronted with color and shading). Under Munroe's generous definition, such absence of shock means that a subject is remarkably passive or unmoved under conditions to which most people will respond more strongly. Like constriction, or rigidity of thinking, it implies a tendency to shut oneself off from experiences instead of being a willing participant in them.

C+ and CF+ (response to color without use of form, and response to color dominant over form), the last two scores, are based on an over-reaction to color at the expense of form. They imply extreme impulsiveness.

These seven categories tend to be associated with

poor ESP scores, even in the records where one of these appears without the other six categories (Appendix III).

Decision as to which factors to include in this list depended on two considerations: how many subjects with a certain Rorschach score had poor ESP scores; and how poor the ESP scores were. Thus, when the only subject who showed very marked shading shock also did very badly at ESP, it seemed an inadequate basis for concluding that marked shading shock indicates poor paranormal ability. And again, when the twenty-four subjects with checks for "K,k" (undifferentiated shadings) had ESP averages that were low but in the predicted direction, it seemed safer *not* to draw any conclusion from their low mean scores.

It will be noted that when we exclude the records in which any of these seven scores occur, the remaining poorly adjusted subjects score about as well in ESP as do the well-adjusted ones (for maladjusted sheep, Mean = 5.39, and for maladjusted goats, Mean = 4.86). This listing of specific factors, relating to *specific maladjustment,* offers therefore an alternative to Hypothesis II, relating to *total maladjustment.*

Two difficulties in the listing will occur to the reader. One is the point already mentioned: the doubtful categories, for which the scores are so few or so ambiguous that we cannot be sure whether the item should be used even provisionally as an indicator of poor ESP scores. The other difficulty is the uncertainty that attends every research hypothesis: we cannot be sure, until we have more cases, whether any of our apparent relationships are due only to coincidence. With these points in mind, I can offer only as extremely tentative the following hypotheses.

Hypothesis IV: Sheep who are well-adjusted, not constricted, not inclined to impose rigid barriers on their creative thinking and not needing to impress others with their intellectual prowess, will tend to have higher ESP scores than other sheep. Goats with these characteristics will tend to make lower ESP scores than other goats.

TABLE IV. *Summary of ESP scores according to Hypothesis IV: that sheep who are well-adjusted, not constricted, not inclined to impose rigid barriers on their creative thinking and not needing to impress others with their intellectual prowess, will have higher average ESP scores than other sheep. Goats with these characteristics will make lower average ESP scores than other goats.*

	SHEEP		GOATS	
	Subjects expected to have high ESP scores according to Hypothesis IV	Other subjects	Subjects expected to have low ESP scores according to Hypothesis IV	Other subjects
No. of S's	44	73	62	71
No. of runs	396	653	557	640
Deviation	+167	−56	−173	+46
Mean	5.42	4.91	4.69	5.07

But if we summarize the tables presented in Appendix II and Appendix III, an alternative hypothesis would do as well, namely:

Hypothesis V: Sheep who are not constricted, not inclined to impose rigid barriers on their creative thinking, responsive to change, not needing to impress others with their intellectual prowess, not too over-active in their inner life, and not over-impulsive, will have higher average ESP scores than other sheep; and goats with these characteristics will tend to have lower ESP scores than other goats.

TABLE V. *Summary of ESP scores according to Hy-pothesis V: that sheep who are not constricted, not inclined to impose rigid barriers on their creative thinking, responsive to change, not needing to impress others with their intellectual prowess, not too over-active in their inner life, and not over-impulsive, will have higher average ESP scores than other sheep; and goats with these characteristics will tend to have lower ESP scores than other goats.*

	SHEEP		GOATS	
	Subjects expected to have high ESP scores according to Hypothesis V	Other subjects	Subjects expected to have low ESP scores according to Hypothesis V	Other subjects
No. of S's	51	66	71	62
No. of runs	459	590	638	559
Deviation	+204	−93	−175	+48
Mean	5.44	4.84	4.73	5.09

Hypotheses IV and V are equally appropriate at this writing; they make equivalent separations of ESP scores, and only further research can decide between them. But because it is more specific, the latter may, if it is verified, be more fruitful. It indicates that any one of three patterns is unfavorable to good classroom ESP scores: extreme intellectuality, extreme impulsiveness, or extreme reserve. This is susceptible to experimental test, both with the Rorschach and with other methods. Like every other working hypothesis, it is by such tests that it must eventually stand or fall.

Summary

The Rorschach test of personality and ESP tests were given to 250 college students. Relationships between personality patterns and success in the ESP tests were described in the form of five hypotheses. The first three hypotheses proposed have been supported by the later investigations. Further research is needed to provide an independent test of the later hypotheses.

References

1. Klopfer, B. and Kelley, D. M.: *The Rorschach Technique,* World Book Company, Yonkers, 1942.
2. Martin, D. R. and Stribic, F. P.: "Studies in Extra-Sensory Perception: III. A Review of All University of Colorado Experiments," *Journal of Parapsychology,* Vol. 4, December, 1940, pp. 159–248.
3. Munroe, R. L.: "The Inspection Technique: a Method of Rapid Evaluation of the Rorschach Protocol," *Rorschach Research Exchange,* Vol. VIII, 1944, pp. 46–70.
4. ———: "Prediction of the Adjustment and Academic Performance of College Students by a Modification of the Rorschach Method," *Applied Psychology Monographs,* No. 7, September, 1945, p. 104.
5. Murphy, G.: "Personality Appraisal and the Paranormal," *Journal A.S.P.R.,* Vol. XLI, January, 1947, pp. 3–11.

6. Riess, B. F.: "Further Data from a Case of High Scores in Card Guessing," *Journal of Parapsychology,* Vol. 3, June, 1939, pp. 79–84.
7. Pratt, J. G., Rhine, J. B., Smith, B. M., Stuart, C. E., with Greenwood, J. A., *Extrasensory Perception after Sixty Years,* Henry Holt, New York, 1940.
8. Schmeidler, G. R.: "Predicting Good and Bad Scores in a Clairvoyance Experiment: A Preliminary Report," *Journal A.S.P.R.,* Vol. XXXVII, July, 1943, pp. 103–110.
9. ———: "Predicting Good and Bad Scores in a Clairvoyance Experiment: A Final Report," *Journal A.S.P.R.,* Vol. XXXVII, October, 1943, pp. 210–221.
10. ———: "Separating the Sheep from the Goats," *Journal A.S.P.R.,* Vol. XXXIX, January, 1945, pp. 47–49.
11. ———: "Progress Report on Further Sheep-Goat Series," *Journal A.S.P.R.,* Vol. XL, January, 1946, pp. 34–35.
12. Soal, S. G. and Goldney, K. M., "Experiments in Precognitive Telepathy," *Proc. A.S.P.R.,* Vol. XLVII (1943), pp. 21–150.

MENTAL HYGIENE

Hospitalization and the Mental Patient[*]

BY *Henrietta B. DeWitt, D.S.Sc.*

One of the greatest obstacles to the acceptance of hospitalization that the mentally sick person has to face is the present-day attitude of society toward mental illness. While psychiatry as a scientific branch of medicine has received limited recognition, it is dissociated from the general cultural attitude, which still looks upon mental illness with ignorance, superstition, and prejudice. As a member of society, the patient shares the attitude of the group, and it operates to intensify his feelings of difference as a mentally ill person. He sees in the tragedy that has befallen him a threat not only to the self, but to his status as a member of the group, and the terrible totality of the separation is almost more than he can bear.

Society tolerates the mentally ill person only as long as his sickness is his private affair. He can be as queer

[*] From *Mental Hygiene*, Vol. XXXI, April 1947, No. 2. Reprinted by courtesy of the author and publishers, The National Committee For Mental Hygiene, Inc., New York.

as he likes as long as he can maintain his place in the community. He may have his private analyst or attend a psychiatric clinic or even have a "nervous breakdown" in a private institution without losing caste, but as soon as commitment to a state mental hospital becomes imminent, a different set of values begins to operate. He becomes an outcast. A stigma is placed upon him and his family, and he is set apart as different. Even though he recovers sufficiently to return to the community, the disgrace of his unfortunate lot follows him. He is looked upon with suspicion. The hardships he must undergo in order to regain a social status acceptable to him are sometimes insurmountable.

Society looks upon hospitalization as a finality and not as a therapeutic process. It harbors fear of the insane person and is concerned for its own protection. State mental institutions are designed primarily to imprison their inmates and to provide for their care and welfare. They are poorly supported, understaffed, and overcrowded. Little emphasis is placed upon treatment and recovery.

Another obstacle to the acceptance of hospitalization is the existence of antiquated commitment laws. In his sick and confused state, the mentally ill person often feels that he is being treated like a legal offender. It is hard to believe that in some localities mental patients are still subjected to court hearings prior to commitment, and that the permission of the court is necessary to effect their release. Sojourns in jail while awaiting admission, transportation by police, and overprotective parole regulations are also examples of the implied punitive attitude of society.

To the average citizen, the mental institution, with its isolated surroundings and jail-like appearance, is wrapped in mystery. He hears weird stories of harsh treatment and of sane people unlawfully held. He believes that most of the inmates are "wild maniacs," and he would be afraid to walk through the grounds alone. The patients whom he sees strolling about seem as different from him as people from Mars. He does not see them as sick people who may recover and return to the community.

The family physician, as well as the layman, has little understanding of mental illness and the therapeutic aspects of hospital care. He is poorly prepared to help the patient and his family when this catastrophe strikes. If the patient sees himself as sick or "nervous," his physician is apt to treat his physical symptoms with no understanding of the psychological implications. He recommends hospitalization only when all else has failed. He seldom takes the patient into his confidence or has the courage to try to help him face the reality of his necessity, but connives with his relatives to trick him into hospitalization. After commitment he feels relieved of all responsibility.

This to me presents a vital problem because it is the family physician more than anyone else who is called upon to interpret mental illness in critical situations. His insecurity and attitude of hopelessness are conveyed to the patient and his family, who are often misled by the confidence they have in him.

To-day committment to a state mental hospital is usually a traumatic experience both for the patient and for his relatives—sometimes it is even more difficult for the relatives than for the patient, although there are relatives who, consciously or unconsciously, look upon it as an escape from a painful responsibility. In any event, the surrendering of personal liberty on the part of the patient and the relatives' feeling of "putting him away" are hard to face. Regardless of the need or the circumstances that have brought it about, commitment is a measure of desperation—a dead end. It is true, however, that the same intensity of emotion is not associated with all admissions.

Many patients are committed because of a failure in the social structure which supported them rather than as a result of any progressive pathological change in them. These consist of the people with primary or residual defects and some seniles who find their way to state hospitals because something happens to the near relative whose care made it possible for them to live in the community.

The use of the state mental hospital as a refuge for this group has long been questioned, since they present problems that community agencies could solve through recognition of the need for foster-home placement for these adults. They clutter up the family-care programs, or, even worse, occupy beds in the hospital often to the exclusion of the acutely mentally ill. This group also contributes to the lack of initiative and the discouragement with regard to therapy and movement that are sometimes felt by chronic-service physicians. It is hard for the patients, too, especially for the old people who could live in a protected situation in the community instead of having to end their days in a mental hospital.

Then there are patients who, in spite of the fearful implications of commitment, welcome hospitalization. In it they hope to find a haven from a hostile world and an opportunity to regain sufficient security to go on living. Also, there are patients who feel the need of the protection of hospitalization, yet who have not the courage to admit it even to themselves. They haunt dispensaries or court arrest, unconsciously hoping that their difference will be noticed and that someone will act for them. They come into the hospital protesting, but go willingly enough to the ward.

The group for whom hospitalization is least difficult are the completely disoriented individuals who are seemingly unaware of what is happening to them.

The largest number of patients committed, however, are those who have only partial insight or none at all. Too often they are trapped into coming to the hospital or are brought in by the police. It is these patients to whom commitment seems such a tragic experience. Even if they can admit illness, they do not believe that they belong in a state hospital. They project their feelings upon distressed relatives who identify with the patients' fear and resistance and are overwhelmed with conflicts and feelings of guilt. The relatives have little more conviction than the patients regarding the validity of this step. They find themselves in the admission office, precipitated there by the emergency of their problem. Beset with doubt and bewilderment, all their past concepts of such places converge upon them with the shock of the present reality.

There are few situations in which there is greater need of understanding and reassurance than in the admission office of a state mental hospital. Here is where treatment begins, and the manner in which this service is conducted may determine the success or failure of the patient's entire course in the hospital. Because of the pressure under which state hospitals operate, the importance of the admission service is usually underestimated. Too often cold, impersonal physical surroundings confirm the worst fears of patients and relatives, while indifferent and unskilled handling at the time of admission lends justification to their feelings of hostility and rejection. Here the need is to focus not on the patient's illness alone, but on the problems of the patient as an individual and of the relatives, in relation to admission. Here it is important that they face together as far as possible the real issues involved and are helped to accept responsibility for their respective rôles in the admission process. To be effective, this service requires the skill of a trained psychiatric social worker as well as that of the psychiatrist.

At Springfield, a social worker receives the patients and their relatives in a warm, attractive admission office. After making an effort to put them at ease, she checks the commitment certificates, and addressing her questions as far as possible directly to the patient, she fills out with his help the statistical sheet. When this form has been completed, the worker talks informally with the patient and his relatives about the rest of the admission procedure, the hospital rules, and the hospital routine.

This interview varies in nature, of course, depending upon the condition of the patient and the problems that the particular situation presents. For instance, if the relative has failed to tell the patient that he is to be admitted to the hospital as a patient, the worker explains the situation, and uses her skill in trying to help the patient and his relatives accept it as a reality.

The physician is then called, and after he has interviewed the patient, he summons a nurse, who appears in a few minutes to take the patient to the ward. Goodbyes are said, and when patient, nurse, and physician have left, the worker proceeds to obtain the history from the relatives. The admission process is completed the following day, when the social worker visits the

patient on the ward to answer his questions and to break
down his feeling of incarceration.

The following case illustrates the rôle of the worker
in helping the patient and his relatives to a more realistic acceptance of hospitalization.

Mrs. Otto, her husband, and her mother-in-law
came into the office together. Mrs. Otto was a young,
rather shabbily dressed woman, who sat quietly
twisting her hands together in her lap. The social
worker from St. Andrews Hospital had driven the
family to the hospital, as Mrs. Otto was a transfer
from there. The social worker handed the papers to
me with a hushed air, saying that she would be glad
to wait for the family, but that she had only driven
them here and had had nothing to do with this.

When I started talking with the patient, her face
was wreathed in smiles and the whole family seemed
to be unusually cheerful, with a contented air about
them. I began by asking the patient if she knew
where she was. She shook her head, saying that it
certainly did look like a hospital. I explained to her
that this was Springfield State Hospital. The husband
sat slouched in his chair, apparently not knowing
quite what to do.

I asked the patient whether she had known that
she was to come here. The mother-in-law explained
that they had fooled the patient. The husband nodded
and said violently that he had not wanted to do this—
that the doctor had felt it wise not to tell her. I said
that I wondered if they could tell us just how this
had happened. Mr. Otto said hesitantly that the doctor
had said this would be a good place to help his wife's
nerves.

When Mrs. Otto heard this, she suddenly remarked
that this must then be a "crazy house." I explained
to her that it was a hospital, a place for people who

were nervously and mentally ill. She started crying silently, saying over and over again that she did not feel she belonged in a place like this. The other two were silent.

I explained that she had come here to-day because two doctors felt that she needed to come. Our doctor would be coming to talk to her, too, so she would have a chance to tell him how she felt.

Her husband then said quietly that he felt very badly about his wife's coming here; they had not told him what sort of hospital this was. Then, turning to his wife, he said that if the doctors felt she needed to come here, maybe a short rest would help her.

She stopped crying and asked me how long would she need to stay. I told her that this would depend on how she got along here. I also asked her if she had other questions about the hospital, now that she had come. I gave the visiting rules to the other members of the family, saying that I would answer their questions later.

She hesitated and asked if she could have visitors. I told her the visiting rules and when she heard that she would not be able to see her husband for a month, she broke down again. I was silent a few minutes. Then I suggested that she might like to help us with the face-sheet information. She stopped crying and eagerly answered questions about her name, marital status, and so on.

I asked her if she had any children. She said she had four. She went on to say that she wondered how they would be taken care of if she had to be at this hospital for some time. I asked her husband what his plans were, and he quietly explained to his wife that he hoped his mother could help until something else could be worked out. I told her, too, that she could feel free to write to her husband and that he could write to her.

Then suddenly she added that she had not brought any clothes with her to-day, and what would she do about this? I explained that her husband could mail things to her and that meanwhile we could supply some. She seemed to have more questions. I told her that I would come to see her the following day and at that time we could talk about these matters more in detail. She nodded and completed filling out the blank. She then asked me if she would have a chance to say good-bye to her husband. I assured her that she would. With a resigned air, she left the room with her husband close by her.

After she had talked to the doctor, she went quietly to the ward and I talked with her husband. He came into the office saying that he felt they had done a terrible thing. I asked him what he meant, and he explained that he felt he should have told his wife she was coming to the hospital. He really had known only that this was a hospital for nervous people, not a "crazy house."

I told him again that this was a hospital for those who were ill, mentally ill. I did know that his wife had been sent to one of the quieter wards and that probably by the time he came to visit her, the doctor could talk with him about how she was. He listened eagerly, and when we made a history appointment, agreed to come in at that time.

As he was leaving, he asked about what financial arrangements would be necessary for his wife's care. He explained that after the war, he had been out of work for some time and was afraid that he could not pay for his wife's hospitalization. I suggested that he could work this out with the department of public welfare. He said that he knew his wife would worry about that, too. He thanked me as he left, saying that he felt much better now about leaving her here.

The following day, when I went to see Mrs. Otto,

she greeted me warmly. She said that she wanted to talk to me about some of the things that had happened to her. She was neatly dressed in one of the state dresses and had no make-up on. I asked her how she felt about being here in the hospital. She said that she did not feel that she belonged here. The people here all seemed so very peculiar. I agreed with her that it was very difficult to get used to.

I asked her if she would like to tell me how she happened to come here—just what did happen. She explained that she had gone to St. Andrews Hospital for a rest and that she had known nothing about coming here. I asked her if she could tell me exactly what had happened. She explained that the social worker had come and told her to get dressed—that they were taking a ride, and that it would help her.

I nodded and said that the worker had told me that she had not told Mrs. Otto she was coming to the hospital on the doctor's advice. She shook her head. I asked her how she would have felt if she had known. She said indignantly that of course she would not have liked it, but she would at least have known what was going to happen to her. It would not have been such a shock. I told her that it certainly must feel as if a terrible thing had happened to her. I wondered what she was going to do now while she was at the hospital.

She listened quietly and said that after all she did not need another physical examination because she had already had one at St. Andrews. I asked her if she felt we could help her at all. She said frankly that she did not see anything here that could help her, but she was going to do her best to get along. I appreciated how she must feel about it and added that she could do pretty much as she wanted here, and that we were here to try to help her get out of the hospital and return to her family. She nodded and said that she was worrying about her children. She had written her husband the previous evening to see what arrangements he was making for their care. I asked her if there was anyone who could be counted on to help. She said that her mother-in-law would help, for a while anyway, but that she was not well either.

I also explained that I might be seeing her husband before visiting day and would talk with her about that later. She said that she would like to know about the clothes she had left at the other hospital. She would like to wear her own things and asked if I would tell her husband to send her clothes to her. I said I would, but also suggested that she write to ask him for just exactly what she wanted.

She went on then to ask how the expense of her care would be met. I explained to her just what could be arranged and she said that she knew her husband could not pay for it. At this point I asked her if she had talked over most of the things that worried her and she nodded, thanking me warmly and adding that she felt much better, having talked to me.

The help that this woman and her husband received during the admission process not only helped them clarify their relationship to each other, but formed a sound basis for their relationship to the hospital. Imagine this patient's anxiety if she had found herself locked in the ward with the added anonymity of state clothing and so many vital questions unanswered. Many of her doubts regarding hospitalization, the care of her children, her clothing, and her financial responsibility could not have been answered satisfactorily by the nurses or the ward physician. It is likely that her husband, for fear of upsetting her, would have answered her letters with meaningless reassurances.

Having started on a sound and frank basis, the patient and relative are helped to move step by step toward an acceptance of the reality of their situation. The support that the patient finds in the protection of the hospital environment replaces rejecting community attitudes, and gradually, with the aid of what therapy is available, he begins to regain security. He may never recover sufficiently to leave the hospital or he may. Considering the limitations under which state hospitals are forced to operate, a surprising number of patients do recover and leave.

Until the discovery of the various shock therapies, recovery from mental illness was appreciably slower and it was necessary for patients to remain in the hospital for longer periods of time. Now physicians and relatives alike are stimulated by the remarkably rapid change they observe in many patients and can see leaving as a reality. Furthermore, many patients are now ready to leave before they have had an opportunity to take root in the hospital. In many state hospitals, however, especially on the chronic services, the old situation still exists. Change in patients is slow, and in the meantime they become useful and are given little help toward leaving.

While the patient's usefulness often operates to keep him in the institution, yet the very fact of his feeling needed is probably the greatest dynamic to recovery that the state hospital has to offer. Many physicians, probably somewhat motivated by the security that they personally find in the institutional setting, are inclined to hold on to patients too long. Complexities of community living loom large, and they are loath to see patients who are well adjusted in the hospital leave and experience possible failure. Therefore, when there are no interested relatives or adequate social-service departments, patients tend to remain overlong in the hospital.

Return to the community is indeed a threatening experience for the recovering mental patient. He may approach it with all the insecurity of a person recovering from an illness, or he may prefer to regard himself as never having been sick, but in either event he is fearful of the rejecting attitudes of society and the overprotection that the hospital seems to exercise over him. He dislikes the fact that physicians are inclined to plan for him instead of with him, and resents the apparent lack of confidence of the hospital in his ability to act as a responsible individual.

An adequate social-service department, in its understanding both of hospital and of community facilities, can do much to break down the separation that exists between them and to combat alike hospital overprotection and community rejection. The social worker is related to the individual patient as he is able to function in a practical situation, and with her knowledge of the community and its resources, can often help him realistically to take the first steps into the community. It is unfortunate for state-hospital patients that the recognition of the need for psychiatric social work in these institutions is not greater.

The community is skeptical of the returning patient's ability to get along. It sees only his difference and is unwilling to accept him as responsible within his apparent limitations. Family physicians and social workers rarely see the recovering individual in relation to his particular family, but only the problem he presented prior to hospitalization, and regularly express their fears of his influence on family members. Although prior to his illness his difference went unnoticed, they are unwilling to accept it, once it has been labelled insanity. Unidentified, he may be able to find a room or a job, but if he frankly admits that he is on parole from a mental hospital, he has a difficult time.

Parole is regarded by the hospital as a convalescent period during which the patient's condition is evaluated by the way in which he is able to adjust in the community and handle his problems in personal relationships. To the community, parole from a state mental hospital is not very different from parole from prison. Its authority is looked upon as a means of controlling the patient's behavior. When he gets into trouble, instead of allowing him to accept responsibility for his behavior and experience its consequences, the first reaction is to try to return him to the hospital. Just the fact of his being on parole is sufficient to create prejudice against him when problems arise.

The punitive connotation that the term, "parole," carries no doubt accounts to some extent for the general misinterpretation of its function. For this reason some states have substituted such terms as "on furlough," "on visit," or "on leave."

The rôle of the relatives frequently proves a vital factor in the patient's adjustment on parole. This is particularly true in situations in which the patient feels needed and has a real place in the home. There are many instances in which the relatives are no longer interested in the patient, or in which the patient has been hospitalized for so many years that they of necessity have had to plan their lives without him. In good faith they have kept unpleasant facts from him and as a consequence their relationship has grown progressively unreal.

If relatives can learn to deal with the patient frankly and respect his integrity as an individual, he will then have a basis of security in reality on which he can build. Therefore, when he becomes ready for parole, painful situations, such as the one I am about to describe, could never arise.

Mrs. Sponsor was admitted to Springfield in May, 1925, with a diagnosis of schizophrenia, paranoid type. She was then thirty-four years old, married, and had two girls, aged six and eight. She had been a responsible wife and mother until several months prior to hospitalization. One year after her admission her husband took her home against medical advice, but had to return her to the hospital. For years she remained hallucinated, but was an efficient worker in the hospital's sewing room. Her daughters remained interested in her and continued to visit.

Gradually her mental symptoms disappeared and she talked of going to live with one of her daughters, both of whom were now married and had children. They, however, kept postponing the time when they would be able to take her.

On October 5, 1944, at the age of fifty-four, she was presented to our social planning staff with the request that the social-service department get into contact with the daughters to see if they could take their mother, since she was now able to leave the hospital and wanted to live with one of them. The case was assigned to a worker who, after seeing the patient, visited one of the daughters. The following is an excerpt from the first interview with the daughter:

"Mrs. Brown said that she was glad that I had come because ever since receiving the letter from the hospital saying that her mother could be released, she had been so disturbed over the situation that her stomach had become upset. She and her sister did not know what would be best to do. They had thought of their mother as always remaining in the hospital and had not told any of their friends about her illness or even that she was living. Mrs. Brown would not object to having her mother in the home, but her husband would, thinking that her influence upon the children would not be good. He had never met Mrs. Sponsor, and Mrs. Brown could easily see how he would feel that way.

"Mrs. Brown was torn between her responsibility to her mother and to her own family. She lives in a small four-room apartment. She has two small daughters and much of her time is taken up with them. I could see that with her housework and the two children, she did have a great deal to do. Mrs. Brown's sister, Mrs. Kramer, was situated equally as badly as far as taking her mother was concerned. Mrs. Kramer's husband has just been sent overseas and it is necessary for her to work to be able to meet her expenses. She has a small three-room apartment and puts her little daughter in nursery school.

"Another thing that would complicate matters would be her father. It was his understanding years ago that Mrs. Sponsor's illness would be permanent and the chances were she would never leave the hospital. He had obtained a divorce, had remarried, and the stepmother was very close to Mrs. Kramer and Mrs. Brown. If Mrs. Sponsor lives in the home of either daughter, it will necessarily interfere with the relationship between them and their father and stepmother.

"I told Mrs. Brown that I did not think their mother realized that her daughters were seeing very much of their father. Mrs. Brown was sure that her mother did not realize it because they did not speak of their father to her. When they came to see her, they tried to talk of pleasant things, wanting to make her as happy as possible.

"I said that Mrs. Sponsor seemed very sure that her daughters could arrange to take her and had told me that they had invited her to come. I asked Mrs. Brown if they had made her feel that she could come home whenever she was well. Mrs. Brown replied that she had told her mother that she could come home whenever she was able. They had said this, trying to make her feel better, thinking all along that she would never be able to leave the hospital. That was one thing that made it so difficult for them.

"At this point Mrs. Brown began to cry. I told her that I understood how she felt that her first responsibility was to her children and her husband, and that she need not have guilt feelings about that. Mrs. Brown seemed to feel better. I pointed out how much better her mother was and what good work she had done in the sewing room, but that after being in the hospital so many years, it would be quite a change to come into a home and to live in an urban community.

"Mrs. Brown realized all this and said that she wanted to assume responsibility for her mother, but she did not see how she could face some of the problems that had to be faced. I asked her if she and her sister had any other suggestions to make.

"Mrs. Brown wondered about the possibilities of putting her mother in a convalescent home and perhaps trying to get help from some Jewish society. I said that might be one solution and also suggested finding her a place in a private home where she would help a little with the sewing or perhaps just pay board. I asked Mrs. Brown how she felt about such a plan, pointing out that after her mother had been out of the hospital for a while, she and her sister could see what kind of adjustment their mother made and whether they felt that they could take her into their homes.

"Mrs. Brown said that she thought that would be a wonderful plan—that if her mother could get used to staying out of the hospital, she could visit them occasionally and their friends could get accustomed to knowing that they had a mother. After further discussion, she agreed that she and her sister should be the ones to explain the true situation to their mother. They planned to visit her the following week."

By recognizing with the patient's daughter the real problem this situation presented, the social worker was able to help her release her guilt feelings and look at the problem objectively. The daughter was then free to bring out her real desire to help her mother in the way that was possible for her. However, much of the pain and anxiety could have been avoided had the daughters followed a more realistic course from the beginning.

In this paper I have presented what seem to me to be the basic problems that confront the mentally ill person in relation to his commitment to a state mental hospital—namely, the attitude of our culture toward mental illness, and the lack of wholehearted recognition accorded psychiatry by the medical profession. Cultural attitudes, I believe, will change as medicine leads the way.

New terms have been invented to describe new concepts and much time and effort is being spent on disseminating mental-hygiene information, but not until the medical profession places the same emphasis on sound psychiatric training as it does on other branches of medicine will state mental hospitals become institutions of treatment and research. Many of their fearful aspects for patient, relative, and physician will then disappear. This has been proved by the greater ease with which the mentally ill person is now able to accept care in a private mental hospital, in which the emphasis is placed on therapy and commitment is more often on a voluntary basis.

The pathway to this goal lies, as I see it, along the lines now represented by what we call psychosomatic medicine. As this approach becomes generally accepted, the status of psychiatry will be recognized as an integral specialty of medicine itself.

The Individual and Society[*]

BY *Thomas A. C. Rennie, M.D.*
AND *Luther E. Woodward, Ph.D.*

An individual's mental and emotional ill health is a reaction of his personality to the multiple stresses of the
total environment, whether the stresses be in the external
environment or in his own complicated emotional imbal-
ances. The point at which any individual becomes sick
depends upon his constitutional stability and toughness
to withstand stress, upon the severity of the stresses in
his external environment, upon the severity of his internal conflict, or upon a combination of these factors.
Our knowledge of how these forces interact in any given
patient is considerable. If prevention of mental ill
health is to become a reality for the millions, we must
learn how to remove stresses in the environment as
well as to strengthen the inner resources of individuals,

[*] Reprinted by permission of the authors and publishers and the
Commonwealth Fund from T. A. C. Rennie and L. E. Woodward's *Mental Health in Modern Society*, Cambridge, Mass.:
Harvard University Press. Copyright, 1948, by The Commonwealth Fund.

and to apply corrective principles there as we now apply them in the treatment of the individual patient.

Mental health cannot be developed in a social vacuum. Powerful factors operate against it as our present society is constituted. To promote positive mental health will therefore require the coöperation and help of many individuals and groups. Medical and social scientists need to look squarely at these factors and, abandoning professional isolationism, coöperate in an effort to counteract them. Mental health can only be achieved in an environment which provides opportunities for self-expression, social usefulness, and the attainment of human satisfactions. Preventive psychiatry is only beginning, and its only sure tool at present lies in educating the public in the meaning and causes of mental disorders and the ways of developing positive mental health.

We have had two world wars in twenty-five years. Obviously our approach to war prevention and peace building has been ineffective. Hitherto we have relied on moral principles and political procedures. Appeals to morality have had little effect on international policy because nations, unlike individual human beings, are motivated by considerations of their sovereignty rather than by principles of right and wrong, and have no sense of responsibility toward other nations comparable to the average citizen's sense of responsibility toward the people of his community. The political procedure which would establish international machinery for settling disputes and maintaining security has not yet succeeded because nations have not been willing to delegate to an international federation the necessary power and—what is still more important—have failed to win for this organization the loyalty, confidence, and good will which citizens feel toward the nation-state. (1)

Lacking loyalty the international organization cannot secure voluntary compliance, and lacking force it cannot compel it. Now that the atomic bomb hourly threatens the actual destruction of civilization, there can be no peace of mind. Blind terror compels us to seek for new solutions.

A warring society is a sick society. As Chisholm has noted:

> The necessity to fight wars whether as aggressor or as a defender who could have, but has not, taken steps to prevent war occurring is as much a pathological psychiatric symptom as is a phobia or the antisocial behavior of the criminal who has been dominated by a stern and unreasonable father. They are alike irrational behavior patterns resulting from unsuccessful development and failure to reach emotional maturity. (2)

For the recovery and the acquisition of health, a sick society, like a sick person, needs therapy and the continuing application of hygienic principles. Thus we must seek to develop those healthy behavior patterns, attitudes, and feelings that are the best insurance against war and at the same time fashion the ideational framework and organizational structure for a peaceful world that will enlist the interest and active support of all the citizens. As stated in the preamble to the Constitution of the United Nations Educational, Scientific, and Cultural Organization: "Since wars begin in the minds of men, it is in the minds of men that the defenses of peace must be constructed." (3)

Developing Emotional Maturity and Leadership

Underlying the collective insecurity that precipitates war is the individual insecurity that comes from emotional immaturity. It is in the home, in the interrelations of parents and children, of brothers and sisters, that healthy personalities and constructive social attitudes, are developed, and it is there that insecurity, dependence, emotional instability, and faulty habits of thinking most often emerge. Therefore, it is in the home that the training for emotional maturity must begin.

The authors believe that [understanding] home training and guidance and the emphasis on human relations in education will go far toward giving the oncoming generation such a satisfying experience in their relations to other people that they can without too much difficulty evolve a workable philosophy or system of beliefs which will serve them as a basis for healthy and coöperative relationships throughout their lives. We express that conviction because the sort of home guidance and school experience we have described not only implants basically sound ideas about human relationships, but develops the even more important patterns of feeling which make a constructive social philosophy possible. Certainly no philosophy will be adequate for the years ahead which fails to draw upon and use the greater depths of human emotion. As Leighton has stated:

Most people use their intelligence to attain ends dictated by their feelings and convictions and not as a matter of their basic motivations. With ourselves, no less than with a foreign or "primitive" people, the choice of a career, of a marital partner, of religion, of friends, of political candidates, of a place to reside, of food, of a doctor, of a lawyer, and many other crucial steps in life are carried out far more on the basis of feeling than on the basis of reasoning—and feeling means systems of belief and related patterns of sentiment in varying combinations, powered by needs, drives, aspirations and insecurities.

Societies move on the feelings of the individuals who compose them and so do countries and nations. Very few internal policies and almost no international policies are predominantly the product of reason. To be sure, reason and thought are components, but they take the form either of rationalization to justify or of scheming to attain ends already decided upon at the dictates of feeling. (4)

A generation of children who have been well loved, who are wholesomely self-confident, who have disciplined their instinctive drives and harmonized self-interest with enjoyable give-and-take with others, who can think critically and objectively, who have become accustomed to making decisions while adapting to change, and whose personalities are well integrated and mature, are the best guarantee that problems of human relationship can and will be worked out. When the dynamic processes of growing up are made to serve positive and constructive ends, conflict, fear, and hostility can be kept within bounds and the danger of disabling psychoneuroses diminished.

The basic training and education provided by families and schools go far to promote the mental health and stability of children. But the efforts of understanding parents and teachers are likely to be partially defeated unless neighbors and friends appreciate children's psychological needs and encourage the educational processes by which sound personality growth can be fostered. Studies of children have shown that variations in personality structure are largely dependent on the familial and other cultural patterns to which the children are exposed. (5)

During the war, the key to morale in our fighting forces was leadership. In building and maintaining a peaceful society, leadership is equally important. The number of people capable of true leadership in our complex world is of course limited, although much less limited than the self-appointed leaders in fascist governments would have us believe. One of the secrets of a healthy society, nationally and internationally, is the selection and training of potential leaders in all professions and major fields of activity. Such leaders must have an understanding of individuals and groups and of the history and heritage of different nations. They must have a mature personality, enough dissatisfaction with the status quo to call forth aggressive, constructive effort, and enough social concern and devotion to hold them to their course while a healthier society is slowly but surely constructed. They need thorough grounding in the knowledge of human motivation, and their training must include understanding of the findings of psychiatry and the other social sciences.

Strengthening Economic Security

One of the most effective means of building morale and preventing psychiatric disorders in the armed forces was the prompt discovery and alleviation of such environmental stresses as discomfort, inconvenience, wasted effort or unfairness, and defective or untrustworthy leadership. The experience of psychiatrists, social workers, and plant managers shows that in a peacetime society the same relationship between mental health and environmental stresses holds. As stresses are multiplied in number and increased in intensity, there is a corresponding increase in the number of people who can no longer function effectively, and, conversely, as stresses are removed or alleviated, the number of people who are mentally healthy is proportionately increased. One of the most powerful environmental stresses, and one to which millions of people are exposed, is economic insecurity.

The extent to which economic insecurity contributes to psychoses, psychoneuroses, delinquency, crime, and other social problems is not yet clear. There was no appreciable increase in admissions to hospitals for the mentally ill during the economic depression of the nineteen-thirties, but there was a marked increase in the number of psychoneurotic persons whose illness became so serious that they had to be hospitalized. This suggests that "economic factors, whether primary or not, do act as inciting and precipitating influences in functional and mental disorders." (6) The total psychological effects of economic insecurity cannot, of course, be measured in terms of gross pathology alone. The anxieties created by unemployment and loss of income have been experienced by so many millions of people, and their expression—in irritability toward members of the family, heightened group conflicts, loss of self-respect and the esteem of the community, and many other ways —has been so commonly observed that statistical proof of such ill-effects is not needed.

Through social insurance in the form of unemployment compensation and old age security and through public assistance, the federal and the state governments have attempted to prevent the worst effects of economic insecurity. As Falk and Hirsch have stated, "To the extent that such measures do provide assurance of income they serve as preventive measures by securing society to some degree against the development of mental deviation arising out of economic fears and worries." (7) There is clearly need to extend social insurance to the many groups of employees not now covered by the provisions of the law and to extend security against accident and health hazards to those who become disabled and are left without earning capacity by reason of nonindustrial disablements.

If our free enterprise system is to function adequately, private business and industry must do much more to stabilize employment and guarantee economic security, and labor groups must develop real leadership and take steps to assure full productivity. Both management and labor have great power, but each group is dependent on the other and each lacks an adequate measure of freedom, enterprise, and security. In the opinion of the authors, this situation will continue until the two groups find a positive common goal, in the pursuit of which a more meaningful way of life can develop. During the war period full production for the sake of the Allied cause was such a positive common goal, with the result that there was not only less distrust and less friction between management and labor than there had been for many years, but—what is just as important—much greater satisfaction in their work on the part of both groups. During the war, to some degree at least, the fiction of economic man motivated only by the lure of financial reward was supplanted by the reality of the individual human being at work on a special task. There was a new realization that managers and workers are creatures of multiple desires, feelings, social needs, and purposes, to whom work is satisfying only when it gives them a sense of comradeship in a shared and truly worthwhile enterprise. To retain this gain it is necessary for both groups, perhaps with the financial aid of the federal government, to take aggressive steps to achieve and maintain full employment, that is, to give everyone the opportunity for steady, gainful, satisfying employment on a year-round basis.

Many economists agree that this is both possible and practical. The American Management Association in a recent study of two decades of experience with guaranteed wages concludes that stabilized employment is an obtainable goal. It points out:

> Most companies could make at least a beginning toward the objective of guaranteed employment. Experience has shown that the big stumbling block of seasonal fluctuation can be systematically reduced or even eliminated by many companies. The annual wage can improve morale, increase output by lowering production and labor costs per unit, afford greater utilization of plant and equipment, reduce labor turnover costs, increase versatility and flexibility of employees and provide eligibility for special government benefits which reduce costs. Moreover widespread guaranteed annual wage could reduce savings accumulated in fear of unemployment and thereby stabilize consumption much more to help eliminate seasonal fluctuations. (8)

It has become clear that economic insecurity is one of the causes of war. While ideological differences were the immediate cause of World War II, behind these ideologies and giving them real power were the hard facts of economic need. Leaders in the aggressor nations sold their ideology to the people by promising to remove the causes of their anxiety and to satisfy their economic and social wants.

It appears to the authors that the psychological aspect of economic need has been too much ignored by those who are seeking to prevent war. The affluence of small minorities within the group of nations can be viewed with some equanimity by those who are fairly comfortable, but among the impoverished, the unemployed, the hungry, and those who are poorly clad and housed, such inequality breeds hostility as inevitably as night follows day. Faced with sharp differences in standards of living, the underprivileged cannot avoid the conclusion that there should be a larger measure of economic justice and of social equality. The human submissiveness characteristic of periods of slavery and serfdom has passed in Western civilization, and is slowly disappearing in the East. The common man will not accept hardship and poverty when plenty and comfort abound. Fighting comes easy to those who by fighting hope to gain needed comforts, possessions, and opportunities, and easier still to those whose resources have been exploited by powerful interests in other lands. As many thoughtful people see it, the greatest hope for peace lies in the Social and Economic Council of the United Nations, which among other things proposes to study the economic needs and to develop the economy of the various nations in the interest of fuller opportunity and a higher standard of living for the people of these nations. The greatest danger to peace is that the efforts of the Council will be blocked by powerful groups of self-seeking individuals in all nations.

Building Interracial and International Understanding

Schreiber in a well-documented article (9) has described realistically the interdependence of democracy and mental health and has pointed out that whatever fosters and promotes democracy also guards and advances mental health. Conversely, whatever breeds racial, religious, or other group prejudices and intolerance accentuates the tensions of all the members of the outgroups and gives them handicaps which largely negate the values of democracy.

Prejudicial attitudes are acquired largely from parents, relatives, and neighbors during early childhood, and are confirmed by habitual emotional reactions that are so strong and so deeply imbedded in the personality structure that they yield only to prolonged critical examination in a social situation that puts a premium on their opposite. In the case of many individuals release from prejudice can be affected only by psychological or psychiatric treatment which allows the unconscious hostility to express itself. As Levy has pointed out:

> Intolerant people are people who hate. Their degree of intolerance is a measure of their hate. When a person is characteristically intolerant, he belongs to the group of the psychologically hostile, whose features I shall attempt to describe. The most distinctive finding among the psychologically hostile is a stultification of the personality. In a well-known personality test such individuals, for whom hatred is so vital a function, are found to be characterized by a marked narrowing of the thought, feelings and imagination. The generalization applies equally well to the haters who have repressed their hate and to

those who express it directly, in words or action . . .

The disseminator of intolerance, operating on the fertile soil of the psychologically hostile, may initiate an epidemic of hate, as readily comprehensible as an epidemic of typhoid fever. The source of either epidemic, whether of typhoid or hate, would be considered equally dangerous and criminal, if public understanding of mental health were at all effective. (10)

The current interest in intercultural education in primary and secondary schools and in adult education circles is a great gain. In communities where the schools strive to bring about better relations between majority and minority groups in the school world and in the community, much is being accomplished. An outstanding example of this is the work done in Springfield, Massachusetts.(11)

In the last five or six years a wealth of material has been published (12) which suggests constructive ways of dealing with the problems of minority groups who are not fully accepted or who are actively rejected. An interesting series of pamphlets has been recently published by the National Institute of Social Relations under the title *Talk It Over.*(13) A concerted program of education and social action directed to individuals of all ages, utilizing various methods and in all community groups, is required to reduce the tensions to which outgroups are now exposed, be they Negro, Jew, Catholic, Protestant, or immigrant. (14) In at least a few communities, group prejudice is becoming unpopular, and although the federal government has not passed any permanent Fair Employment Practices Act, at least a few states have done so. Even in states having no such law some business firms observe fair practices.(15)

An understanding of the cultural background of our fellow nations and of our own is no less important for the maintenance of peace. A knowledge of the history, the characteristic viewpoints, and forms of government of other peoples will give us an understanding of what they need to make their lives full and secure.

To accomplish a satisfactory degree of mutual understanding and to make it possible for the people of different nations to identify with one another and accept one another as kinsmen and neighbors, free and extensive interchange of teachers, students, artists, and technicians who can develop natural resources will be required. In this field the United Nations Educational, Scientific, and Cultural Organization, if properly implemented, promises much of constructive value. Its fourteen-point program should go far to consolidate the findings of the social and psychological sciences and through the contributions of science, education, and art to create international understanding and cooperation.

A Working Philosophy and a Philosophy of Work

The discoveries and inventions of the physical sciences have bridged time and space and have made neighbors, however unfriendly, of all the people of the world. They have greatly multiplied the number of ways people have to work together. On the other hand, the social and psychological sciences have not put to similar practical use the knowledge of human beings that they have achieved, and have not shown a corresponding initiative in extending the limits of their knowledge to include further areas of human activity, both social and individual.

While applied science has brought about radical changes in our mode of living, most people are guided by the same standards, goals, and attitudes which made for a good measure of security in an earlier age, but which no longer help to deal with today's increasingly complex problems. For example, many are committed to the political dogma of national sovereignty notwithstanding the fact that world federation is possible only on condition that national sovereignty is partly surrendered. Again, multitudes who profess belief in the particular plan of personal salvation that was a part of their religious heritage find that their religion gives them neither peace of mind nor social effectiveness in dealing with the major issues of the day. The tendency to hold to static sets of value in a world undergoing phenomenal changes presents a major threat to mental health and social stability.

What is needed today is a new philosophy which does justice to our social and emotional needs and which builds a new and more inclusive morality based on these needs. We need a clear understanding of the nature of our world and a conviction regarding man's place in it that is scientifically tenable, socially acceptable, and emotionally satisfying. Such a faith springs from an appreciation of harmonies of sight and sound, evidences of cosmic purpose and a sense of personal integrity—experiences which have been to a great extent the basis of established religion. But it builds also on our scientific knowledge that the natural world is governed by laws which are fully trustworthy and quite as wonderful and awe-inspiring as the mysterious powers of the supernatural to which our forefathers gave allegiance.

A faith adequate for our age must embody a view of man and society which gives purpose and meaning to each man's life, allays men's fears and distrust of one another, and induces and maintains such mutual confidence, coöperation, and support as are needed for living together in families, groups, societies, and nations. To build and implement such a working faith is one of the big psychological tasks of this age, for unless men believe in their own worth and in their ability to manage their lives with self-satisfaction and social acceptance, and unless they have a similar faith in the worth and ability of their fellow citizens and the citizens of other nations, they will continue to be plagued by a sense of futility and by fears of want and of war.

William James(16) suggested many years ago that to maintain peace one must provide moral equivalents for war. That this will not be easy is clear from Flugel's summary of the values that war has for the individual and the nation:

> The problem of providing a substitute for war that shall have something approaching war's peculiar combination of moral and instinctive appeal, is far from easy. In its danger, its hazards, its call for heroism, effort and sacrifice on the part of whole communities, war is without parallel—as also in the sense of social cohesion that it brings and the amount of aggression it permits. (1)

Such a challenge to personal heroism and group morale need not go unanswered in a peacetime world. Proper attention to personal and social values in connection with work would go far to give workers a genuine sense of contributing to a collective effort. Work that is challenging, that gives people a sense of belonging to a worth-while organization, and that helps satisfy the needs of other people supplemented by concerted efforts toward community improvement, yields a quality and a degree of personal satisfaction and a sense of social cohesion which are essential to both peace and progress. Such a moral equivalent to the values of war can be provided if home and school encourage personality development and social relationships, and if business and industry, government, and voluntary community groups provide maximum opportunities for people to work together in a common cause.

The Responsibility of Medical and Social Scientists

The symptoms of our sick society are multiple. In merely cataloguing them, the authors have added nothing new to the diagnosis. The implications of these factors, however, do need reassertion. For unless individuals are taught to realize the significance of these multiple factors for their own emotional health and security as well as for that of the nation, they cannot be expected to join in concerted efforts at correction. One difficulty is to see the problem as a whole and the other is to break it down into encompassable tasks which individuals and groups can undertake and succeed in. Bomber crews, every man of whom was trained to do a specific job, and who counted on each and every member of the crew to do his part, went out on missions with confidence notwithstanding great danger. Their course was clearly charted. Each man was prepared to do his job and all knew the significance which the success of the mission would have in the total task of winning the war. If our peacetime goals can be defined with something of the same precision, and if the individual's part in the total task can be made as clear and as meaningful for the group, we shall have gone a long way toward removing our basic insecurities and achieving individual stability and group morale.

Multiple factors operate to cause wars, and constant efforts must be made to define and to expose them. Some are ideological, some are economic and sociological, and some operate at the level of the personal emotional motivation of mankind. The latter factors have been long neglected. They need the most vigorous study and research, utilizing all the ingenuity and skill that our social sciences can muster.

An effective safeguard against war would be an international research institute devoted to the study of individual and group aggression, hatred, and fear and their etiology in terms of personality development, cultural heritage, and social conditions. Admittedly, social psychiatry, psychology, and anthropology cannot be as exact sciences as physics and chemistry, for the factors are too complex to admit of control for experimental purposes. There is every reason to believe, however, that research into the causes of aggression and fear and into effective methods of control will yield results just as startling as the discoveries and practical applications of physics and chemistry. Now that the world is becoming one society, it is imperative that we should learn how to live together in groups and nations. The social sciences must take up the challenge. Guesses and fumbling and outworn viewpoints and methods result in too many "accidents" in the form of group conflict and international strife.

It is the peculiar obligation of medical and social scientists—psychologists, psychiatrists, anthropologists, sociologists, social workers—whose field of interest is man as an individual human being and man as a member of

human society, to widen their knowledge and to dissem-
inate their findings, thus confirming the experience and
stabilizing the inner faith of the more naïve. The security
so won will minimize the dangers of conflict, individual
and national, will build satisfying human relationships,
and will tend to free and direct the energies of man for
the service of the community. The safeguarding of mental health and the development of satisfactory human
relations are very large tasks, and they must be shared
by parents, teachers, doctors—especially psychiatrists—
social workers, psychologists, clergymen, business, industrial, and labor leaders, and by all others who are in a
position to lead and influence the lives of people.

Public Education in Mental Hygiene

The material of this chapter sums up inevitably to the
need for a vigorous program of public education in the
principles and dynamics of individual and societal emotional health and happiness. This is the only possible
means of implementing the suggested program for
health and security. Public education will take much
time and great energy, but all of us in our particular
specialties have a deep obligation to assume it. And
while no direct approach at the intellectual level can
hope to touch the deep, unconscious, motivational forces
of the human personality, here and there a beginning
may be made in applying the principles and procedures
outlined in this book toward a fuller mental hygiene
program. This is the task for the years ahead.

During the war, it was necessary in the armed forces
not only to provide for the prompt discovery and treatment of men who were showing early signs of mental or

emotional disturbances, but also to give all officers and enlisted men basic mental hygiene orientation. Such educational measures did not prevent men from being afraid under combat conditions, but it did enable them to understand and accept their reactions as natural and normal under the circumstances, and to use their fear in constructive rather than destructive ways, that is, for their own protection and that of their units.

Although the factors that threaten mental health are harder to isolate in peacetime than in war, and although the tensions of normal civilian life are less acute than those to which military personnel are exposed, it is possible to extend to our population as a whole an orientation in mental hygiene similar in some respects to that which was provided for officers and enlisted men. There are, of course, differences. In the Army a man's interest in himself and his immediate unit occupies almost all his time and energies. In civilian life there are many other influences and relationships, involving people's various roles as workers, mates, parents, club members, and citizens. Consequently, the task of educating people in the mental hygiene of everyday living is more complex.

The major objectives are clear. As an aid to the treatment of the ill such education should (1) strive to remove the stigma which still attaches to mental and nervous disorders and to secure their acceptance as valid and treatable illnesses; (2) supply information in regard to existing and desired facilities, kinds of illness and maladjustment that can be treated respectively by private psychiatrists, outpatient psychiatric or mental hygiene clinics, and psychiatric hospitals, and measures to be taken by families in behalf of the seriously ill; (3) create a demand by the people for adequate facilities for the treatment of nervous and mental disorders, including hospitalization and opportunities for consultation and clinical treatment in all communities.

On the constructive and preventive side, mental hygiene education should (1) develop a broad understanding of what constitutes a healthy-mindedness at each stage of development, what the danger signs are, and what people can do to prevent psychological liabilities from becoming serious blocks to health and happiness; (2) develop increased appreciation of the dynamic quality of family living and of the special significance of healthy and happy relations in the childhood years; (3) bring about fuller recognition of the stabilizing influence of satisfying work and economic security and of the threat to mental health which lies in neglecting the personal, human values of a job and their importance to the worker; (4) acquaint the public with the potential contributions to mental hygiene which can be made by the physician, social worker, teacher, and other professional persons; (5) outline the essentials of a healthier society, with emphasis on the most needed changes and on the appropriate next steps to be taken by citizens.

Fortunately, the professional groups having most to offer in mental hygiene education recognize more than ever before the need for interpreting their knowledge to the layman and for enlisting the coöperation of the non-professional public in efforts to improve the mental health and stability of our people. For example, the Group for the Advancement of Psychiatry (recently formed within the American Psychiatric Association) and organizations of social workers and clinical psychologists are eager and ready to share with other groups the insights developed by their professions, so that these may be applied more effectively in family relations, education, medicine, industry, religious organizations, governmental services, and other phases of community life. Their interest is a hopeful sign. But as Ridenour points out:

> The psychiatric professions are as yet fulfilling only a fraction of their potentialities as interpreters of human behavior. Effectiveness in interpretation requires a public health point of view and continuing development of consultative skills and interpretive techniques. These, in turn, require familiarity with the special problems of related teaching and healing professions and with those of the interpretive professions (press, screen, stage, and radio), and an awareness of the mistakes common to those who, though well trained clinically, are relatively untrained in interpretation. (17)

In-service training in mental hygiene and opportunities for consultation with experts in the field are now available to nurses, teachers, pediatricians, and others who have frequent contacts with young children and their parents. It is also necessary to use mass media for acquainting the public with sound principles of mental health. In all programs of mental hygiene education the cultural pattern, system of belief, and special needs of the particular group to whom the information is addressed must be carefully considered.

The National Committee for Mental Hygiene, a voluntary organization dating from 1909, has done much to promote awareness of mental hygiene needs and opportunities through community social and health services, schools, and other local groups, but its staff and its finances are at present too limited to carry on an adequate over-all educational program. It is significant that the amount of money devoted annually to the dissemination of information regarding tuberculosis and poliomyelitis has been from twenty to forty times as much as the amount spent by all national, state, and local agencies, to educate the public regarding mental hygiene needs and opportunities. In per capita terms, $600 has been spent per case of poliomyelitis as against $1.00 per case of mental illness.

Beginners' information, together with some misinformation, has already been given the American public. A really fine job of public education remains to be accomplished. The psychiatric and allied professions are already overburdened, but they have many socially minded members who will rise to the responsibility. Once the need is seen clearly, sound education will go forward, because it must. Professional persons and enlightened laymen can surely justify their existence in the world of today only by working where and how they can to implement the convictions of Professor Henry DeW. Smyth as stated in the War Department's report on the atomic bomb: "If men, working together, can solve the mysteries of the universe, they can also solve the problem of human relations on the planet. Not only in science, but now in all human relations, we must work together with free minds."

References

1. Flugel, J. C.: *Man, Morals, and Society*, chapter XIX. New York, International Universities Press, 1945.
2. Chisholm, G. B.: "The reestablishment of peacetime society." (In The Psychiatry of Enduring Peace and

534 AN OUTLINE OF ABNORMAL PSYCHOLOGY

Social Progress, William Alanson White Memorial Lectures.) *Psychiatry* 9:1–35, February 1946.

3. United States National Commission for UNESCO, Report on the First Meeting, September 1947, p. 1. United States-United Nations Information Series 14, Department of State Publication 2726. Washington, D.C., Superintendent of Documents, U. S. Government Printing Office.

4. Leighton, A. H.: *The Governing of Men,* p. 362. Princeton, N.J., Princeton University Press, 1945.

5. Jenkins, R. L. and L. E. Hewitt: "Fundamental patterns of maladjustment and dynamics of their origin." (Springfield), State of Illinois, 1946.

6. Malzberg, B.: "The influence of economic factors on mental health." In *Mental Health,* edited by F. R. Moulton and P. O. Komora. (Lancaster), Am. Assn. for the Advancement of Science, 1939.

7. Falk, I. S. and N. D. M. Hirsch: "Social Security measures as factors in mental health programs." In *Mental Health,* edited by F. R. Moulton and P. O. Komora. (Lancaster), Am. Assn. for the Advancement of Science, 1939.

8. Annual Wages and Employment Stabilization Techniques. New York, American Management Association, 1945.

9. Schreiber, J.: "Interdependence of democracy and mental health." *Ment. Hyg.* 29: 606–621, October 1945.

10. Levy, D. M.: "The toll of intolerance upon the intolerant." In *The Family in a World at War,* edited by S. M. Gruenberg, p. 117–124. New York, Harper, 1942.

11. Chatto, C. I. and A. Halligan: *The Story of the Springfield Plan.* New York, Barnes & Noble, 1945.

12. Brown, F. J. and S. Roucek: *One America; The History, Contribution, and Present Problems of our Racial and National Minorities.* Revised edition. New York, Prentice-Hall, 1945.

National Council for the Social Studies, National Education Association. "Democratic human relations"; 16th yearbook. Washington, D.C., the Council, 1945.

Powdermaker, H. *Probing Our Prejudices.* New York, Harper, 1944.

Vickery, W. E., and S. G. Cole. *Intercultural Education in American Schools.* Bureau for Intercultural Education Publication Series. New York, Harper, 1943.

13. National Institute of Social Relations, Inc. "Talk it over." Washington, D.C.

14. Watson, G. B.: *Action for Unity.* New York, Harper, 1947.

15. MacDonald, E. P.: "The publisher who made a better world; education for democracy." *Reader's Scope* 4: 83–86, August 1946.

16. James, William: "The moral equivalent of war." Association for International Conciliation, Leaflet No. 27, 1910.

17. Ridenour, N.: "The job ahead; a philosophy of mental hygiene education." To be published in the 25th Anniversary Volume of the Am. Orthopsychiat. Assn.

The Prevention of Abnormal Behavior[*]

BY *James C. Coleman, Ph.D.*

Aims and Principles in Prevention

Precisely what kind of preventive measures might be expected to be directly conducive to mental health, in the light of what we now know of personality and stress and the individual's efforts to solve internal and external problems? We will find our most important clues in the concepts [which hold] that behavior could be viewed as a matter of need-satisfaction sequences, with our many and varied psychobiological needs patterned to serve homeostasis, ego integrity, and self-actualization. Assuring the satisfaction of our psychobiological needs will mean establishing a favorable climate for certain basic types of adjustment to take place—physiological, occupational, social, philosophical, and so on. Satisfactory adjustment in these and other essential areas will insure mental health.

Although there is still considerable controversy over

THE PREVENTION OF ABNORMAL BEHAVIOR

the most effective means of implementing these principles, and even to some extent over which types of adjustment are more basically important and necessary to
us, we are in a position to outline the many types of
adjustments that contribute to mental health, and the
kinds of measures that can be taken to foster them and
hence prevent abnormal behavior.

Biological Preventive Measures

The biological preventive measures proposed have
involved two rather different approaches. On the one
hand, emphasis has been placed on the physical health
of the individual; on the other, attempts have been made
to manipulate heredity and to insure an adequate prenatal environment so as to get a healthier breed to start
with.

GENERAL HEALTH MEASURES. Clearly, it is important to
maintain the optimum physical vigor and health of the
individual as a means of increasing his resistance to all
types of stress. In this sense the entire field of preventive medicine is important in the prevention of both
physical and mental illness.

In addition, however, the early detection and eradi-
cation of brain tumors, syphilis, and other specific organic pathology associated with mental disorders is a
paramount factor in the effective treatment and control
of these particular disorders. Paresis alone accounts for
some 4 per cent of mental hospital admissions. It is directly preventable. Public health measures for the
control of syphilis and other diseases have been undertaken throughout the United States, and increasing im-

portance is being placed upon periodic medical examinations in order to discover early any evidences of organic pathology. The coöperation of the general public with our health agencies should be particularly effective in reducing the number of organic psychoses through early detection or prevention of the organic pathology known to underlie them.

EUGENIC MEASURES. Eugenic measures include efforts directed toward insuring good heredity, good embryonic and fetal development, and a normal, safe birth —in short, a good prenatal endowment. In discussions of eugenics, most emphasis is usually placed upon the importance of good heredity and upon measures (such as the control of marriage, sterilization, birth control, and abortions) designed to prevent the birth of children with adverse heredity. Several states have legalized the sterilization of mental defectives, and many advocates of controlled breeding would like to have the same provisions extended to antisocial personalities, schizophrenics, and other mentally ill persons. Certainly, it is reasonable to emphasize the importance of good heredity for a good start in life. For the future of the species, there are possible advantages in selective breeding—or at least in exercising some control over who provides society with the bulk of its children. For example, until the last few years the college-trained population has not reproduced itself (that is, the average number of children per family among college graduates has been only 1.7) whereas in the lowest socio-economic levels families are traditionally large. But the role of heredity in schizophrenic disorders, antisocial personalities, neuroses, and other mental disorders is so poorly defined that the value of applying genetic regulations would be extremely questionable except perhaps in very isolated cases where the entire family tree appears tainted with psychopathology. Disturbed parents probably pass their characteristics on to their children more through education and example than through genetic transmission.

Measures carefully designed to prevent accidents and to insure a healthy development during the embryonic period are usually a part of good obstetric practice and are not ordinarily considered a part of a preventive program against psychopathology. But, as we have seen, there is reason to believe that injuries and developmental deviations occurring prior to birth are often an important factor in later faulty personality development. As medical research progresses in this area and as the conditions necessary for optimal prenatal development are worked out, there is every reason to believe that we will be able to do a great deal toward reducing constitutional predispositions to psychopathology. At present, the frontier of constitutional medicine is just beginning to open up.

Psychological Preventive Measures

The psychological aspects of prevention center around the development of strong, socially adequate, and well-integrated personalities. It has been only recently that we have fully recognized the importance of psychological factors and particularly of early personality development in the development of psychopathology.

Although childhood is an especially crucial stage for future happiness, difficulties can develop at any stage of life. Our needs and problems change considerably as we pass through different life periods, for each age has its own particularly pressing needs and important adjustments to make. Thus psychological measures for preventing abnormal behavior must be aimed toward preparing and helping people to deal effectively with the normal life stages through which all human beings pass. Both present and future welfare will be at stake, for successful and happy adjustment at any one stage, while a goal in itself, is also essential for preventing serious difficulties from developing at a later stage. Thus the early detection and treatment of pathological trends or adjustment difficulties will be an important aspect of prevention.

Later in the chapter we shall find that many agencies have been established to deal with specific types of problems arising at different ages—child guidance clinics, marital counseling, vocational guidance, parent-teacher groups, youth centers, activity projects for older people, and many other programs attempting to help people with the normal difficulties of life that even the "well-adjusted" person may have considerable trouble in handling successfully.

SPECIAL NEEDS DURING CHILDHOOD. Concepts of child-rearing and of children's needs have changed radically in recent years. At the present time there is quite general agreement on the following principles with regard to infants and preschool children: (1) adequate mothering during infancy; (2) self-demand feeding schedules; (3) freedom for the child to follow his own pattern of developmental needs, which implies that toilet training, "manners," and other lessons in social living are to be given casually and in a friendly manner, when the child is ready and not before; (4) consistent parental discipline and other values which provide the child with adequate reality and ethical models but which do not unnecessarily restrict his reality testing; (5) most important, a loving atmosphere in which the child is respected as an individual and made to feel that he is an important member of the group.

We have seen continually . . . what a very large part faulty parent-child relationships do play in the development of abnormal behavior; thus one of our most essential areas of psychological prevention must be parent education. Partly, this will mean a spreading of information about children's needs and developmental patterns, but this is only the first step. Parents have their own needs and limitations, and in many cases the faulty relationships they establish with their children are a reflection not of their ignorance of principles of child guidance, but of their own insecurities, tensions, dependency needs, hostilities, and so on. In addition, problems arising in connection with their children are apt to be highly ego-involved: misbehavior or slow development on the part of the child is often evaluated by the parent as a threat to his own capabilities and general worth. Hence it is something he cannot tolerate, and we often see parents protecting themselves from self-devaluation by various defenses such as "denial of reality" or attempting to "stamp out" or suppress the misbehavior at all costs. Parent education, then, will often necessitate parent *counseling*—counseling which will be concerned both with the children's problems and with the parents' own (Whitman 41).

As a child reaches school age and begins to move out from the family into the world outside, the conditions that made good adjustment possible in his earlier years will no longer suffice now. He still needs emotional support from his parents, but it becomes increasingly im

portant for him to have the experience of close
friendships with other children, and membership in a
group of his peers. He becomes more actively interested
in his "gang" than in his family, and is often more responsive to its opinions and standards than to those of
his parents. Though this tendency is often difficult for
parents to accept, it is healthy and normal for him, and
is suppressed by them only at great cost to his normal
development. For it is in such activities that he acquires
the social skills and independent self-reliance essential
for group participation then and in later life. During
these grade-school years, too, we find rapid development
of conscience: the child learns to inhibit his sexual and
aggressive impulses, and with his contemporaries sets up
standards of group behavior that may be even stricter
than the standards of parents or teachers.

The difficulties a child may experience in this period
are many. Traumatic experiences or parental overprotection may undermine his self-reliance and lead him
to cling to his parents instead of forming close relationships with his peers. Parental rejection or lack of physical or social skills may lead to emotional and social withdrawal, and so on. The tensions and anxieties resulting
from such difficulties often lead to antisocial and other
undesirable adjustive reactions which may not only ag-
gravate the immediate adjustive situation but interfere
with his subsequent adjustment during adolescence and
later life. Thus parents and adults close to the child
can have an important part in preventing abnormal behavior if they provide conditions essential to normal
personality development in childhood and prepare him
for the physical and emotional changes that adolescence
will bring.

ADJUSTMENT IN ADOLESCENCE. As we have noted, adolescence is a particularly difficult period in our society, due partly to the lack of adequate preparation for the problems to be encountered in the adolescent period and partly to the fact that our society offers no clear-cut and consistent rules and standards and gives its teenage members no important social or economic role which could channel their energies and lead to feelings of adequacy and personal worth. The adolescent has several specific problems too: he must learn to deal with a sexual drive that his biological maturation is bringing to great intensity, work out less direct, socially acceptable channels for the discharge of hostility, and prepare himself for induction into his role as an adult member of society. In the process, he must emancipate himself from his parents and assume responsibility for his own life and the pursuit of his individual interests His relationships with his age-mates become of increasing importance. For the first time, the adolescent begins to see his parents and home "as they really are," and to understand that adult social institutions—government, business, the church—are not the perfect institutions he has believed.

All these changes in the adolescent lead him into tremendous conflict not only with his parents but within himself. Depending on his individual childhood experience with sex, he accepts his strange new sex drive and his new sex role with equanimity or with concern.

Often parents are reluctant to have the child leave home, are outraged to have him question or criticize them, are offended by his new attitudes toward himself and society. Often they resent also his extreme interest in the opinions of his fellows and his dependence upon their tastes and fashions. The strength of the group opinion in the adolescent culture is enormous, since the adolescent, in his breaking away from home, is usually unsure of himself and feels strongly the need to "belong." The average teen-age boy or girl, feeling it imperative to be an "in" rather than an "out" at school or college, is usually afraid to voice any opinions or interests that will make him appear "different."

The adolescent, in the midst of all these conflicts and new experiences, badly needs the emotional support of parents who have sufficient insight themselves to understand what he is going through and to interpret it to him. And again, for parents who do not have this insight or seem unable to cope with problems that arise, counseling services in the community may be of invaluable assistance.

Crucially important, too, is the school, for more and more our society is coming to regard the school as responsible not only for the intellectual development of students but for their emotional and social development as well. Classes are given in many subjects which prepare students specifically for problems in adult life: community health problems, marriage relations, and so forth. The modern school fosters the adolescent's criticism of existing conditions and his glowing idealism, and tries to direct them toward useful ends. It tries to help him gain some understanding of his own and others' emotional problems, through courses in mental hygiene and through interpretations of novels, plays, poetry, movies, and radio dramatizations.

In addition, the schools are taking increased responsibility for determining students' abilities and special interests and helping them to plan academic work that is best suited to them. Educational adjustment during high school and college years is a prerequisite to the best vocational—and emotional—adjustment later on. A course of study that is too easy or too hard or that is uncongenial to the individual's interests and special talents may lead to a feeling of frustration because of abilities not actualized or because of unrealistic or too-high aspirations. If the individual's feelings of confidence and adequacy are to be fostered he needs the experience of succeeding in school, so he will not be left with feelings of failure, envious comparisons with more successful students, and inevitable self-devaluation.

Adolescence is not a time of stress and turmoil in all cultures. Where the adolescent has a well-structured role, contributes to the social group, and has assured status, he does not suffer the insecurities and fears of our adolescents or exhibit the extreme behavior many of our adolescents manifest in their attempts to feel important and worth while. In proportion, then, as we encourage and plan for a useful part for our adolescents to play in their community, and in so far as we are able to solve our own uncertainties and provide a stable social and economic setting in which they can see a meaningful place as they reach adulthood, we shall be fostering mental health and preventing abnormal behavior.

Along this line—speaking particularly of the shortcomings of our society in the vocational roles it offers its young people—Frank (16) says:

> If we are persuaded that mental hygiene has the significance we have here assumed, and if we are to be guided by the implications of our growing knowledge of personality development, we must acknowledge that most of the contemporary careers we urge upon youth are in truth but defenses against anxiety

and emotional defeat—competitive struggles for power, prestige, or property that reflect the child-hood insecurities from which the individual is fleeing and that threaten him with new insecurities from the other aggressive individuals he must challenge. Such designs for living are neither mentally hygienic nor socially desirable. . . . The youth of today, no less than the youth of other days, wants to be given tasks that arouse his enthusiasm and promise fulfillment of his aspirations. If we are to be sincere, we can but point out the futility of the competitive struggle that leads to no personal fulfillment because it arises from inner personal distortion and insecurity which no achievement, property, or prestige can assuage. In contrast, we can try to give youth an understanding of how his or her personal life may be made significant and enriched, not merely by achievement or acquisition but by the quality of human relations he or she can sustain.

VOCATIONAL ADJUSTMENT. It is sometimes startling to realize the amount of time that the average employee spends away from his family, at work. A saleswoman may spend more time behind the counter with her fellow-clerks than she does with her adolescent children. A businessman may spend more time talking to his colleagues than he does talking to his family. In economic and social terms, the importance of work is enormous. Upon a society's economic efficiency and productivity depends the standard of living of all its members. For the individual worker and his family, the general "standard of living" has very specific and important consequences. Adequate wages are necessary to insure minimum physical conditions of life; work commensurate with his abilities and friendly coöperative relationships on the job are essential to his mental equilibrium; reasonable security is necessary to avoid the harmful effects of worry and uncertainty. Freedom from worry, a sense of self-respect and accomplishment, hope for the future—all of these underlie happy family life and are fostered by healthy occupational adjustment. Later in this article are briefly listed some of the accomplishments of psychiatry in industry in fostering vocational adjustment and mental health. As we have gradually come to realize the role of the individual's whole life situation in his degree of mental health, the contributions of occupational, marital, and other adjustments have been given increasing attention.

MENTAL HYGIENE IN INTERPERSONAL RELATIONS. Currently, a flood of literature has welled from the realization that in order to achieve an effective adjustment to the surrounding world, an individual must learn to get along successfully with other people. Of great importance to all of us is a feeling of competence in dealing with people, of having good friends, and of "belonging" to a group. From a more materialistic point of view, "success," as measured by occupational advancement and the accumulation of material possessions, is heavily dependent upon one's social skills.

The goals of the "how-to-make-friends-and-money" literature are important ones. Modern psychiatry has not found, however, that such material really helps people to attain these goals. First, it does not tell the reader how to change himself so that he *can* follow the rules and formulas it lays down. Information about etiquette and grooming can be helpful to people who are basically well socialized and need only to learn a few social techniques for greater poise and self-confidence in their relations with others. Often the "advice" given, however, is impossible to follow because the individual is blocked by underlying personality maladjustment. Concentration of techniques and rules of behavior will not conceal or change one's basic attitudes. If one feels intense hostility toward people, it will show through his best attempts to create a charming exterior. Such hostility may be thinly disguised, or it may come out in more devious ways.

The second difficulty with the "how-to-be-successful" literature is that too often it is used with the idea of exploiting others, of making people do what we want them to do regardless of their own needs and interests. In so far as this is true, such techniques are not conducive to healthy interpersonal relations or to the mental health of the person using them. Over a period of time, devices motivated by a desire to gain an advantage rather than by a positive interest in others, will lead to a deterioration in interpersonal relationships and human values.

Generally speaking, what *can* modern psychiatry offer in helping us to get along with others and to feel more accepted and happy? *First,* in order to have good interpersonal relationships, we must have a sincere, positive interest in other people. We must share their successes, hopes, and failures, sincerely wish them well, and regret seeing them pushed down, as often happens in our highly competitive society. *Second,* we must like and accept and understand ourselves if we are to like other people and be able to get along with either them or ourselves. As Liebman (26) puts it: "Self-understanding rather than self-condemnation is the way to inner peace and mature conscience." We have already seen that self-acceptance is one of our basic psychological needs,

THE PREVENTION OF ABNORMAL BEHAVIOR

and that the lack of it is found repeatedly to be an important part of neurotic, psychotic, and other abnormal behavior. We now see its role in everyday interpersonal relationships. If we cannot accept ourselves and are so maladjusted that our main energies are directed toward the solution of our own conflicts and frustrations, we will have little time or energy to expend on others, our ego defense mechanisms will be working overtime, we will not be in a position to be completely honest with either ourselves or others, and our relations with others will suffer from our own irrational actions—regardless of how many "techniques of human relations" we may study in books and magazines.

Nor can we decide, by an act of will, to acquire an interest in people. Because our adjustive techniques and habits are rooted in our whole cumulative history of self and environmental evaluations, largely unconscious, it may be necessary for an individual to have psychiatric help in resolving inner conflicts before he will be able to accept himself and come to feel a real interest in others.

MARITAL ADJUSTMENT. Among the adjustments typically involved in adult life is marriage. A compatible marriage is based upon the meaningful sharing of experiences and the formation of deep emotional bonds. It helps both partners feel adequate, wanted, needed, socially approved, and secure—to a degree which cannot be achieved in any other human relationship. Where a compatible marriage is made even more meaningful and worth while through children, it becomes a strong family unit which contributes to the parents' sense of accomplishment and happiness, increases their security and satisfaction in middle and old age, and at the same time provides the good emotional environment so important to the children.

Unfortunately, many modern marriages are contracted without adequate preparation and lead to bitterness, disillusionment, and unhappiness. One out of every three marriages is now ending in the divorce court. These cold statistics represent a serious failure in human relations. Both partners may have entered marriage with high hopes and confidence of success which, when shattered, leave both of them shaken and bewildered. When a divorce breaks up a marriage of many years' duration, the wife particularly may find life difficult. For while the husband may remarry a younger woman with relative ease, the wife, especially after thirty-five, may find her marital possibilities considerably reduced so that it is increasingly difficult to establish a successful new marriage. The children suffer from divorces, not only in terms of the immediate trauma of the breaking up of their homes, but through subsequent divided loyalties, a lack of adequate models, and other factors which may influence their entire development thereafter.

The question that concerns us here primarily is what can be done to promote better marital adjustment. What are the basic factors underlying successful marriages and what conditions are conducive to unhappy marriages?

A number of studies in this area have emphasized some of the following factors in unhappy marriages: (1) emotional immaturity of either or both partners, often with unrealistic and "idealistic" attitudes toward marriage and little conception of the duties and responsibilities involved; (2) incompatibility due to differences in age, intelligence, religion, values, etc.; (3) physical or sexual incompatibility; (4) lack of common goals concerning children, how to spend money, leisure time, etc.; (5) adverse environmental factors such as interfering in-laws, poor health, or insufficient income; (6) faulty parental training in sexual attitudes; (7) an unfavorable early home life, including bickering, tension, or parental rejection, making for later difficulties in giving and receiving affection.

Such studies, confirming what has been generally discovered in clinical practice, suggest that the prevention of maladjustment in marriage can best be conducted along three lines: (1) insurance of an adequate home life and early childhood conditions conducive to healthy emotional development, and an adequate home "model"; (2) specific preparation for marriage in terms of an understanding of duties, responsibilities, functions, and various other reality and ethical considerations relating to marriage and family life; and (3) early psychiatric attention to marriages which are "sick." This last point may involve treatment of the personality problems of one or both partners. In addition, it has been found possible through tests, discussion groups, and counseling, to help engaged and married couples clarify their motives in connection with marriage and understand the factors essential for achieving a happy marriage. Later, in our review of present mental hygiene facilities, we shall see that the prevention and treatment of marital difficulties has received a great deal of attention, and that many groups have been active here.

PHILOSOPHICAL ADJUSTMENT.   It is an accepted fact that "man does not live by bread alone." In our present stage of world history, the truth of this statement cannot be questioned, but it is another matter to find the "something more" than bread which will prove satisfactory amid world conflict, ideological warfare, and rapid social change. Modern technology, in its tearing down of our older social and religious values, has not yet given rise to new values fully productive of human happiness. Many people, unable to find any enduring faith, conclude that life is isolated, trivial, and ultimately meaningless. They find themselves living in this "Age of Anxiety" without any adequate, socially rooted philosophy of life. Unable to order their ideas and feelings and experiences, they begin to lose effective understanding of and direct relation to their environment. They fall victim to weird attitudes, philosophies, and practices. Such states of mind are fertile ground for mental disorders. Thus it becomes highly relevant to our search for preventive measures in mental hygiene, to consider some of the factors which now appear essential to an adequate philosophical adjustment: one that will predispose an individual to mental health and generally effective adjustment.

Although different persons find meaning and reward in different areas of life—some in family life, some in social service, some in intellectual or professional work —certain basic assumptions are commonly made by mentally healthy people. Some of these assumptions are accepted on faith, some are accepted in the light of our historical development, and some are well bolstered by experimental evidence. Those listed below are not presented as eternal values, nor as the only values held by rational and healthy people in our society. Nor are we even arguing for their validity. Our chief interest in them here is that the holding of them seems to be coexistent with mental health and social usefulness in those who share them.

1. A belief in the importance and worth of every individual.

2. A belief that social progress is both possible and worth while.

3. A belief in the value of the "truth" that we try to approximate by means of modern scientific techniques, and in its usefulness for social progress.

4. A belief that democracy, with its respect for the individual, provides the most congenial atmosphere for the pursuit of truth, and for the happiness and progress of both the individual and the group.

5. An acceptance of individual responsibility for carrying forward the social progress made by preceding generations.

6. A belief in mankind as a functional part of the universe, with potentialities for evolution that can be fulfilled.

7. A belief that brotherly love and other fundamental tenets of Christianity and other great religious philosophies are not only compatible with modern, democratic society but actually indispensable to it.

The "philosophy" we are talking about here is not just an intellectual set of principles, but an expression of one's own *Weltanschauung* or world-view, as determined by his emotional as well as intellectual experience. When people report great difficulty in finding "meaning" in life, it usually indicates that their experience in life has been unsatisfying and that due to inner conflicts, their personalities are not well integrated. Young people, who do not yet know how to organize all the conflicting elements of their life experiences, and people in situations of extreme or long-continued stress, such as war or poverty, typically report difficulty in understanding "what life is all about." With a change in the environment or in their way of looking at it, they no longer seek to find some single, mysterious, inner "meaning" to life, but can organize their attitudes and experiences in some such working philosophy as we have outlined above. In more serious instances, when an individual is completely unable to find coherence or satisfaction in his life experiences, psychiatric treatment is indicated. Psychiatry does not itself provide him with a philosophy, but it can help him to become emotionally mature enough to work out new evaluations—values— which will be conducive to greater mental health.

PREVENTIVE MEASURES IN LATER MATURITY. As people move on through maturity into their later years, they are faced with many new and difficult problems of adjustment. Again, as in childhood, they become more dependent upon other people, economically, socially, and physically. Their children grow up and take up full lives of their own away from home, often leaving the parents feeling lonely, insecure, and unneeded. Their sexual life diminishes somewhat with the climacteric, frequently arousing strong anxieties and adding further to feelings of loneliness and inadequacy. For the man, retirement or joblessness represents an additional adjustive burden. And for most older people, the difficulties of this life period are accentuated by the loss of contemporaries (perhaps including husband or wife), physical infirmities and chronic diseases, and the psychological problem of accepting the inevitable changes in one's self-evaluation and life situation brought about by aging.

As we have seen, older people are a growing proportion of our population. In 1800, a newborn child had a life expectancy of 35 years; in 1900, 45 years; in 1950, 70 years. With so many more people now reaching old age than ever before, the occupational, health, and general social problems presented by this segment of our population are engaging increasing national attention.

Attention to the problems of older people in our culture shows that their uncertainties are reflected in the high incidence of senile psychoses and cerebral arterio-sclerosis. The development of psychosis is more closely related to the individual's psychological stresses than to brain deterioration, and a senile psychotic reaction might even be reversed with a change in the life situation of the patient that gave him a new feeling of being needed. Thus it becomes vitally important for us, as individuals and as a society, to do everything within our power to make it possible for older people to achieve satisfaction of their basic psychobiological needs for physical and emotional security, belonging, adequacy, approval, and so on. Older people need to know that they and their lives are appreciated, wanted, valued, that they are still loved even though they are no longer at the peak of material usefulness and that they can continue in creative activities.

Sociological Preventive Measures

In the preceding section we have focused our attention upon the kinds of psychological adjustment that contribute to mental health, but the problems of occupational adjustment, marital adjustment, and so on are also, of course, sociological problems as well. Thus our emphasis upon the prevention of mental illness leads us a step beyond psychiatry proper, into the realm of *sociology*, or the study of societies.

As we have come to realize more clearly the importance of "social pathology" in the production of individual abnormal behavior, there has been a trend toward the fusion of sociological and psychiatric concepts and research, and of sociological corrective measures with mental hygiene programs. Since the sociological level of prevention of abnormal behavior involves the diagnosis and correction of social as well as individual pathology, there is reason to believe that this coöperation in research will be increased. For before we can undertake effective preventive measures, we must be more clear as to just what constitutes social pathology and what methods will be most efficient in correcting it.

Despite our present limitations in knowledge, the accumulation and coördination of facts to date and the ramified research under way forecast a not too remote day when we shall be actually grappling with the social causes of mental illness—not on the basis of guesswork, moral indignation, and hit-or-miss remedies, but on the basis of scientifically established knowledge. We may, in short, be able to reach as directly and immediately into those environmental conditions contributing to mental illness as we now do, with trained specialists and effective techniques, into the poor sanitary conditions favoring epidemics.

Sociological research into the environmental factors relating to abnormal behavior is being carried on along at least four fronts:

1. Studies of the incidence of abnormal behavior.
2. Research into the social origins of abnormal behavior.
3. Evaluation of current preventive and therapeutic efforts.
4. Planning of more effective preventive measures.

We can best understand the importance of such studies by briefly considering what has been done and what is being done, and what studies are proposed or indicated. Here we shall be concerned with the United States, and shall defer until a later point our discussion of research undertaken and proposed on an international level.

STUDIES OF INCIDENCE. The incidence of mental illness has not yet been thoroughly studied sociologically. Studies of the "ecological" type in which the patterns of abnormal behavior have been described with respect to the geographical areas of large cities. [There] have also [been] studies based upon draft and Armed Forces data and census statistics, and other studies indicating the socio-economic distribution of various types of abnormal behavior. These studies have revealed much interesting and valuable information. For example, one finding from ecological studies was that

> Persons residing in areas not primarily populated by persons of their own ethnic or racial groups show much higher rates [of mental illness] than those of the numerically dominant group. (Dunham 11)

Similarly, studies based on Selective Service data have shown an increasing incidence of mental disorders from higher socio-economic levels to lower ones. Although these findings do not indicate much about the origin of mental disorders, they do indicate ways in which geographical "trouble spots" can be determined where preventive action should be concentrated.

In general, we must admit that the amount of usable, reliable information we have on the extent of abnormal behavior and its pattern of distribution within our population is very slight. With more adequate knowledge our mental hygiene program will become increasingly effective.

RESEARCH INTO THE SOCIAL ORIGINS OF ABNORMAL BEHAVIOR. Studies of social factors have done much already to illuminate the influence of the social setting in general upon the content and orientation of the personality. Studies of widely differing cultures indicate certain basic personality configurations in certain societies, or in sub-groups within them (class, ethnic group, and other status sub-groups). For example, paranoidal suspiciousness may pervade the reaction patterns of one society or group, self-effacing noncompetitiveness those of another, and passivity and occasional violent release those of still another (Fortune 15, Benedict 5, Bateson and Mead 3). In fact out of such studies has emerged an important hypothesis: that within each society there exists a basic character or personality structure, with variations among individuals determined by class and other differentials (Benedict 4, Kardiner 19, 20, Dubois 9, Fromm 17, Bateson and Mead 3, Gorer 18, Linton 27). This literature not only is fascinating to the student of abnormal psychology, but has great potential importance for mental hygiene and treatment. If developed much further along present lines, it can eventually give us a social etiology on which we can base the treatment and prevention of mental illness in our particular society, and in the special sub-groups within our society.

Some studies of "primitive" peoples have revealed the personality disorientations occurring when Western civilization has disrupted the old tribal patterns. From this knowledge of the effect of cultural patterns and cultural changes on individual personality, it has become possible to understand, partially, certain comparable effects in our own society. Thus,

> The highest incidence of certain types of mental disorder, of suicide, of crime, and other forms of deviant behavior has been found in areas of high mobility and disorganized community life, with their accompanying anonymity and loneliness. (Felix and Bowers 13)

From Army psychiatric experience, Dr. William Menninger (31) emphasizes the apparent importance of the *group factor* in the etiology of mental illness:

> . . . Far more impressive in the adjustment process than the history [of maladjustment in the individual or his family] or the personality make-up or the internal psychodynamic stresses, was the force of factors in the environment which supported or disrupted the individual . . . We seemed to learn anew the importance of the group ties in the maintenance of mental health. We were impressed by the fact that an individual who had a strong conviction about his job, even though his was a definite, unstable personality, might make a remarkable achievement against the greatest of stresses.

Such studies, bearing directly upon mental illnesses, are supplemented by broad sociological studies of communities, classes, and other population groups, illuminating individual problems by filling in the social background—group standards, ideals, mores, and the degree of individual conformity expected (Lynd and Lynd 29, 30, Veblen 39, Warner 40, Myrdal *et al.* 32). All this information is invaluable in understanding personality development, origins of maladjustment, and the effects that the individual's interactions with group forces have on his mental health. It is especially useful in combination with the other types of research described and with the main body of psychiatric and clinical psychological findings.

But while social science has made great progress in the last twenty or thirty years, much research remains to be done if we are to understand how to change society in such a way as to promote mental health. As Felix and Bowers (13) say of this research, "The literature is fragmentary and presumptive rather than experimentally compelling." They sum up as follows the amount and type of research we need in this field:

a) We need intensive socio-clinical studies of various types of mentally disordered people, including their families. These will help us in relating clinical symptoms and the dynamics of the disorder to the broad psychological and social setting.

b) We need similar studies tracing individuals from birth through all the stages of life.

c) Cross-cultural and cultural group studies should be intensified by adequate life-history and clinical data.

d) Pediatricians, physicians, and psychiatrists should obtain full data on their patients, including sociologically relevant information, which could then be centrally analyzed and utilized in sociological research and preventive action.

e) Personality reactions to the many abrupt and often traumatic changes in life, such as unemployment, death of parents, divorce, old age, imprisonment, and so on should be studied.

f) Finally, we need more laboratory studies of specific personality mechanisms, such as frustration, repression, substitutive processes, et cetera.

EVALUATIVE RESEARCH. Mental hygiene programs carried on by public and private organizations, nationally and locally, have not been intensively evaluated to determine their effectiveness in remedying unfavorable environmental factors. The same is true of the many loose-knit community efforts—counseling services, social work, psychotherapy undertaken by psychiatrists and clinical psychologists, and many community-sponsored projects. It is the general feeling of those working in the field that these measures are proving highly effective in fostering mental health. If they are to be modified in the direction of maximum efficiency, however, we must have additional experimental research data on which to base our improvements.

PLANNING OF PREVENTIVE MEASURES. Present group programs of prevention—such as anti-delinquency projects, the establishment of psychiatric clinics, public education, racial tolerance drives—may eventually do much to improve the mental health of our nation. Their value should not be underestimated. But there is still need for more effective coördination of biological, psychological, and sociological preventive measures based on greater knowledge of the extent, origin, development, and most effective treatment of abnormal behavior. All aspects of our prevention programs are handicapped by a lack of precise data and guiding principles based upon comprehensive research. Likewise we must increase the scope of our preventive measures so that more people will be able to benefit from them.

The responsibility for carrying out sociological preventive measures—for establishing a healthful environment for people and modifying society in the light of research findings—falls heavily upon all the institutions to which we belong and so upon us as members. Primarily, in the twentieth century it falls upon the home, the school, industrial organizations, and the government (local, state, and federal). Gone is the relative self-sufficiency of a hundred years ago, and the old idea that each individual should be able singlehandedly to make a sucessful adjustment to life. With greater interdependency has come greater mutual responsibility for each other's welfare and greater need for careful joint planning in the best interests of all. We now feel that it is up to society to see that the individual is provided with certain essential skills and with sufficient security to enable him to make successful occupational, marital, social, and philosophical adjustments. An intelligent society will take all possible steps to set up a general sociocultural climate which not only permits healthy personality functioning and growth but is actively conducive to it.

The following sections will be concerned with a description of the preventive measures that our society and certain international organizations have undertaken and are carrying forward, in an attempt to fulfill the public responsibility for the mental health of individuals here and in other countries. To allay the fears and anxieties that make for so much unhappiness and abnormal behavior in our age, a mental hygiene movement of truly staggering proportions has developed.

Organized Efforts for Mental Health in the United States

As public awareness, interest, and effort have been directed toward our contemporary mental health problems, an increasing number of professional and lay organizations—employing preventive measures or treatment or both—have begun a coördinated attack on the prevention of mental illness and the promotion of mental health. These include governmental agencies, private professional organizations, volunteer organizations, and various professional groups not directly concerned with psychiatry which nevertheless use its concepts every day as an integral part of their work.

The Government and Mental Health

Growing public awareness of the inadequacy of existing mental health facilities eventually led to the passage in 1947 of *The National Mental Health Act,* which has launched a far-flung program to attack the nation-wide problem. It not only finances directly many needed specific projects but also coördinates and assists in the activities of private organizations, institutions, and individuals already working in the field. The program under the Act is outlined above. Fifty-one states and territories now participate with mental health programs and receive federal funds on the basis of population, financial need, and extent of program. Each state must provide one dollar from its funds for every two federal dollars granted to it.

Through the combination of these appropriations

Government Program under the National Mental Health Act

Assistance ($8,666,000 in 1950)

1. Research grants to expand laboratory and clinical research.
2. Grants for training of psychiatrists, psychologists, psychiatric social workers, nurses.
3. Grants to states for mental health services and community activities (seminars, workshops, clinics, surveys, etc.).

Operational activities

1. National Institute of Mental Health at Bethesda, Maryland—training center and clearing house for psychiatric information; conducts surveys, research projects, and educational activities, and functions as nerve center for activities under the Act.
2. Prince Georges County (Maryland) Clinic—model community clinic, set up by Public Health Service in coöperation with numerous local organizations to show other towns and counties how to undertake mental health measures. Provides regular diagnosis and treatment and studies each case for its community as well as its individual significance, with the hope of establishing principles for prevention of abnormal behavior. Staff includes 2 psychiatrists, 1 clinical psychologist, 2 psychiatric social workers, and a mental health nurse.
3. Mental Health Center at Phoenix, Arizona—field demonstration unit to show potential influence of a clinic on general community health by fostering psychiatric orientation in existing organizations; training and assistance given to staff members of local agencies occupies 70 per cent of the Center's time, case consultation and clinical service 30 per cent.

with state funds, a wide range of vital mental health activities has been made possible. States have made surveys of mental health facilities. Clinics have been expanded in number and scope, with thirty-six new clinics established in the first year of the Act alone. Funds have been made available for research, and for increasing the staffs of hospitals and clinics. Perhaps most important of all, extensive educational campaigns have been conducted for the general public, and for professional workers—general physicians, nurses, teachers, and others dealing with the public—aimed at developing a general psychiatric orientation in the nation, especially in professions most directly concerned with mental health and social welfare. For example, in one month in 1949 the following educational measures were undertaken: a three-day neuropsychiatric seminar in Orangeburg, South Carolina, was conducted by some thirty speakers of national reputation, discussing such topics as alcoholism, schizophrenia, court psychiatry, and prevention; a thousand Cleveland school delegates attended a workshop on "Emotional Health"; in Minnesota, a sex-education seminar was sponsored by the State Departments of Education and Health; an institute for physicians was held in California and one for nurses in Illinois.

In addition to the program under the National Mental Health Act, both federal and state governments carry on numerous other activities relating to mental health. Under the Social Security Administration, the Children's Bureau, through its Mental Health Unit, extends many kinds of aid, including mental health measures and many free pamphlets for the guidance of parents throughout the country. The Veterans Administration, following the modernization of its methods after World War II, has now become a leader in the treatment of the mentally ill, providing funds and facilities for the education and training of psychiatrists and clinical psychologists and pioneering in research and practical programs for the more effective handling of mental patients. These activities have spurred improvement of state institutions.

The states have in the past established, maintained, and supervised their own mental institutions as well as welfare departments and, in some cases, separate mental hygiene departments. With each state, there are county and municipal organizations operating welfare departments, social work agencies, local clinics, juvenile bureaus, educational programs, and other activities, often working in collaboration with private organizations.

Private Nation-Wide Professional Organizations

An inestimable amount of valuable work has been done by the numerous private organizations operating in the mental hygiene field on a national basis. Undoubtedly their nation-wide memberships and their activities of many years have played a major part in bringing about the public awareness of the critical importance of mental hygiene which led to the National Mental Health Act. Their usefulness has not ended, however, with the initiation of federal aid and leadership. They still have vital missions to carry out, and still form the backbone and preponderance of the forces working for improvement of mental health conditions.

Perhaps the two best-known national groups devoted to the promotion of mental health have been The National Committee for Mental Hygiene and The National Mental Health Foundation, which have now merged to form The National Association for Mental Health. In the past, the National Committee, founded in 1909 by

National Professional Organizations Concerned with Mental Health

American Psychological Association (APA)

Professional organization of American psychologists. Publishes periodicals concerning all phases of personality development and functioning; establishes training and professional standards and coördinates research.

American Psychiatric Association (APA)

Professional organization of American psychiatrists. Coördinates research and sets up standards. Works directly with American Medical Association to promote general mental health. Especially concerned with improving standards of mental hospitals, clinics, and other agencies.

American Social Science Association

Professional organization of American sociologists. Carries on preventive measures: community health, education, etc.

Group for the Advancement of Psychiatry

Organized in 1946, led by Karl and William Menninger, to stimulate effective and speedy progress in psychiatry.

Association for the Advancement of Psychotherapy

Composed of psychiatrists, psychoanalysts, physicians, and others. Sponsors seminars for advanced training and interchange of different viewpoints. Publishes a magazine and scientific papers.

American Psychoanalytic Association

Composed of analytically trained psychiatrists. Engages in research and professional-level discussion groups.

American Orthopsychiatric Association

Composed of psychiatrists working especially with problems of children and young people. Sponsors seminars and research projects.

Clifford Beers, concerned itself with direct attempts to improve mental health, largely by working through other organizations (through surveys, advice to mental hygiene agencies, help to communities in setting up clinics, demonstration projects in schools, production of films and dramatic sketches, giving of awards, dissemination of information through books, pamphlets, lectures, and radio programs, and so on). The National Foundation, on the other hand, founded more recently through the initiative of conscientious objectors who had served as hospital attendants during World War II, worked directly with the public and had as its primary purpose the improvement of conditions in mental hospitals, through public education and through various projects to improve the work of mental hospital attendants (training projects, a monthly magazine for attendants about their work, an annual award for the outstanding attendant). Through the merger of these two organizations their many diverse activities have gained impetus and duplication is being avoided.

THE CHILD STUDY ASSOCIATION. The Child Study Association was founded in 1888, for parent education. It has a workshop in New York and serves both parents and professional workers in promoting wholesome family life. (1) It runs study groups which offer parents an opportunity to discuss, under professional leadership, normal problems of family life. In group participation, parents gain the understanding and opportunities for personal growth that come through shared experiences. Parents needing individual guidance may make appointments for interviews with psychiatrically trained counselors. The study groups consider child-parent problems from infancy through adolescence. (2) The

Association sponsors lectures and conferences on views and findings of specialists; for example, a recent lecture was concerned with "natural-childbirth," which has aroused much controversy in this country, and with the rooming-in plan, by which a baby stays with his mother in the hospital to receive her affection and care . . . (3) Speakers are sent over the country to extend the Association's experience to smaller communities. (4) Low-cost literature is distributed to parents and professional men and women and advisory service and bibliographies are given to parents in other parts of the United States who want to start study groups. Many such study groups are being established.

OTHER NATIONAL ORGANIZATIONS. The complex of organizations and activities in the mental field is far too great to permit of adequate discussion here. There are several other professional psychological and psychiatric groups, however, with whose aims and functions the student should be familiar. These are briefly summarized in the [above] chart.

All these professional and other organizations are of the greatest importance in meeting the challenge of mental illness. Without their impetus, without their support, the public would not know *what* action to take, *when, why,* or *how.* Their work is indispensable to research; to government; to states; to educational, parent, and industrial groups working for mental health. They are also of the greatest value in guiding volunteer activities for mental health.

Special Community Facilities

To fill specific needs in the community, several types of community clinics, associations, and guidance services have been established. These are often limited to the problems of a particular age group, or to problems arising in connection with a certain type of adjustment— vocational adjustment, marital and general family adjustment, and so on. Only a few of the many local organizations of this type can be mentioned here. In many cities throughout the nation, comparable services are functioning, though the details of their organization and activities vary.

FAMILY LIVING PROBLEMS. An organization concerned with family problems is the Association for Family Living, in Chicago, which through several activities aims at helping people to develop satisfying relationships in the family and in the community: (1) Group work is carried on by leadership activities in churches, schools, and organizations in the community, by discussion groups conducted directly by the Association, and by consultative work with schools and other groups. (2) Direct counseling service is offered in the field of family, marriage, and premarital adjustments, and as a corollary, consultative service is offered for professional persons to give them psychological insights into the problems of their clients. (3) As do many other organizations in the field of mental health, the Association prepares and distributes to individuals and organizations valuable low-cost literature discussing specific problems. It has made special efforts toward eliminating racial and religious discrimination, and toward securing better schools.

In its efforts to promote better marital adjustment, for example, the Association for Family Living works along several lines:

a) It sponsors group discussions for engaged and married couples, in which questions like these are discussed:

For engaged couples: How well do we really know one another? Will qualities that bother me now in my future partner be more, or less, annoying later? To what extent can I expect him (or her) to "grow up" after marriage? How well do we understand the sex relationship?

For married couples: What have proved to be sensible ways of handling such matters as the wife's contribution to the family income? Getting along with in-laws? "His friends," "her friends," and "our friends"?

Groups of young couples meet in schools, churches, colleges, settlements, other community agencies, or at Association headquarters. Under staff leadership, they discuss these and other questions of family relationships and preparation for marriage. Each series is especially planned to meet the needs of the particular group concerned. Other communities may also call upon the Association for Family Living for help in planning family-life education programs.

b) In addition to group meetings, the Association staff gives training to community leaders, including ministers, social workers, teachers, nurses, and so forth, who have occasion to deal with marriage problems.

c) Individual counseling is carried on by properly qualified counselors at the headquarters, where engaged or married people can come for help with difficulties.

d) If personality maladjustments are too great, individuals who come for counseling are referred to other community agencies, such as psychiatrists or clinical psychologists.

CHILD GUIDANCE AND PARENT EDUCATION. We have discussed the crucial need for parent education, and the
fact that such education involves not only imparting of
information, but help in changing attitudes. A unique
combination of child guidance and parent education
has been worked out in four Community Child Guidance Centers in Chicago, sponsored by the Individual
Psychology Association and supported by community
organizations and interested individuals. Because individual counseling is so slow and can reach at best only a
small number of those who need it, these clinics conduct
their sessions on a group basis, with several mothers and
a counselor or psychiatrist discussing child-rearing problems in round-table style, while the children enjoy supervised play and psycho-dramatics in the next room.

Sessions last two hours and are free to all comers. Two
to four cases are discussed at a session. Often the child's
teacher and other adults concerned attend. The procedure is for the mother to present the problem as she sees
it; then she and the teacher or other relatives go out of
the room and the child comes in and talks over with the
counselor whatever has been suggested in the discussion with the mother or in a previous interview by a
social worker. If there are brothers or sisters, they are
present too and the counselor talks to them together,
for singling out one child is apt to increase existing
antagonisms. Treating them as a group, on the other
hand, lessens mutual hostility and gives the counselor
an opportunity to study the relationships and attitudes
that may be contributing to the problem.

The experience has been that children have discussed
their problems freely under these circumstances, so that
when the children return to the playroom and the
mother comes back in, the counselor, in advising her, is

able to give to her as well as to the whole group a much better insight into the factors responsible for the problem. Because misbehavior in a child is usually a symptom of faulty relationships between parents and child and between siblings, correction of the misbehavior is almost automatic once the intrafamily relationships are made conducive to healthier attitudes and evaluations of self and surroundings. The necessary changes in parental attitude and understanding have often been found to come far more quickly in this group setting than in individual counseling, for each mother quickly gains a new objectivity as she sees her own problems reflected in the others being discussed and realizes that her situation is not unique or something to be ashamed or resentful of, but something that can be analyzed and corrected.

DAY CENTERS FOR THE AGING. One of the most outstanding programs more recently developed is the system of Day Centers for the Aging in New York City, established since 1943. These centers, when combined with suitable, supervised boarding arrangements, are proving a satisfactory way of relieving strain on institutional facilities, and more important, keeping older people active and interested and well. The fundamental principle of the Centers is that senile deterioration occurs "between nine and five"—that is, during the hours of inactivity and loneliness when younger people are about their work. Therefore these Day Centers provide older people with opportunities for friendship and recreation during these daytime hours. Activities include painting, writing, editing a magazine, writing and performing plays, classwork in English, in poetry, in arts and crafts, and many social activities.

As the New York City Day Center program now stands, it is a useful model to other communities. Although "Oldtimers" and "Golden-age" and "Seniors" clubs hold periodic meetings in other communities, this is the only government program which attacks the problem on a city-wide, *daily* basis. However, there are many promising indications that similar action is being taken elsewhere by the federal government, by industry, and by local communities. In Los Angeles, for example, the City Recreation and Park Department puts out a booklet listing the city's recreational activities and classes, starring over seventy that are planned especially for older people. And a national committee has recently been set up to survey available services for older people and provide counseling, under the auspices of the National Social Welfare Assembly and with the sponsorship of prominent church and welfare groups, as well as representation from the federal government.

COMMUNITY PROBLEMS. A successful combination of infant welfare work, feeding and health measures for children, numerous educational programs, family counseling, employment advising, legal and financial assistance, combatting of racial and religious prejudice, and solving of other local problems has been carried on since 1939, on a community basis, by the Back of the Yards Neighborhood Council of Chicago and more recently, under sponsorship of the Industrial Areas Foundation, by similar neighborhood councils in Los Angeles and South St. Paul, Minnesota. In a slum neighborhood back of the Chicago stockyards, where six or seven nationalities had huddled, each around its own church, bitterly hating and refusing any contact with the others except by way of feuds and persecutions, the Council, composed of about 185 organizations representing some 125,000 people, now practices democratic solving of neighborhood problems. The CIO and the Catholic churches (at least 90 per cent of the people in the area are Catholic) work willingly together in the Council for projects that they realize are for the social betterment of the people, and both admit that they are stronger as a result of this coöperation. Local merchants, too, find that business is better since the racial groups have stopped persecuting each other and begun to trade in each other's stores. The basic theory behind the movement was (1) that delinquency or substandard housing conditions or high infant mortality were all symptoms of the basic social disorganization and could not be meaningfully isolated or successfully treated unless the causes of the disorganization were attacked, and (2) that any such program must be carried out by the local people, not by outside reformers (Alinsky 2).

One of the measures that most effectively counteracted the former bitter and racial enmity was the early successful lobbying for state and federal aid for a hot lunch and free milk program, badly needed because of the widespread malnutrition and the high percentage of working mothers. Children who had been taught to avoid and hate each other now found that refusal to eat together meant no food—and so, for the first time, began to get acquainted.

The work of the Council is almost infinitely varied. Some aspects are unique. For example, there is an active program to combat all rumors that foster racial hatred. Any individual found spreading such a rumor is summoned before the Council and publicly reprimanded; his parish priest, the heads of his union, and other groups he belongs to also admonish him. In addition, the accuracy of the rumor is checked; if it is found to be untrue, this fact is publicized.

A juvenile delinquent apprehended from this area sits down to talk things over with a committee consisting of the district captain of police, the adult probation officer, the delinquent's school principal, his clergyman, his nationality leader, his parents, and a representative of his father's labor union. Together they try to get at the root of the trouble and work out a solution. Another unique job of the Council is done through its Credit Union. Money is loaned for only 1 per cent interest; its people may obtain really needed financial assistance but are discouraged from unnecessary borrowing and are counseled instead in better family budgeting.

The community facilities mentioned here represent, of course, only a sample of the many types of activities that are being carried on all over the country. Many communities have coöperative nursery schools, community workshops and recreation centers, and playground programs with instruction in handicrafts and dramatics. All these efforts reflect the increasing recognition that skills, interests, good interpersonal relationships, and the satisfaction of basic needs all make for mental health and that adjustment of the individual in modern life is a group responsibility.

Volunteer Activities

The mental hygiene movement has always gained a great deal of its strength from volunteer work and funds. Since World War II, popular interest in mental health activities has reached unprecedented proportions. Magazine articles and books on the inadequacy of our mental hospitals, on the extent and seriousness of mental illness in the United States, and on the need for community action to provide funds and personnel have led to responsive action by an increasing number of community organizations—the Red Cross, women's clubs, men's clubs, civic welfare committees, parent-teacher associations, and so on.

Women's groups, for example, are taking increased interest in mental health activities. The League of Women Voters studies legislation concerning mental hospitals. The National Council of Jewish Women has been conducting an educational program on mental illness. The General Federation of Women's Clubs has been carrying on a survey of the incidence of mental illness as a first step toward stimulating local concern about mental health problems. These and other community organizations have taken the initiative in promoting the establishment of mental hygiene clinics. The range of community organizations taking an interest is illustrated by the list of organizations represented on the advisory board of the Prince Georges County pilot clinic: Community Chest and Planning Council, county health department, county schools, county courts, parent-teachers associations, the county medical society, the local university, a Negro community, Catholic churches, the County Ministerial Association, the Federation of Women's Clubs, Rotary, Lions, and others.

Psychiatry in the Nonpsychiatric Professions

Psychiatric principles of mental hygiene are gradually coming to be known and applied in many areas of modern life, in the same way that principles of physical hygiene once spread. Modern sanitation procedures began with the discovery of germs in the laboratory, then

Psychiatry in the Nonpsychiatric Professions

In medicine

Rapidly becoming an established part of medical training. Increasing psychiatric and psychosomatic orientation of medical men toward organic illness.

In nursing

Emphasis on psychiatric aspects of illness in nurses' training. Psychiatric orientation in practice: helping families adjust to illness, detecting cases needing psychiatric care.

In public health work

Psychiatric training of health officers to see emotional aspects of economic and health problems.
Individual and public education in mental hygiene, especially for mothers and for families with emotional and other problems.

In social work

Psychiatric orientation in helping clients to deal with their problems of whatever kind—economic, health, emotional, etc. Social workers are active in (1) family case work; (2) child welfare work; (3) court social work; (4) medical social work; (5) direct psychiatric social work to implement and reinforce work of psychiatrists, doctors, and other members of psychiatric staff; (6) social group work in connection with community centers, settlements, YWCA, YMCA, Boy and Girl Scouts, etc.; (7) community organization work, coördinating work of welfare agencies in a community; (8) social research.

In industry

Provision of psychiatric help for employees by either employing psychiatric teams (as is done by Macy's, General Electric, and Metropolitan Life Insurance Company) or helping employee to get needed help.
Institution of conditions in plant conducive to satisfaction of employees: (1) adequate channels of communi-

cation between employees and management; (2) job security and opportunities for advancement commensurate with ability; (3) friendly work relationships; (4) making the worker see the part his job has in the whole picture; (5) effective handling of complaints and frictions.

Careful testing of employees' abilities and interests and attempts at placement best suited to them.

In education

Psychologist or mental hygiene worker on school staff helps children, teachers, and parents, individually and in relationships with each other.

Adjustment of school curriculum at all levels to meet emotional, social, intellectual, and physical needs; special courses in personal and social problems.

Coöperation with other community agencies to help youth.

In the churches

Training courses in psychiatric principles for clergy. Psychiatric orientation in counseling.

Sponsorship of classes in mental health, child training, personality growth, etc., as well as traditional religious education and guidance.

In law

Campaigning against traditional punitive attitude toward lawbreakers; new attitudes toward criminals as people who need help being fostered among lawmakers, penal administrators, and the general public. Direct work with criminals in retraining and rehabilitation, occasionally with the aid of extensive psychotherapy.

See the following sources for a more intensive study of the role of psychiatry: in public health work, Bobbitt 6; Lemkau 23, 24; MacDonald 30; Schumacher 36; and Zimmerman 42; in the ministry, Felix 12; Peale and Blanton 33; Kemp 21; in industry, Rennie *et al.* 34; Dunbar 10.

spread to the hospital; later, through pressure from scientific and medical men, they were incorporated into legal requirements for sewage disposal, food handling, etc. At the same time, principles of hygiene were publicly expounded in schools, doctors' offices, factories, offices, newspapers, and magazines. Now every school child knows the elementary principles of cleanliness and practices them routinely in countless everyday situations. Today, in like manner, psychiatric principles and information are in the stage of progressing from the clinic and laboratory to the public, via medicine, nursing, public health, social work, the ministry, the schools, industry, and the law. The chart on these pages gives only the briefest summary of the role psychiatry is already playing in these varied fields.

International Measures for Mental Health

Mental health is the Number 1 problem not only in the United States, as the President of the United Nations General Assembly recently asserted, but also of the entire world. Indeed the unfavorable conditions in this country are magnified throughout most of the world. The incidence of psychological disorders in the world has not been estimated at all accurately, but it is known to be tremendous. The need for treatment facilities is correspondingly great: Whereas the 150,000,-000 people in the United States have a total—quite insufficient—of 5,000 psychiatrists and 700,000 psychiatric beds, the 350,000,000 of India have only perhaps 80 psychiatrists and 20,000 beds, and other underdeveloped countries also show inadequate ratios. In China there are less than 50 psychiatrists and about 6,000 psychiatric

hospital beds for a population of 450,000,000 people
(Bowman 7). There are similar deficiencies in the number of clinical psychiatrists, psychiatric social workers,
nurses, and other members of the psychiatric team.

The question has arisen as to whether we or any
other advanced industrialized nation can achieve mental
health in isolation from the rest of the world, however
great our efforts. Can one nation save itself while others
remain stagnant, a prey to famines, plagues, and the
frustrations and evils attendant on such conditions? The
answer—becoming increasingly obvious to all of us—is
No. Today we realize that mental illnesses, wars, international tensions and conflicts, and similar troubles are
interrelated, and what happens in the rest of the world
affects us also, directly and indirectly.

We have learned from our terrible experiences of the
last two wars that a sane and peaceable attitude toward others does not prevent war, does not save us
from the holocaust. Humanitarianism does not preclude
deadly hostility and aggression on the part of others.
Nor can we free ourselves from socially rooted anxieties
as long as we are forced to devise ever more powerful
armaments and explosives against the imminent threat
of war. For not only do such preparations directly breed
anxiety over the future in the minds of all of us, but they
also absorb vast funds and labor efforts which otherwise
could be turned to educational, recreational, and other
more profitable pursuits.

Just as our own mental health activities are retarded
and made less effective by world-wide tensions, so too,
conversely, every measure undertaken on an international scale to cure or prevent mental illnesses contributes in turn to our own national programs. The
international outlook—in contrast to the isolationist—

thus expands our field of operations. We must not slacken our efforts within this country, but at the same time we will find it increasingly essential to participate —even take the lead—in international campaigns.

It was this attitude, in general, which brought about the new international organizations at the end of the war—the United Nations, and more especially, its allied organizations concerned immediately with mental health, the World Health Organization and UNESCO (the United Nations Educational, Scientific, and Cultural Organization), as well as the World Federation for Mental Health.

The World Health Organization (WHO)

It is the general function of the World Health Organization to formulate recommendations to be carried out by member states of the United Nations. Brock Chisholm (8), Director-General of WHO, stated: "The desperate need of the human race at this most precarious stage of its development is for understanding of man and for the development of methods by which he can learn to live in peace with his kind." . . . Through the international efforts of WHO, and more particularly, its "Expert Committee on Mental Health" (and UNESCO can be included as well) the individual, organizational, and governmental activities to develop such understanding and methods can be planned, coordinated, and in some cases directed.

The Expert Committee on Mental Health of WHO had its first meeting in 1949 to formulate and agree upon principles and priorities in mental health work. In view of the tremendous needs and the present shortage of psychiatric personnel and facilities throughout the world, the Committee considered that it will be impossible to provide therapeutic facilities for all the needy peoples of the world, within the foreseeable future. We must turn, then, to preventive measures for the ultimate solution of the problem of mental illness. The Committee lays great emphasis on the incorporation into public health work—already widely established throughout the world—of responsibility for promoting the mental health of the community as well as its physical health.

Other salient recommendations, among the many made, refer to (1) extensive educational programs, including psychiatric teaching, psychiatric orientation in medical training, public mental hygiene courses, training of nurses in mental hygiene measures, fellowships, education of the public, and research, and (2) the fostering of psychiatric orientation to the treatment of juvenile delinquents and criminals both before and after prison terms, to be carried out by the WHO in coöperation with the UN Study on the Prevention of Crime (WHO 38).

UNESCO

The UNESCO Project on International Tensions is probably the most elaborate international undertaking involving psychiatric perspectives and aiming at better mental health. The Project is under the Social Sciences Department of UNESCO, directed by Robert C. Angell, the Acting Department Head. The project was outlined, and specific tasks assigned to coöperating personnel at two general conferences, at Mexico City in 1947 and at Beirut in 1948. Much of the work is still in progress, but some is already completed. Two books embracing extensive findings have been prepared. One, entitled *National Aggression and International Understanding*, contains contributions by eight social scientists edited by Prof. Hadley Cantril. The other, by Dr. Otto Klineberg, former head of the Tensions Project, is *Tensions Affecting International Understanding—A Survey of Research.*

The major efforts of the Tensions Project are focused on the problem of war. Social studies are made on factors contributing directly toward the development of war; and general studies are made on national attitudes, ways of life, and other over-all sociological aspects (Klineberg 22). Only a few of its multitudinous projects can be mentioned here:

1. A series of monographs on differences in national cultures or "characters" including sociological descriptions, life histories, Rorschach responses, and other psychological data concerning individual members of the societies studied, and with an attempt to synthesize existing information.

2. Studies of national "stereotypes" or ready-made conceptions of nationals of different countries.

3. Studies of attitude formation and change, particularly with regard to international prejudice; attempts to combat prejudice by exchange fellowships, visiting professorships, elimination of hostility-inducing material from textbooks, etc.

4. Research concerning the forces making for aggressive nationalism.

5. Studies of the relationship between population problems and international understanding.

6. Investigation of the influence of modern technology on attitudes and relationships between people, changes in ways of living, and so on.

The best conclusion to such a brief discussion of the

multifarious activities of WHO, UNESCO, and the participating countries and personnel, is the warning given by Dr. Klineberg (22):

> Our goal is, of course, research leading to action. There is a real and obvious danger in action which is premature. There is an equal danger in delaying action until it is too late. Our major difficulty lies in steering the proper course somewhere in between. . . .

This realistic appraisal of the difficulties and dangers should prevent any repetition of the quick but ineffective "reforms" which the peoples of the world have too often been duped into adopting.

The World Federation for Mental Health

In 1948 an International Congress on Mental Health was held in London, under the auspices of the International Committee for Mental Hygiene (an international counterpart of our National Committee for Mental Hygiene) and the British Association for Mental Health. At this Congress the World Federation for Mental Health was set up. The Federation is a group of nongovernmental organizations concerned with mental health, and at present groups from thirty-three different countries hold memberships. This is an important step toward the coördination of nongovernmental activities. The Federation has been admitted to consultative status by WHO and UNESCO, so that the work of the United Nations for mental health can receive the benefit of work carried out by private organizations both nationally and internationally.

In this chapter we have tried to outline the aims and

principles that must be used as a blueprint for successful preventive measures, and have seen something of
the veritable maze of local, national, and international
measures which have already been undertaken. It is
the first time in history that the social problem of mental health has been so attacked—as a phenomenon
subject to discoverable natural laws, and hence, potentially at least, within our control.

References

1. Adlerblum, Evelyn D.: "Mental Hygiene Begins at
   School." *Mental Hygiene,* XXXI (1947), 541–555.
2. Alinsky, Saul D.: "Youth and Morale." *American Journal
   of Orthopsychiatry,* XII (1942), 598–609.
3. Bateson, G. and Mead, M.: *Balinese Character.* New
   York: New York Academy of Sciences, 1942.
4. Benedict, Ruth: *The Chrysanthemum and the Sword.*
   New York: Houghton Mifflin, 1947.
5. ———: *Patterns of Culture.* Boston: Houghton Mifflin,
   1934.
6. Bobbitt, Joseph M.: "Counseling and Psychotherapy in
   Public Mental Health Work." National Institute of Mental Health, Federal Security Agency, Washington, D. C.
7. Bowman, Karl M.: "Psychiatry in China." *Digest of
   Neurology and Psychiatry Series,* XVI (1948), 328–335.
8. Chisholm, Brock: "The Future of Psychiatry." *American
   Journal of Psychiatry,* CIV (1948), 543.
9. Dubois, C.: *The People of Alor.* Minneapolis: University
   of Minnesota Press, 1944.
10. Dunbar, Flanders: *Mind and Body: Psychosomatic
    Medicine.* New York: Random House, 1947.
11. Dunham, H. W.: "Current Status of Ecological Research
    in Mental Disorder." *Social Forces,* March 1947.
12. Felix, Robert H. (Chief, Division of Mental Hygiene,

U.S. Public Health Service): Speech presented before the Mental Hygiene Society of Monroe County, Rochester, New York, March 23, 1949. Distributed by the National Institute of Mental Health, Federal Security Agency, Washington 25, D. C.

13. Felix, Robert H. and Bowers, R. V.: "Mental Hygiene and Socio-Environmental Factors." *Milbank Memorial Fund Quarterly*, XXVI (1948), 125–147. This authoritative article, by the Medical Director and Chief and Social Science Research Consultant, respectively, of the Mental Hygiene Division, U.S. Public Health Service, has been drawn on heavily throughout the preparation of the section on sociological preventive measures. It contains a full summary of activities in this field, with bibliographical references.

14. Fink, Arthur E.: *The Field of Social Work*. New York: Henry Holt, 1949.

15. Fortune, R. F.: *Sorcerers of Dobu*. London: Routledge, 1932.

16. Frank, Lawrence: "The Reorientation of Education to the Promotion of Mental Hygiene." *Mental Hygiene*, XXIII (1939), 529–543.

17. Fromm, Erich: *Escape from Freedom*. New York: Farrar and Rinehart, 1941.

18. Gorer, Geoffrey: *The American People: A Study in Character*. New York: Norton, 1948.

19. Kardiner, Abraham: *The Individual and His Society*. New York: Columbia University Press, 1939.

20. ———: *Psychological Frontiers of Society*. New York: Columbia University Press, 1945.

21. Kemp, Charles (Pastor, First Christian Church, Red Oak, Iowa): "The Minister and Mental Hygiene: His Opportunity and Responsibility." Distributed by the National Committee on Mental Hygiene, and reprinted from *Mental Hygiene*, XXXII (1948), 72–79.

22. Klineberg, Otto: "The UNESCO Project on International Tensions: A Challenge to the Sciences of

Man." *International Social Science Bulletin,* UNESCO, I (1949), Paris, No. 1–2.

23. Lemkau, Paul V.: "Mental Hygiene in Public Health." Reprint No. 2800 from the *Public Health Reports,* LXII (1947), 1151–1162.

24. ———: "What Can the Public Health Nurse Do in Mental Hygiene?" Distributed by the National Institute of Mental Health, Federal Security Agency, Washington 25, D. C.

25. Levine, Harry (Administrator of Special Services for the Aged and Community Services Section, Division of Field Operations and Services, Department of Welfare, New York City): "Recreation and Services for the Aged." A speech presented at the National Conference of Social Work, Atlantic City, New Jersey, April 22, 1948.

26. Liebman, Joshua Loth: *Peace of Mind.* New York: Simon and Schuster, 1948.

27. Linton, Ralph: *The Cultural Background of Personality.* New York: Appleton-Century, 1945.

28. Lynd, Robert and Lynd, Helen: *Middletown.* New York: Harcourt, Brace, 1929.

29. ———: *Middletown in Transition.* New York: Harcourt, Brace, 1937.

30. MacDonald, Martha W.: "Mental Hygiene in the Child-Health Conference." *The Child,* IX (1944), August, 27–30.

31. Menninger, W. C. "Psychiatric Experience in the War, 1941–1946." *American Journal of Psychiatry,* CIII (1947), 577–586.

32. Myrdal, Gunnar, *et al.: The American Dilemma.* New York: Harper, 1948. (On the Negro problem.)

33. Peale, Norman V. and Blanton, Smiley: *The Art of Real Happiness.* New York: Prentice-Hall, 1950.

34. Rennie, T. A. C., Swackhamer, Gladys, Woodward, Luther E.: "Toward Industrial Mental Health: An Historical Review." *Mental Hygiene,* XXXI (1947), 66–88.

35. Ross, Mabel: "Pilot Mental Health Clinic: First Annual

Report of Prince Georges County Clinic." Federal Security Agency, *Public Health Reports,* LXIV (1949), 797–801.

36. Schumacher, Henry C. (Medical Director, U.S. Public Health Service, District No. 5, San Francisco): "The Integration of Mental Hygiene Concepts and Practices in a Public Health Program." Reprinted from the *Canadian Journal of Public Health,* September 1948. Available from the National Institute of Mental Health, Federal Security Agency, Washington 25, D. C.

37. Stokes, Warrington: "Social Worker Plays Part in Court Process." *The Child,* December 1947.

38. United Nations, World Health Organization. *Report on the First Session of the Expert Committee on Mental Health* (29 August–2 September 1949, at Geneva), p. 39. William C. Menninger was chairman at this session.

39. Veblen, Thorstein: *The Theory of the Leisure Class.* New York: Viking, 1931.

40. Warner, W. Lloyd: *Yankee City Series.* New Haven: Yale University Press, 1941 *et seq.*

41. Whitman, Samuel: "Stop Sniping at Parents." *The Child,* May 1947.

42. Zimmerman, Kent A. "Mental Health Services in the Health-Department Program." *The Child,* September 1946, p. 50 ff.

Glossary

aberration a deviation or abnormality

abulia inability to make voluntary actions or decisions

affect emotion and feeling

agnosia impairment or loss of ability to recognize objects or individuals familiar before

akinesia (der.: **akinetic**) pertaining to the loss of movement for any reason

alkalosis a condition in which the alkalinity of the body increases beyond a normal limit

ambivalence existence of opposing or contradictory feelings simultaneously expressed towards a person or situation

amentia mental deficiency

amnesia anterograde amnesia is loss of memory for events occurring after a trauma; retrograde amnesia is loss of memory for events occuring before the trauma

anamnesis psychiatric case history of events happening in patient's life before mental disorder

anomaly a deviation from the usual or normal

anorexia loss of appetite

anoxia oxygen deficiency

aphasia   loss of or impairment of ability to communicate or understand such symbols as writing and speech

asynergia   lack of coördination between muscle groups, resulting in serial rather than simultaneous movements

athetosis   repeated movements, slow and lacking in volition, indicative of brain lesion

autistic thinking   the gratification of needs through the use of imaginary wishes and fantasies instead of realistic action

Babinski reflex   the extension of the toes when the sole of the foot is stroked

baragnosis   inability to estimate weights

benign   eventuating in a favorable outcome

catalepsy   a loss of consciousness accompanied by rigidity of muscles, allowing for limbs to be kept in any position in which they are placed

catharsis   the discharge of tension accomplished by the release of emotionally charged material which has been repressed

cephalo-caudal   pertaining to the development of the embryo which occurs first, literally "head to tail" (see *proximo-distal*)

cerebellum   the area of the brain which lies beneath the cerebrum, above the medulla oblongata and the Pons Variolii

cerebrum   the major area of the brain consisting of the two hemispheres which contain the higher centers for sensation, movements and association

chorea   spasmodic muscle twitching or jerky movements indicating disorder of motor control centers

claustrophobia   fear of enclosed spaces

clonus   alternate spasmodic contraction and relaxation of muscles

CO₂   carbon dioxide

confabulation   a use of illogical, unwarranted or false assumptions

congenital   existing at birth, as for example, a heart condition

cortex (cerebral)   the surface of the cerebrum

cretinism   a type of mental deficiency resulting from a deficiency in thyroid secretion

cyanosis   a bluish or grayish discoloration of the skin caused by a deficiency of oxygen and an excess of carbon dioxide in the blood

cyclothymia   oscillation in mood, usually considered to be from joy to sadness

cytology   the science of cell life and formation

delusion   an idea or belief expressed by a person which has no apparent basis in reality

dementia   mental disorder resulting from factors not associated with congenital or hereditary characteristics. Example is seen in senile dementia, resulting from brain changes in aged

dissociation   separation of certain mental elements or functions resulting in their splitting off from the main personality components

dysrhythmia   a disturbance in rhythm

ego   the self. In psychoanalytic usage the portion of the mind which is in contact with the outer world, mediating the primitive desires of the unconscious (see *id*) and the demands of the external world

electroencephalography a method of recording electrical impulses emanating from the brain

encephalitis inflammation of the brain

enuresis involuntary urination, "bed-wetting"

epidemiology the study of epidemic diseases

etiology the study of causes or significant factors leading up to a situation, usually in terms of disease

euphoria a feeling of well being

genesis the origin of a thing, *e.g.*, psychogenic—originating in the mind

group therapy group psychotherapy, *i.e.*, treatment of several patients simultaneously, in a group

hallucination sense-impression without external physical stimulus

hemorrhage a discharge of blood from the blood vessels, resulting from an abnormal cause, such as an injury

hyperkinesis excessive general muscular activity

hypokinesis decreased general muscular activity

hypothalamus part of the forebrain which controls the body temperature

id in psychoanalytic usage, the deepest part of the unconscious mind, reservoir of primitive drives and desires, dominated by pleasure-needs (see *ego*)

idiopathic of unknown cause

illusion misinterpretation of the meaning of sense-impressions of external, physical stimulus

intracranial within the skull or cranium

Jacksonian epilepsy a form of epilepsy with local spasm of muscle, limited to one limb or part of the body, usually without the loss of consciousness

lesion an injury or damage to a part of the body

libido in psychoanalytic usage, sexual desire or in a broader meaning, life force or instinctual drives of the person

macrocephaly abnormal condition involving enlargement of the head

masochism desire to experience pain

meninges the three membranes which surround the spinal cord and brain

meningitis inflammation of the meninges

metabolism the processes concerned in the building up (anabolism) and breaking down (katabolism) of protoplasm which the living creature undergoes

metrazol a drug formerly used to produce convulsive seizures in psychiatric patients undergoing shock therapy; no longer widely used, electrically induced seizures being current (electro-convulsive-therapy, called ECT)

myxedema a disorder of nutrition resulting from a lack of thyroid secretion. Main psychological symptoms are lethargy and dullness

narcissism (also **narcism**) self-love

narcolepsy an abnormal episodic attack of sleepiness

neologism a new word which is created or a new meaning given to an old word usually with significance only to the person who coined it

neurosis (also **psychoneurosis**) a mild personality disorder in which the person maintains good contact with reality but which is used to handle what may be overwhelming anxiety or stress

nosology the study of, or the classification of, diseases

Oedipus complex erotic attachment to the parent of the opposite sex with hostility toward parent of the same sex Usually used of boy, the Electra complex indicating girl's attitude

orthopsychiatry field of psychiatry which is concerned with the development of healthy growth in children

paroxysmal pertaining to paroxysms, periodic attacks of any disease; also refers to convulsions, as, *e.g.*, in epilepsy

pathogenesis origin and course of a disease

penis-envy in psychoanalytic usage, a repressed wish in the female to have the male sex organs

petit mal mild form of epilepsy with momentary lapses of consciousness

phallus symbolic representation of the male sex organs

projection ascribing to other individuals ideas, feelings or wishes which the individual himself has but which he may unconsciously feel are not acceptable

projective technique psychological examinations using ambiguous or unstructured stimulus material, allowing the individual to interpret these in a way reflective of his own needs and conflicts, *e.g.*, Rorschach Ink-Blot Test

proximo-distal pertaining to the axis extending from the midline of the body outward toward the extremities. Second in development (see *cephalo-caudal*)

psychogenic (see *genesis*)

psychoneurosis (see *neurosis*)

psychosis a personality disorder involving a disturbance in the perception of reality in which the individual frequently manifests delusional ideas or hallucinations

psychotherapy treatment of emotional disorders by psychological methods

rapport an attitude of mutual acceptance and confidence between two persons; in psychotherapy between patient and doctor

repression the closing out from conscious awareness of thoughts which might be found disturbing or unacceptable

sadism a sexual perversion in which pleasure is obtained from inflicting pain on other individuals

superego in psychoanalytic usage, that portion of the mind which produces distress when the *ego* accepts primitive urges from the *id*. It is synonymous with conscience

syndrome a symptom complex characteristic of a certain disease or disorder

thrombosis the formation of a blood clot (a thrombus)

tonus partial contraction of muscle leading to firmness (see *clonus*)

transference the aggregate of the reactions a patient develops toward a therapist during treatment, in which he may cast the therapist in such rôles as that of a father-figure, etc.

trauma a shock or injury, either physical or psychological

unconscious in psychoanalytic usage, that portion of the mind which is not accessible by direct means through volition. It is the reservoir of repressed thoughts and desires (see *ego, superego, id*)

uremia a toxic condition of the blood resulting from the accumulation of constituents which normally would be excreted in the urine. Results from faulty kidney metabolism

The Best of the World's Best Books
COMPLETE LIST OF TITLES IN
THE MODERN LIBRARY

MODERN LIBRARY GIANTS

A series of sturdily bound and handsomely printed, full-sized library editions of books formerly available only in expensive sets. These volumes contain from 600 to 1,400 pages each.

THE MODERN LIBRARY GIANTS REPRESENT A
SELECTION OF THE WORLD'S GREATEST BOOKS